How I Cook

Ben Lippett

'Cooking?
Maybe keep it as a hobby…'
Dad, circa 2016.

Sorry Dad

How I Cook

A Chef's Guide to Really Good Home Cooking

Ben Lippett

Photography by Sam A Harris

HarperCollins*Publishers*

For my wife, Lou

CONTENTS

Introduction

Welcome 9

How to Use This Book 12

How I Cook: 15 Rules I Live By in the Kitchen 14

How to Taste, Season and Use Flavour 16

How to Choose Ingredients 22

Dry-store Essentials 30

Kitchen Equipment 32

Mise en Place: Before We Begin 40

1.
Eggs Come First 42

2.
Salads & Raw Bits 66

3.
Stocks, Soups & Broths 90

4.
Pastas & Grains 114

5.
Flour & Water 148

6.
A Flash in the Pan 178

7.
From the Oven 202

8.
Back Burner 230

9.
Over Fire 254

10.
Sweet Things 280

Conversion Charts 312
Index 313
Acknowledgements 319

WELCOME

Listen, I didn't come out of the womb knowing how to cook. The first time I tried to make bread, I was rubbish at it. The recipe I'd selected as my debut called for a slightly-too-ambitious plait, and it wasn't going well. In front of me were five thin, wet cords of dough, each a different length and shape, all inelegantly mashed together at the top like a fist. I grew up with sisters, so plaiting hair was supposedly within my skill set, but I'd lost my way somewhere between strands three and five. 'Is this what bread dough is supposed to look like?' No, it wasn't. My 'dough' was a blobby mess of flour, water and yeast, too sticky to handle and about as alive as my will to carry on baking. A slightly turbulent adolescence had led me here, baking alone in my mum's kitchen in Portsmouth, and by now I was ready to tear my hair out, fling the 'dough' at the wall and quit.

Why had I spent the last three hours of a sunny afternoon making nothing more than a mess? Why wasn't the bread behaving? Why wasn't this easy? What was I doing wrong? I've been asking 'why' and 'how' ever since, and it's the answers to those questions that hold the keys to really good home cooking.

When people see the word 'chef' on the cover of a cookbook, it can set off alarm bells. It's intimidating, I get it. The c-word either drags up images of overly shouty men throwing plates at walls or ultra-polished TV shows that deify a succession of silver-haired maestros holed up in their cathedrals of gastronomy. It's either deeply unappealing or feels completely out of reach. For me, cooking like a 'chef' is all about confidence, and the secret to unlocking confidence is constantly asking 'why'. Learning to cook well is about so much more than just blindly following a recipe. To feel true confidence behind the stove, you need to understand what's happening on your chopping board, in your pan and on your plate. If you approach a pile of ingredients with an empty stomach and a healthy dose of know-how, you'll be turning out utterly delicious, effortless food in no time. Best of all, you'll enjoy it, I promise.

In my book, the most important ingredient in any recipe is hunger. To be a good cook, you must be a good eater. I spent the first years of my life cultivating this maxim; from an early age, I devoured food. Variety wasn't my forte, but quantity was. My mum and dad were fantastic cooks with a wealth of skill behind the stove. We ate well growing up and it was obvious they had done too. My dad's folks laid out sprawling 1970s spreads whenever we visited. To be welcomed with platters of just-lettuce salad, cubed cheddar, ox tongue and Grandpa's homemade pineapple cake was to feel like a boy-king. Mum's parents were no different and the memory of eating ham sandwiches after school with my Grandpa lives as close to my heart as is possible. But it's my nanny, a phenomenal cook and a lifelong

> **TAKE PLEASURE IN TASTING, EXPLORING, MESSING UP, TRYING AGAIN AND – CRITICALLY – ASKING: 'WHY?'**

food educator, that I have to thank for countless food memories and for stoking the fire of my appetite so early. I would eat bowl after bowl of her mac and cheese, followed by 'splodge pudding', a deeply English, microwaved syrup sponge served with thick canary-yellow custard. It's hardly surprising, then, that by the time I hit my teens, unlike that infernal plaited loaf, I had become quite doughy. In an attempt to remedy that, I wanted to learn more about food and, more importantly, how to cook.

I was living with my mum in Portsmouth and we were both figuring a few things out at the time. After some very typical teenage (bad) decision-making, I had been left behind by my mates to complete an extra year of school and was very much at a loose end. That year was deeply boring and wholly embarrassing; it was time to refocus, knuckle down, escape my hometown and get my shit together. I was craving control. Almost instinctively, I turned to the kitchen. When you're in a bit of a hole, easy wins like making a broccoli soup can toss you a rope ladder and drag you right up out of it. Leafing through a cookbook to a page that catches your eye, and then just making something can really scratch an itch. So I did that for a little while, making dinner for me and my mum, taking pleasure in the control it thrust back into my life. I found home cooking a salve, something I could work on and progress at, read and practise and mess up and then eventually, attritionally, nail and devour. Food had muscled its way into my brain and dug its claws in.

Fast-forward to completing a largely useless (but very interesting!) degree, throughout which I had continued to fantasise about the world of cooking, I printed out some pretty irrelevant CVs and went knocking on the back doors of restaurants. I cut my teeth in New York, pan-shaking in a cocktail bar that took itself a teeny bit too seriously for cash under the table. Once I could afford my rent, New York became more of a playground. Cooking had swung a booze-soaked, cash-rich door wide open, and at the ripe old age of twenty-one, I jumped right through it. Cooking can be fun! Scary! Exciting! Sexy! Following a formative year in Brooklyn I headed back to the UK to really dive into professional cooking. It's commonplace to dart about in the restaurant game, so after a few years on the south coast, my partner and I upped sticks and moved to Australia. Melbourne was home for a while before we made a hasty, pandemic-driven retreat to the UK. With no restaurant industry to speak of, I undertook a brief spell as a butcher in the Sussex countryside, before finally snaking back to the big smoke; London. Along the way, I spent time on every section of a professional kitchen, covering meat, fish, garnish, larder, grill and – of course – bread and pastry. Within each of these disciplines live a million questions. Why salt the steak now and not right before cooking? Why am I using the expensive olive oil for this? Why has my custard turned lumpy? Why does this taste so good?! I was soaking up cooking like a kitchen porter's sponge.

Without a doubt, the thing I enjoyed the most about restaurants is that you cook, almost non-stop, for fifteen hours a day. It's fierce, fast, unforgiving, beautiful and a complete riot. I don't need to tell you that working in hospitality is hard. A lot of people have done it. You, reading this, might have done it, or still do it, and the rest of you have seen the TV shows that present a dystopian image of the industry. I had a blast, but when the day to interrogate my future in restaurants arrived, I chose the door. It was a basement kitchen in North London that finally got me. I'd hit the wall. The higher you rise in the ranks of the kitchen, the less actual cooking you do. Graduating from cook to chef means more responsibility. You manage the team, write the rotas, do the paperwork, fix the dishwasher, call the suppliers and stroke the investors' egos. That's a hell of a lot, and almost none of it is cooking. I had squashed in as much learning and downloaded as much knowledge and experience as I possibly could.

I'd schlepped a heavy bag of knives around the world, racked up hours sweating behind stoves, been yelled at, cut fingers, burned forearms and dropped pans on toes, and what did I have to show for it? Almost no cash, a heaping pile of cracked friendships to rebuild (turns out no-showing parties and birthdays because you're grilling John Dory all night doesn't help in that department) and a big black cloud over my head. The silver lining? I now had a hefty measure of culinary knowledge and experience.

The idea of writing about food was sitting in the back of my mind – it was something I'd always loved and had been doing on and off as a hobby, so a handful of days into my post-restaurant existence, I turned to it with more purpose. I'm now in my early thirties and, having spent most of my twenties at the stove in a professional kitchen, I've boomeranged all the way back to the home kitchen. Home cooking is now one of the most significant parts of my life. What was once a mental salve, discovered purely by chance thanks to a dog-eared baking book, ended up evolving into an obsession, a love, and now, by some miracle, I've managed to manhandle it into a career.

This book is about making great food approachable to everyone. It's not always going to tick the midweek box; good food takes time and patience and sometimes you'll have to go to the butcher and ask them a question or two. This is a book of 'real' food. Food that you can make with a concise collection of equipment, some great ingredients and a little technique. Food that gets your heart pumping and saliva flowing. It's food that exists in that sacred space between the home and the restaurant: easily achieved and could be enjoyed in both. Be warned, you won't find any dainty tweezers, fancy gels or sous-vide machines here. Cooking with feeling, understanding ingredients and seasoning, and learning how to handle hot pans and tame elements like fire and smoke is far more useful, and affords you the freedom needed to cook from the hip.

The most effective way to learn to cook is to understand the sights, sounds, smells and taste of food. As this is a book and we can't physically stand side by side and make an omelette together, I've done my best to talk you through these sensory cues and describe in detail what you should be looking for as you cook your way through a recipe. There are plenty of words, but don't be dissuaded by a chunk of text. An overly brief recipe is a useless one!

Ultimately, I hope that once you've spent some time with this book you'll be ready to take on a new recipe, technique or ingredient and appreciate the hows and whys of the food you choose to eat. If you can grasp these simple elements, you're one step closer to finding the root of your own cooking. Be hungry. Read the words, make the recipes, mess them up and then try them again. Take pleasure in tasting, exploring, messing up, trying again and – critically – asking: 'why?' After all, you've got to cook and eat three times a day for the rest of your life, so you might as well be good at it.

HOW TO USE THIS BOOK

This book is as much about how I cook as it is about how you cook. Through the lessons, tips, tricks and recipes in the following chapters, you should explore how you naturally cook. On this culinary journey, you'll scoop up little tips and tricks, techniques and learnings through tasting, cooking, practising, nailing it and messing it up. I've done it too, so this is a collection of recipes that contain a whole host of those little teachable moments. Through years spent at the stoves of restaurant kitchens, and via a deep obsession with food, I've picked up a few things that you might not often come across in the home kitchen. Some are usually found in the professional setting but are applicable and deeply useful when transplanted into a domestic setting, with very few extra steps. There are so many tips and shortcuts that are used by chefs that look and feel intimidating but in reality are dead simple and will seriously level up your cooking.

The recipe collection is by no means exhaustive, but if you cook your way through this book, I guarantee you'll come out the other side equipped with some new tools in your kit.

Before your brain barges its way to the front and picks which recipe and techniques to tuck into, listen to your stomach. Being guided by your stomach and appetite when cooking is invariably the best route to take. Identifying what you really want to eat is a direct pathway to a pleasurable cooking experience. Your eyes and nose will be instrumental in this, too. Head to the market, the grocer or the butchers and something will always catch your eye. What we crave is often dictated by the seasons; in summer you want a tomato salad, or a salt-baked fish with sauce vierge. In winter, it's a big, bold short-rib glazed with molasses and vinegar and a sticky date pudding to finish. It can also be influenced by your mood. Do you need a dose of comfort food? Or are you feeling a little sluggish and need something zippy and bright to wake things up? Perhaps you had a few drinks last night and only a big bowl of mac and cheese will do.

Right after you've figured out what you fancy eating, the hows and whys of the recipe are the most important questions you can ask. Why am I adding salt now and not later? How can I make these scrambled eggs even silkier? Why am I patting this chicken breast dry before it hits the pan? Why has my chocolate mousse split? How do I fix it?! Why does this taste so good? Understanding the answers to these questions to a slightly deeper level, along with learning some basic cooking principles, is akin to holding the keys to the culinary kingdom and will ultimately make your life in the kitchen a fulfilling and enjoyable one. Skills and techniques are vital to a cook's arsenal and are the culinary tools they carry with them and pass forward, whether that's teaching their partner, their kids or their mates. In my book, knowledge is far more valuable than a fancy slow cooker or blender.

NEVER PREPARED RAW FISH? DON'T BE AFRAID, I'VE GOT YOU.

I've split the book into ten chapters. Each chapter has a specific focus and contains a variety of recipes, each designed to leave you with a little nugget of knowledge, a teachable moment that you can apply to other recipes, whether they're found in this book, another book, or you're just shooting from the hip. There will be dead easy 'cook with your eyes closed' recipes, recipes that make you roll your sleeves up, and a few that aim to challenge the home cook and are a bit more of a project. Nothing beats mastering a new skill in the kitchen, and I'm here to hold your hand through the whole process. Never deboned a chicken? Prepared raw fish? Whipped up a meringue? Made your own pastry? Don't be afraid, I've got you. Whether it's prepping a midweek meal or a weekend project, you'll be set up to succeed. Via a mixture of classic dishes and new, contemporary cooking we'll explore a broad spectrum of culinary lessons. The classics demonstrate technique, are unshakably delicious and furnish a cook with a fundamental understanding of how different ingredients behave and how flavours develop, but there's always room for the new. These days we have an ever-growing variety of ingredients at our disposal, and it'd be a crime not to use them.

> Dietary requirements? No worries, each of the recipes has a handy label that'll let you know what's going on at a glance.
>
> V = Vegetarian
> VE = Vegan
> P = Pescatarian
> DF = Dairy-free
> GF = Gluten-free

You'll see a few little boxes alongside each recipe: **chef's tip**, **notes** and **shoot from the hip**. These'll help you identify some things to think about while you're cooking, some shortcuts and hints, a fact or two, and how to substitute ingredients, riff and play off the different recipes. Yes, there's a little bit of science scattered along the way, but don't worry: this science-y bit is grounded in everyday kitchen moments, rather than in a lab or a Michelin-starred restaurant.

Ultimately, the goal is for you to finish this book feeling nourished in more ways than one: maybe you learnt something new or changed the way you thought about an ingredient or technique; had a eureka moment; imagined eating something delicious; actually ate something delicious; or, even better, shared it with someone in your life. Just making a recipe for your dinner is brilliant, too. I want you to close this book and walk to the pantry and the fridge equipped with a new understanding, be able to swing the door open with the panache of a confident cook, ready to employ fresh skills and techniques to turn out a delicious, thoughtful, well-crafted plate of food.

INTRODUCTION

HOW I COOK

15 RULES I LIVE BY IN THE KITCHEN

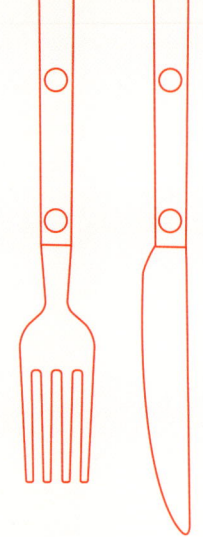

1.
Be a Good Eater and Listen to Your Stomach.

Be hungry, devour knowledge, eat other people's food, ask questions, be curious and taste as much as you can. When deciding what to cook, always be led by your cravings. Don't let the brain get in the way too much. Be a 'live to eat' person, not an 'eat to live' person.

2.
Eat With the Seasons.

Good cooking is all about the ingredients. If you pay attention to restaurant menus, you'll see them change and evolve throughout the year, cycling through the ingredients as they're grown and at their peak. This isn't boring cooking, it's smart and if you approach your home cooking with this in mind, you'll be one step closer to cooking like a chef, and supporting farmers and producers while you're at it. Whatever you do, don't be eating fresh strawberries in the middle of winter.

3.
Trust Your Gut.

There are so many variables in the kitchen. Our ovens are all a little different, my cut of steak will be slightly different to yours, your hob might be a little fiercer, or your yeast might take 10 minutes more than mine to rise. Use the recipes as a guide, read the sensory cues and ballpark the timings. Above all, pay more attention to your senses and your gut when making the call about when to pull something out of the oven or turn the heat down a little.

4.
Taste, Taste, Taste.

Your tasting spoon should be by far your most-used tool. It's how you learn, grow and deliver delicious food over and over again. Taste at the beginning, throughout the process and right before you serve. It's like a little adventure, always with a happy ending.

5.
Learn the Basics. Respect the Classics.

Nothing will prepare you for a life of delicious food like learning the basics, the classics, the time-tested combinations and age-old techniques that lay the foundations for all contemporary cooking. This will give you the tools to go out there on your own and whip up something magical.

6.
Work Clean.

Try your best to keep things clean and tidy and look after your little workspace. Take pride in giving everything a home and sticking to it. Have a plan and read your recipe through a couple of times before you kick off. A tidy space and clean workflow will make you feel efficient and keep your mind clear so you're better able to enjoy the process.

7.
Look After Your Tools.

Keep your knives sharp, your pots clean and your chopping board well-scrubbed. Your tools will be by your side for a very long time, so choose them wisely and treat them with respect. They're going to help you make some really good food. Look after them, and they'll look after you.

8.
Go Steady.

Has anyone ever told you that you can add a potato to an over-salted bolognese or soup to fix things? Well, it doesn't really work. Whatever the ingredient, go steady when adding it to a braise or sauce you've been working on for a few hours. You can always add more, but once it's in, you can't get it back.

9.
Consider Doneness.

Medium-rare is for so much more than a steak! Planning and considering to what degree you want to cook any ingredient is so important for both texture and flavour. How do you want your courgette to be cooked? The same question should be asked of pork, fish and vegetables: there are levels of doneness for every ingredient.

10.
Break New Ground.

Every new recipe, technique or ingredient you take on becomes a little piece of the wider puzzle, another brick to play with, a potential new character in your next dish. Don't be afraid to buy the spice you've heard about but never tasted, to cure your own fish, to cook ox tongue. Don't stop pushing yourself or get too comfy.

11.
Always Use Herbs.

Herbs are such a powerful ingredient in the kitchen, and it's rare for me to cook anything savoury without there being a herb at play somewhere. Whether it be a handful of parsley, some torn basil or mint leaves right at the end, or a little bunch of rosemary or thyme at the beginning of a cook. Use them often and with abandon.

12.
Fruit Belongs Everywhere.

Fruit belongs on your dinner plate. It's not just for dessert! Duck and orange, pork and peaches, seared fish and gooseberries . . . You can and should try pairing fruit with savoury dishes. It's delicious and feels very 'cheffy'. Just make sure you're adding enough savoury elements to offset that natural sweetness.

13.
Can I Be Bothered?

Be sure that whatever you set out to create, you are going to be present and up for every single step. After work on a Wednesday might not be the time to start that big kitchen project you've been dreaming about all week, maybe it's just time for a bowl of pasta.

14.
Patience. Patience. Patience.

The answer to so many problems in cooking is simply to wait a little longer. Don't rush your way through fried rice or your first loaf of bread and don't expect to master a tricky technique in seconds. Good things take time and learning to cook is a lifelong practice. Stick with it, enjoy the journey.

15.
Don't Worry, You'll Eat Again.

I used to get so, so mad at myself when I tried a new recipe and it was not quite going to plan. An early, failed attempt at viennoiserie springs to mind here. After trying to roll nearly-frozen butter into an over-proofed, underdeveloped dough, I tore it to shreds, tossed it into the bin along with my hopes and dreams of light, ethereal French pastries and swore off cooking for the next week. Once you learn to relish these moments and lean into the things that don't go to plan, you can transform them into teachable moments and opportunities to grow. You're going to mess up, and that's good! The feeling of getting back on the horse, then dialling in a technique or recipe that gave you a hard time before, tastes better than the best chocolate mousse in the world.

HOW TO TASTE, SEASON AND USE FLAVOUR

'What does this need?' I'm standing in the middle of a busy kitchen holding a pan full of mint gelato base. It's Kermit green, silky smooth and, in my mind, nearly ready to freeze and churn, but there's something missing. We've bought a bunch of Peruvian black mint from a local grower and have grand ambitions of it hitting the menu that evening. It's destined to be scooped into a roche then perched atop a chocolate fondant. The fondants will be perfect, the little sprinkle of flaky salt will be just right, the drizzle of grassy olive oil that has been imported from Italy will bring a bitter edge to the plate, and the ice cream is the final piece of the puzzle. But I can't figure it out. I taste the base for what feels like the 256th time and it still tastes like mint, but not a full, rounded mint. Like a half-formed idea of a mint ice cream or somebody shouting the word 'mint' down a very long, empty corridor. You can just about hear it, but it's not right there, it's not in your face, it's not, well, minty.

My head chef, Michael, plunges his spoon into the green pond and tastes. You can see his mind whirring, drawing on years of tasting experience, a thousand spoons dipped, a million flavours tasted, a well-seasoned palate. Within seconds, he spits out the word, 'salt'. 'Salt . . . in the ice cream?' 'Yes. Use the nice sea salt.'

I grabbed a handful and tossed it into the mix, whisking the two together, convinced I'd just ruined the custard I'd spent about an hour making. I grabbed a clean spoon, dunked and tasted. In a moment, the flavour had transformed, the mint had come into focus. It had been enlarged and now stood proud at the front of the room. The salt brought balance and a subtle salinity that gave the custard a rounded, full flavour. The mint tasted mintier, the cream tasted creamier; it had adopted a lip-smacking, moreish quality that five minutes ago I didn't think possible.

Without seasoning, food is flat, drab, boring and limp. To season food is to taste, to identify the missing pieces, the little tweaks and additions that'll make a good plate great. To learn to taste and adjust like Michael is a kitchen superpower, and guess what? You can teach yourself to do it.

What is tasting?

I'm going to ask you to taste your food, and, to be honest, I don't really shut up about it. What do I mean when I say taste? Well, first, let's clear something up: taste and flavour are not the same thing. To get all science-y for a second, taste refers to the five basic sensations our tongues can detect. For a very long time, it was thought there were only four: salty, sour, bitter and sweet. Most foods can be largely grouped into these categories. Fish sauce? Salty. Honey? Sweet. Biting into a lime wedge? Bitter and sour! You get the idea . . . these four didn't quite cut it, though.

In the early 1900s, Professor Ikeda of Tokyo Imperial University was slurping on a bowl of rich, moreish, deeply savoury soup. How do you describe the taste of something so earthy and meaty? And just like that – *voilà* – umami was born.

So why these five tastes? Like most things anatomical, it boils down to evolution. We're sensitive to these five because they are all related to what our body needs a lot of and what we don't want too much of. We're super-sensitive to salt: we need salt to live, but too much salt can cause problems. On the flip side, we need heaps of carbohydrates and protein to keep us going, so we're not overly sensitive to sugar or umami. We're about ten times less reactive to sugar and umami than we are to salt, but about ten times more sensitive to bitter and sour, tastes that indicate something might be awry – maybe this apple is rotten, or the chicken has started to turn. Of course, with enough willpower, you can override these warnings and eat as many sour sweets and salty pork scratchings as you like, just before you sip on a bitter espresso or pint of stout. If taste can help us identify which foods are good for us, and which foods might not be, can aroma and texture help, too? When you sniff the milk before making your cup of tea, you're looking for similar signs, right? Absolutely! When all three of these – taste, aroma and texture – come together, you get flavour.

Taste vs flavour

Flavour happens in the brain, rather than on the palate. Taste and aroma collide between the nose and the mouth, sending signals up to the brain that are registered in tandem and spit out a flavour. When your olfactory organs (they are what enable you to smell stuff!) join the party, and your brain starts to assess textures and aroma alongside the five tastes, suddenly your brain transforms all that information into flavour. Try this: make a cup of strong coffee and inhale the aroma. Have a sip, hold the liquid on your tongue for 4–5 seconds, inhale and exhale through your nose, then really interrogate the flavour left on your palate. You'll taste coffee, obviously, but you might also pick up some caramel, chocolate, a fruity twang, or a touch of umami. Now, pinch your nose and try again. The flavour will vanish. You'll still feel the texture of the coffee, the heat of the liquid and the underlying bitterness, but those flavour notes you were relishing just moments ago have gone. You can try this with pretty much any ingredient and the effect will be the same. It's a fascinating experiment, isolating the taste of something and almost completely bypassing its flavour. While taste is definable, packaged into five neat little categories, flavour is a devilishly subjective thing. What works for me might be your idea of hell. This is where personal preference comes into play. Our eating habits, food memories and DNA all help to define our flavour preferences. They can change and evolve, but they're at their most malleable in our youth, so if you want to live a life full of adventurous flavours and have a well-seasoned palate, get going and eat as many different things as soon as possible.

Palate fatigue

Have you ever been making something and tasted it, added a pinch of salt or a dash of vinegar, and tasted it again, 'nope still not right . . .', adjusted and tasted, and after a while, you just can't put your finger on what's missing, it just all tastes the same? You might be suffering from palate fatigue. Also known as sensory enervation, this is when your taste buds and olfactory organs stop reacting to the same stimulus due to over-exposure. You can avoid palate fatigue by practising tasting – the more you taste, the more physically fit your tasting faculties become and you'll be able to taste more and for longer – but once it hits, there's not a huge amount you can do about it besides asking for a second opinion or drinking some water and taking a quick break, giving your taste buds time to recover and forget what they've been relentlessly smashing into.

INTRODUCTION

Practise, practise, practise

You aren't born with a naturally impeccable palate; it needs training. You need to teach your brain and taste buds what they think is tasty via a lifetime of practice and information gathering. That is good news on two fronts: first, to develop a good palate you need to eat loads of food; second, there are no hard or fast rules when it comes to flavour – you like what you like and no one can really say otherwise. When you taste something for the first time, you don't have any building blocks with which to build an assessment. For example, the first time you taste a tomato, you think okay, that's what tomato tastes like. After your 500th tomato, each has tasted a little different, and your knowledge of the tomato spectrum has broadened. You've tried different varieties – some large, meaty ones, some sweet baby ones – and the flavour has been moulded and changed with different salts, vinegars, oils, each bringing out different qualities of the fruit. You have a wealth of experience to draw from, an idea of what tomatoes can and should taste like. You pick up a tomato, slice into it, have a taste and think, this could be better. The next step is figuring out how to get it there. Enter, seasoning.

What is seasoning?

Broadly speaking, a seasoning is anything that amplifies or elevates flavour. When I say 'check the seasoning' or 'taste and adjust the seasoning', I'm talking about more than just salt. I'm talking about how you use tertiary ingredients to celebrate your hero ingredient(s). Salt, yes, but I'm also calling for acidity, heat, fat or fragrance. To season effectively is to arrive at the moment when your food tastes spectacular, sailing past the point that it tastes dull or flat and just before it becomes overly salty, sour, sweet, fatty, rich or bitter. You can bring these seasonings to the party using so many different ingredients – citrus, vinegar, sugar, honey, chilli, hot sauce, pickles, Worcestershire sauce . . . the list is endless. When it comes to levelling up your home cooking, nailing your seasoning will bring you one step closer to cooking like a pro. Understanding when and how you apply seasoning is vital to your success in the kitchen. Let's kick things off with the big dog: salt.

Salt

Salt is the backbone of pretty much everything we eat, it's the most powerful ingredient out there when it comes to enhancing, manipulating and modifying flavour and texture, and without it the word 'delicious' would cease to exist. The fancy scientific name for salt is sodium chloride. It's a mineral that we need to stay alive, so much so that we actively crave it. Salt can come from many sources – from the ocean, ancient lakes, salt flats or mountain streams. These are the most common forms of salt that you'll find in the supermarket.

TABLE SALT Cheap and cheerful, this is the commonplace salt out there. It's quite heavily refined and sometimes contains additives, anti-caking agents and other bits and bobs you don't necessarily want to be tossing into your food. It can also have an artificial, metallic flavour and it is super salty.

FINE SEA SALT This is the salt I use the most. It's the salt that is left over after a pool of seawater evaporates. Sea salt carries the best flavour for me. It tastes like the sea in the best way possible, rarely has any additives and works with any ingredient. A fine sea salt can be used to season pasta water, salt a chicken prior to roasting or add a savoury edge to a caramel for a tarte tatin.

KOSHER SALT Traditionally used in the Jewish process of koshering, this salt has a fluffy, unique texture and is the go-to for a lot of cooks across the pond. It can be trickier to get hold of in the UK, but it is a great product. It's not overly salty and has a clean flavour.

FLAKY SEA SALT The magic salt. Flaky sea salt should be used right at the end of the cooking process when you want an active crunch of sea salt. If used too early, the huge, complex crystals dissolve and are then no different to regular sea salt. Flaky salt is a little pricier than its finer counterpart, so use it wisely. You'll feel like a true chef, grabbing a pinch of flaky salt to finish a chocolate mousse, a big fat steak or whipping it into homemade butter.

How to use salt

So, you've got the right salt for the job. Now, how do you best use it? These are a few things I keep in mind when reaching for the salt.

THE SALT SANDWICH PRINCIPLE Seasoning should start early. I like to season my food at the beginning, keeping tabs on how the recipe is progressing by tasting, and adjusting the seasoning right at the end. If you don't season at the top of the cook and just hurl in a big handful of salt at the end, your food will taste super salty.

USE YOUR HANDS Your hands are the best way to distribute salt effectively. Salt mills and shakers are okay, and they get the job done, but getting to know the texture and feel of your salt and being able to gauge exactly how much you're using is the best way forward. Buy a pinch pot, fill it with salt, and you're on the right track.

CAN'T TASTE? USE YOUR SCALE Sometimes you can't taste the food until it's cooked and too late to adjust. For bread and pastry recipes, always measure with a teaspoon or digital scales before adding salt.

DON'T BE AFRAID OF HEIGHTS The higher you sprinkle, the better the distribution, so always make sure you're sprinkling a good distance from your food. This is especially important when you're seasoning a piece of fish or meat before cooking. Grab a pinch of salt and sprinkle it over your chopping board from 2cm, 10cm and 30cm high. You'll see that the higher you get, the better the spread of the salt.

HOLD YOUR HORSES Salt needs a second to work its magic. Once you've added it, hold on for ten seconds before tasting again.

BE BOLD, BUT GO SLOW I want you to cook like a chef and be bold with your seasoning, but go steady. Once you've added it, you can't get it back, so take your time and taste the whole way. If you're nervous, you can whip out a little bowl of whatever you're seasoning and experiment with just that to avoid spoiling the bigger batch.

This might sound completely wild, but you should taste your salt. If you're going to taste your food throughout the cooking process, knowing the qualities of the most important ingredient you're using will give you a better understanding of how to use it properly. Fine sea salt doesn't mean it'll taste the same as table salt. Some salts are saltier than others, so a pinch of one brand won't be exactly the same as another. Dip your finger in and give it a try! It should taste clean, oceanic and pure.

WHEN SHOULD YOU ADD SALT?

When you choose to add your salt is so important to how food tastes. When you season something with salt two things can happen. The salt sits on the surface of the ingredient and begins to draw out moisture; moisture then creates a solution, and the salt can then begin to penetrate the ingredient via osmosis. This is how you season meat and fish well, and why curing with salt is so effective. As osmosis draws water out of the ingredient, the salt moves in, seasoning the food. Genius! Once the salt is in, it diffuses through the ingredient, creating an even balance of salt throughout.

Some recipes require you to add salt years in advance (like cured meats, fish sauce and Tabasco), a handful call for a week (such as pastrami, corned beef and salt cod), a few need a day or two (roast chicken, leg of lamb, porchetta) and most require salt on the day – right before you cook or during the process. When cooking meat or fish, you want to get your salt on ahead of cooking. For example, when you cook a piece of chicken breast, the proteins within the meat contract and denature, squeezing moisture from the meat. If, ahead of cooking, you sprinkle the chicken breast with salt and allow it to penetrate the meat, the salt will begin to break down those proteins. When the breast is cooked, the proteins won't tighten and contract to the same degree; instead, they'll help to retain moisture. The larger the piece of protein, the longer it needs to be salted. If it's a steak for one, 20 minutes will do. A prime rib for 15, then you'll want to salt it at least a day in advance. Seafood is a little more delicate, and I find 15–20 minutes is more than enough for a portion of fish destined for the pan, though you'll want to salt it for longer if you're aiming to cure or dramatically change its texture.

OTHER SALTY THINGS

Sometimes you don't want to use salt, you want to reach for something that brings salinity, but also can offer other qualities. There's a whole cast of salty ingredients that can help liven things up. As well as the classic miso, soy and fish sauces, you can introduce olives, cheese, cured meats and ferments. Check out the list of salty bits for more inspiration on page 30.

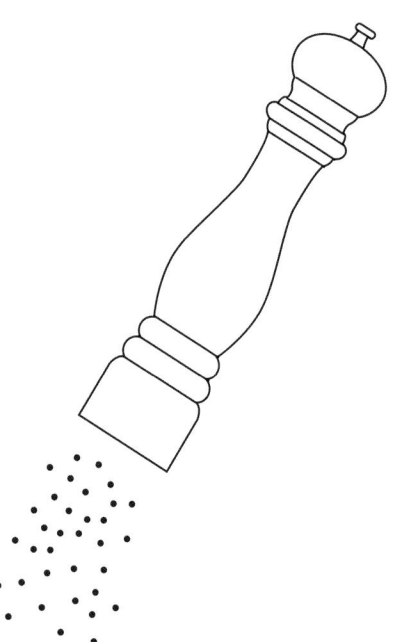

Black pepper and other spices

It's rare to see or mention one without the other, but in reality, salt and pepper are worlds apart. Salt is a mineral that has a direct effect on the texture, flavour and makeup of the food it meets, while black pepper is a spice and can't quite pull off those feats. Black pepper can't penetrate ingredients in the same way salt can, but it can elevate flavour. A good-quality pepper can add a fruity heat to a recipe, enhance a meaty steak, bring out the sweetness in a roasted piece of monkfish, or heighten the salty funk of guanciale in a proper carbonara. While they can't affect the texture of another ingredient, spices like black pepper give life to dishes, adding depth and texture (Sichuan pepper will literally make your mouth tingle! Check out the recipe on page 241 and try for yourself).

Spices come in all shapes and sizes, and in most cases, you should buy them whole, not ground. Walk away from ground black pepper forever, please. The aromas of spices are held in the essential oils that are released once you smash the spices up with a peppermill, pestle and mortar, or when you chew on them. Some spices are better bought ground, like turmeric, chilli powder and mace – grinding them yourself would be a nightmare. But spices like pepper, fennel, cumin and coriander will taste ten times better when freshly toasted and ground right before you add them to your food. The heat from the toasting warms and wakes up those oils before you grind and release them into your recipe.

Fat

When you add fat to a dish it can deliver silky, unctuous texture and richness. To use fat as a seasoning is to use it to finish a dish – a drizzle of olive oil over a ripe tomato, an egg yolk on a beef tartare, or a blob of crème fraîche with a lip-puckering lemon tart. Fat offers a soothing quality to balance spicy recipes, a respite from bitter and sour flavours, and a gentle foundation for sweet things to build upon. You can find fat in different forms all over the pantry and fridge. Here are some of my favourite fatty things:

1. Oils (olive, seed, nut and vegetable)
2. Butter and ghee
3. Animal fat (pork, beef, duck)
4. Nuts and seeds
5. Avocados
6. Oily tinned fish (sardines, mackerel)
7. Dairy products (cream, yoghurt, kefir)
8. Cheese
9. Egg yolks
10. Chocolate

Sugar, acid and spice

After salt and spices, there's sugar. Sugar is a serious flavour enhancer, especially in the savoury kitchen. A pinch of sugar or a squeeze of honey in a ragù can work wonders in the balancing act of seasoning. Sugar is vital to a balanced vinaigrette, and when caramelised and burnt, it can add a serious depth to glazes and braises.

Lemon is a staple ingredient in my kitchen. It's my favourite source of acidity – a lemon wedge plonked on the side of a plate is rarely a bad idea. Vinegars and citrus bring zip and life to a recipe, brightening up the heaviest, richest flavours with ease. Why do you think a pickle works so well on a burger? Or why salt and vinegar crisps are objectively the best flavour? Acid. Try to buy really good-quality wine vinegars; they have an incredible sweet and sour flavour that the cheap stuff completely misses. Citrus must be fresh (bottled citrus juice tastes nothing like the fresh stuff). I also like to splurge on a special bottle of aged balsamic. I use it to finish plates like I do Maldon salt. It has a complexity that is hard to find in other ingredients and the texture of a sticky, rich, aged balsamic is crazy good.

Fresh herbs should also be considered under the umbrella of seasoning. Herbs are used across so many cuisines to add vibrance and fragrance to a plate of food. Vietnamese cookery is perhaps the champion of this. When ordering pho, you're often given a huge heaping tangle of fragrant herbs like basil, perilla and mint to add to your bowl at will, the aroma and texture elevating the flavours of the broth and proteins within. The right herb can accentuate umami, highlight sweet and sour notes and bring a thwack of aroma like no other. When using soft herbs (parsley, dill, coriander, chives, etc.), you can eat the whole thing, and the stems are usually some of the most flavoursome parts, while also adding great texture. For hardier herbs you'll want to strip the leaves off their woody stems (unless you're using them to season a dish from the start, and removing them at the end).

EMBRACE THE SOUR AND BITTER

So, those tastes that are supposed to indicate that food might be out to get us, how can we use them to our advantage? It's best to live life a little close to the edge, and a measured dose of sour and bitter in your food will help you live an exciting life in the kitchen. A bitter edge in cooking is an under-celebrated thing: when folks think of bitter citrus, they typically associate it with the wince-inducing act of chomping into a slice of raw lemon or grapefruit. But the truth is, we love bitter things. Consider your morning coffee, your evening beer, a chunk of dark chocolate, your 'skin glow' matcha – it's all bitter! If you've travelled in Italy, you'll know the Italians love a bitter edge with their meals. A glass of Campari and Aperol are great examples. A meal often starts with something bitter to excite the palate. After that, plates of bitter braised chicory or raw *puntarelle alla Romana* are commonplace and help bring another (bitter) dimension to a table full of food. Rich, fatty roasted pork with a hint of bitter grapefruit, or chopped lemon rind through a butter sauce for fish, not only lends the acidity needed for culinary balance but a savoury bitterness and hint of sour that amplifies the natural sweetness and richness of the other ingredients. Learn to embrace the sour and bitter, and you'll enjoy a new dimension in your cooking.

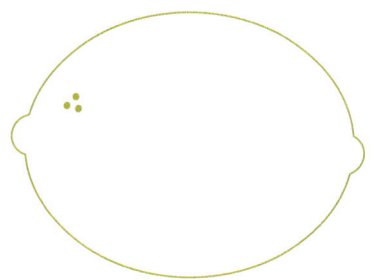

INTRODUCTION

HOW TO CHOOSE INGREDIENTS

Always remember, a cook is only as good as their ingredients, whether you're making a porchetta, a tomato salad or just cheese on toast. It's very hard to cook entirely with the seasons – sometimes, you need to break the rules, and that's okay: I use citrus all year round, but when it comes into season in January and February, I really go for it. Whether it's meat, fish, fruit or veg, buy what you can afford, and take a moment to think about what you're buying and when you're buying it.

Vegetables, herbs and fruit

Every time you buy and eat a vegetable or a piece of fruit, it's a bit of a gamble. When your teeth pierce the skin of an apple, are you met with an offputting, furry texture, or a crisp burst of flavour? Does your watermelon taste like water and no melon, or is it alive with intensity? If it's the former, it can sometimes be down to bad luck, but more often than not, it's because you might be eating produce at the wrong time of year. How do you tip the odds of eating good fruit in your favour? Eat with the seasons.

The majority of the fresh ingredients you buy will be fruits and vegetables, so check out each month and get to know what's in season in your region. What grows together goes together, so things in season at the same time are often good bedfellows! These lists are far from exhaustive, but it's a solid round-up of everything I like to eat and when I like to eat it.

SALAD Baby Gem, Butter Leaf, Frisee, Iceberg, Oak Leaf, Rocket, Romaine
BITTER LEAVES Castelfranco, Endive, Radicchio, Tardivo
VEG THAT ARE 'SECRET' FRUITS Avocados, Chillies, Cucumbers, Peppers, Tomatoes
ROOTS Beetroot, Carrots, Parsnips, Radish
BRASSICAS Broccoli, Cabbages, Cauliflower, Cavolo Nero, Kale, Purple Sprouting
PODS Broad Beans, French Beans, Peas
STEM VEGETABLES Asparagus, Kohlrabi, Rhubarb
STARCHY VEGETABLES Potatoes, Sweet Potato, Sweetcorn
MUSHROOMS Cep, Chanterelle, Chestnut, Field, Girolle
SOFT HERBS Basil, Chervil, Chives, Dill, Mint, Parsley, Tarragon
HARD HERBS Bay, Marjoram, Oregano, Rosemary, Sage, Thyme
STONE FRUITS Apricots, Cherries, Nectarines, Peaches, Plums
POMES Apples, Pears, Quince
MELONS Cantaloupe, Charentais, Honeydew, Watermelon
BERRIES AND SOFT FRUITS Blueberries, Raspberries, Strawberries
CITRUS Blood Orange, Clementines, Lemons, Limes, Navel Oranges

VEG Brussels Sprouts, Cauliflower, Celeriac, Jerusalem Artichoke, Kale, Leeks, Purple Sprouting, Radicchio, Spinach, Spring Greens, Wild Garlic
FRUIT Blood Oranges, Forced Rhubarb, Grapefruit, Lemons, Limes

 VEG Brussels Sprouts, Cauliflower, Celeriac, Jerusalem Artichoke, Kale, Leeks, Purple Sprouting, Radicchio, Spinach, Spring Greens, Wild Garlic
FRUIT Blood Oranges, Forced Rhubarb, Grapefruit, Lemons, Limes

 VEG Cauliflower, Celeriac, Leeks, Purple Sprouting, Radicchio, Spinach, Spring Greens, Wild Garlic
FRUIT Blood Oranges, Forced Rhubarb, Grapefruit, Lemons

 VEG Asparagus, Beetroot, Broad Beans, Cauliflower, Leafy Spring Greens, Mint, Peas, Purple Sprouting, Spinach, Spring Garlic, Wild Garlic
FRUIT Citrus, Grapefruit, Lemons, Rhubarb (unforced)

 VEG Asparagus, Beetroot, Broad Beans, Leafy Spring Greens, Mint, Peas, Radishes, Spring Carrots, Spring Garlic, Spinach
FRUIT Elderflower, Gooseberries, Lemons, Rhubarb (unforced)

 VEG Artichokes, Asparagus, Basil, Beetroot, Broad Beans, Broccoli, Carrots, Chard, Courgettes, Fennel, Green Beans, Kohlrabi, Lettuces, Mint, New Potatoes, Peas, Peppers, Radishes, Sweetcorn, Tomatoes
FRUIT Apricots, Cherries, Elderflower, Gooseberries, Lemons, Melons, Nectarines, Peaches, Raspberries, Rhubarb (unforced), Strawberries

 VEG Artichokes, Aubergine, Basil, Beetroot, Broad Beans, Broccoli, Carrots, Cavolo Nero, Celery, Chard, Courgettes, Fennel, Green Beans, Kohlrabi, Lettuces, Mint, New Potatoes, Peas, Peppers, Radishes, Sweetcorn, Tomatoes
FRUIT Apricots, Blueberries, Cherries, Gooseberries, Melons, Nectarines, Peaches, Raspberries, Strawberries

 VEG Artichokes, Aubergine, Basil, Beetroot, Broccoli, Cabbage, Carrots, Cavolo Nero, Celery, Ceps, Chanterelles, Chard, Chestnut Mushrooms, Green Beans, Kale, Kohlrabi, Lettuces, Mint, Peas, Peppers, Radishes, Sweetcorn, Tomatoes
FRUIT Apples, Apricots, Blackberries, Blueberries, Cherries, Figs, Grapes, Melons, Nectarines, Peaches, Plums, Raspberries, Strawberries

 VEG Artichokes, Aubergine, Basil, Beetroot, Broccoli, Cabbage, Carrots, Cavolo Nero, Celery, Ceps, Chanterelles, Chard, Chestnut Mushrooms, Early Pumpkin, Green Beans, Kale, Kohlrabi, Leeks, Lettuces, Radishes, Sweetcorn, Tomatoes
FRUIT Apples, Blackberries, Blueberries, Figs, Nectarines, Peaches, Pears, Plums, Raspberries, Strawberries

 VEG Beetroot, Broccoli, Brussels Sprouts, Cabbages, Carrots, Cauliflower, Cavolo Nero, Celeriac, Celery, Ceps, Chanterelles, Chard, Chicory, Fennel, Kale, Kohlrabi, Leeks, Pumpkin, Squash
FRUIT Apples, Dates, Figs, Pears, Plums, Quince

 VEG Broccoli, Brussels Sprouts, Cabbages, Carrots, Cauliflower, Cavolo Nero, Celeriac, Ceps, Chanterelles, Chard, Chestnuts, Chicory, Jerusalem Artichoke, Kale, Kohlrabi, Leeks, Parsnips, Pumpkins, Purple Sprouting, Radicchio, Winter Squash
FRUIT Apples, Clementines, Cranberries, Dates, Quince

VEG Broccoli, Brussels Sprouts, Cabbages, Carrots, Cauliflower, Cavolo Nero, Celeriac, Chard, Chestnuts, Chicory, Jerusalem Artichoke, Kale, Kohlrabi, Leeks, Parsnips, Pumpkins, Purple Sprouting, Radicchio
FRUIT Apples, Clementines, Cranberries, Dates, Grapefruit, Quince

Meat

In 2020, I spent a happy six months working as a butcher on a farm in West Sussex. Pork, lamb and beef were reared on the farm, and every Thursday we'd bring roughly 11 pigs, 4 lambs and half a cow into the butcher's shop to break down over the week. By the end of my stint, I'd made thousands of sausages, cured and smoked sides of bacon, learnt to break down a fore and hind quarter of beef and could debone a pig's head with my eyes closed.

Walking down the aisle of a supermarket after having been thrust into butchery was pretty revelatory. The disconnect between source and table is stark. For the most part, the only whole animals that home cooks deal with are chickens. Of course, the idea of a whole pig, lamb or – God forbid – cow in your kitchen is out of the question, but there is certainly a chasm between the steer chewing grass in the field and the neatly packaged sirloin you see on a supermarket shelf.

Even working as a chef, when the meat delivery arrives, it comes in boxes, often full of pre-portioned steaks or chops, along with bones and trim for stocks and sauces. Buying and breaking down whole animals in restaurants is a rarity. Being involved in the process – from whole animal, to primals, to sellable cuts, to steak-on-plate – gave me a new perspective on meat and how it travels from the field to your table. It also taught me how to really embrace nose-to-tail eating, how to transform the trim from prime cuts into pies, sausages and terrines, and how to respect every last bit of the animal.

We were dealing with beautiful produce, heritage breeds and very high-quality meat. I learnt to identify the best cuts for braising, what the optimum amount of fat for a pork chop looks like and how thick to cut your T-bone for the grill. I want to pass on some of that knowledge, plus a few butchery tips and tricks I picked up on the farm. Butchery is intuitive, fun and easier than you think. By taking the time to learn a few basic cuts and anatomy, you can seriously level up your home cooking. You'll be deboning chickens, butterflying pork belly and whipping out wishbones like a pro.

What being a butcher also taught me is that good meat will never – and should never – be cheap. It takes an awful lot of work and a load of hands to rear, slaughter, butcher and process the meat we cook with and enjoy. Meat is a treat, a privilege to be enjoyed on occasion and with thought. Speak to your butcher, ask them about their produce – they're itching to talk to you about it. Try not to eat meat every day, and when you do eat meat, buy happy meat from a good source! Trust me, it'll taste about a million times better.

FAT IS YOUR FRIEND

It doesn't matter if you're buying chicken, pork, lamb or beef. Fat = flavour. On both tender and tough cuts, you want there to be a decent amount of fat present, whether it's intramuscular or wrapped around the exterior. There was a time when a large fat cap on your pork or lamb chop was undesirable. We need to change the narrative here, big time. When properly rendered, the fat cap on a pork chop delivers flavour with every bite and helps support the leaner portion of the cut. Don't be shy, look for good marbling or a generous fat cap and remember, meat is a treat!

Let it rest

This is probably the most important step of the process of cooking a steak. You can nail the air-drying, the seasoning, the render, the sear and the baste, but if you cut right into that thing before it's had time to chill out, it's game over. No matter how well you've cooked your beef, it's going to give up all its juices to the chopping board. Happy chopping board, sad chef.

Steaks are muscles, and when you expose muscles to heat, they contract and tighten. These muscles are full of little fibres that hold on to water, the 'juice' of the steak. The fibres contract and squeeze on that water, so when you open an exit route (the moment you carve), it's going to get the hell out of dodge. It's all about temperature. As your steak rests and cools, those muscle fibres relax and allow the juice in the steak to be under far less pressure.

Choose your fighter

TENDER CUTS

Tender cuts are unique as they're often just seasoned, cooked quickly and then celebrated for exactly what they are. Broadly speaking, the tender cuts are found towards the middle of the animal. To stay nice and tender, the muscles don't do a lot of work and are supported by the extremities of the animal: the legs, shoulders, neck, etc.

Tender cuts demand a higher price as there are fewer of them on the animal. Depending on where it was cut from, a sirloin or ribeye from one end of the cow can contain more different muscle groups than one cut from the other. You're after a steak that is mostly made up of one muscle. The more muscles that make up the steak, the more collagen there will be in the steak, and collagen needs to be cooked for a longer time. With something like a ribeye or a sirloin, you want to serve it blushing pink. If you've ever had a gristly, tough steak, it's likely it had a good amount of connective tissue and collagen in it. The story is the same for pork, lamb or venison.

Examples: fillet, ribeye, chop, T-bone, porterhouse, bavette, rump cap

TOUGH CUTS

Tough cuts are taken from the parts of the animal that have worked pretty hard. They have thick, visible muscle fibres (referred to as the grain) and are often made up of pockets of smaller muscles, stitched together with collagen and connective tissues. A good tough cut will also have heaps of intramuscular fat.

Why are these cuts so good for slow cooking? These larger, tougher cuts are made up of a whole bunch of smaller muscles grouped together. You can look at a cross-section of a pork or lamb shoulder and identify muscle groups surrounded by white lines. Between each of the muscles, knitting them together, you'll find connective tissue, mostly made up of collagen. When slow-cooked, collagen proteins unravel and transform into gelatin, which gives your dish the creamy, unctuous texture and rich flavour that we're looking for in a ragù, stew or braise.

Examples: shoulder, shin, cheek, neck, leg, rib, brisket, belly

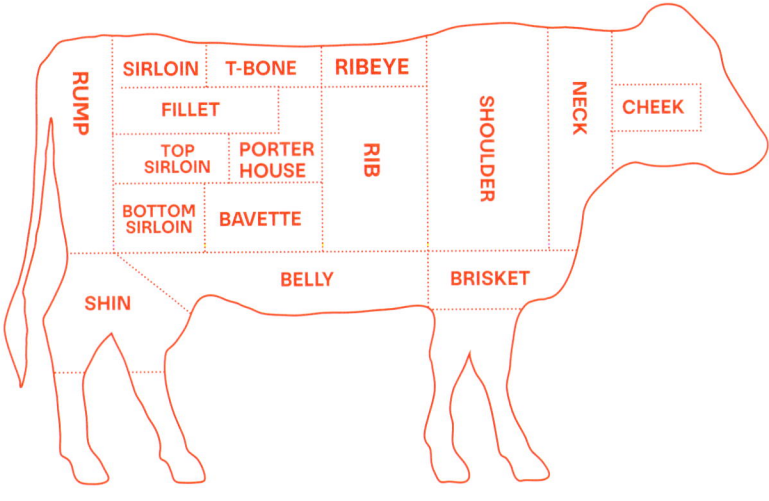

Chicken

It's the world's favourite meat, and it's utterly delicious. It's also a great way to learn about cooking tough and tender cuts as well as the benefits of rendering fat and crisping up skin. We're going to poach, roast, sear, grill AND braise chickens throughout this book, so you'd better learn how to buy a good one. What are the visual clues that point towards a healthy, happy bird? Look for taut, firm skin that has some heft. If the skin seems very thin, especially on the breast, then the bird won't have much natural fat on it and has likely lived a short life. If you notice a yellow-ish tinge to the skin, it probably means the chicken has had a diet containing corn (healthy!), not that it's jaundiced. Try to skip chickens with oversized, inflated breasts. You might think you're getting good bang for your buck, but this is often a sign that the bird has been hurried through life, likely encouraged to eat more than necessary to hit the minimum weight requirement as soon as possible. The result is meat that is pappy, largely flavourless and dries out very quickly. You're after a well-proportioned bird; a slightly skinnier bird is often a sign of a healthy, happy life, especially in the legs.

Beef

You can get really lost in beef. There are hundreds of breeds and about a million different ways to cut steaks, with each having a different name, some well-known, some more obscure, but all delicious. For the purposes of this book, however, I'm keeping things general. After you've landed on whether you're after a tough or tender cut, it's time to distil your decision: which one on the butcher's counter is catching your eye? The things you're looking for with beef are colour, fat content and the visible texture of the meat. Run your eyes over the display and look for cuts and chops with a deep red colour, ideally with little veins of intramuscular fat running like lightning bolts across the meat. The surface of the meat should look dry and smooth – if it's rough, it's been cut badly. If the surface is greying or has a sticky quality, it might have been sitting out a little too long. If you're buying mince, you can ask your butcher to make it fresh for you and pick the cuts you want to include. Check out the burger recipe on page 196, pick up some dry-aged steak trim, ask the butcher to mince it, and you'll never buy a pack from the supermarket again.

Pork

The first time I remember sitting up in my seat and thinking 'woah, pork!' was at a little restaurant in Vinegar Hill, Brooklyn. A thick-cut, bone-in pork chop was plonked down between my dad and me, dressed with little roasted gooseberries and carved into thick, blushing slices. In general, pork chops have had a pretty bad rap in the home kitchen and been criminally overcooked for a fairly long time. You should cook your pork chops pink, the shoulders and belly until melting and the skin, if present, should crackle. To tick all these boxes, you need to start with the right product. Similarly to beef, you're after meat that has plenty of fat. You'll see less intramuscular fat in a pork chop, but the cap on the back of the chop should be generous. The meat should be a deep pink colour and look dry rather than really moist. If buying a shoulder or belly, look for thick, firm, creamy white fat and plenty of it. For glassy, puffy crackling, ask your butcher for pork that has been hung or even dry aged. This'll ensure your skin has had a head-start on the way to crackling. You probably won't find this at the supermarkets, and if that's the only option, you can help the skin along the way yourself by placing it on a rack and giving it some time uncovered in the fridge.

Lamb

For special occasions, I love to buy lamb. When you're at the butcher's counter, look for a deep, pinky-red colour in the meat rather than a pale, chalky pink. The fat should be thick, firm and stark white. If you're feeding a crowd, a shoulder or whole leg is the way to go. Sheep are animals of routine. After the frost of winter has thawed, they are gunning to give birth at the start of spring. Late spring and early summer are when British lamb is at its very best, so I try to cook lamb predominantly during this time of year. This supports domestic farming, limits the amount of imported lamb on plates (it mostly cruises in from New Zealand, the other side of the world!) and the meat tastes really good. If you want lamb at any other point in the year, don't shrug off the idea of hogget or mutton. Technically, lamb is any sheep that is under a year old, hogget and mutton is meat from a sheep over a year old. It's a cheaper option and the flavour is sensational. A slow-cooked hogget shoulder is a homerun for an Easter lunch.

Seafood

Perhaps the food that I enjoy buying, cooking and eating the most is seafood. Seafood cookery can take just seconds or hours, it can be dead simple or technique-heavy, and it can be a midweek meal or a weekend treat. Seafood also boasts that rare quality of being both incredibly delicious and extremely good for you. It requires a little more thought and planning than meat cookery, but the payoff is exceptionally satisfying. Nothing beats searing a fresh wild bass fillet in a pan, taking down a bowl of saucy clams or grilling a whole fish over fire. Home cooks always seem so petrified of cooking fish: a nuclear combination of limited availability, awareness and willingness seems to have stunted our love of seafood cooking at home. However, if your goal is to elevate your home cooking, seafood is the easiest of wins.

Seafood is an almost perfect food source and is highly seasonal. It can be cheap as chips (mackerel, sardines, mussels) or a real treat (brill, trout, clams). Seafood has a pretty short shelf life and wild produce is always dearer than farmed. When sourced responsibly, it can be good for the planet, too.

You'd think that as an island that boasts some of the finest seafood on the planet, it would be easy to scoop up sparkling seafood in the UK at the drop of a hat. Unfortunately, independent fishmongers are dropping like flies as supermarkets hoover up the lion's share of the market. How can you help? Find out who your local fishmonger is and get to know them! Ask them what's best, when it was landed, how it was caught and where it's come from. Knowledge is power and I promise you a good fishmonger will have all the answers and be itching to share their expertise. I very rarely go to my fishmonger with my heart set on something. Thanks to its wild nature, buying seafood can be unpredictable and what jumps out of the counter at you can and will change daily, so be ready to think on your feet. If you don't have a fishmonger near you, there are now a great number of online fishmongers and sustainable retailers that source directly from regional fisheries and deliver straight to your door.

Seafood basics

ROUND FISH

Round fish make up 90% of the seafood you'll see. They are cylindrical, swim upright and their bodies taper towards the tail. Typically, they have two fillets, one on either side of a central spine.
Examples: cod, bass, hake, mackerel, red mullet, gurnard, bream, trout

FLATFISH

These are a much tighter bunch than the catch-all of round fish. They have a similar flavour and texture across the board, with the bigger fish offering a meatier flesh. Flatfish swim horizontally across the ocean floor, with both eyes on one side. They have four fillets, two on either side of their spine.
Examples: plaice, turbot, brill, halibut, sole

SHELLFISH

There are heaps of different types of shellfish, but we're going to focus on just a few here. Crustaceans and molluscs are sometimes collectively referred to as shellfish. The common denominator is the fact that they don't have a backbone, relying on a shell or exoskeleton. Crustaceans (prawns, lobster, crab) have a hard shell, a segmented body, and jointed legs and claws. Molluscs and bivalves make up the rest, and this also encompasses squid and octopus.
Examples: clams, mussels, prawns, crab, squid, octopus, lobster

SMOKED, TINNED AND PRESERVED FISH

To extend the shelf life and transform the flavour and texture of fish, it is often preserved: frozen, smoked, cured with salt or acid or packed into a tin and pasteurised. Always check the sustainability credentials of your preserved fish.
Examples: salted anchovies, smoked trout, smoked eel, caviar/fish roe, frozen fish

Buying whole fish

So, you've walked up to the counter and a few things have caught your eye. How can you check what's super fresh and what to swerve? A fish's eyes are the best way to gauge how recently it was caught: they should be bright, shiny and crystal clear. If you can, ask to see the fish's gills and check they're bright red and vibrant and that the fins are moist, shiny and intact. Also, if the fillets are dry or cracking, the fish ain't fresh. The skin should have a clear sheen to it, if the slime has begun to turn opaque, walk away! The fillets should feel smooth, firm and bounce back when prodded. A good fish will smell clean and oceanic and not fishy. Trust your nose, it's rarely wrong.

Buying portioned fish

More often than not, you're buying portioned fish, i.e. smaller cuts of a larger fillet designed for one or two people. When looking at fish that's been prepped, you can't check the eyes, gills or scales and, if they're inside packaging, the smell test is useless. If there's heaps of moisture inside the pack, the fish has either been frozen and thawed a couple of times or is simply losing the ability to retain moisture due to ageing. Check out the flesh and look for cracks or splits within it: if the muscles have started to separate, the fish has started to break down and is old. You want a portion of fish that looks firm, moist and shiny and ever so slightly translucent. If the fish is mushy, has started to turn opaque or looks dry, walk away!

Buying shellfish

A few types of shellfish, such as mussels, clams and oysters, will be alive when you buy them. Their shells should be tightly closed, and they should feel dense and heavy when picked up. If they're open and don't close after a sharp tap, don't buy them. These are dead and can make you sick! Crabs and lobsters are either sold live or just cooked. The crab recipe in this book (page 129) calls for picked white and brown crab meat, and you can easily buy this in little pots.

Gutting and scaling

A good fishmonger will offer to gut and scale your fish for you if they haven't done it already. You can do this yourself, if you really want to, but it can be a messy job and you'll probably be finding scales all over your kitchen for a while afterwards. Once the fish has been gutted, make sure the cavity is clean and dry before you pop it into the fridge.

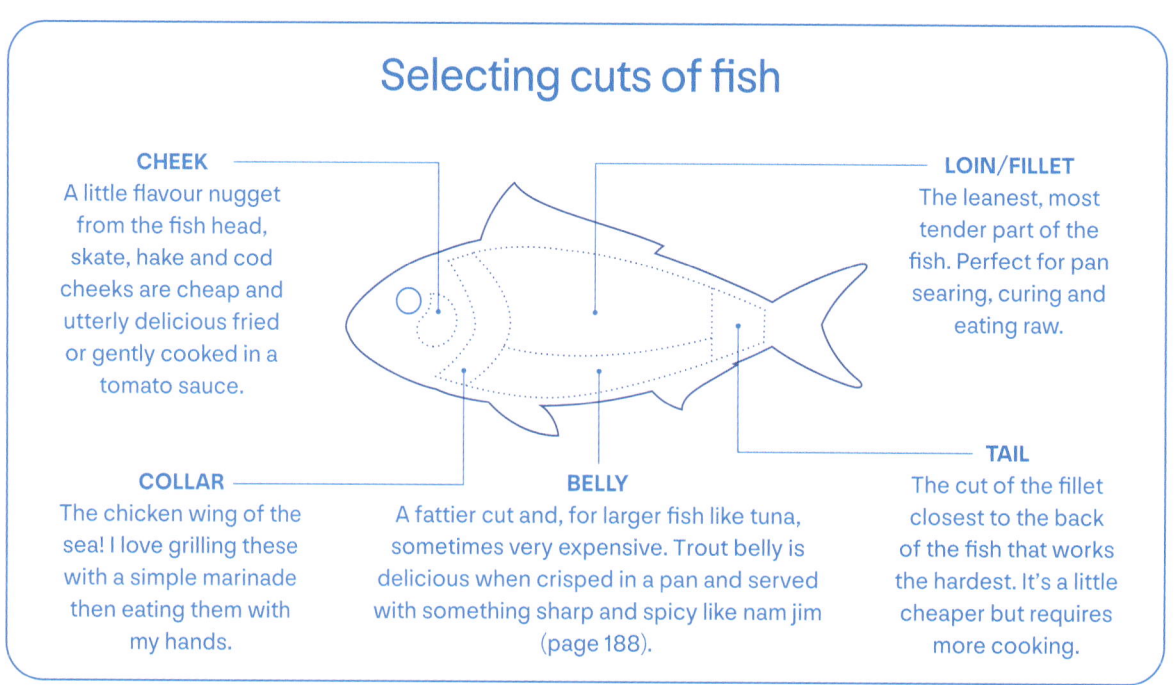

Selecting cuts of fish

CHEEK
A little flavour nugget from the fish head, skate, hake and cod cheeks are cheap and utterly delicious fried or gently cooked in a tomato sauce.

LOIN/FILLET
The leanest, most tender part of the fish. Perfect for pan searing, curing and eating raw.

COLLAR
The chicken wing of the sea! I love grilling these with a simple marinade then eating them with my hands.

BELLY
A fattier cut and, for larger fish like tuna, sometimes very expensive. Trout belly is delicious when crisped in a pan and served with something sharp and spicy like nam jim (page 188).

TAIL
The cut of the fillet closest to the back of the fish that works the hardest. It's a little cheaper but requires more cooking.

Storage

Keep your fish as dry and cold as you can in your fridge (sub 5°C) and don't put live shellfish in an airtight container. It's a total myth that you need to eat fish the same day you buy it: in fact, some fish benefit from a day or two exposed to circulating air in your fridge. I like to keep fish that is going to hit the grill or pan on a rack set over a tray to help air dry the skin so I can get it super crispy. If you've got space, you can even tie the fish up and hang it in your fridge by its tail.

Crudo and cured fish

Crudo literally means 'raw' and is as simple as buying an immaculate piece of fish, removing the skin, trimming it up, slicing it beautifully and serving it with a simple garnish. All you need in order to pull it off is a good fishmonger and they'll guide your hand. I like to serve sea bass, bream, tuna, mackerel or fresh scallops raw. You can pick these up from any fishmonger worth their salt and be super confident they're fresh and delicious. If you're feeling a little nervous, you can freeze the fish, which kills almost anything that might make you unwell. Most sushi restaurants around the world are required to freeze and thaw their fish before serving. Speak to your fishmonger, ask when the fish was landed, if it's sushi grade or okay to be eaten raw.

Eating fish sustainably

A huge chunk of the fish and shellfish we buy and eat in this country is caught in the wild. With advancements in technology and more efficient, greedy fishing practices, the once cat-and-mouse game of fishing and hunting is far from a fair fight. Overfishing, wasted bycatch and poor farming conditions can make buying fish responsibly a total minefield, so your best bet is to talk to your fishmonger and get their advice. If shopping at a supermarket, look for MSC labelling. All you can do is your best!

DRY-STORE ESSENTIALS

This is a solid list of the key players in my kitchen cupboards. They all feature in this book, see action regularly, are widely available, affordable and not considered specialist (no super-pricey, aged, dried tuna or bottles of olive oil from Mount Olympus lurking here). You don't need them all at once, so scoop up new items when you're ready to use them and buy ingredients in quantities that make sense. I live in a pretty small flat in London and space is at a premium, so keeping a tight, concise crew of flavour-boosters is super important. You can then draft in a few wildcards at a time.

SALT AND SALTY STUFF

I've talked about the importance of tasting and seasoning your food, so where better a place to start than with the salty stuff. Whether it's straight-up sea salt or a dash of fish sauce, all of these ingredients bring salinity and depth to your cooking, and some have the added bonus of umami.

- Flaky Maldon salt
- Fine sea salt
- Light soy sauce
- White miso paste
- Fish sauce
- Worcestershire sauce
- Salted anchovy fillets in oil
- MSG

OILS AND FATS

To deliver richness, lubrication and flavour, all of these ingredients are either pure fat or have a high fat content, and can be used to sizzle, fry or roast, or to finish dishes, sauces and marinades.

- Extra virgin olive oil (for finishing)
- Olive oil (for cooking)
- Neutral oil (sunflower/vegetable)
- Toasted sesame oil
- Unsalted butter
- Ghee
- Tahini

VINEGARS AND ACIDITY

Put some zip and brightness into your food with acidity. There's a very large list of delicious things that tick this box, but these are my staples. My eyes were opened to the world of vinegars in restaurants, and it goes deep: all have a different balance of sweet to sour – some are rich, some are tannic and bitter, all are tasty. Start here and you're in a great place.

- Sherry vinegar
- Wine vinegars
- Aged balsamic vinegar
- Rice vinegar
- Apple vinegar (cider)
- Pomegranate molasses
- Fresh lemon
- Fresh lime

CORE SPICES AND DRIED HERBS

I keep a pretty tight spice cupboard and try to buy whole spices where possible. Some are only available ground (this is totally fine!), but whole spices will last a lot longer and better retain their potency. When I use whole spices, I always try to toast and grind them fresh.

- Fennel seeds
- Cumin seeds
- Coriander seeds
- Cinnamon sticks
- Dried oregano
- Ground turmeric
- Fresh vanilla pods
- Vanilla paste

CHILLIES AND HOT STUFF

My appetite for heat is pretty generous. I love the sensation of spice and heat, and these are my go-tos for bringing a robust kick to my cooking. Some are punchier than others.

- Black peppercorns
- Sichuan peppercorns
- Aleppo pepper
- Dried chilli flakes
- Whole dried chillies
- Harissa
- Chilli oil
- Vinegar-based hot sauce (Tabasco/Crystal/Frank's)
- Chilli-forward hot sauce (Cholula/Sriracha/Encona)
- Prepared horseradish
- A few good mustards (Dijon, English, American, wholegrain)

PICKLES, PRESERVES AND BRINY THINGS

Where would we be without pickles? Nowhere, that's where. These are a two-for-one, delivering a good thwack of acidity as well as salinity.

- Green olives – gordal, nocellara or manzanilla
- Black olives – kalamata or taggiasche
- Brined green peppercorns
- Cornichons
- Pickled jalapeños
- Pickled guindilla chillies
- Nonpareille capers
- Pickled ginger
- Kimchi

TINS, JARS AND A TUBE

With these six ingredients, you can make so many of the recipes in the book. I'll always have a couple of each in stock.

- Good-quality tinned tomatoes
- Tomato purée/concentrate
- Jarred chickpeas
- Jarred white beans
- Coconut milk
- Good-quality tinned tuna

SUGAR AND SWEET THINGS

You can go deep on different sugar varieties, but you can get most jobs done with the three sugars in this list. And honey and maple syrup are some of the most magical naturally-occurring ingredients out there.

- Caster sugar
- Light brown sugar
- Dark brown/muscovado sugar
- Honey
- Maple syrup

BAKING

The kind of baking I like to do is pretty simple. I keep a couple of good-quality flours in the cupboard, a bag of semolina for baking and pasta-making and that's about it! Start here then build your heritage flour collection later!

- Plain flour
- '00' flour
- Strong white bread flour
- Semolina
- Instant yeast
- Baking powder
- Bicarbonate of soda
- Ground almonds

ALCOHOL

I don't cook with alcohol an awful lot, but I'm a huge fan of having a good-quality boxed wine on hand for a splash here and there. Boxed wine is such an underrated product – once you've cracked the seal, the wine stays fresh for weeks and you can use it a glass at a time, no dramas. I'll keep a box of white and red knocking around to dip into as well as a good stout for braises and a bottle of whisky or rum for baking.

READY-TO-GO CONDIMENTS

I'm an absolute condiment fiend. A collection of good condiments is a collection of good mates: they wait, ready and eager to make a good bite great. These are entirely subjective and should remain so. They're about what you're into, what you like to spread on your toast or dash over a grilled cheese. Buy what you love and use them as a little crutch when you can't be bothered and need big flavours straight away.

KITCHEN EQUIPMENT

In the kitchen world, there is an endless line-up of useless tools you don't need in your kitchen drawers. I'm looking at you, egg slicer . . . I like to have a concise collection of tools that have purpose, are multi-functional, versatile and are built to last. Be minimalist with your kit and maximalist with your cooking. A clutter-free kitchen is a happy one.

Sharp things

On my first stage (pronounced 'stah-j', the fancy chef term for work experience), I witnessed the horrifying moment a bleary-eyed chef realised that he'd left his knife roll on the train, ruining his day and costing him about £1k. Knives are hyper-personal items in the professional kitchen. Chefs are fiercely protective of their roll, like a bear with its cub. Pick up a knife without permission and you could find yourself on the sharp end of a bad temper. In the kitchen, everyone wears the same jacket, same apron, even the same shoes. A chef's knife is an opportunity for individual expression – the style of blade, the brand, the geometry, the weight, the feel of the handle and how sharp you keep it, says a lot about who you are as a cook.

I'm a firm believer that less is more when it comes to kitchen knives. I know chefs who have amassed enormous collections of knives over their lifetime – we're talking 100+ knives. Some of my old colleagues might come back into work after a day off with a shiny new blade, proud as punch, reinvigorated with new life, a pep in their clog-bound step. It was never really my thing. That being said, I do take great pride in the concise collection I have put together over the years. While there are myriad more specialist knives, these are the essentials.

CHEF'S KNIFE

Every cook needs an all-rounder. This is a larger knife that you'll spend the most time with in the kitchen, and one that should be able to handle 90% of tasks. There are few different styles, materials and geometries to choose from. A chef's knife usually ranges between 15 and 30cm. I opt for a 27cm knife, principally because it has a large handle (which I favour), and the blade is long enough to cut through larger, more stubborn items with ease. My Misono UX10 was the first serious knife I ever bought, and it's an absolute workhorse, gliding through vegetables and proteins while still being capable of pulling off the finest chiffonade or a laser-precise shallot brunoise. It holds a mean edge for weeks and it's light – it's my favourite knife of all time and probably will be for ever. It wasn't cheap by any measure, but 21-year-old Ben thought 'I reckon this might stay with me for the rest of my life' and in the period of my life where questionable decisions were a forte, this was one of my better ones.

BREAD/PASTRY KNIFE

A serrated knife that is, of course, excellent at carving up crusty loaves of sourdough, baguettes and trimming pastry. These are also very handy for slicing big, fat, juicy tomatoes. Buy a good serrated knife and it'll last you a very long time. The rosewood Victorinox serrated knife I have has lasted me over eight years and still gets the job done.

PETTY KNIFE

If you find a knife you love, chances are they make a mini version. You'll use this for more finicky, precise tasks and it should be nimble and light. This is my favourite knife for mincing garlic, preparing herbs and some smaller meat and fish butchery. Essentially, you want a knife that you can wield with ease, one that can cut around corners. Ideally, it'll also have a little flex to it which makes it great for filleting smaller fish and breaking down poultry.

PARING KNIFE

The smallest knife in your collection. A key thing to look for when picking a paring knife is finding one that you can use away from the board. You should be able to hold a veggie in one hand, your knife in the other, and use it in the air. With a good paring knife, you'll find yourself preparing artichokes, or peeling shallots or onions like a real chef.

SCISSORS

A vital piece of equipment for the home cook is a very solid pair of kitchen scissors or shears. I use these principally for fish and chicken butchery, but find they come in handy for so many different jobs. You want them to be properly sturdy, snipping through anything with relative ease. The key thing to look for is that you can separate the blades so you can clean them properly and can sharpen them! Yes, that's right, sharpen your scissors – it can (and should) be done.

MANDOLINE

A razor-sharp mandoline offers you complete consistency when it comes to slicing veggies or shaving cheese. There are a handful of styles out there, but the classic Japanese style is the one for me. It comes with a little guard, and I suggest you use it. Mandolines are incredible tools, but they can be a little dangerous. Trust me, I've been bitten a few times!

MICROPLANE

Oh boy, are these useful. The microplane is one of my top five kitchen tools of all time, it's just a fantastic bit of kit. For the uninitiated, it is a very fine, very sharp grater that can do things a box grater never could. You can mince garlic, ginger and horseradish in seconds, transform cheese into a fluffy cloud and whip the fragrant zest off any citrus fruit with ease. They become blunt over time, but I've had mine for four years and it's still going strong, so they do have a pretty long life.

STEEL/HONING ROD

A sharp-adjacent tool and a must-have for any cook wanting to look after their knives. A common misconception is that these tools sharpen your knife. While they might improve the edge ever so slightly, they really just straighten the edge on your knife. When you use a brand-new knife, it'll have a perfectly straight or 'true' edge. That means that the two bevels are perfectly even. When you use the knife, you smash the edge into the cutting board repeatedly, and the edge rolls over onto one side, bending the sharp edge out of whack, forming what's called a bur. The goal with a honing rod is to straighten that edge out, bringing it back to 'true'.

KNIFE ROLL

The majority of you reading this will likely never need to delicately pack up your knives, sling them into your bag and leave the house, but I still think it's worth investing in a roll. It's a comfy little house for your knives, one that can sit snugly in a drawer and save the blades from rattling around. A knife roll is a sign of respect, a nod to your tools.

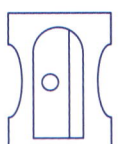

Stay sharp

Knife maintenance is everything. I'd use a £1.50 knife that's razor sharp over a £1,500 blade that's dead dull any day of the week. A blunt knife increases the likelihood of injury and food waste; a sharp blade is peaceful, predictable and oh-so satisfying to use. So, how do you keep your knives sharp? Invest in a whetstone or find someone who can sharpen your knives with one on your behalf. Whetstones are made from a composite of natural and artificial stones used to grind away material on your knife, resetting the edge. They come in different 'grit' levels, similar to sandpaper. You start low and slowly make your way up the grit levels until you're left with a razor-sharp knife.

INTRODUCTION

Cookware

28CM CARBON-STEEL FRYING PAN

I used carbon-steel pans in pretty much every restaurant I worked in. They're very, very good at searing and roasting proteins, can fly in and out of an oven, they're heavy, super durable, very affordable, they hold on to heat for dear life and are indestructible. The more you use them, the more seasoned they become, developing a natural non-stick coating over time.

24CM STAINLESS-STEEL HIGH-WALLED PASTA PAN

Perhaps the pan I use the most. It's a great midweek pan and it can nail pastas, grains, smaller portions of soup, braises and one-pot dishes. Stellar, Mauviel and Made In all make very good pasta pans.

28–30CM STAINLESS-STEEL LIDDED SAUTÉ PAN

A larger pan that'll be another staple of your midweek rotation. I favour stainless steel for recipes where you need to create a solid foundation of flavour. Build sauces and whole dishes in this pan and zip it in and out of the oven. Fast dishes, slow dishes, big or small, a good sauté pan is your best mate. All-Clad is my go-to brand.

20–25CM STAINLESS-STEEL FRYING PAN

For any recipe that needs a super-hot pan, I reach for stainless steel. Carbon steel can get pretty smoky and if you need something clean, quick and effective, stainless is the way to go. You can also add wine, tomatoes, or vinegar and not panic about your seasoning flying off. All-Clad is my favourite brand.

3 STAINLESS-STEEL LIDDED SAUCEPANS

A small, medium and large saucepan are must-haves for boiling pastas, making pilaf, soup, sauces, desserts . . . The list is endless. Look for a pan that is a made with a few plies (layers) of good-quality stainless and has a tight-fitting lid.

28–30CM ENAMELLED CAST-IRON CASSEROLE/COCOTTE

You need one of these in your kitchen, but you only need to buy one and, if well cared for, it'll last for literally generations. Perfect for slow cooking and braising, these pans are iconic. Staub or Le Creuset are the brands to look for.

ROASTING TINS

I have two roasting tins, one large, heavy, handled guy and a slightly smaller, more agile one. These are perfect for roasting large cuts of meat like porchetta or a lamb shoulder, have enough depth that you can braise in them, and have nice thick walls so they hold on to and distribute heat efficiently.

BAKING TRAYS AND WIRE RACKS

These are, of course, very handy for baking, but they go beyond that. I like to organise all my ingredients onto trays and map everything out in my head, even if it's a simple tomato pasta. Having a good stack of stainless-steel baking trays, in a few different sizes, is perfect for this. Have a few wire racks that sit neatly on top, too. These are great for cooling bakes or resting meat or fish.

How to look after your pans

New carbon-steel or cast-iron pans will be squeaky clean and shiny so need to be seasoned before first use. You can either use your hob or your oven, but be warned, it's going to get smoky! Rub a thin layer of neutral oil across the surface of the pan, top and bottom, leaving the handle untouched. Heat the pan until smoking hot, then remove from the heat and rub with another thin layer of oil as it cools. Repeat this process four or five times to develop a naturally non-stick coating.

In terms of aftercare, stainless steel is pretty much bulletproof: you can go at it with scourers and soaps, run it through the dishwasher and let it air dry. Cast-iron and carbon steel are a little fussier: always wash by hand and never use anything acidic or aggressive to clean them. I wipe mine out with a damp cloth then repeat the seasoning process once before allowing them to cool completely. You want to make sure no water sits in them either, as they'll rust.

General tools

WOODEN CHOPPING BOARDS

Next to your chef's knife, these ought to be your second most-prized possession. I favour wood above any other material. It's easy to clean and maintain, extremely knife-friendly and can be lovely to look at. I use a large, butcher's block-style chopping board. It's made of American maple wood by a company called Boos and it's excellent. I also keep a couple of other, smaller wooden boards of the same style for raw meat and fish, and one for chopping chocolate and fruit for desserts.

COOKING SPOONS

These are one of the things I've carried with me from the professional kitchen to the home. A good stock of large stainless-steel spoons, to be used for cooking and tasting, kept separate from your dining cutlery, will encourage you to commit to tasting as you cook. They're good for basting, plating and everything in between, too. You can complete so many tasks with the humble spoon, you'll be amazed.

BENCH SCRAPER

A bench or dough scraper is a must-have for me. A plastic one is super cheap and endlessly handy. Whether you're shaping bread rolls, picking up a load of chopped chives or cleaning out a bowl, a plastic bench scraper is always there to help.

Y-PEELER

Where would I be without my peeler. This humble little tool makes light work of peeling veggies, fruits, shaving cheese and thinly slicing cabbage. Ditch any other style, the y-peeler is superior.

CAKE TESTER

These are perfect for testing the doneness of cakes and your meat and fish. You can get an idea of the internal temperature of your proteins by sticking a cake tester in for a couple of seconds and then holding it to your lip. If it's cold, it's raw. If it's warm, it's about 40°C. With a little practice, you get to know exactly what a medium pork chop or a perfectly cooked piece of cod feels like on your lip. They're also less intrusive than a digital probe thermometer as they're so thin.

DIGITAL SCALE

A good-quality scale will be your right hand in the kitchen. Whatever you're cooking, being able to identify an accurate gram amount of both solids and liquids is so useful and will make sure your more precise cooking, like bread and pastry, works every single time. You want a scale that can hold up to 5kg and ideally can measure to 0.1g.

BOX GRATER

Box graters chomp through cheese, mirepoix and raw veggies with ease and the first good one you pick up will be the last one that you buy.

METAL TONGS

I have two sets of these. The first is a bog-standard metal tong used for flipping, turning and inspecting whatever I'm cooking, whether it's in the oven, in a hot pan or over fire in the back garden. The second is a pair of long metal tweezers for more delicate foods like prawns, baby veg or scallops.

OVEN THERMOMETER

I hate to break it to you, but your oven isn't running at the temperature it says it is. An analogue oven thermometer hangs out on one of the racks and tells you exactly how hot things are in there. When you're baking a lasagne or finishing off a chicken breast, a difference of 10–12°C doesn't make a whole lot of difference, but when you're baking your partner's birthday cake, every degree counts.

DIGITAL PROBE THERMOMETER

To cook through this book properly, you're going to need one of these. A digital thermometer removes the guesswork from

INTRODUCTION

cooking and will help you in so many recipes. Cooking meat, fish, pastry, custards, bread or frying is zero stress. You know exactly what's going on, all the time.

NEST OF MIXING BOWLS

You can never have enough mixing bowls. I use stainless-steel ones and buy as big a bowl as my kitchen can hold. You can then fill it full of smaller bowls and it'll tuck neatly away into a cupboard.

OFFSET PALETTE KNIFE

I cruise around the kitchen with this in my back pocket, ready to flip things in a pan, ice a cake, spread mayo for a BLT. You might see it referred to as an offset spatula or 'crank'. It is super useful for sweet and savoury cooking. If you want to get fancy with your plating, it's ace for that, too. Small but mighty.

FISH SPATULA

A proper fish spatula is a more graceful tool than the big fat plastic thing you might be used to. They're made of thin, flexible metal that you can really scoop things up with. The flex allows you to press down into the pan and slide under a piece of fish (or anything, really) without smashing it to pieces. They're a much smarter design than your bog-standard spatula, with large holes that let liquids and cooking fat drain away from your ingredients.

SILICONE SPOONULA/SPATULA

This is essentially the only big spoon you need in your kitchen. It's good for scooping and cleaning out any bowl, blender or food processor, it can fold together a chocolate mousse or fondant, scrape chicken sauce out of a pan and help you clean dough out of a bowl. You can get flat, spatula versions of these but you want, no, you need, the spoon version. Thank me later.

PAN WEIGHT

When you're searing ingredients, a pan weight is a great little tool. Steaks and fish will buckle in a pan if left unattended, leaving you with blonde spots, and an uneven texture overall. A pan weight helps an ingredient to maintain full contact with the cooking surface throughout the cook. There are a few options out there, something heavy and flat is all you need.

SPIDER

These are the chef's answer to the slotted spoon; a shallow basket that resembles a spider's web on the end of a long handle, perfect for fishing pasta or veggies out of boiling water and whipping things out of a deep fryer.

BALLOON WHISK

This whips up salad dressings, mayonnaise, custards and cream with ease. Thanks to its large bulb-shaped design, a balloon whisk is great at aerating, mixing and emulsifying ingredients. It's the classic whisk, and it's the best.

ADJUSTABLE PEPPER MILL

Get your hands on a high quality, refillable pepper mill. Ideally you want one that is adjustable, too. I think folks often think that a mill is just for black pepper, well, guess what, it isn't! You can fill them with whatever the burrs can handle – different styles of peppercorns, spice blends, etc. For my money, Peugeot makes the best mills.

PESTLE AND MORTAR

I love my pestle and mortar. This tool has been around for as long as we've been cooking and it's like a little portal to the past. A pestle and mortar is great for making dressings, pastes, pestos and grinding spices. Try to get one that's a decent size, at least 15cm, and made of granite or stone.

FINE-MESH SIEVE

These are used an awful lot in professional kitchens for passing/straining stocks, sauces, purées and mash. These are great for sifting ingredients for baking, too.

DIGITAL TIMER

Stop using your phone! A bog-standard digital timer is really useful for cooking and not using my phone helps me to focus on what's going on with my cooking. You can get magnetic ones too, so you can stick it on your hob, fridge or cupboards.

SALAD SPINNER

An underrated tool. Efficiently washing and drying salad or herbs without one is a real challenge.

ROLLING PIN

A good-quality wooden rolling pin is a must for making schnitzel, pastries, breads and, well, anything flat. I prefer wood over plastic, marble or metal. They're easy to maintain, are surprisingly non-stick and develop a lovely natural patina over years of use. Never, ever wash your rolling pin with water – this might cause it to warp. Use a damp cloth or a soft bench scraper to remove any residual flour or dough.

PASTRY BRUSH

A baking essential. Brush on egg wash and brush off excess flour like a pro. Silicone versions are pretty rubbish, so buy a proper bristly brush.

BLOWTORCH

A blowtorch is a very easy thing to scoop up for not too much money and can really elevate the way you cook at home, achieving a level of char and smoke on savoury food that a domestic oven never could. Aside from brûlée, I use mine to add a bit of char to steamed broccoli, finish off melting the cheese on a burger or quickly add a touch of smoke to a piece of fish. I like to buy blowtorch heads that simply screw onto a gas canister.

Appliances

Appliances are a luxury, not a necessity. These are all things to work towards as you lean into your cooking journey. Don't run out and buy them all at once, just buy what you can afford. Ultimately, appliances like air fryers and food processors facilitate convenience. You can achieve very similar results with a handful of basic tools and that all-important power – knowledge.

FOOD PROCESSOR

If you're going to own one electric appliance in the kitchen, let it be a food processor. To be clear, food processors are quite different to blenders. They use their blades to chop and slice ingredients and with some nifty attachments can also shred, grate, grind, purée and even knead. They're a much gentler machine than a blender, which gives you the ability to chop and process your food to a more precise texture.

STAND MIXER

These are expensive, but if you're a big baker then they're worth it. Kneading dough, creaming butter and sugar and whipping up meringues are literally effortless with a stand mixer, and you and your whisk will never be able to compete. KitchenAid is the industry leader and my go-to brand, especially with the plethora of attachments you can get for them now.

IMMERSION BLENDER

Also known as a stick blender, these handy little gadgets are good for making mayonnaise, aerating sauces and blending custards and soups. They're agile, easy to clean and you can stick them straight into a bowl, jug or pan.

HIGH-POWER/JUG BLENDER

To make an ultra-smooth soup or purée you're going to want to get your hands on a high-power or jug blender. It's not just the blades of the blender at play here, these blenders use some clever physics to literally smash your food against the sides of the jug by creating a shearing force that drags food down towards the blades and then hurls it outwards into the walls of the jug. This, along with the blades of the blender, can turn the most stubborn of foods into silky smooth purée with ease.

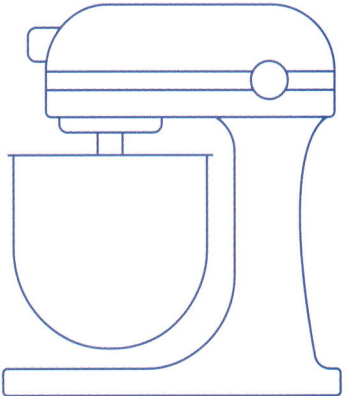

Cooking over fire

A guide to barbecues

Grills come in all shapes and sizes. Some have lids, some are big enough for pork shoulders, some just large enough for a few skewers. It depends on what you're cooking and how big your space is. As a baseline, you want a grill that has adjustable vents to control airflow (more on that shortly). Here are four commonplace, classic grill styles that might work for you.

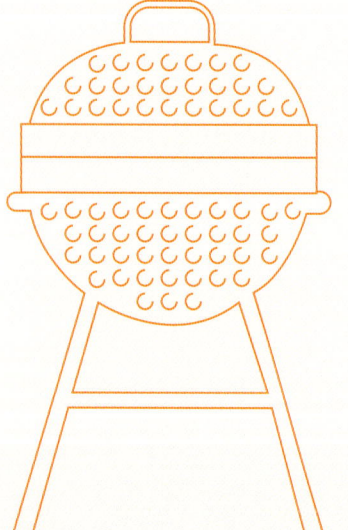

KETTLE

An iconic style of grill, kettles are large round grills. This is my everyday grill. You can do pretty much anything with them, they're great as an all-rounder, are super affordable and tick all of my barbecue boxes. Whether it's high-heat fish cookery, low and slow smoking or just grilling a few sausages, a kettle never fails.

KONRO/HIBACHI

A fantastic option if you have limited space or are usually just cooking for 2–4 people. Perfect for skewers and smaller items, these are made of porous clay or ceramic and retain heat very well.

KAMADO

Based on ancient Japanese cooking pots, these are serious grills for a serious cook. The enormous, egg-shaped grills are prized for their ability to create and maintain high heat and their unparalleled fuel efficiency.

Fuel

What is charcoal? In simple terms, it's wood that has undergone a process called pyrolysis, removing all the water and other bits and bobs in the wood, leaving just the carbon behind. On the whole, I think the world sleeps on the idea of what good quality charcoal is.

I know I did until I worked at a restaurant on the grill section and used the top-tier stuff for the first time. Try to avoid cheap charcoal if you can afford to – it's pretty nasty stuff, often packed with chemicals and made using illegally sourced wood. The distinct difference between using this and a good-quality, responsibly sourced charcoal is the smell. Good-quality charcoal makes barbecuing incredibly easy. It lights so much faster than the cheap stuff, burns hotter and for longer, and you can tip more onto your barbecue during cooking without infecting your food with nasty tastes and smells of burning chemicals. If you take anything away from today's read, let it be this!

COMPACTED BRIQUETTES

These little pillow-shaped pieces of charcoal are reliable, easy to get hold of and super cheap. They burn the coolest of all the charcoal but last a long time and are pretty consistent. They're made of wood trimmings, sawdust, charcoal and paper. All of this is compacted together into a uniform shape and then sold cheap. If you're slow roasting or smoking on the barbecue, these are probably your best bet.

EXTRUDED BRIQUETTES

A step above the compacted briquette is the extruded briquette. These are much more expensive than the pressed variety, but burn for even longer, and thanks to the clever hole that runs through the middle to allow for consistent airflow, they can reach much higher temperatures. Extruded briquettes also burn with very little smoke, so if you're cooking somewhere where smoke might be an issue, this is the fuel for you.

HARDWOOD CHARCOAL

Also known as lump charcoal, this is my go-to fuel. I like to cook hot and fast on the grill and that's exactly what this charcoal is built for. Made of burned pieces of hardwood, the charcoal burns very quickly and can reach very high temperatures. The pieces in a bag are all different – some large, some tiny – and this can make building a grill with plenty of airflow a bit finicky. It's a bit pricier than briquettes, but for good reason: the smoke flavour given by hardwood is hard to beat, it's easy to light and you can feed the barbecue with more as you go without worrying too much about stifling the heat. I love it.

Barbecue tools

You don't need many tools, and I find that most of the ones I use when grilling I also use indoors. The crossover is enormous – whether it's tongs, spatulas, trays, scourers – what works indoors works outdoors, too. Aside from a barbecue and a chimney starter, I don't have any tools that are just designed for grilling, so when the guy down at the barbecue shop tries to upsell you a huge pair of tongs or a chisel-esque spatula, walk away! Don't be afraid to use your saucepans and frying pans on the grill either. Some things just can't be cooked directly on a grill (enter frozen peas . . .). Utilising pans on the grill isn't cheating, or a waste of charcoal – it will level up your grilling game infinitely. Warming up sauces or marinades, reducing glazes or rendering fat in pans on the grill is just smart cooking. In the pork chop recipe on page 273, we use a couple of pans to make burnt butter and to render the fat from the chop to avoid a shedload of flare-ups. Don't be afraid to stick a pan on the grill – it won't screw it up. It might come off with a bit of soot on it, but you can clean that right off.

Another ace way to cook is to pick up a metal sieve and use it to cook veggies. If I want to grill a load of peas, small mushrooms, corn, or even cherry tomatoes, setting a little metal sieve straight over the coals is a great way to pick up the smoke of the charcoal while grilling an ingredient that is logistically impossible with a classic grill grate.

BINCHŌ-TAN

The hallowed charcoal . . . the king! This is about as clean a charcoal as you can buy. Made with strictly oak wood, it burns super hot, is smokeless and can maintain heat for up to 4–5 hours! You can also quench it in cold water once you're done cooking, allow it to dry and then reuse. It's a pretty wild product, and you'll pay top dollar for it. I would only recommend using binchō-tan if you have a small konro-style grill. Filling up a kettle will be big bucks.

WOOD CHIPS

These are really a bonus fuel to add flavour to your cooking. A few soaked apple or hickory wood chips scattered over some cheaper briquettes can bring great flavour on a budget.

MISE EN PLACE: BEFORE WE BEGIN

Mise en place is a very restaurant-y thing to consider, and realistically, you don't need to get too much ready when cooking at home. Unless you're juggling a few recipes and cooking for a crowd, you can crack on with any of the recipes in this book without a shedload of planning.

However, it's the principle of mise en place that really matters. My mental prep list is always in the works. When I get ready to cook at home, I set up my little pot of spoons and my little bin, and top up my salt, and go through the ritual of getting my kit sorted, taking a moment to think through what I'm doing. Do the same and you're in for a smooth ride.

READ YOUR RECIPE

Read through your recipe from start to finish before you go to the shops. Identify any potential sticking points or moments you'll need to focus on. Read the chef's tips and notes, and decide on any shortcuts or swap-outs you might want to make. Not having to guess what your next move is while you're at the hob taking on something new is comfy, smart cooking.

GET READY!

Once you've been through your recipe, you can get everything ready to rock. A skim of the recipe will give you an understanding of what you're going to get up to in the process. Get your ingredients out, your tools prepared and, if you need to, get a pan of water on the hob to boil or get the oven preheating.

BE PRECISE WHEN IT COUNTS

You'll notice that sometimes I'm very specific when it comes to the amount of salt or oil you need to add to a recipe, and sometimes I'm using words like 'a glug', 'a shot' or 'season to taste'. In the world of baking and pastry, a few grams either side of the amount called for can have a huge impact on the end result: when I call for 10g of salt or 80g of olive oil, you should reach for the scale. For the most part though, you can shoot from the hip and cook with feeling and relative abandon. A drizzle here, a glug there . . . it's all good, don't overthink it.

A GUIDE, NOT GOSPEL

With that in mind, recipes are guides, not gospel. Sometimes a recipe requires you to be fluid, loose and agile, to rely on what you're tasting, smelling and seeing rather than counting the minutes from the moment you slide the pie into the oven, only to watch it burn and then call me saying 'but you said 40 minutes?!'. Not every oven or hob, or tomato or block of cheese is created equal – sometimes you've got to think on your feet! Sure, sometimes you'll get it a little wrong, but we embrace those moments. Your sensory faculties should always win out, and if it says to whip it out the oven when it's golden brown, go right ahead, whip it out, even if you're a little ahead (or behind!).

I've provided rough prep, cook and total times for every recipe, but these are just a guide! Everybody works, chops and cooks at a different pace. What might take me five minutes to do might take you a little longer and vice versa. In my experience, it's repetition and confidence that are the main variables that affect how long something takes in the kitchen. The first time you make a bowl of tomato soup will invariably take a little longer than the twentieth time. Be patient and remember that the more you cook, the more natural your movements become, the more confident your decision making and the speedier you'll get.

CAN I ADD FLAVOUR HERE?

If you're reaching for water to add to a recipe, consider whether you could add something with more flavour and if that would help build a better dish. Stock? Wine? Vinegar? Tea? Even if the answer is no, always have a think. Similarly, at the end of a recipe, can I introduce some acidity or a fresh herb to add a little lift?

COOKING FOR A CROWD? MAKE A LIST AND MAP IT OUT

If you're juggling multiple recipes at once, it's always a good idea to draw up a little prep list, breaking down each of them into a handful of smaller jobs. These can be as simple as 'cut chives' or 'preheat oven'. Lists are little roadmaps to success and without them, professional kitchens fall apart.

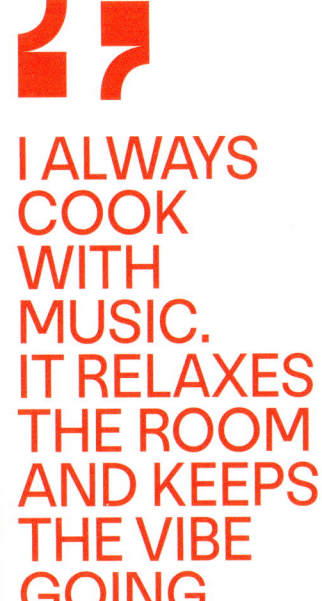

> I ALWAYS COOK WITH MUSIC. IT RELAXES THE ROOM AND KEEPS THE VIBE GOING.

STICK SOME MUSIC ON

I always cook with music. The best kitchens I worked in played music throughout the day while the chefs worked away, preparing their mise en place. It relaxes the room, keeps the vibe going and it's another way to express creativity. It's not for everyone, but when cooking at home I'll always stick a record on to accompany me, whether it's a new recipe or one I've cooked a thousand times. What should you play? Well, that's up to you.

SERVE WARM FOOD ON WARM PLATES

If the food is warm, the plate should be, too. I give my plates a quick zap in the microwave but, failing that, you can warm plates in a low oven. If my oven is already hot, I drop the plate in, count to 15, and by then it's usually good to go.

EGGS COME

Chive Soft Scramble 46

Fudgy Boiled Eggs & Comté on Rye 48

The French Omelette 50

Diner-style Stuffed Omelettes 52

'Baked' Eggs, Two Ways 54

Poached Eggs with Garlicky Greens 56

Sweet Onion Tortilla 57

Pommes Rösti with Crispy Sage Fried Eggs 58

Oeufs Mayonnaise 60

Pecorino Pain Perdu 62

Deep-dish Leek & Guanciale Quiche 64

FIRST

It all starts with eggs – life, your day, and most people's culinary education – and there's good reason for this.

If you can cook an egg, you can cook pretty much anything. Eggs are inexpensive, ubiquitous, magical and, in the right hands, utterly delicious. Let's make those right hands your hands. My dad taught me to scramble an egg when I was about 7 or 8 years old, standing on my tiptoes by the stove. This lesson enabled me to make my mum breakfast in bed on her birthday (nailed it, Dad), and I'm still making them today. Good technique stays with you forever.

The recipes in this chapter will demonstrate that with boiling water, an oven or frying pan, a whisk, a spoon or fork and, more often than not, a knob of butter, you can cook, shape, mould and manipulate the humble egg into a multitude of forms, textures and flavours.

How does knowing how to fry an egg help you cook a steak? Cooking an egg as a standalone ingredient in a pan is all about temperature. The way you apply heat to an egg will dramatically alter the way it cooks and it's easy to watch this happen in front of you. Eggs are a very visual ingredient; while cooking they change colour, opacity and texture before your eyes.

The most basic expressions of cooked eggs hold the most teachable moments: creating perfect, fine curds without colour for the French omelette, soft-boiling an egg for a perfect runny yolk, or nailing a crispy fried egg into a searing-hot pan. Similarly, if you can identify exactly when your water is the exact right temperature to drop in an egg to poach, then you're halfway to perfect poached chicken or Dover sole. You can buy about 40 eggs for the price of a Dover sole, so if I were you, I'd start with the eggs. If you screw it up, no biggie! The stakes are as low as they come in the kitchen, and that's the beauty of them.

Cooked and raw eggs demonstrate the sheer magic of food science. Yolks are used to create rich mayonnaises (page 60), silky custards (page 305) and add a luxurious texture to chopped raw beef (page 84) whites are whipped into ethereal meringues (page 302) and used to lift a chocolate mousse (page 286).

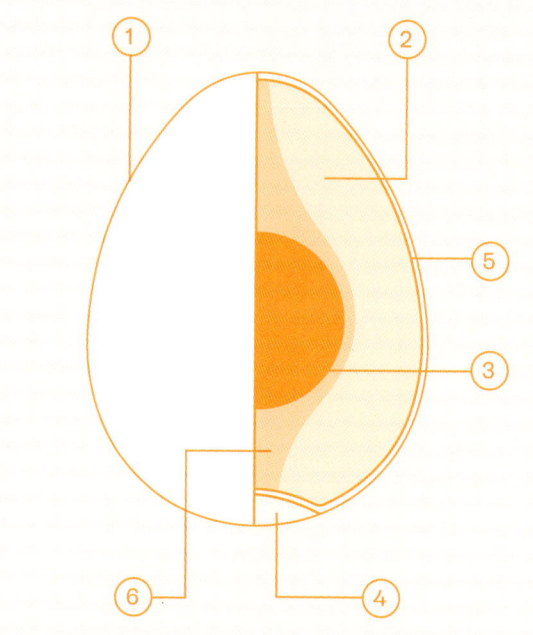

1. EGG SHELL – Egg shells, mostly made up of calcium carbonate, are permeable and have microscopic holes all over the surface; this allows water and air to pass through the shell.

2. EGG WHITE/ALBUMEN – Made up of layers of thick and thin egg white, which offer a protective cushion as well as holding lots of water and protein. As the egg gets older, the white thins out.

3. EGG YOLK – The most luxurious part of any egg, and where you'll find most of the calories, fats and nutritious stuff. The primary roles of yolks are to enrich and emulsify.

4. AIR POCKET – The bubble of air between the two internal membranes of the egg is the first breath of air a chick will get as it develops.

5. MEMBRANE – The very thin but surprisingly robust layer between the white and the shell, which protects the egg from contamination.

6. CHALAZA – A little twisty chain/knot either side of the egg yolk that keeps it centred.

EGG + HEAT

So, what happens to all these eggy bits and bobs when we add heat? Essentially, the heat transforms the makeup and order of the water and proteins inside the egg. When raw, the amino acids that make up the proteins are twisted together like a tangled pair of headphones in a body of water. As you add heat, the proteins untangle, unfurl and separate, cruising about in the water. As they do this, they start bumping into each other. As they collide, the strands begin to connect and bond, forming a complex, 3D network of protein with the water suspended inside the network. Mastering egg cookery is all about knowing when this network is formed just enough to yield the texture you're looking for, the goldilocks moment. Too little heat, and you've got a raw, underdeveloped network, but too much heat and the network will become too tight, like a tensed muscle, and squeeze out all the water. For example, if you overcook your scrambled eggs, you get a pan of watery residue and dry, pappy curds (not dissimilar to overcooking a steak).

EGG + OTHER STUFF

You can influence the network of protein with other ingredients. If you add milk or cream, you interrupt that tight network of proteins with fats and water. This changes the texture and form of the egg completely. If you cook this out, stirring, and keeping those proteins moving, you might get something close to custard, the protein structure adding viscosity and body to the liquid. If you were to bake them undisturbed, the protein structure will set the eggs into a solid mass, but be much more tender than if you baked some plain whisked eggs without the extra stuff. Whatever you add to your eggs, think about how it will interrupt the structure and affect your recipe.

AN EGG'S AGE

It might sound a weird thing to say, but the age of your egg might impact what you choose to do with it. If you've got an egg that's super fresh, straight from the farmer, you'll want to poach it (see poached eggs with garlicky greens on page 56), as the albumen will still be super thick and yield a perfect, bouncy, burrata-looking poached egg. If the eggs have been hanging out for a week or so, they're great for whipping up a meringue or an easy-to-peel boiled egg.

EMULSIONS

What is an emulsion? If you pour a shot of oil into a glass of water, it'll float to the top, unable to blend with the water. An emulsion is the process by which water and fat are bonded together via the helping hand of protein or an emulsifying agent (egg yolk! mustard!). Yolks, specifically, are required to pull off the impossible: mix oil and water. Egg yolks contain emulsifiers, including the mighty lecithin. Lecithin molecules are long, fat-like molecules that at one end love water, and at the other, hate it. This means that fat binds at one end of the molecule and water the other, holding them together and creating that magical emulsion. This emulsification process is used in heaps of recipes. Without egg yolks, there's no mayonnaise, hollandaise or bearnaise. There's also no crème brûlée or custards, no light, fluffy sponge cakes – no fun at all!

Emulsions can break if you try to combine the ingredients too quickly, or try to add too much fat. If you add too much oil, there simply won't be enough protein in the egg yolk to handle the quantity of oil, and the emulsion will break. To fix a broken mayonnaise, try whisking a teaspoon of water into it. If that doesn't work, grab another egg yolk or two, add a teaspoon of mustard and whisk the split mayo right into these. It'll create a new emulsion and your mayo will be all good.

AIR, AIR, AIR

Next, we're going to take those egg whites and whip them up, creating a foam that can hold on to heaps of air and be used in many ways. Albumen is 90% water and about 10% protein. The whipping process behaves in a similar way to when heat is applied to an egg. As you whip egg whites, those bundles of proteins begin to unfurl and create a 3D network, with the water suspended in the network. As you continue to whip, you incorporate air bubbles, which are captured by the network, too. You can over-whip egg whites, and similar to overcooking scrambled egg, you'll notice water flying out of the mixture and some sad-looking egg protein left behind. When whipped, the protein structure will naturally deteriorate over time as the proteins haven't firmed up and stabilised through exposure to heat. This is why French meringue (raw) needs to be baked after whipping, while Italian or Swiss meringue is cooked during the whipping process and so doesn't require any time in the oven.

EGGS COME FIRST

Chive Soft Scramble

- SERVES: 2
- EYES CLOSED
- V
- TOTAL: 15 MINS
- PREP: 5 MINS
- COOK: 10 MINS

For me, the secret to a great scramble is not found in the extras. Good scrambled eggs require only eggs, butter, salt and pepper, chives and a little know-how. Nothing more! Adding a shedload of extra dairy in the form of cream, milk or crème fraîche is a corner cut. The more 'stuff' you add to your eggs, the less they taste like eggs! Dairy can lend a more tender curd to your eggs, but so can good cooking. Eschew the cream-laden extras in favour of good technique!

small bunch of chives
6 eggs
40g unsalted butter, cold
2 slices of toast
fine sea salt
black pepper

CHEF'S TIP
Salt your eggs ahead of cooking for a richer, more tender curd. Letting your eggs hang out for 15 minutes or so with a pinch of salt will help break down those proteins in the egg, preventing them bonding as tightly and squeezing out moisture. We want to hold on to that moisture, so a little early seasoning can give your scramble a push in the right direction. While effective, it doesn't make a **huge** difference, so don't sweat it if you forget or don't have time.

1 Begin by finely chopping your chives. Often, chives come in a neat little bundle, held together by an elastic band. If this is the case, shimmy the elastic band to one end and slice away. If not, I like to wrap a damp piece of kitchen paper around the chives to keep them together. Using a sharp knife, slice the chives as finely as you can. We want them to perfume the scramble with that lovely, gentle oniony flavour but not interrupt that luxurious texture too much. The finer you slice them, the stronger the aroma. Once chopped, set aside.

2 Crack your eggs into a small mixing bowl, add a pinch of salt and use a fork to beat them until homogenous; that is, until you can't see any streaks of egg yolk or white. Don't add your black pepper yet – if you add it too early the eggs will go grey. Cut the butter into small dice and add to the bowl.

3 Preheat a medium (roughly 20cm) non-stick or well-seasoned pan over a medium-low heat. Once the pan is warm, tip in the eggs and butter and use a spatula to get things moving. You'll notice the egg mixture slacken out and become more liquid as it warms and just before that protein network begins to set. Use your spatula to keep things moving at all times, cleaning the bottom of the pan, bringing the eggs from the outside into the middle.

4 Once the eggs begin to set, you can use your spatula to create larger curds by stirring less, dragging the cooked egg around the pan gently, or create finer curds by being more vigorous. Don't be afraid to remove the pan from the heat at any time if you think things are moving too quickly. Take your time: the slower you go, the more control you'll have.

5 Just as the last of the liquid egg is beginning to loosely set, tip in the chives and remove the pan from the heat. They should be 80% of the way there at this point. Give the eggs a final stir to incorporate the chives and break up any curds at the bottom of the pan, the residual heat finishing the cooking. Season with black pepper, taste and adjust the salt if you need to, then serve immediately on hot buttered toast.

SHOOT FROM THE HIP
Swap out the chives for dill or any soft herb, or leave them out entirely. For added crunch, sprinkle over toasted seeds or crispy diced chorizo. Stir grated parmesan through these right at the end for a salty, umami twang. Tabasco is encouraged.

Fudgy Boiled Eggs & Comté on Rye

SERVES: 2
EYES CLOSED
TOTAL: 15 MINS
PREP: 5 MINS
COOK: 10 MINS

A soft-boiled egg is such an easy win in the realm of eggs. It's almost completely hands off and, following two or three simple steps, you have results worthy of the finest brunch spot. This is a lovely breakfast, inspired by a friend, Clare Cole. Nutty, sharp, well-aged Comté is a complete dream with a nicely boiled egg. I like a 36-month-old cheese, so if you can get your hands on some, don't hesitate. Toast your bread good and dark and don't be shy with the butter. For the egg, I favour a 7-minute cook; I'm not after yolk spilling everywhere, rather a slightly firmer, fudgier set. The rich, barely set yolk can be squashed down onto the toast like a second spread. This is my preference, but it's totally up to you! Use the guide on this page to pick your perfect doneness.

- 4 large eggs
- 4 slices of rye bread
- 120g Comté cheese
- 2 tbsp butter, softened
- 1 tbsp Dijon mustard
- olive oil, for drizzling (optional)
- flaky sea salt
- black pepper

1 Grab your eggs and pierce a small hole in the base of each shell, being sure to pierce the membrane to allow that air to escape (see Chef's Tip).

2 Bring a small pot of water to a rolling boil over a high heat. Using a slotted spoon, spider or a fork, lower the eggs into the boiling water and set your timer for 7 minutes.

3 Grab a bowl and fill it with very cold water. Drop a couple of ice cubes in there and set aside for your eggs. As soon as the timer goes off, carefully lift your eggs out of the boiling water and plunge them into the iced water. Allow them to sit for 10 seconds or so, then fish them out and use a flat surface (chopping board or your kitchen counter) to lightly crack the shell. I start with the bottom (where we pierced the hole) and gently tap my way around the shell. Once the shells have been cracked, return the eggs to the water for a couple of minutes, this makes peeling much easier.

4 While the eggs hang out, pop your rye bread into the toaster and cut the Comté into chunky slices. Spread the toast liberally with butter and mustard and top with the cheese. Finish peeling the eggs and then cut each one into halves and then quarters.

5 Top each slice of bread with 4 quarters of egg and season liberally with flaky sea salt and freshly cracked black pepper. Add a little drizzle of olive oil, if you like, and get stuck in.

CHEF'S TIP

The pro move here is to make a little hole in the bottom of your egg (the round end, not the pointy end) with a pin or the heel of a sharp knife before you pop it into the boiling water. This will pierce the membrane, allowing the air held at the base of the egg to escape, preventing the shell from popping or cracking, making peeling easy later down the line and giving you a perfectly egg-shaped boiled egg.

EGG BOILING 101

A guide to boiling eggs from room temperature.
4½ minutes – Just-set white with a runny, liquid yolk
6 minutes – Set white with a slightly thicker liquid yolk
6½ minutes – Set white with an oozy, jammy yolk
7 minutes – Set white with a fudgy, spreadable yolk
8 minutes – Soft-set yolk, getting towards hard-boiled
10 minutes – A hard-boiled egg, before the yolk starts to become dry and chalky

The French Omelette

SERVES: 1	TOTAL: 10 MINS
EYES CLOSED	PREP: 5 MINS
V / GF	COOK: 5 MINS

This is the omelette for the egg connoisseur. The French omelette is a tender, buttery sheet of gently cooked egg, infused with fine herbs, beautifully folded into a parcel that envelops a delicate, fluffy, soft scramble. It should take on little to no colour in the pan and is a show of great technique. Of the basic egg recipes, this is the final boss. Chefs are often put through their paces on trial shifts by cooking this omelette for their prospective boss; I've done it, it's equal parts thrilling and terrifying. I try to cook myself one of these at least once a week for breakfast; not only because they're delicious, but it's good to keep your eye in and make sure that skill is well practised.

3 eggs
small bunch of chives, dill or chervil
25g butter, plus extra to finish
fine sea salt and flaky sea salt
black pepper

1. Crack the eggs into a small mixing bowl. Finely chop your herb of choice, bung the herbs into the bowl and, using a fork, beat the eggs until there are no big streaks of white remaining, but try not to incorporate too much air.

2. Put the butter in a 15–20cm non-stick or well-seasoned frying pan, place over a medium heat and allow the butter to melt. Once it starts to sizzle and foam, tip in the egg mixture and begin cooking the eggs.

3. Using a spatula, keep stirring the eggs – moving them around, cleaning the bottom of the pan and gently beating – until you've created a little texture in the mix, small curds are forming and the pan looks like it's full of very undercooked scrambled eggs. Now give the pan a gentle shake to distribute the eggs evenly across its surface and allow the bottom of the omelette to set. Season with fine sea salt and pepper.

4. You still want the majority of the mixture to be pretty loose, as when you fold up the omelette the residual heat will keep cooking the egg. The goal here is to finish cooking the omelette without letting it brown, so don't let it hang out too long here.

5. Give the pan another little shimmy to make sure nothing's sticking, before flipping the edge of the omelette that's closest to you into the centre, enveloping the custardy middle. Keep rolling away from you until you have 50% of the pan visible. Now give the pan a tap to free up the backside of the omelette and slide it away from you into the curve of the pan.

6. When the top of the omelette looks just about set but not quite there, flip the back lip of the omelette over and turn it out onto a plate, sealing the deal. Your omelette should be a lovely oval shape, with a custardy interior and a smooth, light exterior. If you want to be extra fancy, rub the omelette with a little butter to give it some gloss and finish with extra cracked black pepper and flaky sea salt.

SHOOT FROM THE HIP
If you want to drop in some little dollops of goat's cheese or any other filling, do your thing. You'll want to add it just before you fold the omelette up. Whatever you're adding, don't add too much. Like a good pizza, the beauty of a French omelette is its simplicity, so always remember, less is more!

CHEF'S TIP
You won't get this right the first time, but guess what? Neither did I! I've been making these for years and still have good and bad days. The best thing about them is, they all taste delicious, despite not being perfect. Don't be afraid to move the pan away from the heat if you think it's overcooking! I do this all the time, and it gives you ultimate control.

EGGS COME FIRST

51

Diner-style Stuffed Omelettes

- SERVES: 1
- EYES CLOSED
- GF
- TOTAL: 25 MINS
- PREP: 5 MINS
- COOK: 20 MINS

My days as a New Yorker taught me a few things: how to work 6 days a week, how to work very hard on those 6 days and how to make a proper diner-style omelette. The best way to approach this is to think of the omelette and filling as two different things that are brought together right at the last minute. When you watch a short-order cook churning these out, you'll see them spooning pre-cooked, hot fillings into stacks of omelettes. This is not only efficient, but really smart. Spooning a hot filling into an omelette will help you cook the thing evenly. Add a handful of cold cheese and vegetables into the centre of an omelette, the egg on the outside is going to be very overcooked by the time the filling is warm and the cheese is gooey and melted. Work smart, not hard.

3 eggs
50g diced smoked pancetta
3–4 asparagus spears
10g pickled jalapeños
2 spring onions
1 tsp sherry vinegar
25g mature cheddar
25g butter
olive oil
fine sea salt
black pepper

1 Crack the eggs into a mixing bowl, add a healthy pinch of salt and beat them with a fork. Set aside.

2 Add the pancetta to a 20cm non-stick pan (or similar) with a shot of olive oil, place over a medium-low heat, and cook for 9–10 minutes, allowing the fat to render and the pancetta to crisp. While the pancetta cooks, trim the woody ends from the asparagus and cut into 1cm chunks at a steep angle to make pointy pieces. Roughly chop the jalapeños and thinly slice the spring onions, separating the white from the green.

3 When the pancetta is crispy, fish it out of the pan and transfer it to a small mixing bowl. Crank the heat up to high and when the fat is smoking hot, tip in the asparagus and spring onion whites, holding back the spring onion greens. Season with salt and toss in the hot pancetta fat. Cook for 2–3 minutes over a high heat then tip into the bowl with the pancetta. Add the sherry vinegar and pickled jalapeños to the mixture, coarsely grate in the cheddar and mix.

4 Return the pan to the hob, reducing the heat to medium, and toss in the butter. Allow the butter to melt, foam and lightly brown before tipping in the beaten eggs. Shake the pan and use a spatula to create large curds, drawing the outside of the omelette into the middle and tipping the raw egg into the open space. Once the omelette is 85% cooked, with just a small amount of uncooked egg on the top, give the pan a tap on the hob to make sure the whole base is covered. Carefully tip your filling onto one half of the omelette. If you need to, cover with a bowl or a lid for a moment or two to steam the top of the omelette.

5 Give the pan a little shimmy to make sure nothing is sticking and then fold the omelette over, enveloping the stuffing. Don't worry if a little spills out of the sides, that's a proper stuffed omelette! Slide onto a warm plate and get stuck in.

> **CHEF'S TIP**
> The sherry vinegar elevates this omelette from good to great but if you've only a lemon or lime to hand, that'll work too. You want to balance the fat of the bacon and cheese with a shot of acidity.

'Baked' Eggs, Two Ways

SERVES: 2
EYES CLOSED
TOTAL: 40 MINS
PREP: 10 MINS
COOK: 30 MINS

So, hear me out, the best baked eggs don't ever hit the oven... When testing these recipes, I found that simply adding a lid creates a steamy environment to cook the top of your eggs, delivering a gently cooked, perfectly poached egg with a tender white and a warm, runny yolk. The intense, dry heat of the oven is much more aggressive than steam and can dry everything out and overcook the yolk. I've given you two sauces as a jumping off point, but get creative. The first is a super simple turmeric coconut curry, and the merguez ragù is a riff on eggs in purgatory, or to the likes of you and me, eggs baked in spicy tomato sauce.

FOR THE TURMERIC COCONUT CURRY

- 1 onion
- 2 garlic cloves
- 10g fresh ginger
- 1 tbsp ground turmeric
- ½ tbsp cumin seeds
- 6–8 curry leaves
- 200ml coconut milk
- 400g tin chickpeas
- pinch of basil leaves, plus extra to serve
- 4 eggs
- 2 green finger chillies
- olive oil
- fine sea salt

FOR THE MERGUEZ RAGÙ AND PICKLED PEPPERS

- 2 merguez-style lamb sausages
- 2 garlic cloves
- pinch of flat-leaf parsley
- 1 lemon
- handful of pickled peppers
- 1 tbsp harissa, plus a little extra
- 1 tsp cumin seeds
- 400g good-quality tinned tomatoes
- 4 eggs
- 3 tbsp thick Greek yoghurt
- olive oil
- fine sea salt

TURMERIC COCONUT CURRY

1 Preheat an ovenproof 25cm frying pan or similar over a medium-high heat. Finely chop the onion, garlic and ginger. Add a shot of olive oil to the pan and toss in the onion with a pinch of salt. Cook for 5–6 minutes until starting to crisp and caramelise, then add the garlic, ginger, turmeric, cumin seeds and curry leaves. Sizzle for 3–4 minutes before adding the coconut milk and chickpeas and their tin liquid. Bring to the boil, then reduce to a simmer and let it tick over for 30–35 minutes until thickened and the colour is a deep yellow. Season with salt and finish with the basil leaves.

2 Use the back of a spoon to create four little pockets in your sauce then crack an egg into each. Sprinkle the top of each egg with a little salt then cover the pan with a lid. Cook for 2–3 minutes over a low heat, until the white is set and the yolk is just warm. Remove from the heat and finish with some extra basil leaves and thinly sliced finger chillies.

MERGUEZ RAGÙ AND PICKLED PEPPERS

1 Preheat a 25cm frying pan or similar over a medium heat. Add 2 tablespoons of olive oil and, once warm, remove the skins from the merguez sausages and pinch small amounts into the pan, almost like little meatballs. Reduce the heat and slowly brown the sausage, rendering out the spicy, flavour-packed fat. Roll the merguez pieces around the pan as they cook to colour all sides.

2 While the merguez cooks, thinly slice the garlic, finely chop the parsley, cut the lemon into wedges and roughly chop the peppers. Once brown add the harissa, cumin seeds and sliced garlic to the pan, increase the heat to medium and cook for 3–4 minutes until fragrant and the garlic has lost its raw edge. Tip in the tomatoes, season with salt and bring to a simmer, then turn the heat to low and let it blip away for 20 minutes. The ragu will reduce, thicken and deepen in colour while the oils split out and rise to the top of the pan.

3 Use the back of a spoon to create four little pockets in your sauce then crack an egg into each. Sprinkle the top of each egg with a little salt then cover the pan with a lid. Cook for 2–3 minutes over a low heat, until the white is set and the yolk is just warm. Remove from the heat and finish with chopped pickled peppers, parsley, a blob of yoghurt, a drizzle of oil and a lemon wedge.

NOTES
A heavy, cast-iron pot or sauté pan is your best bet for an even cook on your eggs. They usually come with a snug lid to trap in the steam and the thick, heavy metal holds on to heat well, and evenly distributes it, ensuring a balanced cook.

CHEF'S TIP
Crack your eggs into an egg cup or espresso cup before gently sliding them into your sauce. This way, if any broken shell sneaks in there, it's easy to whip out before it gets lost in the sauce.

Poached Eggs with Garlicky Greens

- SERVES: 2
- TOTAL: 50 MINS
- EYES CLOSED
- PREP: 10 MINS
- V / DF
- COOK: 40 MINS

When poaching an egg, you not only want a super-fresh egg, you want your water to be sitting in the right temperature range. If your water is too cold, the egg white won't set quick enough and it'll become a wispy, flat, soggy mess. If the water is too hot, the egg will explode, as the convection of the water throws the egg around the pot and separates the white from the yolk. Game over. For mozzarella ball-looking eggs, the golden temperature range is 82–86°C. If you've got a thermometer, you can pinpoint this exactly. If not, you can still approximate it pretty well by looking for bubbles.

400g mixed greens

4 fat garlic cloves

1 red chilli

4 very fresh eggs

2 slices of your favourite bread

1 lemon

olive oil

fine sea salt and flaky sea salt

black pepper

> **CHEF'S TIP**
> Use the freshest eggs you can get your hands on: fresh eggs have a much higher ratio of thick white to thin and will give you a more uniform egg. To test how fresh that egg is, drop it into a cup of water – if it sinks on its side, it's super fresh; if it sinks on one end, it's been around a few days; if it floats, it's on the older side.

1 Start by preparing the greens. Roughly chop or tear them into bite-sized pieces. Don't worry about separating the leaves and stems – everything is going to be cooked down together until super soft.

2 Peel and thinly slice 3 of the garlic cloves. Deseed and finely chop the red chilli. Add 5–6 tablespoons of olive oil to a cold medium saucepan and chuck in the sliced garlic. Place over a medium heat and allow the oil to come up to temperature. As it heats, the garlic will begin to sizzle and sputter. Once it's sizzling away, reduce the heat to low and cook the garlic and chilli for 3–4 minutes or so, or until the garlic has lost its raw edge.

3 Pile in the greens. If you can't quite fit all the greens in at once, don't worry, as you toss and turn them in the garlicky oil, they'll wilt down. Keep adding your greens to the pot, stirring and wilting them down as you go, until all the greens are in. Cook, stirring now and then, for 30–35 minutes, or until super soft. Season well with fine sea salt and pepper and keep warm while you poach the eggs.

4 Fill a saucepan with water and place over a medium-high heat. Bring to a simmer, then drop the temperature to low. If you've got a thermometer, look for that golden range of 82–86°C. If not, bring the pot to a rolling boil and then reduce the heat so only a few gentle bubbles are floating to the top. No salt, no vinegar, no fancy tricks. This is a temperature game.

5 Crack each egg into a ramekin or small coffee cup. If it looks a little runny, you can crack the egg into a fine-mesh sieve first to remove any excess white. If your egg is super fresh, this isn't necessary. Confidently lower the egg into the water and tip it out of the ramekin, cup or sieve. Don't play with the egg too much – just let the gentle bubble of the water keep it moving and just let it do its thing. After 3 minutes, lift the egg out of the water with a slotted spoon. Give it a prod: the yolk should feel soft, and the white should have a bit of bounce. If you're not totally confident, cook the eggs one or two at a time at first.

6 Toast or grill the bread with a little olive oil until slightly charred. Cut the remaining garlic clove in half and rub it over the toasted bread. Load your braised greens into bowls and top with a couple of poached eggs. Season them with flaky sea salt and pepper, a drizzle of olive oil and a little lemon zest. Serve your grilled bread on the side with a lemon wedge for squeezing.

Sweet Onion Tortilla

SERVES: 2
DIG IN
V / DF / GF

TOTAL: 1 HOUR
PREP: 10 MINS
COOK: 50 MINS

A traditional *tortilla de papas* is a thing of beauty, but requires a shedload of olive oil and a good dose of patience. We're swapping olive oil-confited potatoes and onions for sweet, caramelised onions and a humble bag of crisps. A tortilla is also one of life's finest leftovers, packed into a crusty roll with plenty of aioli and a few twists of black pepper for lunch.

4 sweet white onions
20g thyme sprigs
6 large eggs
75g salted crisps
shop-bought or homemade Aioli (page 209), to serve
olive oil
fine sea salt

CHEF'S TIP

This recipe is all about confidence. Any hesitation may result in a hob glazed with raw egg and crisps. Move quickly and with purpose. Defining the perfect set in the centre of a tortilla is down to you. If you like it runny, run the pan a little hotter and slide out onto the board sooner than you think. If you like it firm, cook for a minute or two longer at a slightly lower heat.

1 Peel and thinly slice the onions. You want to go as thin as you can here. Place a frying pan over a medium heat and add a shot of olive oil. Tip in the onions, season generously with salt and throw in the thyme, sprigs and all. Get the onions going, stirring as they cook, then top with a cartouche (page 233). Cook over a gentle heat, stirring now and then, for 35–40 minutes, or until golden brown, caramelised and sweet.

2 Crack the eggs into a large mixing bowl and season with a tiny pinch of salt. Don't go too hard on the seasoning – the crisps and onions will bring a fair amount of salt to the party, too.

3 Once your onions are ready, fish out any woody thyme sprigs then tip the warm onion into the beaten eggs. Pile in the crisps and stir everything together, saturating the crisps with the eggs.

4 Preheat a 20cm non-stick or well-seasoned pan over a medium-high heat. Add 2 tablespoons of olive oil and swirl around the pan. Once hot, dump in the egg mixture – you should hear a tiny sizzle as it hits the hot oil. Quickly shake the pan to even out the mixture and use a spatula to balance out the onions and crisps across the pan. Drop the heat to low and cook the omelette for 3 minutes or so. The goal here is to set the perimeter of the omelette and the bottom third before flipping. Shake the pan every now and then to check everything is loose and nothing is sticking to the bottom.

5 Grab a plate wide enough to cover the top of the pan and invert it over the top. With confidence, flip the pan over, turning the omelette out onto the plate. Pop the omelette down while you wipe out the pan and add a shot more oil. Let the pan hang out on the heat for another 20–30 seconds before carefully sliding the omelette off the plate and back into the pan, wet side down.

6 Cook for another 1–2 minutes. During this second cook, use your spatula to 'tuck in' the edges of the omelette, creating a rounded edge, achieving the classic puck-like shape of the Spanish omelette. You'll know your tortilla is ready when it has a slight jiggle in the centre, but the edges are firm and a little bouncy. Slide onto a chopping board, let it rest for a moment, then cut in half. Serve immediately with a generous dollop of aioli.

Pommes Rösti with Crispy Sage Fried Eggs

SERVES: 2
TOTAL: 55 MINS
ROLL YOUR SLEEVES UP
PREP: 15 MINS
V / GF
COOK: 40 MINS

There ain't no fried egg like a crispy fried egg. Listen, if we're frying an egg, we're going to really fry that egg. I want the oil to blister, sputter and crisp the white into a super-lacy, crunchy egg perfumed with caraway seeds. Pommes rösti are basically big, beautiful hash browns. I serve my rösti with pickles and sour cream for a pop of acidity. You could add grated onions, parmesan, finely chopped herbs or spices to the potato mix to inject more flavour, or keep it classic.

- 500g Maris Piper potatoes
- 10g rosemary leaves
- 100g butter
- 2 eggs
- 15g sage leaves
- 2 tbsp sour cream
- 40g dill pickles (or something else pickled)
- olive oil
- fine sea salt
- black pepper
- hot sauce, to serve

CHEF'S TIP
If you want a slightly fancier finish on your rösti, use a mandoline to cut thin slices of potato, then cut them into a fine julienne. You can also use the grater attachment of a food processor to achieve a similar result.

1 Preheat the oven to 200°C fan/220°C/425°F/gas mark 7.

2 Peel the potatoes and coarsely grate them with a box grater. Tip the potato shreds into a large bowl and thoroughly rinse with cold water. The goal here is to wash away as much of the naturally occurring starch as possible. Swirl the potato around and change the water a couple of times until it runs clear.

3 Now dry the potatoes as best you can – you can use a colander for this, or a salad spinner works well, if you have one. Tip the potato shreds into a medium mixing bowl. Finely chop the rosemary and add it to the potatoes. Melt the butter and add it to the bowl. Toss to coat the potatoes with butter and evenly disperse the rosemary.

4 Preheat a 25cm non-stick or well-seasoned ovenproof frying pan over a medium heat. Gently add the potato mixture and press it into the pan, evenly covering the bottom of the pan and creating a slight dome in the middle. Cook for 8–10 minutes, shaking the pan now and then. Once the rösti is holding together as one mass, slide the pan into the oven for 10–12 minutes.

5 After 10–12 minutes, remove the pan from the oven and carefully flip the rösti over. Do this pancake style, confidently tossing the pancake over, or use a spatula. Another good move is to grab a plate that is just a little bigger than the pan and invert the rösti onto it, before sliding it back into the pan. Return to the oven for another 10–12 minutes, or until the underside is golden brown and crispy. If you need to give the rösti another little blast on the hob, go ahead.

6 Remove from the oven and let the rösti rest while you fry your eggs. Preheat a cast-iron or stainless-steel pan over a high heat. You want it ripping hot – to test if the pan is at temperature, add a few drops of water: they should bead and zip about the pan, but not evaporate straight away. Once you've hit this point, add 2 tablespoons of olive oil. Working fast, crack the eggs into the pan, straight into the hot oil. Season with salt and pepper and scatter in the sage leaves. Allow the eggs to crackle and fry for 1–2 minutes, watching as the whites become lacy and crisp and allowing them to fully set before sliding out of the pan. Keep an eye on the sage and remove the leaves when they stop fizzing and bubbling and become crisp.

7 Cut your rösti into portions and transfer to warm plates. Top with a crispy egg, sage leaves and add a dollop of sour cream and a few pickles. Finish with hot sauce.

Oeufs Mayonnaise

- SERVES: 2
- ROLL YOUR SLEEVES UP
- P
- TOTAL: 30 MINS
- PREP: 20 MINS
- COOK: 10 MINS

A true classic. Egg mayonnaise makes a delicious light lunch when served with a few green leaves tossed with vinaigrette or a great starter alongside some warm baguette with crunchy large-flake salted butter (page 174). I top mine with salty anchovy fillets and a good crack of black pepper. Eggs are used in two ways here: first, to make a rich, emulsified mayonnaise, then more are perfectly boiled. It might seem old-fashioned, but this is one of the great plates of French food and is rather chic!

2 egg yolks
15g/1 tbsp Dijon mustard
8g/1½ tsp white wine vinegar
15g/1 tbsp lemon juice (roughly ½ lemon)
330g neutral oil, sunflower or vegetable
100g olive oil
3 eggs
6 good-quality salted anchovy fillets
fine sea salt
black pepper
warmed baguette and dressed leaves, to serve

NOTES
Be sure to season the mayonnaise with a healthy amount of salt before you start adding the oil, this will result in a much more roundly flavoured emulsion as the salt dissolves into the lemon juice and vinegar and is then evenly dispersed through the mixture.

1 Start by making your mayonnaise. Use a damp tea towel to anchor a medium mixing bowl to your work surface. Tip in the egg yolks, mustard, vinegar and lemon juice. Whisk to combine, then add a good pinch of fine sea salt and whisk until the salt has dissolved.

2 Combine the oils in a jug or squeezy bottle and begin to incorporate them into the yolk mixture slowly, whisking constantly. Gradually drip in the oil and watch as the texture of the mayonnaise transforms from very thin to thick. Use your instincts here: if it's getting too thick and starts to seize up, add a teaspoon of water and just let it back a bit. The golden rule is, you can't go too slowly, so take your time.

3 Once you've incorporated all the oil, you should have a thick, rich, pale emulsion. You want it to have a spoonable consistency, not quite jarred mayonnaise thick, but thick enough to hold its own on the egg. You want it to drape over the top like a blanket. You can adjust the texture with water or lemon juice if it's too thick, and whisk in a drop more oil if it's too thin. Have a taste and add a little more lemon juice or salt if you need to. Cover and set aside.

4 Boil your eggs for 7 minutes and 30 seconds following the tips on page 48. Peel while still just warm and cut in half lengthways.

5 Arrange 3 egg halves on each plate and spoon over some of the mayonnaise. You might be tempted to serve these sunny side up, but serving them cut side down is the pro move. The yolk will stick to the surface and stop your eggs from racing around the plate. Top each egg with an anchovy fillet and a crack of coarsely ground black pepper. Serve with warm baguette and a handful of vinegary dressed leaves.

SHOOT FROM THE HIP
Once you've mastered making mayonnaise you can experiment with different flavours. Try adding some chopped fine herbs (tarragon/dill/chervil/chives) to the mayonnaise at the end or add a dollop of miso, sesame oil and rice vinegar to your mayonnaise for some extra umami. A dash of smoked paprika or piment d'espelette would also be delicious. You can add grated garlic, parmesan and chopped anchovies for a Caesar-style mayo.

Pecorino Pain Perdu

- SERVES: 2
- ROLL YOUR SLEEVES UP
- TOTAL: 25 MINS
- PREP: 10 MINS
- COOK: 15 MINS

You're never going to throw away stale bread again. Pain perdu means 'lost bread', and in the spirit of all great working-class foods, it refers to the magic of transforming something lost, on its way to the bin, into a delicious plate of food. This is a levelled-up version of the eggy bread a friend used to make us the morning after a few too many drinks, hence the Marmite. I wouldn't blame you for dipping it into ketchup, either. Eggs are used to create a rich, savoury custard here, packed with sharp pecorino romano and spicy, fruity black pepper. While the custard is still raw, the bread soaks it up and is then fried off in butter, gently setting the eggs.

1 tbsp black peppercorns
200g whole milk
100g double cream
3 eggs
100g pecorino romano
4 thick slices of day-old bread
60g unsalted butter, plus extra for spreading
4 tsp Marmite (optional)
4 slices of ham, prosciutto or jamon (optional)
fine sea salt

1 Tip the peppercorns into a large non-stick frying pan and place over a medium heat. Toast for 1–2 minutes, or until fragrant, then use a pestle and mortar to coarsely crush. Set aside.

2 Grab a mixing bowl and tip in the milk and double cream. Crack in the eggs, season with salt and half of the toasted pepper. Finely grate in around half of the pecorino and then beat the mixture with a fork. Tip this custard into a small, shallow baking tray – you want it to sit roughly 2–3cm deep.

3 Lightly butter the slices of the bread on both sides and divide the Marmite between them (if using). Lay two slices of prosciutto (if using) onto two slices of bread and add some extra grated pecorino and a little of the pepper. Lay the other two slices, Marmite side down, on top to make two sandwiches.

4 Briefly re-stir the custard to reincorporate any cheese or pepper that might have sunk to the bottom then dunk the sandwiches into the custard, allowing them to hang out for a good few minutes before flipping and repeating. You want the sandwiches to be totally saturated with the custard.

5 Preheat a large non-stick frying pan over a medium heat. Once hot, add half of the butter and allow them to melt and then foam. Fry the pain perdu for about 3 minutes on each side, adding the remaining butter just before you flip. You want the cheese and pepper to caramelise on the outside and take on a golden hue with the centre being just cooked. The pain perdu will firm up and should feel bouncy to the touch as the custard cooks and the egg gently sets. Once cooked, slide out of the pan and finish with a cloud of extra grated pecorino. Get stuck in.

SHOOT FROM THE HIP
You can lose the ham and use vegetarian pecorino to make this vegetarian, and the Marmite if it ain't your thing. This also works well with a fried egg on top – a nod to the mighty croque madame.

BEST BREAD?
White bread works best – a tin loaf, farmhouse bloomer or French-style country loaf. A sourdough will work but as they're a robust bread, they won't give you the rich, tender finish we're after. If you've got it, brioche makes a wonderful pain perdu – it might even be worth buying a loaf and letting it go a little stale! The trick here is making sure your bread is thick enough to soak up plenty of custard. You want a crispy, caramelised crust and a luxurious, barely set interior.

Deep-dish Leek & Guanciale Quiche

- SERVES: 6
- DIG IN
- TOTAL: 180 MINS, PLUS CHILLING
- PREP: 50 MINS
- COOK: 130 MINS

Shop-bought quiches are largely terrible, and I'd go as far as to say most people have never had a good one. Well, the wait is over, it's time to make a great quiche. There are two things to focus on here, the savoury custard (the eggy bit) and a shatteringly flaky, deep, golden brown crust. This recipe takes some time, and it ought to! Any recipe that claims a good quiche can be made in an hour is lying to you.

FOR THE PASTRY

| 300g strong white bread flour, plus extra for dusting |
| 8g fine sea salt |
| 20g sugar |
| 225 unsalted butter, very cold |
| 135g very cold water |

FOR THE FILLING

| 550g whole eggs (roughly 11 medium or 9 large) |
| 300g whole milk |
| 100g double cream |
| 9g fine sea salt |
| ¼ whole nutmeg |
| 180g guanciale or unsmoked pancetta |
| 2 leeks |
| 60g pecorino romano, finely grated |
| 90g Gruyère, coarsely grated |
| 25g chives, finely chopped |
| black pepper |

1 Weigh all the pastry dry ingredients into a bowl. Toss the butter in the dry mix then cut it into thin slices, then matchsticks and then into tiny cubes. Dump it back into the flour mixture, then use your fingertips and thumbs to rub the butter into the flour. Once the mixture has the texture of coarse breadcrumbs, add the water and bring together into a rough, shaggy dough. Tip out onto a work surface lightly dusted with flour and press together into a dough. It will seem dry, but don't be tempted to start adding more water! Once the dough is holding together, press it out into a long rectangle, roughly 10 x 20cm, then fold it into thirds over itself. Press down again into that rectangle and repeat the folding process. Press into a rough disc, wrap in cling film and chill for at least a few hours to rest, ideally overnight.

2 Once rested, roll the cold pastry out on a lightly floured surface until it's roughly 3mm thick and large enough to line a 20cm springform cake tin with plenty of overhang. Lower the pastry gently into the tin and press it against the sides, along the base and right into the corners, using a piece of excess pastry to prod the corners into shape. Pop it back into the fridge for another 30–45 minutes.

3 Meanwhile, combine the eggs, milk, cream and salt with 9–10 twists of pepper and plenty of finely grated nutmeg in a large bowl. Using a hand blender or whisk, mix until completely smooth. Cut the guanciale into generous lardons and put them in a large frying pan. Place over a medium heat and cook for 6–7 minutes, or until the guanciale is crisp and the fat completely rendered. Remove from the pan, leaving the fat behind. Trim the leeks, cut them into 1cm-thick rounds and sweat them down in the residual guanciale fat for 3–4 minutes until soft and bright green. Remove from the heat, toss through the crispy guanciale and set aside.

4 Preheat the oven to 200°C fan/220°C/425°F/gas mark 7. Line the pastry case with foil, fill with about 600g baking beans and blind bake for 45–50 minutes. Remove the foil and beans and slide the case back into the oven for a further 25–30 minutes until a rich golden brown. Remove from the oven and reduce the temperature to 170°C fan/190°C/375°F/gas mark 5.

5 Layer the leeks and guanciale into the baked pastry, scatter over both cheeses and pour over the custard. Cover the surface with the chives and return to the oven for 60–70 minutes until just set, with a tiny wobble in the middle. Remove from the oven, cut away the excess pastry using a serrated knife and allow to cool for at least 2 hours.

6 Remove from the tin, slice into chunky wedges and serve warm.

SALADS &

The Green Salad 70
The Chopped Salad 72
Tomato, Anchovy & Smashed Olive Salad 74
Mustardy Beans & Hazelnuts 76
Cucumber, Cherry & Almond Crunch Salad 78
Iced Veggies & Three Easy Dips 80
Roasted Peppers, White Beans & Tuna 82
Fennel & Bitter Leaf Slaw with Smoky Apple Vinaigrette 83
Chopped Beef Tartare & Rosemary Crisps 84
Fish Crudo with Jalapeño & Apple 86
Cured Mackerel with Soy Vinaigrette 88

RAW BITS

On paper, a salad is a simple plate of food, but an awful lot can happen in a salad bowl.

On the larder section of a kitchen you look after salads and cold starters. Using a series of seasonings, dressings, emulsions and other flavour enhancers, you bring inherently bland ingredients to life, give them a voice and allow them to hold their own alongside the big, loud, brash hot plates. A salad perhaps presents the best opportunity to add texture and bright, vibrant flavour to a meal, whether as a standalone dish or as a side. I have fond memories of working and learning on every larder section I was trusted with: dressing raw venison with salty parmesan and earthy pickled walnuts; learning to cure fish with salt, sugar and acid. Salads and raw bits, in the right hands, are some of the best bites out there.

BALANCING THE BOWL

The salad bowl is a great place to learn how to build a dish. We've covered the five tastes and enhancing flavour, so what goes into a good salad?

FRESH/RAW The main body of any salad, think fresh lettuces, bitter leaves, raw vegetables and fruits.

PICKLE/ACIDITY Adding pops of acidity to a salad using capers, kimchi, little pickled shallots or cornichons is like using a secret weapon.

CRUNCH/TEXTURE This can be delivered via a crouton, a toasted nut or seed or something like an iced piece of raw celery. Crunch is a vital element.

FATTY/RICH Salads can be fun, too. This is where you get to add a bit of indulgence to the bowl, maybe some cheese or a few olives.

FLAVOUR/AROMATICS If your dressing is quite mellow, it's tasty to add some high-impact flavours to the salad, such as whole herbs, salty anchovies, sliced chillies or toasted spices and seeds.

THE DRESSING The dressing should work in harmony with all your other ingredients, elevating them and making the bowl more than the sum of its parts.

If you're after a heftier serve, you can of course add meat, fish, eggs or other proteins to your salads. The ratio of how much of each of these elements you add is entirely up to you. You are the master of your bowl. If you like super-crunchy salads, up the quantity of croutons, nuts or seeds you dash across the bowl. Like a super saucy, rich salad? Add a little more dressing.

THE MECHANICS OF A GOOD DRESSING

In my book, a salad dressing should always be slightly too salty and slightly too acidic. You're going to add it to a load of vegetables that are made up of mostly water. Bite into a slice of cucumber and it's super juicy with a very mellow, clean flavour – that juice and water is going to naturally dilute your dressing. I like my salad dressings to be pretty punchy. A 3:1 ratio of fat to acid is standard, but I prefer somewhere closer to 1:1. If you need more richness, try adding some of the fatty ingredients listed above. These will bring the body your salad is after, without interrupting your dressing.

The seasonings should go in as early as possible, ideally before any fat is introduced. Good salad dressings need to have an aqueous (water-based) ingredient to infuse flavour and seasoning into. Salt can't dissolve into a pure fat like olive oil – it needs water and water-soluble flavours are brighter, punchier and much easier to amplify before you add fat. The salt will dissolve into the vinegar/lemon juice and then spread throughout the whole dressing and be emulsified into the oil. If you add the salt after the oil/fat has been introduced, it won't dissolve as well, and you run the risk of over-seasoning your dressing.

When making a dressing, I aim for roughly equal quantities of something with body and backbone like mustard (this also acts as an emulsifier), something sharp like citrus or vinegar and something sweet to balance everything. These flavours are then rounded out and mellowed by a decent dose of fat. It's important to identify which of the ingredients you want to be the hero here. Is it anchovies and parmesan in a Caesar? Is it the sweet and sour apple vinegar that you just picked up? Maybe it's the grassy green new season olive oil. Adjust the ratio of your dressing to allow those ingredients to shine. The more fat you add, the more subdued the rest of the ingredients will become. For example, if you've got a beautiful sherry vinegar, you want those complex flavours to pop and shine through when you're eating your salad.

Adjusting the amount of fat you add will allow the vinegar to take centre stage. If you're grappling with the balance, don't be afraid to add a drop of water.

Dressing like a pro

If you're making a leaf-heavy salad, you don't need salad tongs – use your hands! Dressing salads with clean hands is the best way to incorporate delicate ingredients and flavours. You also get a much better idea of when everything is dressed nice and evenly. I always start with my dressing in the bottom of the bowl, then tip in the heaviest ingredients, like chopped cucumbers or chunks of cheese, and then build it up, finishing with the lightest, most delicate ingredient, such as leaves and soft herbs. When I'm digging my hands into a big bowl of leaves and dressing, the word that I like to keep in mind is 'tumble'. A light touch will ensure your herbs stay vibrant and the salad leaves retain their texture and crunch.

While leafy salads appreciate delicacy, some call for a firmer hand. Making a salad with potatoes, kale or more robust ingredients? You'll want to get in there and knock them about a bit. This improves the texture and increases their ability to absorb a dressing.

When to dress

How early should you dress your salads? Well, it depends on the ingredients. A leafy green salad should be dressed moments before being served, as the salts and acid begin to wilt the leaves after just a few minutes. A tomato salad should be seasoned and dressed a little in advance to allow the salt to work its magic on the meaty fruit.

Wash your own greens

When planning your salad making, try to buy whole heads of lettuce and vegetables rather than bags of mixed leaves or prepared salad, which will have gone through a pretty rigorous, violent process of being picked, chopped, blasted with water and packed into hermetically-sealed bags, pumped with gas to preserve their freshness. Buying whole heads of lettuce allows you to control the flavours of the salad, adjusting just how much sweet lettuce, how many bitter leaves or spicy radishes you'd like, and ensures that everything is super fresh. Buy a salad spinner, wash your own greens, and thank me later.

RAW MEAT AND FISH

Eating raw meat and fish isn't for everyone, but for me, it's one of the purest ways to engage with these ingredients. It's also about as easy as cooking gets. Is it even cooking? Not really, it's all about seasoning. The secret to serving meat and fish is simply in the ingredients, buying the freshest you can get, and learning how to simply prepare them with a few confident cuts is about all it takes.

USE HIGH-QUALITY INGREDIENTS Use very fresh fish or tender lean cuts for raw and cured serves.

CHILL THE PROTEIN Slightly chill the meat/fish to make it easier to handle and achieve precise cuts.

USE A SHARP KNIFE A sharp chef's knife is crucial for clean, even cuts.

Against the grain

You can manipulate the texture and mouthfeel of raw meat by cutting it in different ways. It's all down to the meat's 'grain' and how you alter, disrupt or celebrate it. In meat, grain refers to the direction in which the muscle fibres run. It's easier to identify in tougher cuts like bavette and almost invisible in cuts like tenderloin – the more prominent the grain, the tougher the meat will be and the more attention you should pay to how you cut it. When you slice meat 'against the grain', or perpendicular to these muscle fibres, you end up with a much more tender product, as the muscle fibres have been disrupted. Preparing beef for tartare offers the most opportunity to tenderise tougher cuts as you can chop and 'break' the grain more.

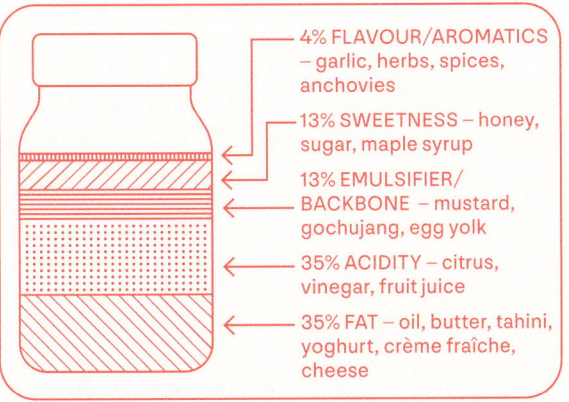

- 4% FLAVOUR/AROMATICS – garlic, herbs, spices, anchovies
- 13% SWEETNESS – honey, sugar, maple syrup
- 13% EMULSIFIER/BACKBONE – mustard, gochujang, egg yolk
- 35% ACIDITY – citrus, vinegar, fruit juice
- 35% FAT – oil, butter, tahini, yoghurt, crème fraîche, cheese

SALADS & RAW BITS

The Green Salad

- SERVES: 4 AS A SIDE
- EYES CLOSED
- GF
- TOTAL: 20 MINS, PLUS COOLING
- PREP: 15 MINS, PLUS COOLING
- COOK: 5 MINS

For me, the green salad is the simplest (and best) expression of what salad is and should be. A tangle of vinegary leaves and herbs topped with salty cheese is a welcome guest on any dinner table and the perfect sidekick to an infinite list of main courses.

FOR THE PICKLED SHALLOTS

2 shallots

75ml white wine vinegar

50ml caster sugar

25ml water

FOR THE DRESSING

1 egg yolk

3 tsp Dijon mustard

50g white wine vinegar

3 tsp honey

50g extra virgin olive oil

50g sunflower oil

fine sea salt

black pepper

FOR THE SALAD

2 heads of soft-leaf lettuce

2 baby gem

90g rocket

10g chives

5g dill

10g flat-leaf parsley

5g tarragon

½ lemon

10g parmesan cheese

1 Start with the pickled shallots. Peel the papery skin from the shallots and cut them into thin rounds. Separate the rounds into individual rings and pop into a heatproof bowl. Combine the vinegar, sugar and water in a small saucepan and gently heat until just below simmering. Stir to combine, then pour it over the shallots while still warm. Cover and set aside to cool to room temperature.

2 To make the dressing, grab the bowl you plan to dress your salad in (the largest you own!). Place it on a scale so you can weigh the ingredients straight into the bowl. Tip in the yolk, mustard, vinegar, honey, 1 tablespoon of cold water, a good pinch of fine sea salt and a few twists of pepper. Whisk together vigorously before slowly adding the oils to create an emulsified dressing. Taste and add more sugar, vinegar or salt as needed. You want the dressing to be sweet, sour, salty and have a pourable consistency. For a super light, fluffy dressing, you can make this in a blender.

3 Scatter in your salad leaves, add a handful of pickled shallots and finely chop the chives before adding them, too. Pick the remaining herbs from the stems, adding them straight into the bowl. Keep them in large, toothsome pieces – they'll add texture and serious pops of flavour to your salad. Season with a little fine sea salt and gently tumble the salad together. It shouldn't need more than a few turns to coat the leaves in the dressing.

4 Build the salad high on a plate, laying larger leaves on the bottom and smaller on top. It should be tall and proud with plenty of herbs and pickled shallots scattered throughout. Top your salad with freshly grated lemon zest and a generous cloud of finely grated parmesan. Serve right away.

> **CHEF'S TIP**
> Don't be afraid to add a shot of water to your dressing. This dressing is a fantastic all-rounder, modelled on a classic French Dijon dressing, but with an egg yolk for a rounded finish. It can sometimes come out punching, a little too salty or sharp or sweet. I find a little drip of water can level the playing field.

The Chopped Salad

- **SERVES:** 4
- **EYES CLOSED**
- **VE / GF**
- **TOTAL:** 25 MINS
- **PREP:** 15 MINS
- **COOK:** 10 MINS

I might make this salad more than any other. Dressing simple crunchy veggies with olive oil and lemon juice is a joy and is a real exercise in seasoning. We're not building a dressing in a bowl for this recipe, we're going to dress the bright, fresh veggies until super sharp and bright and then pair them with a rich, creamy tahini dressing. When you take a bite, you get zippy, cool, crunchy veggies, fragrant with chopped herbs and raw chilli, then a smooth blanket of tahini dressing. One works in harmony with the other. It's a stunner.

FOR THE CRISPY CHICKPEAS

- 400g tin chickpeas, drained, rinsed and dried
- 1 tbsp za'atar
- light olive oil, for frying
- fine sea salt
- black pepper

FOR THE TAHINI SAUCE

- 120g good-quality tahini
- 1 garlic clove
- ½ lemon
- 100g cold water
- fine sea salt

FOR THE SALAD

- 2 large ripe tomatoes
- 1 cucumber
- 1 sweet white onion
- 40g rocket
- 20g mint
- 30g flat-leaf parsley
- 1 red chilli
- 1 lemon
- extra virgin olive oil
- fine sea salt
- black pepper

1 To make the crispy chickpeas, place a small saucepan over a medium heat and add a good layer of olive oil so that it comes 3–4cm up the side of the pan. Heat the oil to around 150°C then gently lower in half of the chickpeas. Cook for 5–6 minutes, or until they stop bubbling and hissing and become golden brown and crispy. Scoop them out, drain on kitchen paper, then toss with salt, a few twists of pepper and the za'atar while still nice and warm. Repeat with the remaining chickpeas. Set aside. If you don't fancy frying them, you can roast the chickpeas tossed in a generous glug of oil in the oven, spread out on a baking tray, at 200°C fan/220°C/425°F/gas mark 7 for 30–35 minutes until crispy.

2 To make the tahini sauce, put the tahini in a small bowl and finely grate in the garlic clove. Add the juice of the half lemon and stir to combine. Start slowly whisking in the water until the sauce has a rich, creamy, spoonable consistency. Season with salt and set aside.

3 Cut the tomatoes, cucumber (removing the seeds) and onion into an even dice. What size? Dealer's choice, but I shoot for around a 3cm cube. Tip them into a bowl and season well with salt. Roughly chop the rocket. Pick the herbs from their stems and finely chop. Split the chilli in half lengthways, remove the seeds and finely chop. Add everything to the bowl. Toss the chopped salad with a good pinch of salt, a few twists of black pepper, plenty of olive oil and lots of lemon juice. Set aside and leave to hang out and macerate for 10–15 minutes.

4 Add a dollop of tahini sauce to the bottom of your plates and swoosh it around, add a pile of the chopped salad and top with a handful of crispy chickpeas. Finish with a few spoons of the juice from the salad bowl and get stuck in.

> **CHEF'S TIP**
> Tahini sauce can tend to split. How can you tell if this has happened? If it looks greasy and a bit like scrambled eggs. You'll notice the sesame paste seize up when you start to add water-based liquid (water/lemon juice). We're creating another emulsion here! It's about taking your time to marry that water and fat. If it splits, you can tip it into a blender with a bit of water and whizz it back together, or whisk for your life with a splash more water.

SALADS & RAW BITS

Tomato, Anchovy & Smashed Olive Salad

SERVES: 4
EYES CLOSED
P
TOTAL: 15 MINS, PLUS MACERATING
PREP: 15 MINS, PLUS MACERATING

There are some things that shouldn't be messed with. Good tomatoes, olives and anchovies achieve a harmony of flavour that is almost unrivalled. Tomatoes need three things to really sparkle: salt, fat and time. I always try to season the tomatoes a good half an hour before I want to eat them. The salt draws the moisture out of the tomato, intensifying the flavour.

FOR THE SALAD

450g large ripe tomatoes

1 ball of good-quality mozzarella

10g basil leaves

12 of the best tinned anchovies you can find

FOR THE SOURDOUGH CRUMBS

2–3 slices of sourdough

olive oil

fine sea salt

rosemary leaves or crushed garlic (optional)

FOR THE DRESSING

½ red onion

25g sherry vinegar or red wine vinegar, plus a little extra for the tomatoes

1 tsp caster sugar

75g nocellara olives

60g taggiasche or kalamata olives

40ml extra virgin olive oil, plus extra for the tomatoes

fine sea salt

black pepper

1 Start by making the sourdough crumbs. Preheat the oven to 150°C fan/170°C/325°F/gas mark 3. Cut the sourdough into even dice and toss with a little olive oil and salt. You can add rosemary or crushed garlic at this point too. Slide into the oven for 13–15 minutes, or until golden and crisp all the way through. Remove from the oven, allow to cool and then blitz in a food processor or crush using a pestle and mortar to your desired texture. Transfer to an airtight container; these will sit in the cupboard quite happily for a week or so.

2 Cut your tomatoes into a few different shapes and sizes. I like to slice one larger, fleshier tomato into thick slices as a good base for the salad and then the rest into halves, quarters or random chunks. Remove the core if it feels too coarse or unpleasant to eat. Season the tomatoes generously with salt, drizzle with a little olive oil and vinegar and set aside for at least half an hour and up to 2 hours.

3 Finely dice the red onion and tip it into a bowl with the vinegar, sugar and a pinch of salt. Stir to combine everything.

4 Use the flat of your knife to squash the olives on your board. Find a natural seam in the crushed olive and peel it apart, exposing the stone. Remove the stones and discard. Roughly chop the pitted olives and add to the bowl with the red onion. Add the olive oil and season with black pepper. Leave the dressing to hang out and macerate for 5–10 minutes. Cut the mozzarella into bite-sized chunks.

5 Lay your seasoned tomatoes out on a plate, adding any residual tomato juice to the olive dressing. Spoon the dressing over the plate of tomatoes, distributing the olives evenly. Add chunks of mozzarella and basil leaves and drape the anchovies onto the tomatoes. Finish with a sprinkle of sourdough crumble and serve.

> **CHEF'S TIP**
> I like to use large tomatoes in this salad. You can go for smaller cherry, baby plum or datterini tomatoes if you like, but for me, the flesh-rich varieties like San Marzano and Cuore Del Vesuvio are the ones to look out for. These tomatoes have a much higher flesh to seed ratio and are super juicy.

Mustardy Beans & Hazelnuts

- SERVES: 4
- EYES CLOSED
- GF
- TOTAL: 20 MINS, PLUS COOLING
- PREP: 15 MINS, PLUS COOLING
- COOK: 5 MINS

A stone-cold classic mustard vinaigrette! It's a lovely nod to a classic French green bean salad, with a few welcome additions. The pro move here is to add crème fraîche to the dressing: the dairy cuts the sharpness of the classic vinaigrette beautifully, rounds out the tarragon flavour and gives everything a punch of lactic acidity.

FOR THE DRESSING

25g Dijon mustard

20g wholegrain mustard

35ml white wine vinegar

25ml olive oil

25ml neutral oil

5–10g fresh tarragon

50–80g full-fat crème fraîche

fine sea salt

black pepper

FOR THE SALAD

400g mixed long beans; green, yellow, runner or pietonne

50g toasted hazelnuts

4 spring onions

20g dill

250g cooked beluga or puy lentils

1 lemon

60g Manchego cheese

1. Start by making the dressing. Put the mustards and vinegar in a bowl along with the salt and 6–8 twists of black pepper then whisk to combine. Working gradually, whisk in the oils one by one to create a thick, emulsified dressing. If it's a little too thick, add a splash more vinegar or a drop of water. Pick the leaves from the tarragon, finely chop and add to the dressing. Mix through the crème fraîche and set aside.

2. Bring a large pot of water to the boil. Heavily season it with salt (roughly 120g per litre of water) – you want it to be much saltier than you think and far saltier than pasta water! Trust me. Set up a bowl of iced water and season that generously, too. Top and tail the beans and cook in the boiling water for 3–4 minutes, or until tender.

3. Remove from the boiling water and plunge into the salty iced water. Jostle the beans around to ensure even cooling then remove. Dry the beans as best you can, using either a tea towel or a salad spinner.

4. Use the flat of your knife to crack the hazelnuts into chunky pieces. Trim and thinly slice the spring onions and roughly chop the dill. Toss the cooked beans into a bowl along with the hazelnuts, spring onions, dill, lentils and the zest of the lemon. Shave in half of the Manchego cheese with a peeler.

5. Pour over the dressing and gently toss to combine everything. Divide among plates, shave over the remaining Manchego and serve.

> **NOTES**
> Before you add the tarragon and crème fraîche, this vinaigrette is extremely shelf stable and will sit happily at an ambient temperature for a good month or so. You can have a bottle or jar ready to which you can add herbs, grated garlic, fresh lemon zest, crème fraîche or whatever you're into. Just remember, as soon as you add anything fresh or 'alive', it'll start to spoil and lose its potency.

> **CHEF'S TIP**
> Always add a handful of salt to your ice bath when blanching – this ensures when you plunge those perfectly cooked, perfectly seasoned beans into the ice bath, you don't wash away all that salt!

SALADS & RAW BITS

Cucumber, Cherry & Almond Crunch Salad

SERVES: 2
EYES CLOSED
GF
TOTAL: 15 MINS
PREP: 15 MINS

This one is all about the texture, with layers of crunchy veggies and toasted almonds. No crazy techniques here, no pickling or roasting or searing, just an ice bath. An ice bath is a really easy way to elevate a salad by ramping up the crisp, juicy crunch of a raw vegetable or salad leaf. It's a clean, simple salad that punches way above its weight, I love it. Try it and you will, too.

150g fresh cherries
50g coriander
25g flat-leaf parsley
1 red onion
2 celery sticks
½ cucumber
2 green chillies
1 lemon
100g good-quality toasted salted almonds
200g feta cheese
1 tsp dried oregano
extra virgin olive oil
fine sea salt
black pepper

1 Use a cherry pitter or chopstick to pit the cherries. If using a chopstick, carefully push through the side of the cherry until you hit the stone, keep pushing and it should pop out the other side. If you don't have either a cherry pitter or chopstick handy, you can remove the stone as you would a peach or plum, cutting around the circumference of the fruit and twisting the two halves apart, then picking out the stone. I prefer to keep some of the cherries whole, and tear some in half, but do whatever works for you!

2 Cut the coriander and parsley into lengths of roughly 5cm, leaving the leaves and stems intact. Thinly slice the red onion and cut the celery and cucumber on a steep angle into chunky slices roughly 2–3cm thick. Thinly slice the green chillies, leaving the seeds in for heat. Set up a couple of bowls of iced water, seasoning one generously with salt and stirring to dissolve. Chuck the herbs into the unseasoned water and add the celery, cucumber, onion and chillies to the other bowl and leave for 10–12 minutes.

3 Drain and dry before adding to a bowl with the pitted cherries. Add a generous glug of olive oil and the juice of the whole lemon. Season well with salt and pepper and gently toss together. Have a taste – the salad should be very sharp with lemon juice, this will be balanced by the fat of the cheese and the almonds.

4 Roughly chop the almonds. Tear the cheese into bite-sized chunks and scatter them across a platter, season with salt, a few twists of pepper and a drizzle of olive oil. Top the cheese with the dressed salad and finish with a sprinkle of oregano and a handful of the almonds.

SHOOT FROM THE HIP
Not a fan of coriander? Statistically, around 20% of you will think it tastes like soap, so no hard feelings. You can swap it out for any soft herb you like (dill, chervil, chives), or simply use more parsley. Whip out the cheese for a vegan serve.

CHEF'S TIP
I like to keep the stems on softer herbs when using them whole. Not only are they delicious and packed with flavour, they bring a lovely toothsome bite to an ingredient that is usually chopped. Texture, texture, texture!

Iced Veggies & Three Easy Dips

Raw veggies dipped into something tasty are a staple when entertaining. Sometimes they can be a bit sad, wilting as they sit out, carrots curling, cucumbers drying out, lettuces drooping. How do you fix it? Serve them over ice. It's a little more effort, but it looks super chic and will keep those veggies fresh, bright and crunchy all night long. We also have three super simple, high-impact dip recipes to pair with your icy-cold crunchy veg. Make one, two or all three and you'll keep any number of diners happy.

THE VEGGIES

SERVES: 6–8 **EYES CLOSED**

- a generous mixture of crunchy, dippable veg (baby carrots, baby cucumbers, celery, radicchio, radishes, mange tout, fresh peas, baby gem)
- 1kg crushed ice
- rock salt

Cut the veggies into dippable pieces, if you need to. If the veggies are good to go au naturale, then stick with that! I like to serve baby gem in little wedges, serve baby veg whole where possible and, if not, cut into bite-sized, sensible pieces. Add a layer of rock salt to your serving vessel before topping with a generous layer of crushed ice. Briefly shock the veggies in iced water then lay them on top of the ice and serve with your dips of choice.

CRÈME FRAÎCHE RANCH

V / GF **TOTAL: 10 MINS PLUS HANGING**

- 235g full-fat crème fraîche
- 1 lemon
- 1 garlic clove
- 1 tsp garlic powder
- 1 tbsp onion powder
- 1 tsp dried dill
- 1 tsp Dijon mustard
- 25g fresh dill, plus extra to serve
- fine sea salt
- black pepper

Line a sieve with a J-cloth or piece of kitchen paper. Set the lined sieve over a bowl and tip the crème fraîche into it. Cover and pop into the fridge for 3–4 hours. Tip the hung crème fraîche into a bowl and add the grated zest of the lemon. Finely grate in the garlic clove and add the garlic and onion powders, dried dill and mustard. Finely chop the dill and get that into the bowl. Beat together and season with salt and around 25 twists of coarsely cracked black pepper. Pour into a bowl and top with a crack of pepper and a little extra fresh dill.

SALADS & RAW BITS

SPICY PEANUT HUMMUS

✓ VE / GF　　● TOTAL: 15 MINS

- 2 shallots
- 2 garlic cloves
- 1 tsp sweet smoked paprika
- 350g good-quality jarred chickpeas
- 1 tbsp hot chilli oil, plus a little extra to serve
- 75g smooth peanut butter
- 2 limes
- 2 tbsp dry roasted or spicy peanuts
- olive oil
- fine sea salt
- black pepper

Peel and thinly slice the shallots and garlic. Preheat a small frying pan over a medium-high heat, add a shot of olive oil and tip in the shallots and garlic. Season with salt and cook for 2–3 minutes over a high heat. Add the paprika and remove from the heat, allowing the residual heat to bloom and wake up the spice. Tip the chickpeas and their liquid into a saucepan and warm over a low heat. Once warm, scoop the chickpeas into a food processor along with a splash of the liquor. Add the shallots and garlic, the chilli oil, peanut butter and the juice of one lime. Season and blend until very smooth – I usually let the machine run for at least 4–5 minutes. Meanwhile, bash the peanuts with a rolling pin to break them up. Scoop the hummus into a bowl and top with extra chilli oil, smashed peanuts and grated zest of the other lime.

SMOKY TROUT RILLETTE

✓ GF　　● TOTAL: 10 MINS PLUS SALTING

- ¼ cucumber
- 100g cream cheese
- 100g full-fat crème fraîche
- 150g hot smoked trout
- 1 tbsp capers
- 40g dill pickles
- 25g dill
- 25g chives, plus extra to serve
- 1 lemon
- 2 tbsp trout roe or caviar (optional)
- fine sea salt
- black pepper

Cut the cucumber into a small dice, season generously with salt and leave to hang out in a bowl for 10 minutes or so. Pour off the excess liquid and rinse briefly with cold water. Drain and dry. Beat together the cream cheese and crème fraîche until smooth. Flake in the trout and add the capers. Cut the pickles into a small dice and fold through the mix. Finely chop the dill and chives and add to the bowl. Finish with the grated zest and juice of the lemon and season generously with 18 twists of pepper and some salt. Scoop into a bowl and serve topped with extra chopped chives and a dollop of trout roe or caviar, if using.

SALADS & RAW BITS

Roasted Peppers, White Beans & Tuna

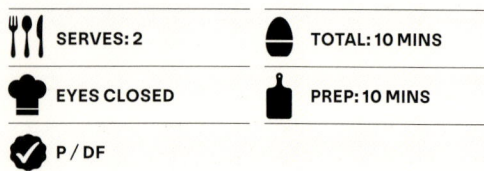

- SERVES: 2
- TOTAL: 10 MINS
- EYES CLOSED
- PREP: 10 MINS
- P / DF

This is very much a one-bowl wonder, and a real showcase of fresh, sunny flavours. It's an achingly simple play on the classic 'fagioli e tonno', or tuna and beans. Open a few jars and slice a handful of ingredients and 10 minutes later you have a damn near perfect lunch. There are a couple of takeaways from this recipe, the most important being that you're only as good as your ingredients, and this salad is only as good as its beans and tuna – you want to find the best you can. Jarred beans are best, they're cooked in the jar and seasoned well, unlike their tin-bound counterparts. Try and get hold of really good quality jarred or tinned tuna that is packed and cooked with olive oil.

1 red onion
700g jar cooked white beans
4 jarred roasted peppers
2 large ripe tomatoes
100g pitted taggiasche or kalamata olives
20g flat-leaf parsley
20g basil
1 lemon
40ml red wine vinegar
1 tbsp capers
200g good-quality tinned tuna in oil, drained
2 tbsp Sourdough Crumbs (page 74)
extra virgin olive oil
fine sea salt
black pepper

1 Peel and top and tail the onion. Cut it in half through the root and top and place the cut side flat on your board. Run your knife from the top to the root, cutting with the grain of the onion, creating slices roughly 5mm thick. Fill a small bowl with iced water and stir in 1 teaspoon of salt. Separate the slices into individual slivers of onion and submerge them in the icy cold water for 10 minutes.

2 Empty the beans into a fine-mesh sieve or colander and rinse under cold running water. Cut the roasted peppers into strips and the tomatoes into a chunky dice. Tip into a bowl along with the beans and tear in the black olives. Finely chop the parsley and add to the bowl.

3 Drain and add the onions and tear in the basil. Add the zest and juice of the lemon, the vinegar, capers and a generous glug of olive oil. Season generously with salt and about 12 twists of black pepper then toss the salad together. Allow to the salad to sit for a minute or two before you have a taste, just to let the ingredients react to the seasoning. Adjust the seasoning as you like then tip in the drained tuna. Toss two or three times to lightly break up the fish and incorporate it into the salad. Divide between plates and top with extra olive oil and a sprinkle of sourdough crumbs.

> **TUNA TEXTURE**
> I like to keep the tuna nice and chunky, so I don't add it until right at the end. If the fish is added too soon, you'll have to toss the salad too much and it'll break down into mush!

> **CHEF'S TIP**
> Take the sting out of the red onions with a little bath in icy cold, salted water before they hit the salad bowl. You can skip this step, if you like, but that onion might spend a few hours with you once you're done eating!

Fennel & Bitter Leaf Slaw with Smoky Apple Vinaigrette

- SERVES: 2
- ROLL YOUR SLEEVES UP
- TOTAL: 40 MINS
- PREP: 15 MINS
- COOK: 25 MINS

This recipe is proof that both butter and pork do belong in the salad world. I discovered the joys of reducing fruit juice as a young, bright-eyed cook in London. Litres of apple juice (preferably cloudy, for extra funky, malic acidity) bubble away quietly, slowly reducing into a sticky, complex distillation of pure apple flavour. It's sweet, sour, rich and can be used all across the kitchen. For me, it makes a great base for a salad dressing, bringing depth and complexity to any bowl of veggies.

600ml cloudy apple juice
125g smoked pancetta
30g unsalted butter
2 fennel bulbs
1 head of radicchio, castelfranco or similar bitter leaf
2 gala apples
2 celery sticks
20g dill or chervil
40ml apple cider vinegar
½ tbsp Dijon mustard
½ tbsp wholegrain mustard
fine sea salt
black pepper

1 Start by reducing the apple juice. Pour the whole lot into a small saucepan, bring to a simmer, then reduce the heat to the lowest setting and allow it to lazily bubble away until thick, caramelly and tart (be sure to allow it to cool slightly before tasting or it'll burn your tongue clean off!). This should take about 20 minutes, but will vary a little depending on the size of your pan (the larger the pan, the quicker the reduction) and the ferocity of your hob.

2 While your apple juice reduces, cut the pancetta into lardons and put them in a small frying pan. Place over a medium heat and allow the fat to render and the lardons to crisp. Once golden brown and crunchy, fish out the lardons, leaving behind the smoky pork fat. Chuck the butter into the pork fat and cook over a low heat until nutty brown, swirling the pan as it cooks. Remove from the heat and allow the fats to cool slightly.

3 Using a sharp knife or mandoline, thinly slice the fennel and roughly chop the bitter leaves. Cut the apples into matchsticks, thinly slice the celery and roughly chop the dill or chervil. Toss everything into a bowl, season with salt and toss.

4 To finish the dressing, combine the reduced apple juice with the brown butter and pancetta fat in a small mixing bowl. Whisk in the vinegar and both mustards. Season with salt and pepper to taste. The dressing should be tart, sweet, rich and smoky, with a decent punch of mustard.

5 Pour the dressing over the veggies and add the pancetta. Toss everything together and serve.

SWAPS
If you're after a vegetarian version you can leave out the pancetta and simply add 40g olive oil in place of its fat. Fully vegan? Swap the pancetta and butter for 75g olive oil.

SHOOT FROM THE HIP
This salad is a great way to use up leftover roasted pork belly or Garlic & Fennel Porchetta (page 226), chopped into generous, juicy chunks and tossed through the salad while still warm.

SALADS & RAW BITS

Chopped Beef Tartare & Rosemary Crisps

- 2 AS A MAIN / 4 AS A STARTER
- TOTAL: 55 MINS
- ROLL YOUR SLEEVES UP
- PREP: 30 MINS
- GF
- COOK: 25 MINS

If I see beef tartare on a menu, chances are I'm ordering it. It's not something amateur cooks take on all that often, which is a shame as it's incredibly easy. There aren't many secrets to a good beef tartare: just spend a few quid on a nice piece of beef, and dress it with beautiful ingredients that boost that meaty flavour. The anchovies and fish sauce might seem out of place at first, but they bring a serious hit of umami to the tartare and are a great background note. The rocket is finely chopped through the mix for extra peppery heat.

FOR THE BEEF TARTARE

- 500g beef rump cap or fillet
- 2 shallots
- 1 lemon
- 50g cornichons
- 2 guindillas or pickled green chillies
- 2 good-quality tinned anchovy fillets
- 10g chives
- 15g rocket
- 2 tsp Dijon mustard
- 6–7 dashes of Tabasco sauce
- 2 dashes of good-quality fish sauce
- egg yolks, 1 per portion
- extra virgin olive oil
- flaky sea salt
- black pepper

FOR THE HOMEMADE ROSEMARY CRISPS (OPTIONAL)

- 20g fine sea salt
- 4g dried rosemary
- 4g MSG
- 400g large Maris Piper or russet potatoes
- vegetable oil, for frying

1 To make the tartare, pop the beef into the freezer for 10–15 minutes to firm up. Using a sharp knife, trim any silvery skin or sinew from the beef and, if using rump cap, remove any of the layer of fat cap that might be left on top of the beef (save the fat and use it for the cheeseburger blend on page 196 or freeze for another day!).

2 While the beef chills, peel and cut the shallots into the finest dice you can (we call it a brunoise!), tip into a bowl and cover with the juice of half the lemon. Set aside. Cut the cornichons and guindillas into thin rounds and drain and finely mince the anchovy fillets. Finely chop the chives and rocket.

3 Whip the beef out of the freezer and cut it into an even dice, as fine or as coarse as you fancy: slice it thinly against the grain and stack the slices then cut crosswise into strips before stacking the strips and dicing. Add to a large mixing bowl and tip in the shallots, lemon juice and all the cornichons, guindillas, anchovies, chives and rocket. Add the mustard, Tabasco and fish sauce. Add a little olive oil, season with a little salt and about 11 twists of black pepper, mix, then taste and adjust the seasoning.

4 Divide between plates and top each with an egg yolk. Season the yolk with a little flaky sea salt and a twist of coarse black pepper. Serve with a handful of crisps, homemade or otherwise.

5 To make homemade crisps, first stick the salt, rosemary and MSG in a spice grinder or use a pestle and mortar to grind to a fine powder.

6 Scrub the potatoes well. Using a mandoline, cut the potatoes into slices around 2mm thick. How do you know you're slicing at 2mm? Cut 10 slices, stack them together and then measure them, each stack should be around 2cm thick.

7 Add the slices to a bowl of warm water and swirl around to wash off the excess starch. Ditch the water and replace with fresh warm water. Leave the potatoes to soak for 20 minutes, then drain and dry them between tea towels or kitchen paper.

8 Preheat a pan half-filled with vegetable oil to 150°C. Working in batches, fry the slices of potato for 3–5 minutes, or until golden brown and crisp. Take your time and keep an eye on the temperature as you go. Fish the cooked crisps out with a spider and drain on a rack. Tip the rosemary powder into a fine-mesh sieve and dust it over the crisps while still warm.

CHEF'S TIP
The way you cut your beef will transform the way the tartare eats. I call this 'chopped' beef tartare as I like to keep the beef pretty chunky. You might see some tartare prepared using minced beef, or meat chopped so finely it looks like it's been through the mincer. You cut any piece of beef fine enough, and it'll lose its character. For me, to celebrate the cut you've chosen, it's best to leave it with a little bite.

Fish Crudo with Jalapeño & Apple

 SERVES: 2

 TOTAL: 25 MINS, PLUS SALTING

 ROLL YOUR SLEEVES UP

 PREP: 25 MINS, PLUS SALTING

 P / DF / GF

This is a bright, zippy way to serve sparkling seafood. 'Crudo' literally translates as 'raw' in Italian and is an easy way to taste the purest expression of a fish. We're going to use sea bream or bass for this recipe – they're a great place to start with raw fish and are widely available and easy to find super fresh. This recipe looks very fancy, and delivers restaurant quality at home, but is so, so simple.

2 fillets of super fresh sea bream or sea bass, skin-on, bones removed
15g fine sea salt, plus extra for the dressing
1 tsp coriander seeds
½ tsp caster sugar
1 shallot
1 fresh jalapeño
1 lime
1 lemon
1 green apple
extra virgin olive oil
flaky sea salt

1 Pat the fillets dry with kitchen paper and set onto a clean tray. Sprinkle a thin layer of the salt on both sides of the fish. Place the fillets back onto the tray, skin side down, and put in the fridge for 1 hour.

2 While the fish salts, prepare the dressing. Place a small saucepan over a medium-high heat and tip in the coriander seeds. Toast until fragrant then tip into a mortar and lightly crush with the pestle until coarsely cracked. Add the sugar and a healthy pinch of salt. Peel and finely dice the shallot and deseed and slice the jalapeño. Either add to the mortar or transfer everything to a small bowl and mix it all together. Set aside for 1 hour.

3 Once the fish and dressing have had time to rest, you'll notice both have exuded some moisture. The shallot and jalapeño will have made the dressing super fragrant, they just need some acidity now. Add the juice of the lime and ½ of the lemon to the dressing. Peel and cut the apple into a very fine dice and tip that in, too. Add 1 tablespoon of extra virgin olive oil and stir together.

4 Using a damp, clean cloth, wipe away the salt and any excess moisture from the fish. Using a sharp knife, remove the skin: starting at the back of the fillet, make a small incision just above the skin. Holding the knife at a shallow angle, towards the board, pull the fillet back towards you, allowing the knife to slice away the skin. Once the skin is removed, discard.

5 Cut the fish into thickish slices, cleaning your knife between each cut with a damp clean cloth, and arrange each fillet on a room-temperature plate. Spoon over lashings of the dressing and finish with flaky sea salt and a little more extra virgin olive oil.

CHEF'S TIP
We're going to very gently salt-cure the fish ahead of serving. It's still very much crudo, but this small amount of time hanging out with salt will dramatically improve the texture and flavour of the fish.

SHOOT FROM THE HIP
The dressing ingredients are up to you – you can play with different citrus (orange, yuzu, grapefruit) and different crunchy, fresh bits (cucumbers, radishes, pear). If coriander seeds aren't your jam, try fennel or cumin!

Cured Mackerel with Soy Vinaigrette

- SERVES: 4
- DIG IN
- P / DF
- TOTAL: 30 MINS, PLUS CURING
- PREP: 20 MINS, PLUS CURING
- COOK: 10 MINS

If you've tried ceviche before, you've probably noticed how the texture of fish changes when submerged in citrus juice. This is a similar process, but vinegar is a little gentler on the fish. To get into how the raw fish changes with acidity, prepare and compare the fish in the crudo recipe on page 86 to this one. Both are salted, but this one is exposed to acidity, completely transforming the flavour and texture.

FOR THE PICKLED MACKEREL

4 super fresh mackerel fillets, skin on

45g fine sea salt

200ml good-quality sherry vinegar

FOR THE VINAIGRETTE

2 tbsp light soy sauce

½ orange

1 lime

1 garlic clove

1 tsp sesame oil

1 tsp caster sugar

1 tsp toasted sesame seeds

4–6 mixed radishes

1 Use the salt to season the fish on both the skin and flesh sides. Pop onto a tray and slide into the fridge, uncovered, for 2 hours. Once it's had 2 hours, whip it out of the fridge and add to a bowl. Cover with the vinegar and add a layer of parchment to ensure the fish is fully submerged. Return to the fridge for 30 minutes.

2 To make the vinaigrette, combine the soy with 2 tablespoons of the vinegar used to cure the mackerel, the zest and juice of the half orange as well as the juice of the lime and a squashed garlic clove in a small bowl. Mix in the sesame oil, sugar and sesame seeds. Taste and adjust the sugar, soy and vinegar as you like. Thinly slice the radishes and pop into iced water with a pinch of salt.

3 Once the mackerel has had 30 minutes in the vinegar, remove and pat the fillets dry with kitchen paper. Put them on a board, skin side up, and use your fingers to remove the silvery membrane on the skin – you might not be able to see it, but it's there. Using your thumb and forefinger, grab onto a corner of the fatter end of the fillet and peel up and towards the tail. Be gentle, you can peel away some of the flesh if you're too rough, so take your time.

4 Once removed, discard the membrane and cut the fish into slices about 1cm thick. Arrange on a room-temperature plate and dress with a generous helping of the soy vinaigrette. Scatter over the radishes and serve.

CHEF'S TIP

The only finicky bit of this recipe is removing the membrane or silvery skin from the mackerel. You can get the process started with a pair of tweezers, but I find you can use your fingers just as well.

SHOOT FROM THE HIP

You could use a variety of vinegars here to imbue the mackerel with different flavours. Rice vinegar would yield a clean, pure flavour, apple vinegar would lend some sweetness . . . experiment! Though I would avoid using a sugar-rich vinegar like a balsamic.

> ### SOUSING
> 'Sousing' is a centuries-old method of preserving fish; you'll probably have seen soused herring. The fish is submerged in a salt brine and/or vinegar to cure the fish and prolong its life. This process is similar, but we're only going to bathe the fish for a fraction of the time you might traditionally sous a herring. This way, the middle of the fillet stays a beautiful, blushing raw.

SALADS & RAW BITS

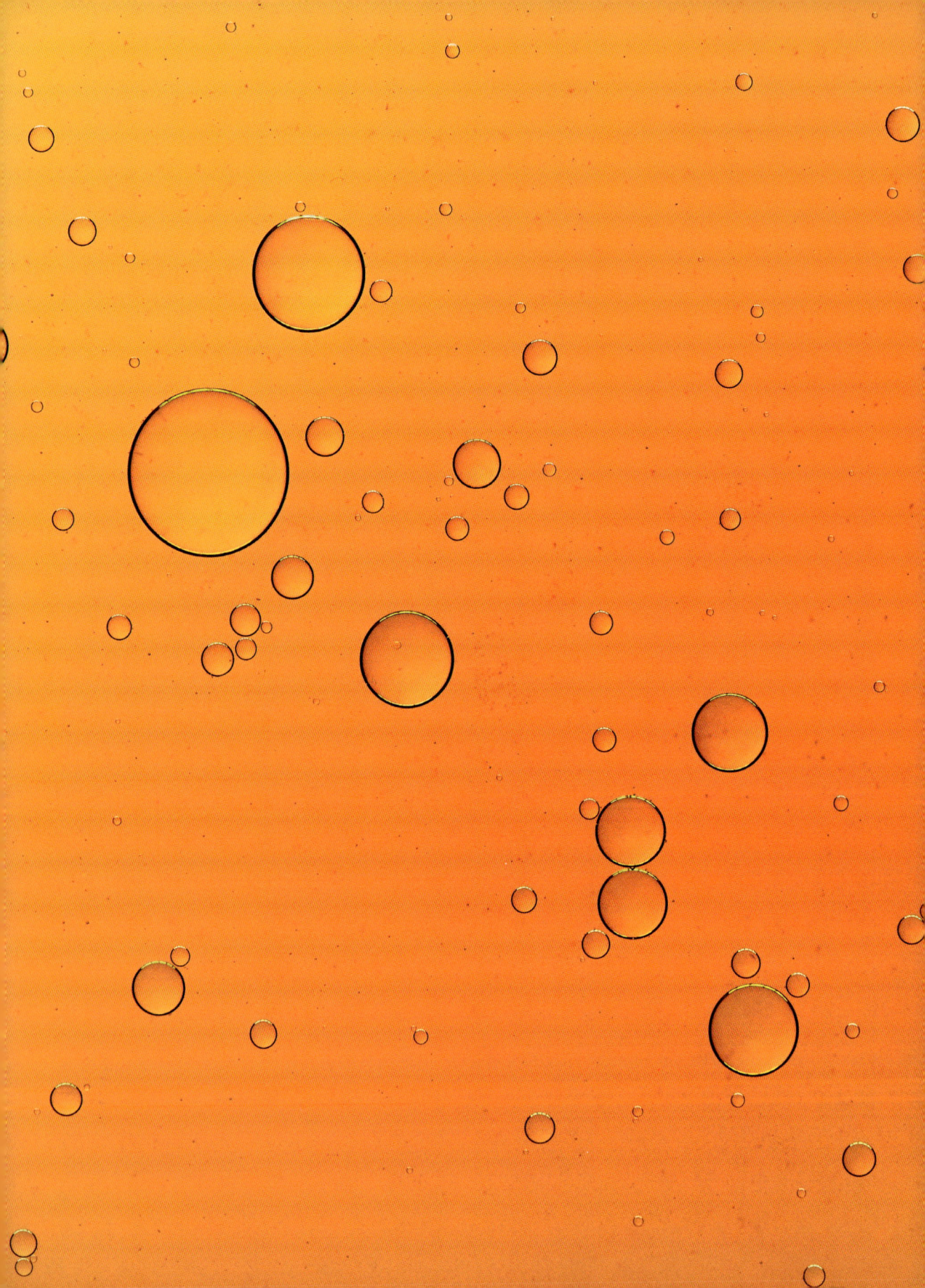

STOCKS, SOUPS

Tomato Soup & Fennel Seed Soldiers 94

Silky Almond Soup with Melon & Cucumbers 96

Brothy Chickpeas with Pancetta & Leeks 98

Smoky Squash, Butter Bean & Citrus Soup 100

Chicken Soup with Crispy Skin & Golden Garlic 102

Roast Chicken Pozole Rojo 104

Fragrant Pork Meatball Noodle Soup 105

Fennel, 'Nduja & Mussel Chowder 106

Chicken Wing Tea with Liver Toast 108

Udon with Ginger Prawn Bisque 110

Beef Bone Broth & Tortellini 112

& BROTHS

Stocks are the main character in so many kitchens, with only the senior chefs or 'sauciers' allowed to make them. In classical French kitchens, sauciers spend days transforming pile of bones and vegetables into complex, rich stocks that are then reduced into elegant sauces.

As the foundation of so many different dishes, stock-making is an invaluable skill when it comes to becoming a more confident cook. Soups, broths, sauces, braises and stews are only as good as the stock used to create them. In the name of zero-waste cooking, learning to make stocks, soups and broths is also a great way to transform scraps and leftovers. While to create a truly delicious stock scraps and trim aren't quite enough, using a few peelings and scrappy herbs is a great way to use up anything that might be looking a bit sad or wilting. If you've got some soggy-looking carrots, roast 'em up and blend into a stunning, silky soup. For a knockout stock there are a few tips and tricks, a few secrets to master.

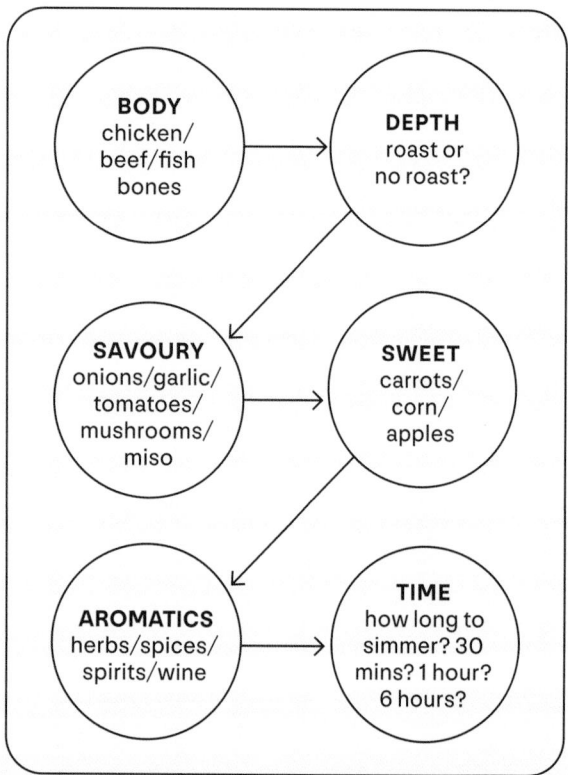

'GOOD-QUALITY' STOCK

You'll notice that a lot of recipes throughout this book call for 'good-quality' stocks. What I'm referring to is a fresh stock rather than a cube. Stock cubes can add flavour to water, but they miss one of the mainstays of a proper stock: texture. A good stock or soup gets its lip-smacking, moreish texture from gelatin. Of course, to make a stock full of gelatin, you'll need to use meat or fish in the recipe. Let's zoom in on chicken stock. I always make brown chicken stock – I think it tastes better than blonde (made with unroasted bones), so I'll usually roast chicken wings or bones first.

Now, you might think that buying chicken just to make stock is wild, and don't let me stop you using your leftover chicken carcass. You absolutely should. But for a really good stock I use chicken wings because they're cheap and contain every bit of the chicken that you need to maximise flavour and texture. A wing is like a tiny chicken – it has a little bit of meat, cartilage, bone and golden-brown skin, just like the whole bird. They also have heaps of surface area for cooking, which means a more crispy, roasted chicken flavour.

A SIMPLE STOCK

Buy a kilo of wings and roast them hard. The next step is adding a few other ingredients to bring depth and complexity to the stock and help enhance the flavour of the chicken. You'll need some savoury ingredients, some sweet, and a few aromatics to perfume the stock. For maximum flavour, cut the veggies very thinly to make the most of the potential surface area. We want to extract every last bit of flavour out of these ingredients and doing that with a big lump of carrot or leek just takes longer. The devil (as always) is in the details. Don't worry about dicing, though – thinly sliced is great and much easier. Then, it's as simple as covering everything with cold water. Starting with cold water yields a much clearer, more flavourful stock as the proteins in the meat form larger aggregates, floating to the top and not being dispersed through the liquid, which would make it cloudy. Slowly bring to a simmer and skim off these scum-like aggregates as they hit the surface. Let the stock tick over for about 2 hours, then strain. Follow these steps and you'll yield a beautiful stock – your soups and broths will thank you with flavour, texture, colour and body.

> ### Short on time? Work smart, not hard
>
> Good meat stock can be a bit of a project to make. You need an abundance of chicken wings, pork or beef bones and a big pot. The yield is pretty small, and it can take hours. What's the solution for the home cook? Well, you have two options. You can carve out some time, make a ton of stock, reduce it and freeze it in little cubes ready to chuck into a pan. (Batch-making stock is smart and something I ought to do more.) Or, you can do what I often do – if I want to treat myself to a decent pork chop, good ragù or steak au poivre, I buy a pouch of good-quality stock.

BROTH

When does a stock become a broth? Well, in my mind, the two aren't a million miles apart. When I make a stock, I keep it pretty light on the salt, sometimes not adding any at all. In the same way you might use unsalted butter, using a neutral, unseasoned stock allows you to have total control of your recipe. Once seasoned, a stock is ready to eat and, for me, is officially broth-certified! Broths usually have some other 'stuff' in there and are rarely just a bowl of flavourful liquid. Whether it's a load of tortellini, some poached or roasted veggies, or leftover roast chicken, the stock is just the starting point, you can build some serious flavour on the way to broth from stock.

FINISHING MOVES – ADDING CONTRAST

Good cooking is almost always about contrast. We've got a big, bold, rich stock here. The handful of herbs added at the beginning have given the stock a deep, earthy flavour, but they've lost their verve. Adding bright fresh herbs at the last minute gives you back that verve. The flavours smack you round the chops. You can also add richness to a soup or broth: add a spoonful of crème fraîche or sour cream to your tomato soup and marble it through just before getting stuck in. The cool, rich dairy is a wonderful contrast to the hot soup. You can also add a fresh note with raw herbs, chillies and raw veggies, and add crispy, crunchy things like nuts, croutons or seaweed.

A SMOOTH SOUP IS JUST A PURÉE

Smooth or chunky soup? This is entirely down to the ingredients you're using to make your soup and how you like to eat it. I remember being taught how to make a golden beetroot purée in Australia, and it clicked in my head that a purée is just a thick, smooth soup. I was shown the steps to a perfectly smooth purée and how you can apply the process to any veg. Here's how.

- **ROAST/CARAMELISE/SAUTÉ** Pick your veg and caramelise quickly in a little fat (butter, oil, ghee) with salt and a few spices, if you like.
- **ADD LIQUID AND COOK** Add just enough stock or water to cover the veg – too much and your soup will be too soupy. You can always add more later.
- **BLEND/WHIZZ AND ADD FAT (OPTIONAL)** The secret to a super-silky purée is to emulsify in a fat while you blend everything together. I stream in a little olive oil or melted butter.
- **LAND YOUR TEXTURE AND SEASON** For a mega-smooth finish, pour your soup through a sieve to catch any lumps. Add a little extra stock or water if your soup is too thick and then season.
- **TOPPINGS** Adding something crunchy, chewy, fresh and flavourful right before you eat a bowl prevents you getting bored – adding a few thoughtful toppings is a surefire way to make sure your soup is firing on all cylinders with every bite.

> ### Hot soup or cold soup?
>
> Some soups really work cold. They are absolutely stunning at the top of a meal or as a light lunch on a hot day. Soups take a little more seasoning when served cold, so once you've made yours, chill it down, then check the seasoning when it's at the temperature you intend to serve it. I'd avoid serving meat stock-based soups cold, unless you're into eating meaty jelly! There are heaps more absolutely delicious cold soups out there. Check out *naengmyeon* from Korea, *salmorejo* from Southern Spain or *okroshka* from Russia.

STOCKS, SOUPS & BROTHS

Tomato Soup & Fennel Seed Soldiers

- SERVES: 4 (OR 2 WITH LEFTOVERS)
- EYES CLOSED
- TOTAL: 35 MINS
- PREP: 10 MINS
- COOK: 25 MINS

Tomatoes scream sunshine, but what do we crave in the winter months when it's cold and grey? Still tomatoes . . . Thanks to the marvellous process of canning, you can make very delicious, comforting, flavour-packed tomato recipes all year round. Combine tinned tomatoes with a few base veg and store cupboard staples and you've got a tomato soup ready to rival Heinz.

FOR THE SOUP

| 1 onion |
| 2 garlic cloves |
| 10g thyme |
| 1 tsp dried oregano or za'atar, plus extra for sprinkling |
| 2 x 400g tins good-quality chopped tomatoes |
| 2–3 tbsp full-fat crème fraîche |
| olive oil |
| fine sea salt |
| black pepper |

FOR THE SOLDIERS

| 1 tsp fennel seeds |
| 1 tsp dried chilli flakes |
| 2 tbsp butter |
| 4 slices of sourdough |
| 50g mature cheddar, grated |
| 50g grated mozzarella |
| 15g grated parmesan |
| fine sea salt |
| black pepper |

1 To make the soup, dice the onion and thinly slice the garlic. Preheat a saucepan over a medium heat and add a generous glug of olive oil. Tip in the onion and cook for 5–6 minutes with a healthy pinch of salt. Drop in the garlic, thyme and oregano or za'atar and cook for 1–2 minutes until fragrant, then tip in the tomatoes. Fill each empty tin halfway with water, swirl to clean out the last bits of tomato and dump that into the pan as well. Season with salt and pepper, bring to a simmer, and cook for 13–15 minutes before blending until super smooth with an immersion or jug blender. If you want your soup to be even more glossy, you can stream in a little extra olive oil while blending. This will emulsify into your soup and give it some extra shine. Once nice and smooth, have a taste, adjust the seasoning and set aside.

2 To make the cheesy fennel-seed soldiers, first preheat the grill to a medium heat. Lightly crush the fennel seeds and chilli using a pestle and mortar or spice grinder. Add the butter to a large, ovenproof frying pan over a medium heat and once melted and bubbling, sit the sourdough on top. Reduce the heat to medium-low.

3 Mix the cheeses and divide them between the sourdough slices, then sprinkle each with a good dose of the fennel and chilli mixture. Toast on the hob for 2–3 minutes, cheese side up, then slide under the grill for another few minutes until the cheese has melted.

4 Now sandwich the 4 slices together to create 2 grilled cheeses. Return to the hob over a medium heat, turning them now and then, until golden brown and crunchy on the outside. I like to sprinkle more of the fennel and chilli mixture into the pan as I'm toasting the sandwiches. The spices are picked up by the bread and melted cheese and form an amazing crust on the outside.

5 Once they're looking golden brown and delicious, fish them out of the pan and cut into chunky soldiers. Divide the soup among bowls and finish with a good dollop of crème fraîche, a drizzle of olive oil and a dusting of oregano. Serve with a handful of soldiers and get stuck in.

GRILLED CHEESE HACK
The easiest way to nail a grilled cheese is to use your grill. Cook both sides of the toastie at once, with the cheese facing up, this way you can control the toast of the bread on the bottom and gently melt the cheese under the grill. Once you've given the cheese a good head start, sandwich the two pieces together and just focus on getting that bread nice and golden. You can relax, the cheese is melted, you've seen it!

Silky Almond Soup with Melon & Cucumbers

SERVES: 4–6
EYES CLOSED
VE
TOTAL: 30 MINS, PLUS MARINATING
PREP: 30 MINS, PLUS MARINATING

This is a soup that I must credit to the great Phil Howard. A version of a gazpacho, it is made with rich almonds, spicy raw garlic and a few surprise ingredients. When you can't cook your ingredients, it's all about maceration. Marrying the ingredients in a bowl and letting them sit, soaking in salt and acid, exuding flavour compounds and becoming one, is the secret to any raw, blended soup.

FOR THE SOUP
- 3 garlic cloves
- 120g blanched peeled almonds
- 2 cucumbers (500–600g in total)
- 130g fresh white breadcrumbs
- 600ml unsweetened almond milk
- 150ml cloudy apple juice
- 150ml extra virgin olive oil
- 25g caster sugar
- 25g fine sea salt
- 100ml ice-cold water
- 40ml sherry vinegar, plus a little extra

FOR THE TOPPING
- 1 shallot
- 1 tbsp sherry vinegar
- ¼ cucumber
- ¼ charentais or canteloupe melon
- 25g toasted salted almonds – I like to use Marcona
- extra virgin olive oil

1 Halve the garlic cloves lengthways and, if there's a little green sprout inside, remove and discard before roughly chopping the cloves. Tip the almonds into a large bowl or Tupperware container with the garlic. Peel and dice the cucumbers and add them to the bowl. Add the breadcrumbs, almond milk, apple juice, olive oil, sugar and salt to the bowl, cover and leave to marinate in the fridge overnight.

2 When ready to eat, tip the contents of the soup into a high-power blender and whizz until extremely smooth. I blend mine for a really long time, maybe 10–12 minutes straight. This will naturally heat the soup, so try not to let the soup heat up too much as you blend, or it can become bitter. Work in batches if you need to, add the water as you go and pause to let the soup cool down. Add the water gradually, using it to adjust the soup to your desired texture. Once blended, pour the soup through a very fine sieve into a bowl and season with the sherry vinegar. Chill the soup until very cold.

3 While the soup chills, prepare the topping. Peel the shallot and cut it into thin rounds, separate into rings and add to a small bowl. Pour over the sherry vinegar and leave the shallot for a few minutes to marinate. Peel and deseed the cucumber, cut the cucumber and melon into even dice and add to the bowl. Tumble in the almonds, add a drizzle of extra virgin olive oil and toss to coat.

4 Pour the chilled soup into chilled bowls and finish with a scattering of the soup topping, a drizzle of olive oil and a drop of sherry vinegar.

> **CHEF'S TIP**
> Olive oil and sherry vinegar are what give this soup its character, so don't be shy with either! I like to use oil and vinegar with real character, so pick one you love. For the oil, I'll go for something grassy and spicy, and for the vinegar a good aged sherry vinegar with a pretty high natural sugar content.

STOCKS, SOUPS & BROTHS

Brothy Chickpeas with Pancetta & Leeks

- SERVES: 4
- EYES CLOSED
- DF / GF
- TOTAL: 35 MINS
- PREP: 10 MINS
- COOK: 25 MINS

A short and sweet recipe and one I lean on for a working lunch. When you serve a hot bowl of this soup with crusty bread and butter, it tastes like a fennel sausage and leek pizza and it's absolutely killer. Not only that, it's really, really simple to make and you're done in 30 minutes flat.

150g sliced smoked pancetta lardons
1 tbsp fennel seeds
3 garlic cloves
1 red chilli
500g leeks
700g jar of good-quality cooked chickpeas
1 litre good-quality chicken stock, bought or homemade (page 92)
25g fresh dill
1 lemon
extra virgin olive oil
fine sea salt
black pepper
crusty bread and butter, to serve (optional)

1 Grab a large pot or saucepan and place over a medium heat. Add a shot of oil and tip in the pancetta. Cook, stirring now and then, for 5–6 minutes until the pancetta is crispy and the fat has completely rendered. Add the fennel seeds and 8–9 twists of coarsely cracked pepper to the pan and cook for 1–2 minutes until super fragrant. Thinly slice the garlic and deseed and finely chop the chilli. Add the whole lot to the pan and stir them through the crispy pancetta. Allow the garlic and chilli to cook for 3–4 minutes, infusing the pancetta fat with flavour.

2 Trim, wash and cut the leeks into chunky rounds, dump them into the pan with a pinch of salt and sauté for 4–5 minutes until just starting to soften. Now add the chickpeas, the liquor from the jar and the chicken stock. Bring everything to a simmer and let the broth bubble away for 15 minutes. Have a taste and adjust the salt as you like – it shouldn't need much, the pancetta will have brought a good amount of salinity to the party. Once you're happy with the salt, finish the soup with a big handful of finely chopped dill and the juice of the lemon. Serve straight away with warm crusty bread and butter.

NOTES
It might seem counterintuitive to crisp up the pancetta before dumping in loads of liquid and killing the crisp, but trust me, there's method to the madness. When you crisp up the pancetta it develops a toasty, caramelised flavour that will carry through the whole soup.

CHEF'S TIP
The liquid in that jar of chickpeas can work wonders in your soup. Not only is it full of natural starches that help thicken the stock, giving your soup a lip-smacking quality, it is also packed full of protein, keeping you feeling fuller for longer. Liquid gold.

Smoky Squash, Butter Bean & Citrus Soup

SERVES: 4
ROLL YOUR SLEEVES UP
V / GF
TOTAL: 70 MINS
PREP: 25 MINS
COOK: 45 MINS

This soup is perfect for using up any odds and ends you've got in the fridge. It's loosely inspired by ribollita, aka the perfect vehicle for transforming leftovers into a delicious, hearty bowl of soup. Hard-roasting squash and onions and then dressing them up with stock, starchy beans and smoky chilli paste makes for a delicious, thrifty bowl of soup. Whether you're using beans, chickpeas or the classic stale bread, it needs to have a high starch content. It's that starch that's going to thicken the soup and give it a lovely, smooth, almost velvety texture.

3 white onions
1 crown prince or butternut squash
3 celery sticks
2 tbsp chipotle paste
3–4 fresh bay leaves
25g rosemary sprigs
1.5 litres good-quality vegetable or chicken stock
700g jar of butter beans and their liquid
25g dill
1 orange
150g feta
olive oil
fine sea salt
black pepper

1 Preheat the oven to 220°C fan/240°C/460°F/gas mark 9.

2 Peel and cut the onions into chunky wedges, peel and cut the squash into bite-sized pieces and discard the seeds and pith. Toss the whole lot onto a baking tray, dress with plenty of olive oil and season with salt and black pepper. Slide into the oven and cook for 30–35 minutes until deeply roasted, completely tender and starting to char.

3 Cut the celery sticks into chunky diamonds. Preheat a large saucepan or cast-iron pot over a medium heat and add a generous glug of olive oil. Tip in the celery and add a pinch of salt. Cook for 8–9 minutes, stirring regularly, until it starts to sweat and soften. Add the chipotle paste and crank up the heat. Stir the pastes through the veggies to coat and cook over a high heat for 6–7 minutes until the mixture starts to caramelise. Drop the herbs in (leave the rosemary stems intact) and cook for a minute or two before adding the stock. Scrape the bottom of the pan to draw up any colour or gnarly flavour that might have developed at the base of the pan. Bring the whole lot to a bare simmer.

4 Tip the beans into a bowl and use a fork or your hands to squash around a third into a smooth-ish paste. Tip the whole lot into the pan of soup and stir through. Bring back to a simmer and notice the soup thicken. Cook for 25–30 minutes.

5 While the soup simmers, prepare your garnishes – finely chop the dill, zest the orange and crumble the feta. Once the soup has been simmering for 25 minutes, add the roasted squash and onions, turn up the heat slightly and bubble for a final 5–6 minutes.

6 Remove the soup from the heat and fish out the bay leaves and rosemary stems. Finish the soup with the dill and the zest and juice of the orange. Season with salt and pepper and then divide among warm bowls. Top with the crumbled feta, a little olive oil and a twist of pepper.

> **CHEF'S TIP**
> This recipe is all about building flavour from the ground up. Take your time and notice how at each stage the flavours develop and deepen. Be sure to get plenty of smoky, roasted flavour onto the pumpkin and onions in the oven before they hit the pan. Build flavour, caramelising the celery and roasting the chipotle paste, and seal the deal with a big hunk of feta. If you take your time at each stage and follow the steps, a relatively simple soup with a short ingredient list can be a big hit.

Chicken Soup with Crispy Skin & Golden Garlic

SERVES: 4
ROLL YOUR SLEEVES UP
TOTAL: 135 MINS
PREP: 15 MINS
COOK: 120 MINS

Poached chicken is a marvellous thing to cook and eat and this method is my go-to. It yields perfectly poached chicken and a pot full of delicious, light, golden chicken stock. Where you go from there is up to you – you've a base stock ready to infuse with so many different things. Add pasta, mirepoix and lots of dill for a classic chicken noodle vibe, or follow me and add miso, fragrant ginger and rice. Sushi rice is my pick; the grains have a heft and chew that doesn't get lost in the soup.

FOR THE SOUP

1 chicken, about 1.5kg
about 2 litres water or good-quality chicken stock
8–10 spring onions
50g fresh ginger
5 garlic cloves
300g sushi rice
150g cherry tomatoes
2 tbsp white or red miso paste
fine sea salt

> **SHOOT FROM THE HIP**
> Leftovers? Freeze the stock for braises and future back-burner recipes (page 230) and use any leftover chicken to bulk up a fennel salad (page 83) or stuff into homemade pitta (page 156).

1 Start by breaking down the chicken. Pull any skin away from the front of the cavity where the neck meets the breasts and use a small, sharp knife to expose either side of the wishbone. Trace up the either side of the bone with the tip of your knife, cut down and through the bottom of each side and then pull the wishbone out. Make an incision in the skin where the leg meets the breast then pull the legs down, away from the chicken and pop out the joint. Run your knife along the line where the leg meets the main body of the chicken without missing the oyster. Repeat with the other leg. Divide the legs into drum and thigh.

2 Remove each wing from the bird by cutting where you imagine its armpit might be, finding the joint and slicing through the cartilage. Sit the chicken back up so the breast is facing up and cut the spine away from the breast by snipping through the ribs. You can use scissors to do this if you find it easier! Once the breasts and breastbone are removed from the spine, turn them over, so they're meat side down, and use a heavy knife to cut them in half through the bone. Carefully remove the skin from the chicken pieces, you'll be able to easily pull it away with your fingers.

3 Pop all of the chicken pieces into a large pot and add around 2 litres of cold water or, if you've got it, chicken stock. Chunk up the spring onions, peel and roughly chop the ginger, smash the garlic cloves, then add them all to the pot along with a tiny pinch of salt. Place the pot over a medium heat, add a lid and gradually bring up to a simmer. Once simmering, reduce the heat to the lowest setting and walk away for 1 hour. You don't want the water to boil, it should sit around 75–80°C. Once the soup has had an hour, remove the breasts and let the wings, legs and bones tick over for another 40 minutes.

4 Add the rice to a bowl and cover with cold water. Use your hand to swirl the grains around before discarding the milky water. Repeat at least three more times until the water is clear. Add the rinsed rice to a lidded pot and cover with 360g of water. Add 1 teaspoon of salt and bring to the boil. Add the lid, reduce the heat to its lowest setting and let the rice cook for 9–10 minutes. Turn off the heat once all the water has been absorbed and allow to rest, with the lid on, for at least 5 minutes.

5 To make the garnish, cut the reserved skin into largeish pieces and lay into a cold frying pan. Add a drizzle of olive oil and place over a medium heat. Allow the skin to render and crisp. It'll curl up a little as it cooks. Keep turning it over and over, encouraging the fat to render and the skin to submerge in the hot oil. After 9–10 minutes, it'll be crispy, like chicken crackling.

FOR THE GARNISH

chicken skin (from the bird)

30g fresh ginger

6 garlic cloves

1 tsp dried chilli flakes

3 spring onions

6 While the skin crisps, peel and cut the ginger into matchsticks and thinly slice the garlic. Once the skin is crisp, whip it out of the pan, leaving behind the chicken fat. Turn the heat down to low and add the garlic. Swirl it through the hot fat, cooking until golden brown and crisp. As soon as it starts to colour, remove the pan from the heat and keep swirling it around in the residual heat. Once it's perfectly golden brown, add the ginger and chilli flakes to the chicken fat and set aside to keep warm.

7 Remove the rest of the chicken from the pot, discard the bones and bring the stock back to the boil. Reduce the whole lot by about a third, using a spoon to remove any scum that rises to the surface. Drop in the cherry tomatoes and simmer until they're just bursting. Whisk the miso through the soup and taste and adjust with salt or a little more miso. Remove the breast meat from the bone and carve into thick slices. Shred the leg and wing meat into bite-sized pieces.

8 Divide the rice among warm bowls and top with some of the chicken. Ladle over the hot broth and tomatoes. Finish the chicken fat dressing with finely chopped spring onions and chives. Spoon generously over the hot bowls of soup, add a few chunks of chicken skin and serve.

> **CHEF'S TIP**
>
> If you've got time, once you've picked the meat from the chicken, pop the bones back into the broth and let it simmer away for another hour or so. This'll double down on the chicken flavour. It's what is known as a 'double stock' in restaurant kitchens.

STOCKS, SOUPS & BROTHS

Roast Chicken Pozole Rojo

- SERVES: 2–3
- ROLL YOUR SLEEVES UP
- GF
- TOTAL: 75 MINS
- PREP: 15 MINS
- COOK: 1 HOUR

You can get some serious mileage out of a roasted chicken and cooking one should never be seen as a one-meal mission. When you're left with a few slices of meat and a whole load of bones, the smartest route is the soup route. *Pozole rojo* is typically made with pork, and is utterly delicious, but I am really into this slightly lighter version designed to hoover up any leftovers you might have. Load up the soup with a handful of crunchy, bright, zippy toppings and you've transformed leftovers into something spectacular. There are a couple of ingredients here you might need to order online or head to a Mexican grocer to pick up, but trust me when I say it's worth it.

FOR THE SOUP

- leftover bones from 1 roast chicken (carcass, wings and legs)
- 1 litre good-quality chicken stock
- 2 dried ancho chillies
- 2 dried guajillo chillies
- 1 onion
- 2 garlic cloves
- 2 tsp cumin seeds
- 1 tbsp dried oregano, plus a little extra
- 250g cooked tinned hominy or cooked chickpeas
- 250g leftover roast chicken
- light olive oil
- fine sea salt
- black pepper

TO SERVE

- ½ avocado
- 4–5 radishes
- 1 fresh jalapeño
- 15g fresh coriander
- 2 tbsp sour cream
- 1 lime
- handful of tortilla chips

1 Take your chicken carcass and use a large, heavy knife to break it down into smaller pieces. We want to increase the surface area to get all that flavour into the soup as quickly as possible. Place a large saucepan or stockpot over a medium heat, add 2 tablespoons of olive oil and, once hot, tip in the chicken bones. Sear for 4–5 minutes until the room smells of roasted chicken and the bones are nicely browned. Pour in the stock, 500ml of water and bring to the boil. Reduce the heat to low and let the chicken blip away in the stock for 40 minutes.

2 While the chicken stock is doing its thing, use a pair of scissors to snip the stems from the chillies and open them up. Remove the seeds and discard. Peel the onion and cut into quarters. Thinly slice one quarter and set aside for later. Peel the garlic cloves and add to a frying pan with the chillies and onion quarters. Place over a high heat and toast for 4–5 minutes, tossing regularly, until charred in places and fragrant. Turn down the heat, then add the cumin seeds for the last minute. Remove the chillies from the pan and add them to a small heatproof bowl and cover with boiling water. Allow to rehydrate for 15 minutes or so. Tip the soaked chillies, spices, oregano and toasted veggies into a blender and whizz until you have a thick, smooth purée. You can add a little of the chilli soaking water if you need to loosen things up.

3 Pop the frying pan back over a medium-high heat and add 2 tablespoons of olive oil. Tip in the chilli purée and cook for 3–4 minutes until it's darkened in colour and reduced a little. Use a slotted spoon to remove the chicken bones. Stir the cooked chilli mixture into the soup and bring back to a simmer. Add the hominy and reduce the heat to low. Let the soup tick over for 20–25 minutes before stirring in the leftover chicken and seasoning to taste with salt.

4 Cut the avocado into chunks, quarter the radishes, thinly slice the jalapeño and roughly tear the coriander. Spoon some of the hominy and chicken into large warm bowls and cover with plenty of the broth. Add the avocado, radishes and a pinch of the coriander. Add sour cream, topped with a little dried oregano, sliced onion, fresh jalapeño and a lick of olive oil. Add a lime wedge and serve with a few tortilla chips on the side.

> **NOTES**
> If you can't get hold of cooked hominy, you can sub in cooked chickpeas. If you're in a pinch, you can use a good-quality chilli paste like chipotle, ancho or a blend instead of whole dried chillies.

Fragrant Pork Meatball Noodle Soup

SERVES: 4	TOTAL: 55 MINS
ROLL YOUR SLEEVES UP	PREP: 20 MINS
GF / DF	COOK: 35 MINS

In the meatball world, beef and lamb steal the show. Enter, pork. This is the kind of soup that I could eat every day for my breakfast and go out ready to take on anything. It's light, delicate and super fragrant while also rich and robust, lifted with fish sauce and fresh lime, kept exciting with the heat of bird's eye chillies. You can make this soup pretty much any time of year, with heaps of different seasonal veggies. It's a winner at the weekend or in the week. Love it.

FOR THE MEATBALLS
- 500g pork sausagemeat
- 3 garlic cloves
- 2 bird's eye chillies
- 6 spring onions
- 1 tbsp coriander seeds
- ½ tbsp ground white pepper
- 2 tbsp fish sauce
- 1 lime
- fine sea salt

FOR THE SOUP
- 40g ginger
- 3 celery sticks
- 120g radishes
- 1 litre good-quality chicken stock or chicken wing tea (page 108)
- 2–4 tbsp fish sauce
- 4 nests of rice noodles
- 25g Thai basil
- 25g mint
- 2 bird's eye chillies
- 2 limes
- olive oil

1 Tip the sausagemeat into a bowl, finely grate in the garlic and finely chop and add the chillies, seeds and all. Trim and thinly slice all the spring onions and add to the mix. Crush the coriander using a pestle and mortar, and add it, along with the white pepper, fish sauce and the grated zest of the lime, to the sausagemeat. Season with a tiny pinch of salt then use a wooden spoon or your hand to vigorously beat the meatball mix together for at least 2–3 minutes until the mixture becomes sticky. Cover and chill for 10 minutes.

2 While the mixture chills, peel and cut the ginger into matchsticks, chop the celery into chunky slices, and halve the radishes. Preheat a large pot over a medium heat, add a shot of olive oil and tip in the ginger and celery. Cook for 3–4 minutes until fragrant, then dump in the chicken stock and half of the fish sauce. Bring to a simmer and whip the meatball mixture out of the fridge.

3 Using slightly damp hands, gently form the mixture into meatballs just a little smaller than ping pong balls. Line them up on a plate or tray and when they're all rolled (you should have about 20) drop them into the warm broth. Cook very gently for 10–12 minutes until cooked through. Drop the radishes in for the last 4–5 minutes to gently poach (they'll still have some nice bite to them when they hit your bowl).

4 Cook the noodles according to the package instructions, I usually pour a kettle of boiling water over them in a heatproof bowl and leave them for 2–3 minutes or until tender. Drain and shake dry.

5 Add the noodles to the broth and have a taste, adding more fish sauce if you need to bring up the salinity. Finish with torn Thai basil, torn mint, thinly sliced chillies and lime juice to taste. Divide among bowls and serve.

Fennel, 'Nduja & Mussel Chowder

- SERVES: 4
- ROLL YOUR SLEEVES UP
- P / GF
- TOTAL: 1 HOUR
- PREP: 15 MINS
- COOK: 45 MINS

Of all the shellfish, I think mussels carry the most flavour. The aroma is intoxicating, and wholly unique. Moules frites is a stone-cold classic, and while utterly delicious, it can sometimes cloud the mind of mussel cooks, forcing them down the same road, really limiting the potential of these little flavour bombs. We're going to treat them a little differently today and whip up a spicy, creamy, punchy mussel chowder.

2kg mussels
300ml dry white wine
2 fennel bulbs
2 white onions
1 red chilli
3 garlic cloves
100g unsalted butter
2 tsp fennel seeds
80g fresh 'nduja
1 litre good-quality fish stock
500g waxy potatoes (e.g. La Ratte, Jersey Royals or Charlotte)
250g full-fat crème fraîche
10g fresh oregano
10g basil
2 lemons
extra virgin olive oil
fine sea salt
black pepper

1. Give the mussels a really good scrub under cold running water and remove any beards, using a little cloth or piece of kitchen paper to help you grip if you need to (the beards look like little hairy strings coming out of the side of the shell, just grip them tightly and pull them up and away from the back of the mussel, they should pop right out). Discard any open mussels that won't close after a sharp tap, or those with broken shells.

2. Preheat a large pot over a high heat. Once very hot, tip in the mussels then dump in the white wine. Quickly cover with a lid and give the pan a gentle shake. Cook for 1–2 minutes until the mussel shells have popped open but the mussels aren't quite fully cooked. There will be lots of liquid in the bottom of the pan, this is the gold! Scoop the cooked mussels out of the pan and into a large bowl. Pour the liquid through a fine-mesh sieve into a bowl or smaller saucepan for later. Remove the mussel meat from the shells and keep in a bowl. Discard the shells.

3. Chop the fennel and onions into even dice. Don't worry about going too fine here, we want everything roughly the same size, so use your mussels as a guide. Finely chop the red chilli and garlic.

4. Preheat a large saucepan over a medium heat, add the butter and allow to melt, foam and start to sizzle, then tip in the fennel and onions and season with a generous pinch of salt. Cook for 8–9 minutes until translucent and starting to catch a little on the bottom of the pan. Tip in the fennel seeds, 'nduja, garlic and chilli and cook for another 5 minutes or so until super fragrant. Add the fish stock and deglaze the bottom of the pan, then bring to the boil and reduce by a third. Add the reserved mussel stock and bring back to a simmer. Cut the potatoes into bite-sized chunks and drop them into the chowder. Cook for 10–12 minutes, or until the potatoes are tender.

5. Turn the heat right down, add the crème fraîche to the soup and whisk through. Season to taste with salt and plenty of black pepper. The soup should be quite spicy at this point, which is what we're after. If it's a little too hot for you, add a dollop more crème fraîche. Add the mussels and tear in the herbs right at the last moment before finishing with the grated zest and juice of the lemons. Divide among warm bowls and top with a drizzle of extra virgin olive oil.

Chicken Wing Tea with Liver Toast

- MAKES: 2 LITRES CHICKEN STOCK
- ROLL YOUR SLEEVES UP
- TOTAL: 4 HOURS
- PREP: 15 MINS
- COOK: 3 HOURS 45 MINS

When thinking about this recipe, I wanted to demonstrate that stocks and soups are one and the same and that home cooks should put the same love and care into making a stock than they would a slow-braised short rib or a birthday cake. We're essentially making a seasoned chicken stock here, one so rich and deep and full of flavour that you can serve it in a mug to clutch with both hands with something delicious to snack on on the side. Later on in the book, if a recipe calls for chicken stock, you can make this recipe and use it as the base for braises, soups, stews and sauces. A good stock will never let you down.

FOR THE CHICKEN STOCK

- 1.5kg chicken wings
- 2 white onions
- 1 carrot
- 1 celery stick
- 1 garlic bulb
- 40g dried porcini mushrooms
- 1 tbsp black peppercorns
- 50g thyme sprigs
- 50g rosemary sprigs
- 10g fresh bay leaves
- olive oil
- fine sea salt

FOR THE LIVER TOAST

- 4 slices of sourdough bread
- butter, for spreading
- 150g chicken or duck liver parfait
- 2 tbsp good-quality honey
- pinch of thyme leaves
- olive oil
- flaky sea salt
- black pepper

1 Preheat the oven to 220°C fan/240°C/460°F/gas mark 9.

2 Tip the chicken wings into a roasting tin, rub with olive oil and season with salt. Slide into the oven and roast for 35–40 minutes, or until a deep golden brown. You want some of those chicken juices to render and catch on the tray, so don't worry if it starts to pick up colour. Colour is flavour!

3 While the chicken roasts, chunk up the onions, carrot and celery. Don't worry about peeling them, just give them a good wash. Halve the whole garlic bulb. Preheat your largest pot over a medium heat and add a generous glug of oil. Once hot, tip in the veg and leave to sear for 6–7 minutes. Don't be tempted to move the veggies, you want to get a good amount of colour on them at this stage. Once nicely coloured, give them a turn and repeat the process.

4 Take the chicken wings out of the oven and add to the pot with the veggies. While still hot, add a splash of water to the tin and scrape up any chickeny flavour that's roasted onto it. Tip all of that into the pot, too. Cover the whole lot with cold water and drop in the mushrooms, peppercorns and just over half the herbs. Bring to a simmer, turn the heat down to low, stick a lid on and let the whole lot blip away, barely at a simmer, for 3 hours.

5 When your stock is ready, fish out the solids with a slotted spoon or spider. While they might look tasty, you probably want to ditch the chicken wings: all the flavour has left town and is now in that golden, delicious stock. Once all the big chunks are out, pass the stock through a fine-mesh sieve and into a new pan. Fire up the heat and bring to the boil. Once boiling, reduce by a third.

6 Have a taste and season with salt. Right before you serve, scrunch up the remaining fresh herbs in your hand and drop them into the soup. Infuse for a few minutes before fishing out.

7 To make the liver toast, rub the bread with olive oil and grill in a hot griddle pan. Toast until a little charred on the outside. You can also do this in a toaster, if you like. Spread generously with butter and liver parfait. Finish with a drizzle of honey, a few thyme leaves, a twist of pepper and flaky sea salt. Serve mugfuls of chicken broth with a couple of slices of liver toast.

COLOUR = FLAVOUR
In a dark chicken stock like this one, colour = flavour. Don't be shy when caramelising the veg and roasting the wings. The deeper you go with the colour, the deeper the flavour. There is a happy medium, though, don't go so dark as to burn the ingredients, or your stock will be bitter! If you've got access to a pressure cooker, use it! You can make this stock in a matter of minutes. Pile in those roasted wings and aromats, cover with water and cook at full pressure for 45 minutes. You'll have a seriously intense chicken stock in no time at all.

Udon with Ginger Prawn Bisque

- SERVES: 4
- DIG IN
- P / DF
- TOTAL: 1 HOUR
- PREP: 20 MINS
- COOK: 40 MINS

A good bisque is all about drawing sweet, aromatic shellfish flavour from the shells of prawns, crab or lobster and into a thick, rich creamy soup. This isn't a traditional bisque, but it definitely follows a handful of the same rules. Bisque is typically made with heaps of double cream and salty butter, so to keep things a little lighter, I use coconut milk, ginger and fresh herbs to make the shellfish sparkle. The herbs are absolutely essential, adding extra fragrance, anise and bite to the bowl.

20 raw shell-on prawns
4 shallots
4 garlic cloves
70g ginger
2 Thai bird's eye chillies
3 tbsp tomato purée
800ml full-fat coconut milk
4 tbsp fish sauce, plus extra to taste
3 limes
350g dried udon or 450g fresh udon
150g mange tout or sugar snaps
25g coriander
25g Thai basil
light olive oil
fine sea salt
crispy shallots, to serve

1. Start by peeling the prawns. Working over a bowl to catch any juice, hold onto the head and the body and twist – the head should come away easily. Drop the head into the bowl, then using your thumb and forefinger, start to peel the shell away from the tail, dropping the shells into the bowl. Work your way down the prawn until you've just got the end left. I like to leave this piece on as it looks pretty, but you can whip it off if you like. Run a knife down the back of the tail and remove the intestinal tract. If you've not done this before, it's the little black line that runs down the back of the tail. Set the peeled prawns aside in the fridge.

2. Peel and slice the shallots into thin rounds, thinly slice the garlic cloves and peel and cut the ginger into matchsticks. Finely chop the chillies, too, removing the seeds if you want to cool things off a little.

3. Preheat a large saucepan over a medium-high heat and add a generous glug of olive oil. Tip in the prawn heads and shells (plus any juice from the bowl) and toast them in the hot oil for 4–5 minutes, keeping the shells moving as they cook and watching them turn pink and then start to caramelise. Add the garlic, shallots, and half of the ginger and chillies and cook for 4–5 minutes until the veggies have taken on a little colour, then add the tomato purée and stir, coating the ingredients. Keep cooking, toasting the purée and letting it catch on the bottom of the pan a little. Now tip in 250ml of water and deglaze, scraping any caramelised sticky bits off the bottom of the pan. Tip in the coconut milk and bring to a simmer. Cook for 20–25 minutes until a creamy red colour and super fragrant.

4. Carefully transfer the bisque and shells to a blender and pulse until smooth-ish. This will unlock all of the magical flavour held in the prawn shells. Pass the mixture through a fine-mesh sieve and back into the pan. Use the back of a spoon or ladle to really squeeze and press all the liquid out of the pulp from the blender. Add the fish sauce and the juice of 2 of the limes. Keep warm on the hob.

5. Cook the udon according to the package instructions. Cut the mange tout into thin slices.

6. Just as the udon are about to come out of the water, drop the prawns into the warm bisque and stir them in. Place over a low heat and gently poach the prawns; they should take no more than 1–2 minutes in the hot bisque.

7. Divide the drained udon among warm bowls and ladle over the hot prawn bisque. Top with the prawns, sliced mange tout and the remaining ginger and chillies, then tear over the herbs. Finish with lime wedges and crispy shallots.

Beef Bone Broth & Tortellini

SERVES: 4
DIG IN
TOTAL: 5 HOURS 25 MINS
PREP: 25 MINS
COOK: 5 HOURS

It's a real flex being able to make a stock so delicious that you just want to drink it, cook little stuffed pasta in it, bathe in it. A proper bone broth takes time, there's no way around it, and when you're making a beef bone broth, it requires long, slow cooking. The bones are absolute whoppers and the cooking process needs lots of time to penetrate the bones and extract the collagen and beefy flavour that this recipe relies on.

FOR THE BONE BROTH

| 2kg beef bones |
| 2 canoe-cut beef marrow bones |
| 500g piece beef brisket |
| 1kg chicken wings |
| 500g white onions |
| 3 carrots |
| 5 celery sticks |
| 50g rosemary sprigs |
| 50g thyme sprigs |
| 8 fresh bay leaves |
| 1 tbsp black peppercorns |
| 3–4 parmesan rinds (optional) |

FOR THE TORTELLINI

| 300g sausagemeat |
| 20g parmesan cheese, plus extra to serve |
| ½ portion pasta dough from page 144 |
| fine sea salt |
| black pepper |

1 Add the beef bones, marrow, brisket and chicken wings to your largest stockpot. Cover with cold water and set over a medium heat. If you don't have one quite big enough, divide across a couple of pans. Bring the whole lot to the boil and let it bubble away for 15–20 minutes. Skim any scum that rises to the surface as the stock cooks.

2 Chunk up the onions, carrots and celery and add them to the pot along with the remaining broth ingredients, then leave the stock to tick over, barely at a simmer for at least 4–4½ hours. No need to check in on it or keep stirring, just pop a lid on and walk away.

3 After that time has elapsed, you'll have a seriously beefy, super-rich stock. Fish out the solids using a spider or a slotted spoon then bring to the boil and reduce until you're happy with the flavour. Once you're happy, it's ready to use straight away, chill in the fridge for the week, or freeze for a rainy day!

4 If making the tortellini, add the sausagemeat to a bowl and finely grate in the parmesan. Season with 35 twists of black pepper and then mix thoroughly. Use a pasta machine or a rolling pin to roll the dough out until it's thin enough to see your hand through (for more tips on how to nail this, head to page 129). Cut the sheet into lots of little squares, the size is up to you, but I shoot for a 3–4cm square.

5 Add a little dollop of filling to the centre of each pasta square and then turn it 45 degrees so it's like a diamond. Use a damp finger to moisten the top two edges. Fold the bottom edges up to the top to fold the pasta in half, envelop the filling and create a little triangle. Press down firmly on the seal, squeezing out as much air as you can. Hold the pasta at the bottom two corners and swing one around so it meets the other, joining them while creating a gap. Press down firmly to join the two ends.

6 Warm your bone broth in a saucepan until just below boiling point, season well with salt and drop in your tortellini. Gently poach them in the broth for 3–4 minutes before ladling into warm bowls and topping with plenty of grated parmesan.

CHEF'S TIP
For an ultra-clear, ultra-clean broth you can clarify it using egg whites. Tip 4 egg whites into a food processor with 200g of beef mince, an onion, a carrot and a bunch of herbs. Whizz into a loose paste and then (trust me) pour it into your stock. Whisk the mixture through the stock and cook over a low heat until it begins to float to the top. Let the solids rise and form a raft. Cook for 12–15 minutes before making a little hole in the raft and scooping out the crystal-clear liquid. You just made consommé!

PASTA

Rigatoni & Sunday Sauce 118

Perfect Polenta 120

Crispy Rice with Za'atar Chicken Livers 122

Kimchi Butter Fried Rice 124

Brown Butter, Orange & Almond Pilaf 126

Crab with Fresh Tagliolini 129

Stovetop Seafood Rice 132

White Sausage & Sage Pappardelle 134

Ricotta Dumplings with Cheese & Tomato Broth 136

Cheesy Spelt with Pancetta, Mushrooms & Yolk 138

Creamed Cabbage Cavatelli 140

Homemade Gnocchi with Smashed Peas & Crème Fraîche 141

Pumpkin Ravioli with Taleggio Fonduta 144

& GRAINS

In 2019, I spent a very happy summer running a little pasta bar. I rolled pasta twice a day, every day – once in the morning before lunch service and then once again in the afternoon before dinner – all while cramming in making ragùs, semifreddo, mousse and sauces.

The pasta bar summer taught me to make and cook levelled-up fresh pasta, choose the right shapes and create silky sauces. It also taught me to make risottos and love food made with seeds in a way I didn't think possible. I now make pilaf, steam sushi rice and prepare bulgur wheat with a newfound respect.

Most of the world is fuelled by seeds. Nuts are seeds, beans are seeds, pasta is made from seeds. The carbohydrates we reach for every day are all derived from the edible seeds of plants and have been around for as long as we have. Pasta is very close to my heart. I make less fresh pasta these days, but cooking with pasta and grains is as much a part of my everyday life as drinking water. Luckily, all you need to do is learn how to combine the two and you are most of the way to nailing pasta and grains.

PASTA AND GRAINS

Without getting too deep into it, the grains and pastas we eat are made up of plant seeds. They can be grouped into four categories: whole, cracked, polished and ground. Whole grains are the seeds in their natural form (e.g. brown rice). The whole seed is left intact, and the cooking time is pretty long; the bran (shell) is robust and takes a long time to become tender. Cracked grains (e.g. rolled oats) have been smashed into pieces or squashed, disrupting the bran and shortening the cook time. Polished grains (e.g. sushi rice) have had the bran and germ removed, leaving just the pure carbohydrate behind, decreasing the cooking time but losing a little earthy flavour. Ground grains (e.g. polenta) are simply dehydrated and milled to a fine meal or powder.

Rice can be split into two broad families: long-grain (Indica) and short-grain (Japonica), and each has distinct textural differences. Reach for the long-grain rice when making steamed rice, pilaf and other light, fluffy dishes. Short-grain rice should be used to make sushi, risotto and paellas. Typically, short-grain rice has chewier, chubbier grains and has more bite and body, whereas long grains are much fluffier and more delicate. Rice can also be categorised as brown or white. Brown rice is the whole, intact seed, whereas white rice has been polished and refined. Brown rice has a nuttier, earthier flavour whereas white rice has a cleaner, purer flavour.

Pasta is a derivative of flour, and whether it's plain old wheat '00' flour or durum wheat semolina, pasta is made with milled, dried seeds and water. The pasta dough is then shaped, either by hand with a large rolling pin called a mattarello, with a hand-cranked pasta machine, or using a machine called an extruder (the dough is forced into shapes through dies a bit like playdough) and then either sold fresh or dried. Just like any other grain, it just needs water!

COOKING METHODS

BOIL Boiling pastas and grains is the easiest way to take them from dry to cooked. It's as simple as bringing a pot of water or cooking liquid to a rolling boil, seasoning it and then dropping in your pasta or grain. Cook until tender, drain and dress with a sauce, vinaigrette or other seasonings.
Best for: pasta, lentils, whole grains.

ABSORB The absorption method is what I use when cooking most of my rice. It relies on the ratio of grain to liquid being spot on, as it all goes into the same pot, with the goal of the pasta or grains soaking up and absorbing just the right amount of liquid to cook perfectly. A lot of rice recipes will call for you to wash the grains pre-cook – this removes excess starch from the rice and helps yield light, fluffy rice rather than sticky, clumpy grains.
Best for: rice, couscous, pearled grains, bulgur wheat.

RISOTTO/PORRIDGE You can cook just about any grain using this method. It's probably the most forgiving method of the three and just requires you to bung in enough liquid, a little at a time, to fully cook the grain. The most famous examples of this method are risotto, polenta or – literally – porridge.
Best for: polenta, rice, spelt, oats.

> ### Get toasty
>
> Toasting your grains before cooking them can add some lovely flavour to your rice, and it also helps with grain separation and produces super fluffy rice. When you cook rice in a little fat before adding water, wine or stock, you're not only adding flavour but also breaking down the starches, limiting their thickening power and yielding a cleaner, less sticky rice. Check out the pilaf recipe on page 126.

SALT

When you're cooking pasta and rice, it's important to salt the cooking water early. Cooking with salt from the beginning ensures an even, thorough seasoning of your food, and it doesn't have any effect on texture.

The amount of salt you add is up to you. Rarely do I measure it by weight – I almost always season by taste here. I season my cooking water to the point of it tasting like a good soup; if it tastes like the sea, it's probably too salty. If you want to measure the amount of salt to water, you can work it out with a percentage. For blanching vegetables, cooking legumes, grains and pasta, aim for roughly 1% weight in salt to the water. So, for every 100g of pasta, you need 1000g of water and about 10g of fine sea salt.

PASTA: DRY VS FRESH

There are a few questions to answer when you're considering fresh versus dry pasta...

- **SAUCE?** What sauce are you serving with your pasta?
- **SHAPE?** Whether it's shells to capture sauce in your mac and cheese, silky pappardelle for a robust ragù or rigatoni tubes for Sunday Sauce, consider how the shape will behave with the sauce.
- **TEXTURE?** Dried pasta can be cooked to a more prominent 'al dente' texture. It sometimes lacks the silky quality that fresh pasta can lend a dish. Fresh pasta also has a delightful chew to it that is lost in the drying process.
- **AVAILABILITY?** Dried pasta is infinitely easier to get hold of and store at home. Fresh pasta, on the other hand, has a much shorter shelf life, and while freezable, is best cooked straight away. If you're making your pasta yourself (gold star!), figure out what you've got the time and patience for that day. If you've spent hours making a ragù, there's no shame in reaching for the dried rigatoni.

The magic of pasta water

Pasta water is the magic ingredient that'll transform boiled pasta and sauce into a rich, silky, homogenous, utterly delicious plate of food.

When you cook pasta, it releases starches into the water. You might notice, as your pasta cooks, that the cooking water gets progressively more opaque. That's all the starch leaching out of the pasta and into the water. This water is now charged with the power to thicken sauces and help build emulsions. It's best not to cook your pasta in a mega pot of water – for 200g of pasta, I'd use about 2–2.5 litres of water. Another way to double down on that starchy magic is to transfer your pasta to the sauce when it isn't quite cooked, and it still has some starch to give. This will help create a creamy, emulsified, homogenous sauce.

> ### How to marry pasta and sauce
>
> - Warm your sauce
> - Salt the cooking water
> - Drop the pasta in and cook until al dente
> - Transfer pasta and a little pasta water to warm sauce
> - Toss, toss, toss
> - Add pasta water as needed
> - Adjust seasoning and serve
>
> It's important not to make your pasta water crazy salty. You're going to be adding spoonfuls of it into your sauce and, if it's too highly seasoned, your bowl of ragù is going to taste like a salt lick. If there's one thing to take away from this, it's that when cooking pasta, use tongs, a spider or a spoon to transfer your cooked pasta from the pan of water to the awaiting sauce, hanging on to that liquid gold.

PASTA & GRAINS

Rigatoni & Sunday Sauce

- **SERVES:** 2
- **EYES CLOSED**
- **TOTAL:** 40 MINS
- **PREP:** 10 MINS
- **COOK:** 30 MINS

Sunday Sauce is a tradition I share with my wife, Louisa. We take turns making it, and each week it varies a little. Versions come back around. We've each got our favourites and, yes, it does get competitive. I'm going to share my favourite version with you, and it's this garlicky number. You'll need to cook the garlic just right so that it's spicy and fragrant, on the right side of raw, and isn't crispy, acrid or burnt. In the recipe below there's a little tip on how to find that sweet spot where the garlic becomes mellow and super sweet.

5 garlic cloves
400g tin chopped tomatoes (Mutti is my preferred brand)
30g basil
200g dried rigatoni
25g parmesan
extra virgin olive oil
fine sea salt
black pepper

1 Start by peeling and thinly slicing the garlic cloves. Add these to a cold pan and cover with more olive oil than you think you need. We are going for luxurious, tomato confit levels of oil here. Our plan here is to cook the sauce until the oil splits from the sauce and separates itself from the other ingredients. We will then re-emulsify the oil into the sauce later via a combo of magical pasta water and vigorous tossing.

2 Place the pan over a medium-low heat and slowly bring the oil up to temperature. As the oil heats up, you'll see little bubbles coming off the garlic. Swirl the slices around in the oil and cook very gently for 4–5 minutes. Now, keep a close eye on the garlic, something cool is going to happen (if you think it's cool too, this is definitely the book for you). As the garlic cooks it'll start to release natural sugars; when these sugars release they make the garlic 'sticky'. Keep swirling away, and you'll notice a point when the garlic starts to stick together and clump up – now it's time to add the tomatoes.

3 Dump in the tomatoes and half the basil, stalks and all. Mix everything together, mixing the oil and garlic through the chopped tomatoes. Crank up the heat and bring the sauce to the boil. Reduce to a simmer and cook for 15–20 minutes until that oil comes back out of the sauce. It'll be a rich, ruby-red colour.

4 Cook your pasta in salted water until just al dente, but not quite fully tender. Add it to the pan with a good ladle of pasta water. Toss, toss, toss everything together, over and over again, adding more pasta water if you need to loosen things up. If things are looking a little too loose, reduce over a high heat. You want to keep tossing until the oil is back together with the sauce and everything is looking glossy and delicious.

5 When you're happy, season with a shedload of black pepper and toss in some grated parmesan. Toss the cheese and pepper through the pasta off the heat. If you cook the parmesan too much, it'll go stringy. Stir in the remaining basil, divide between warm plates and serve right away.

> **CHEF'S TIP**
> We're back in the world of emulsions! There's a healthy dose of olive oil here, and the challenge is to marry that with the pasta water and tomatoes. A key step for this is finishing the cooking of the pasta for the last minute or two in the sauce, so move it over while it's still al dente.

Perfect Polenta

Polenta is endlessly comforting. I absolutely love it and can put down bowl after bowl. Polenta is one of those things that is so often done badly, and I want to help rewrite the rulebook. This is a simple recipe on paper but it really delivers on texture and flavour. Once it's made, you can steer the polenta down so many different roads. I've given you three of my favourite routes: one laced with cheddar and topped with spicy corn and jalapeño salad; the

THE POLENTA

- SERVES: 2
- EYES CLOSED
- V / GF
- TOTAL: 1 HOUR 15 MINS
- PREP: 15 MINS
- COOK: 50–60 MINS

600ml water	olive oil
250ml whole milk	fine sea salt
150g coarse cornmeal	black pepper
30g unsalted butter	

Pour the water into a pan with the milk and whisk in the cornmeal. Place over a medium heat and bring to the boil, whisking constantly until the pan is up to temperature. We're going to cook the cornmeal for 50–60 minutes and, while you don't need to stand there the entire time, you want to check in on your polenta every 5–10 minutes and give it a good stir. When the pan is approaching boiling point, the polenta will thicken considerably and start to plop and spit a little. Turn the heat down to low and let it tick over, stirring now and then to make sure nothing is sticking or scorching. If things start to get a bit too thick, you can add a splash of water to loosen it up. Once it's had 45 minutes or so in the pan, finish the polenta by whisking in the butter. Adjust the texture of your polenta to your liking. If it's too thick, add a little water or milk, too thin, keep cooking! Season to taste then divide between warm bowls. While the polenta cooks away, prepare your chosen topping.

CORN AND JALAPEÑO SALAD TOPPING

- SERVES: 2
- EYES CLOSED
- V
- TOTAL: 25 MINS
- PREP: 10 MINS
- COOK: 15 MINS

fine sea salt	30g coriander
2 cobs of corn	2 limes
2 fresh jalapeños	100g mature cheddar, grated, plus a little extra to serve
80g pickled jalapeños	
1 white onion	olive oil

Bring a pan of water to a simmer and season it generously with salt. Drop in the corn and cook for 3–4 minutes until just tender. Once cooked, drain and shave the kernels from the cobs. Preheat a frying pan over a high heat and add a good glug of olive oil. Once hot, tip in the corn kernels and sauté for 5–6 minutes until starting to caramelise (be careful, they will pop!). Season with salt and remove from the heat. Thinly slice one of the fresh jalapeños, finely dice the other and roughly chop the pickled. Halve the onion and cut it into thin slivers, and roughly chop the coriander. Tip the sliced jalapeños, pickled jalapeños, onions and coriander into a bowl along with the sautéed corn and add the grated zest and juice of the limes. Toss together. Beat the grated cheese into the hot polenta until melted before dividing between warm bowls. Top each bowl of polenta with a generous helping of the warm corn and jalapeño salad. Get stuck in.

PASTA & GRAINS

second topped with jammy onions, rosemary and pecorino; and the third perfumed with nutmeg and topped with baked pancetta, sage and lemon. It's quite hard to pick, honestly. Be mindful of the type of polenta you're buying. A popular polenta is the quick-cook variety, but we don't want that for this recipe, we want a proper coarse-ground cornmeal. The texture and flavour is miles better than the quick-cook stuff and is a lot more predictable.

JAMMY BALSAMIC ONION, ROSEMARY & PECORINO TOPPING

SERVES: 2
EYES CLOSED
TOTAL: 25 MINS
PREP: 5 MINS
COOK: 20 MINS

- 4 red onions
- 10g rosemary (2–3 sprigs)
- 20g light brown sugar
- 20ml aged balsamic vinegar
- olive oil
- fine sea salt
- pecorino romano, to serve

Thinly slice the red onions and strip the leaves from the rosemary sprigs and finely chop. Preheat a frying pan over a medium heat and add a shot of olive oil. Add the onions and half of the rosemary with a pinch of salt, toss in the warm oil, and cook for 10–12 minutes, or until beginning to caramelise. Add the sugar and vinegar, cooking down for 4–5 minutes, or until the onions are jammy. Finish with the remaining rosemary. Spoon the polenta into warm bowls and top with the jammy onions. Use a mandoline or cheese grater to shave the pecorino over the top and serve.

PANCETTA, SAGE & NUTMEG TOPPING

SERVES: 2
EYES CLOSED
DF
TOTAL: 10 MINS
PREP: 5 MINS
COOK: 5 MINS

- ¼ nutmeg
- 8–10 thin slices of smoked or unsmoked pancetta
- handful of sage leaves
- 1 lemon
- olive oil
- black pepper

Season your cooked polenta with the grated nutmeg and a shedload of black pepper. Lay the pancetta in a cold frying pan with a glug of olive oil and place over a medium heat. Bring up to temperature and cook for 4–5 minutes until very crispy. Remove from the pan then drop the sage into the hot fat. Let the leaves sizzle for about 1 minute until crisp – you'll know they're done when they stop bubbling and all the water has cooked out of them. Remove the pan from the heat, allow it to cool slightly, then add the juice of the lemon to the pan and swirl it around the pancetta fat and olive oil. Spoon the polenta into warm bowls and top with crisp pancetta, sage leaves and plenty of the dressing.

PASTA & GRAINS

Crispy Rice with Za'atar Chicken Livers

SERVES: 4
EYES CLOSED
TOTAL: 35 MINS
PREP: 10 MINS
COOK: 25 MINS

Crisping up leftover rice is one of the best ways to use it up, and pairing it with a pile of juicy chopped chicken thighs and livers and a sharp parsley salad sounds like a dinner for the ages. If I don't have leftover rice, but still fancy making this for dinner, I just cook rice! It might sound obvious but just prepare some rice then spread it out onto a tray to dry out. The goal is to get that rice as dry as you possibly can before it hits the pan to crisp. Water is the enemy of crisp, after all.

4 skinless, boneless chicken thighs
250g chicken livers (optional – use an extra 2–4 thighs if not using)
2 garlic cloves
1 tsp cumin seeds
2 tsp smoked paprika
2 tbsp za'atar
3 lemons
400g cooked rice
50g unsalted butter
35g flat-leaf parsley
20g dill
3 shallots
5 dill pickles
2 red chillies
4 tbsp tahini
olive oil
fine sea salt
black pepper

1 Cut the chicken thighs into 4–5cm chunks and add to a mixing bowl. If using the chicken livers, rinse them well under cold running water before adding to the bowl with the chicken thigh chunks. Finely grate in the garlic cloves, then add the cumin, paprika, half of the za'atar and the zest and juice of 1 of the lemons. Add a good glug of olive oil and season generously with salt and 15 twists of black pepper. Toss together and pop into the fridge for 30 minutes.

2 Pull your leftover rice out of the fridge. Preheat a non-stick or well-seasoned frying pan over a high heat and add a shot of olive oil. Roll the oil around the pan then tip in the rice, patting it down into a single layer. Allow the rice to sizzle and crisp for 4–5 minutes. Dot half of the butter around the pan and allow it to melt through the rice and start to brown underneath the rice. Once you can smell the butter browning and the rice toasting, start to turn the rice over in chunks. I like to have big pieces of caramelised rice rather than individual grains. Once flipped, sprinkle the rice with the remaining za'atar and keep warm.

3 Preheat a large frying pan over a high heat and add the remaining butter and a glug of olive oil. Once the butter is sizzling away, tip in the chicken thighs and livers and let them sear. Don't touch them for a good 5–6 minutes; you want that first side to really sear. Once they've had a good cook on that first side, shuffle them around a little and repeat that hard sear. Cook for a total of 12–13 minutes, or until cooked through, the spices and garlic are toasty and the pan is full of a deep red oil.

4 Pick the parsley leaves and dill fronds into a bowl. Peel and cut the shallots into thin rounds then separate into individual rings and pop those into the bowl with the herbs. Dice the pickles, thinly slice the chillies and throw those in too, along with a good squeeze of lemon juice, a pinch of salt and a twist of pepper. Toss together.

5 Slacken the tahini with cool water and a little lemon juice until it has a pourable consistency, similar to double cream. Season with salt.

6 Divide the crispy rice among plates and top with the juicy chicken. Serve with a drizzle of tahini, a handful of the herby pickle salad and a lemon wedge.

> **CHEF'S TIP**
> Be brave with your rice cookery. It'll smell really toasty and nutty with the butter in the pan and you might think it's ready to flip, but give it an extra 1–2 minutes at this point. You want to push that rice to crispy perfection.

Kimchi Butter Fried Rice

- **SERVES:** 2
- **EYES CLOSED**
- **GF**
- **TOTAL:** 40 MINS
- **PREP:** 15 MINS
- **COOK:** 25 MINS

Hungover? This might just tick all the boxes for things that I crave when I've had a few too many the night before. Fried rice should be rich, but light. I like to eat a big heaping bowlful when I make it, so I cook everything very hot and very fast at the end – I like to cook all the different elements separately before marrying them right at the last moment and serving it straight away. This keeps the texture super light, the rice crispy and the ingredients bright and vibrant. Keep the heat high and you'll prevent anything steaming and getting soggy in the pan.

½ white onion
1 garlic clove
4 spring onions
200g kimchi, plus roughly 4 tbsp of kimchi juice
1 tbsp gochujang chilli paste
½ tbsp rice vinegar
40g unsalted butter, softened
75g smoked pancetta or guanciale lardons
300g dried cooked rice (see notes – I like to use short-grain sushi rice)
2 eggs
1 tbsp toasted sesame seeds, nori sprinkle or similar
vegetable oil
sesame oil
fine sea salt

1 Finely dice the onion and thinly slice the garlic clove. Trim and thinly slice the spring onions. Tip the kimchi juice, gochujang, rice vinegar and softened butter into a mixing bowl and beat together into a smooth kimchi butter.

2 Preheat a large heavy-based frying pan over a medium heat. Tip in the pancetta or guanciale, add a shot of vegetable oil, and cook for 5–6 minutes until they've given up their fat to the pan and are starting to become crispy. Tip in the onion and spring onion whites, crank up the heat, and cook for 3–4 minutes until the edges of the onion are starting to caramelise. Add the garlic and cook for 1–2 minutes until fragrant. Tip the whole mix into a bowl.

3 Wipe out the pan and return to the hob over a high heat. Once smoking, add the kimchi and roast it in the hot pan: it'll smell smoky and a bit burnt, but that's what we want! Cook over a high heat for 3–4 minutes then tip into the bowl with the other bits.

4 Wipe out the pan, return the pan to the high heat and, once smoking, add a shot of sesame oil and tip in the rice. Use a wooden spoon or spatula to break down any larger clumps and fry for 3–4 minutes, tossing a lot, until the grains of rice are a toasty colour, have a shiny skin and are starting to get crispy. Add the kimchi butter, pancetta, onion and roasted kimchi and toss them through the fried rice. Once you've incorporated everything, spread the rice evenly across the bottom of the pan, lower the heat a little and leave the bottom layer to crisp while you fry your eggs.

5 Preheat a smaller frying pan over a high heat. Add a shot of vegetable oil, crack in the eggs and fry until the bottom of the whites are crispy, the top is just cooked and the yolk is runny. Season with salt and remove from the pan.

6 Divide the fried rice between bowls and top with a fried egg, toasted sesame seeds or nori, and a handful of spring onion greens.

> **NOTES**
> People always say you must use day-old rice to make fried rice. This is only half true, what you're actually after is dry rice. A very dry, day-old rice will make marginally better fried rice than one that has just been cooked, but the difference isn't as dramatic as you think. You can cook your rice 20 minutes or so before you want to stir-fry and just spread it out onto a tray to allow the surface moisture to evaporate. It's that surface moisture that's going to get in the way of your rice being crisp and light.

PASTA & GRAINS

Brown Butter, Orange & Almond Pilaf

SERVES: 4
EYES CLOSED
V / GF
TOTAL: 45 MINS, PLUS RESTING
PREP: 10 MINS, PLUS RESTING
COOK: 35 MINS

Pilaf isn't a dish, rather a technique. It exists under different names across a whole heap of cuisines. Pilaf is the French name for this rice preparation and is, in its most basic form, rice toasted and steamed with aromatics and fat. All of the variations on pilaf usually follow the same blueprint, so once you've got it down, you can really get creative! This is one of my favourite ways to make and serve rice cooked in the pilaf method.

350g basmati rice
1 tbsp cumin seeds
½ tbsp black peppercorns
3 onions
125g unsalted butter
1 cinnamon stick
440ml vegetable or chicken stock
1 carrot
1 orange
3 tbsp flaked almonds
handful of fresh mint leaves
olive oil
fine sea salt
black pepper
6–8 tbsp thick, full-fat Greek yoghurt, to serve

1 Start by washing the rice. Put it in a mixing bowl and pour in enough cold water to cover. Use your hand to agitate the rice, rub the kernels against each other and give it a good swirl. The water will look milky as the starch is washed from the exterior of the rice. Discard this water and repeat the process at least twice, ideally three or four times. The water should run clear on the last wash. Drain the rice and remove as much water as you can. Set over a bowl in a sieve to drip dry while you prep some other bits.

2 In a small frying pan, or the pot you'll use for the onions, toast the cumin seeds and black peppercorns over a medium-high heat for a few minutes until fragrant. Lightly crush using a pestle and mortar and set aside for later.

3 Thinly slice the onions and place a lidded pot (roughly 24cm) over a medium-high heat. Add 100g of the butter and let it melt. Drop in the onions with a pinch of salt and cook for 12–15 minutes until deeply caramelised and starting to crisp. This will take a little longer than if you were using oil, as you need to cook the water out of the butter. You'll see the onions go from raw, to soft and milky, to golden, to dark and crisp. Stick with it and keep everything moving. The butter will also brown as the onions cook – your kitchen is about to smell really good.

4 Once your onions are looking good, fish them out, leaving behind all that oniony browned butter. Turn down the heat to medium-low and tip in the rice. Stir the rice vigorously to coat the grains with the hot fat. Some grains might stick a little to the bottom of the pot but don't panic – as they cook and toast, they'll naturally release. Stir the rice over the heat for a good 4–5 minutes; you want to get a good toast on the rice here. You should be able to smell the rice caramelising as you go. After 5 minutes or so, add the toasted spices and cinnamon stick, half of the cooked onions and a healthy pinch of salt. This is your moment to season the pilaf, so don't be shy – when you add salt here it's going to cook into the rice, any salt added after cooking just sits on the surface and can taste too salty without properly seasoning the pilaf. Pour in the stock, stir it through the rice and crank the heat up to high. Once the stock starts to simmer, slap the lid on and drop the heat to low. Set a timer for 14 minutes and do not lift the lid. If you lift the lid, you'll allow moisture (stock) to escape and that golden ratio will be thrown off. It won't be the end of the world, but you won't have the light, fluffy pilaf you're shooting for.

Continued overleaf →

5 While the rice is cooking, prepare your garnish. Cut your carrot into a really fine julienne (matchsticks). Peel away a few strips of zest from the orange, remove as much white pith as you can, then cut into very fine julienne, too. Add the remaining butter to a small saucepan and place over a medium heat. Let it melt, foam, then sizzle before dropping in the almonds. Toast the almonds in the hot butter until golden brown and the butter is nutty brown. Remove from the heat just before they're at the colour you're after. They'll carry over a little off the heat.

6 Once your timer goes off, whip the pilaf pan off the heat. Allow to sit for 1 minute before lifting the lid and gently fluffing the rice. Don't be too rough here – the grains are still very tender and need to set, but this is an opportune moment to add the garnish. Scatter the almonds, carrot and orange over the rice along with the remaining onions and finally the mint leaves. Squeeze the juice from the orange over the rice and pop the lid back on. Leave to rest for 10 minutes. Don't worry, it's not going to go cold, the residual heat in the pan will gently steam your garnish and infuse the pilaf with orangey, minty flavour. This step also gives the rice grains time to set and separate. This part is so important to avoiding stodgy rice, so don't skip it!

7 Grab some warm plates and divide the yoghurt between them, spreading it over the plate before topping with heaped portions of pilaf.

SHOOT FROM THE HIP

Any bits and bobs you want to add to your pilaf (chicken/peas/braised lamb/chewy fried onions/herbs/spices) will want to go in at the right moment. Add your herbs too early and they'll be limp and devoid of the fragrance you bought them for. Add the chicken too late and it's a chicken sashimi pilaf for dinner. You'll need to decide if the bits and bobs require a proper cook, or just a light steam in the residual heat of the pan. Any raw meat should go in with the rice before the toast, spices are also good to go in now. Herbs, raw tender veggies, nuts and seeds are perfectly tossed through when you fluff your rice. A squeeze of lemon juice is great at this moment, too.

WASH YOUR RICE!

When you buy a bag of rice, it's been on a journey to get to you. All the grains have been packed into the bag, hit the shelves, then bumped around in your shopping trolley, thrown into your backpack, then all the way back to your kitchen. Along the way, the little grains are colliding with one another, creating a dusty, starchy coating. If you dump rice straight from the bag into a boiling pan of water, you're essentially dumping a load of rice flour (the dust) in there, too. This will give you a gummy, sticky mess of cooked rice.

CHEF'S TIP

Toasting your rice is key and will transform any old steamed rice into a kick-ass pilaf. The toasting works two-fold here. First of all, you're developing flavour. Toasting any grains in hot fat will encourage the Maillard reaction and inject a rich, nutty flavour into the dish. Second, you're actually encouraging grain separation down the line: by cooking the exterior of the grain, you are breaking down the starches found on the surface, reducing their thickening power.

Crab with Fresh Tagliolini

- SERVES: 4
- ROLL YOUR SLEEVES UP
- P / DF
- TOTAL: 1 HOUR 35 MINS, PLUS RESTING
- PREP: 1 HOUR, PLUS RESTING
- COOK: 35 MINS

Crab pasta is such a delicious thing to eat. There are a few little techniques in this recipe that I absolutely adore and add bags and bags of flavour: the first – hard roasting super-sweet cherry tomatoes until caramelised and jammy. This gives you the most amazing foundation for so many pastas. It's like a fresher, sweet, more vibrant tomato purée. The second – blending brown crab with miso. The miso enhances the brown crab, bringing out its salinity and earthy richness. The miso and brown crab create a stunning, silky, umami-rich emulsion that is the perfect base for the sweet white crab meat, sweet and acidic tomato and fragrant herbs. Could be a death row pasta, this.

FOR THE LONG PASTA DOUGH

300g '00' flour
100g whole eggs (roughly 2 medium eggs)
50–60g egg yolks (roughly 2–3 egg yolks)
semolina, for dusting

1 Start by making the pasta dough. You can do this in a food processor or by hand. To make it in a food processor, tip the flour, whole eggs and yolks into the bowl and whizz until you've got a rough, shaggy dough. Tip onto the work surface and knead for 5–6 minutes into a smooth, uniform ball. Wrap and rest for 30 minutes. To make it the old-fashioned way, tip the flour out onto a clean worktop and use a bowl large enough to hold the whole eggs and yolks to make a well in the centre. Tip the eggs and yolks into the well and use a fork to beat the eggs and yolks together. Gradually bring more and more flour into the egg mixture until it is very thick, then use your hands to bring everything together into a rough, shaggy dough. Knead for 8–9 minutes until you have a firm, smooth dough. Wrap and rest for 30 minutes.

2 To roll the pasta, unwrap your dough and cut it in half. If you've kneaded the dough well, there'll be tiny air pockets trapped inside. No air pockets? Knead a little more next time. Open your pasta roller to the largest setting. Use a rolling pin to roll a piece of dough out until it's just about thin enough to pass through the machine. If you try and squash it through when it's too thick, you'll knacker your pasta machine. It's best to get your dough as close to the thickness of the setting you're starting on. Pass the pasta through the machine, working down the levels, getting thinner and thinner, until you can just about see your hand through the dough. Now fold the pasta in half lengthways, and in half again into quarters. Return the pasta to the thickest setting and repeat the process. This will continue to knead the pasta while also giving you a much more uniform shape. Repeat this lamination process twice before rolling the pasta to the second thinnest setting.

3 Cut the pasta into 20–25cm-long sheets and dust with semolina. Stack three of the sheets, fold in the bottom edge up to the top and then cut from right to left into 1.5–2mm-thick strips, then unfold the strips into your tagliolini. Dust the pasta with extra semolina and curl into nests. Set aside.

Continued overleaf →

PASTA & GRAINS

FOR THE SAUCE

500g sweet cherry tomatoes (datterini are my favourite)

2 garlic cloves

1 long red chilli

25g basil

10g tarragon

2 tsp white miso

200g fresh brown crab meat

200g fresh white crab meat

2 lemons

4 tbsp Sourdough Crumbs (page 74)

olive oil

fine sea salt

black pepper

4 Halve the cherry tomatoes, peel and lightly crush the garlic cloves and halve the chilli lengthways. Place a large frying pan over a medium heat. Add enough olive oil to cover the bottom of the pan and, once hot, drop in the garlic cloves and chilli. Swirl them in the oil, allowing them to infuse for 2–3 minutes, but don't let them burn.

5 Once your oil is smelling delicious, remove the garlic and chilli, crank up the heat and dump in all the halved cherry tomatoes at once. Cook the tomatoes over the highest heat for a good 10–12 minutes, stirring and scraping the bottom of the pan and letting the tomatoes catch and caramelise and reduce. You should be left with a jammy, rich paste of tomatoes and the volume will have reduced significantly. Keep warm over a low heat.

6 Tear the basil leaves into pieces and finely chop the tarragon.

7 Bring a large pot of salted water to the boil. Spoon a little of the water into the tomato reduction and add the miso and brown crab meat. Mix together to form a smooth, thick emulsion.

8 Drop your tagliolini into the boiling water and cook for just shy of 1 minute. Add another big ladle of pasta water to the tomato mixture then transfer the cooked pasta straight into the sauce. Start tossing the two together. The pasta, crab and tomatoes will come together to make a rich sauce. If you need to add more pasta water to loosen things up, go ahead; if things are a little loose, just crank up the heat and reduce the sauce. The pasta will require a good amount of water, but add a little at a time until you're happy and things are saucy.

9 Once the pasta is coated beautifully with the sauce, add the chopped herbs, white crab meat and the grated zest and juice of the lemons. Taste and season as necessary. Divide among warm plates and top with the sourdough crumbs and a drizzle of extra virgin olive oil. Serve straight away.

FRESH PASTA?
Making the pasta is completely optional! The sauce is still completely delicious with dried spaghetti or linguine, but for the full experience, I'd urge you to give it a go. If your eggs are just a little shy of the required weight, top them up with a splash of water.

SHOOT FROM THE HIP
If you can't find fresh crab, chopped raw prawns would work well. Omit the brown crab and just use the miso and add the prawns at the same time as you would add the white crab meat. They'll cook through as you toss everything together.

CHEF'S TIP
Getting your dough right is the key to happy pasta making. Adding the correct proportion of eggs to flour is crucial to making a firm but supple dough. Use your instincts and lean towards the drier side if you're unsure. After the rest, you'll find the dough will soften. If it's your first time making pasta, try making the dough the old-fashioned way (by hand) so you can be mindful of how the dough's texture changes.

Stovetop Seafood Rice

- SERVES: 2
- ROLL YOUR SLEEVES UP
- P / DF / GF
- TOTAL: 1 HOUR
- PREP: 15 MINS
- COOK: 45 MINS

Yes, this is absolutely inspired by the mighty paella and no, it is not traditional! If you're from Valencia, look away now. There are some seriously good lessons at play when making paella. It's one of the more challenging rice recipes out there, as it doesn't follow the same rules as others. For this recipe to work really, really well, you want to use the biggest pan you can get your hands on so you can make that layer of rice as thin as possible. The dream scenario is to have a layer of rice just a few grains thick. However, any wide frying pan will turn out delicious seafood rice!

4 large raw shell-on prawns
tiny pinch of saffron
1 litre fish stock
2 large ripe tomatoes
1 onion
3 garlic cloves
100g raw squid (tubes and tentacles), cut into bite-sized pieces
1 tsp smoked paprika
220g bomba paella rice
100g fresh mussels or clams, cleaned
25g rosemary sprigs, tied into a bunch with the rind from the lemons
1 lemon
extra virgin olive oil
fine sea salt
black pepper
Aioli (page 209), to serve

1 First things first, we've got to level up that fish stock. Working over a saucepan so you catch any bits, twist the heads off the prawns, peel the shells and drop them into the pan. Add the saffron then pour over the fish stock. Place over a medium heat, bring to a simmer and let it tick over for 10–15 minutes while you prepare the other bits and pieces. Remove the veins from the prawns (see page 110) and set aside.

2 Halve the tomatoes and use the coarse side of a box grater set in a bowl to grate the flesh into a pulp. Use the flat of your palm to hold the tomato and keep grating until you've just got the skin left. Discard the skin. Peel and finely dice the onion and finely grate the garlic cloves.

3 Place a paella pan or your largest frying pan (30cm+) over a medium heat. Pour in roughly 50ml of olive oil and, once hot, add the squid. Season with a little salt and cook for 4–5 minutes until lightly coloured. Tip in the onion and cook with a pinch of salt for a couple of minutes, then add the garlic, smoked paprika and grated tomatoes. Cook for about 2 minutes, until the oil starts separating from the tomatoes and they've become jammy. Tip in the rice and stir it through the mix. Cook for a couple of minutes, coating the grains with oil and toasting them a little. Add the stock and give the pan a shake to distribute everything evenly. Bring to the boil and cook over a high heat for 9–10 minutes before scattering the prawns, mussels or clams and the rosemary over the top of the rice. Lower the heat, cover the surface of the pan with a tea towel or piece of foil and let it bubble away for another 7–8 minutes. The stock will have almost entirely cooked away by this point and for the final few minutes we're going to crank up the heat to get that crispy bottom.

4 Remove the lid and cook over a high heat for the final 2 minutes until the rice begins to crackle and sizzle – it'll smell like toasted shellfish and will fill your kitchen with aroma. Remove from the heat and let it rest for 5 minutes before serving with fresh lemon wedges and aioli.

> **CHEF'S TIP**
> Once the rice hits the pan, do not stir it. As soon as you stir a short-grain rice like paella rice, it'll start to release starch and make the stock super creamy and the dish will become too stodgy. If you feel the urge, shake the pan gently to even things out, but put the spoon down!

PASTA & GRAINS

White Sausage & Sage Pappardelle

SERVES: 4
ROLL YOUR SLEEVES UP
TOTAL: 2 HOURS 55 MINS
PREP: 25 MINS
COOK: 2 HOURS 30 MINS

Sausage might be the greatest cheat code for homemade ragù out there. A perfect balance of fat, spices and meat, sausage gives you a big head start in the flavour department. Paired with a few simple ingredients, you've got a white ragù for the ages.

FOR THE RAGÙ

- 15g dried porcini mushrooms
- 400g sausagemeat
- 5 shallots
- 2 celery sticks
- 5 garlic cloves
- 1 bouquet garni (thyme, rosemary, bay)
- 250ml white wine
- 500ml chicken stock
- 200ml whole milk
- ½ whole nutmeg
- olive oil
- fine sea salt
- black pepper

TO FINISH

- 400g dried pappardelle or 600g fresh pappardelle
- 200g bitter greens, Swiss chard, broccoli rabe, or chicoria
- 2 tbsp mascarpone
- 10g chopped flat-leaf parsley
- 10g chopped sage
- parmesan
- 1 lemon

1 Making a good speedy ragù is all about being efficient, so we're going to multi-task the hell out of this recipe. Start by grabbing your largest ovenproof saucepan, setting it over a medium-high heat, boiling the kettle and preheating the oven to 160°C fan/180°C/350°F/gas mark 4.

2 Add the porcini mushrooms to a heatproof bowl. Pour enough boiling water in to just cover the mushrooms and set them aside for 30 minutes. Add a shot of olive oil to your preheated pan and tip in the sausagemeat. Break it up a little with a wooden spoon then leave it alone to caramelise. Keep it moving now and then, until thoroughly browned and broken into small pieces.

3 While the sausagemeat is browning, peel and cut the shallots and the celery into even, fine dice. Every step of the way, try to remember to think about your pasta shape and how you want your ragù to 'behave' down the line. We want the sauce to cling to the pasta and with pappardelle, larger chunks of celery or shallot will simply fall off. Thinly slice the garlic and tie up your bouquet garni.

4 Remove the sausagemeat from the pan, leaving behind the fat, and add your shallots and celery. Add a pinch of salt and cook over a medium heat for 10–15 minutes until very soft and starting to caramelise. Add the garlic and bouquet garni and cook for 3–4 minutes. Add the sausagemeat back to the pan, crank up the heat and add the wine, scraping the bottom to deglaze. Reduce by two-thirds then add the chicken stock and milk. Add the mushroom soaking liquid, roughly chop the soaked 'shrooms and get those in there too. Bring to the boil, season with a little salt and pepper, grate in the nutmeg and top with a cartouche (page 233). Slide into the oven for 1½–2 hours until reduced and rich.

5 Whip the ragù out of the oven, fish out the bouquet garni and bring a pot of salted water to the boil. Cook your pappardelle according to the packet instructions, or until cooked to your liking. Preheat a pasta pan over a high heat and add a shot of olive oil. Once very hot, sauté the greens with a pinch of salt for 2 minutes, or until just wilted with a little colour. Spoon the ragù into the hot pan with the greens and reheat.

6 Marry the pasta and the ragù in the pan with a few spoons of pasta water, the mascarpone, chopped parsley and sage. Toss the two together, adding pasta water as you need it, until you have a glossy, rich sauce. Finish with grated parmesan and lemon juice. Season and divide among warm bowls, top with extra grated parmesan and serve.

CHEF'S TIP
To make the pappardelle yourself, whip up a batch of whole egg pasta dough (page 129) and use a pasta machine to roll out sheets of dough on the second- or third-thinnest setting. Cut into 20cm lengths and then into 5cm-wide strips.

NOTES ON RAGÙ
If you don't want to turn the oven on for this recipe, you can absolutely cook it on the hob, just remember to keep stirring it now and then! The benefit of using the oven is that the whole pan is exposed to the even heat of the oven whereas on the hob, it's just the bottom that bears the brunt of the heat. It's up to you, but the oven is way more hands off! A pro tip: cook your ragù the day before you want to serve it, pour it into a tub, and leave it in the fridge overnight. It always tastes better the next day. Trust me.

Ricotta Dumplings with Cheese & Tomato Broth

SERVES: 4
ROLL YOUR SLEEVES UP
TOTAL: 35 MINS, PLUS CHILLING
PREP: 20 MINS, PLUS CHILLING
COOK: 15 MINS

These are similar in principle to gnocchi, but use ricotta instead of potato to give the dumplings a light, fluffy, rich texture. What almost steals the show in this recipe is the cheese broth. It's an incredible way to use up old parmesan rinds. I keep them in the freezer and once I've got a few, make this! The broth is packed with umami and has a lovely, creamy mouthfeel. Finished with sweet little tomatoes and plenty of herbs this makes for a really light, elegant bowl of pasta that has one foot in comfort, but the other in summer.

FOR THE DUMPLINGS

500g ricotta (one with a crumbly texture)

30g grated parmesan

1 egg, plus 1 egg yolk

160g '00' flour, plus extra for dusting

fine sea salt

black pepper

FOR THE SAUCE

80–100g (3 or 4) parmesan rinds

60g grated parmesan, plus extra to serve

1 garlic clove

150g cherry tomatoes

4 spring onions

30g soft herbs (I like a mixture of basil, chives and dill)

extra virgin olive oil

1 Put the ricotta, parmesan, egg and egg yolk in the bowl of a food processor. Add a healthy pinch of salt along with 25 twists of black pepper, then whizz everything together. It'll look a little loose, but don't panic, the flour is going to sort that out. Sprinkle the flour over top and then pulse it into the mixture until everything is homogenous. It should have thickened but still be a tiny bit sticky.

2 Line a baking tray with parchment paper and dust it generously with flour. Grab a spoon (a normal eating spoon will do) and scoop up a little of the mix, then drag it up the side of the processor, with its bowl flat against the wall. The mixture should fill the bowl of the spoon completely, with a flat top.

3 Dust your index finger with flour, then use it to push the mixture from the spoon down onto the lined tray, forming it into a little dollop as you do so. Don't sweat about making these all the same, there's beauty in the imperfections. Repeat with the remaining mix then dust your little dumplings with plenty of flour. Slide into the fridge for 1 hour or so to give the flour time to hydrate and the dumplings time to firm up.

4 While the dumplings chill, make the sauce. Put the parmesan rinds and grated parmesan in a pan and cover with 1 litre of water. Lightly crush the garlic clove and drop it into the pan. Place over a medium heat, bring to a simmer and let it tick over for 1 hour, or until it's reduced by about half. Pass everything through a sieve into a large pasta pan. Have a taste and marvel at your parmesan broth. Halve the tomatoes, trim and thinly slice the spring onions and roughly chop the herbs. Stir the tomatoes and spring onions through the broth and keep them warm on the side.

5 Whip the dumplings out of the fridge and bring a large pot of water to the boil. Drop the heat to medium so the water is at a simmer, season it generously with salt and carefully drop the dumplings in. Cook for 3–4 minutes. They'll nearly double in size as they gently cook. Go easy on them, they're delicate! Once cooked, transfer to the pan of cheese broth and gently warm everything through. Add the herbs then divide among warm bowls. Finish with a drizzle of olive oil and serve.

> **CHEF'S TIP**
> Be super gentle with these dumplings, they will be smashed to pieces if you toss them like you would spaghetti or linguine. Picture swirling them gracefully into your sauce instead of the rough and tumble of a pasta.

NOTES ON CHEESE

You want a pretty dry ricotta for this recipe. If yours comes in a little basket, then it's probably been hung already and is ready to rock; if it looks like it's been dolloped into the pot, then you'll want to either hang it in a sieve for a few hours or press some moisture out of it in a clean tea towel. You're looking for a ricotta with a crumbly texture. No parmesan rinds? No sweat. Just use 100g of grated parmesan instead.

Cheesy Spelt with Pancetta, Mushrooms & Yolk

SERVES: 4
ROLL YOUR SLEEVES UP
TOTAL: 55 MINS
PREP: 10 MINS
COOK: 45 MINS

Making risotto is a well-trodden path and to be honest, I don't *love* eating them. I'm a sucker for chewy grains and pastas, things with real bite. What I do love is using other grains to make risotto-style dishes. Pearl barley, farro, fregola and orzo are all ace for this task, but one comes out tops for me – spelt. Spelt is a fantastic grain for whipping up a risotto-style plate. It retains an amazing chew and isn't so starchy that the resulting plate is super stodgy. It holds its shape, has a delicious earthy, nutty flavour and gives you a beautiful alternative to arborio.

2 onions
2 garlic cloves
2 litres good-quality chicken stock
25g thyme sprigs, tied with string
300g spelt
200ml dry white wine
200g smoked pancetta lardons
60g unsalted butter
300g mixed wild mushrooms
40g parmesan
40g Comté, cheddar or gruyère
25g chives
1 lemon
extra virgin olive oil
fine sea salt
black pepper
4 egg yolks, to serve

1 Finely dice the onions and finely grate the garlic. Place a large pasta pan over a medium heat and add a generous layer of olive oil. Tip in the onion and season with a pinch of salt. Cook for 8–10 minutes, or until just translucent. There should be enough oil in the pan that the onion is almost confiting, so don't be shy! Meanwhile, tip the stock into a saucepan and warm over a low heat.

2 Once the onion is sweet and soft, add half the garlic and half the thyme (stems and all). Crank up the heat a little and cook for a minute or two more. You want to smell the garlic and thyme come to life in the heat of the pan. Now tip in the spelt and stir it through the base veggies. Cook for 3–4 minutes, then add the wine and bring to the boil. Cook for 3–4 minutes, or until the wine is almost completely gone. Now start gradually adding the warm chicken stock, stirring the spelt as you go to make sure everything is cooking evenly. You want all of the grains to be submerged in stock so they cook evenly – any grains that are left stuck to the side of the pan above the liquid line will cook at a different rate, so make sure everything is where it's supposed to be. Cook for 30–35 minutes, or until the spelt is tender and the stock has reduced into a beautiful sauce.

3 When your risotto is about 9–10 minutes away from being ready, preheat a frying pan over a medium heat. Add the pancetta and a shot of olive oil and cook for 5–6 minutes, or until the pancetta fat has rendered and the pancetta is crispy. Remove the lardons from the pan, leaving the pancetta fat behind. Crank up the heat and, once very hot, add half of the butter and allow it to melt, foam and sizzle. Once sizzling, tear in the mushrooms and cook for 3–4 minutes until caramelised. About halfway through, add the remaining garlic and pick in the leaves from the leftover thyme and sauté together for 1–2 minutes. Add the pancetta back to the pan, remove from the heat, and keep warm while you finish the spelt.

4 Remove the thyme stems from the pan. The little fragrant leaves will have come away from the stems and be lost within the pan. Stir in the remaining butter and grate in the cheeses. Stir them in off the heat and have a taste. Adjust the seasoning and add about 20 twists of black pepper. Finish the mushroom mixture with finely chopped chives and plenty of lemon juice.

5 Divide the spelt among warm plates. Pick the plates up one by one and use the heel of your other palm to gently tap the bottom of the plate, this will encourage the risotto to spread evenly across the plate. Scatter the mushrooms and pancetta over the top and crown each plate with an egg yolk. Season the little yolks and serve.

CHEF'S TIP
Whenever I'm making a risotto or similar style of dish, I like to use a silicone spatula as my weapon of choice. A wooden spoon will be okay, but the ability a silicone spatula has to effectively clean the sides of a pan as it stirs is unrivalled. It's a thorough tool, leaving no grain stuck to the pan.

SHOOT FROM THE HIP
I've gone for a nice autumnal garnish for this with the garlicky sautéed mushrooms, but as with a risotto you can finish this spelt with just about anything. It's carte blanche. In spring, top it with blanched asparagus, peas or broad beans. In winter, roasted squash or pumpkins with crispy kale, and in summer you could spoon over a zippy tomato salad.

Creamed Cabbage Cavatelli

- SERVES: 4
- ROLL YOUR SLEEVES UP
- TOTAL: 40 MINS, PLUS RESTING
- PREP: 20 MINS, PLUS RESTING
- COOK: 20 MINS

Cavatelli is one of the simplest, most accessible handmade pastas out there. The dough requires just two ingredients and can be made without any special equipment. I've carried this pasta shape through a few different restaurants with me over the years. We put it on the menu at Marion in Melbourne, I rolled thousands at a pasta bar and a squid ink version made it onto the plates at 64 Degrees.

FOR THE CAVATELLI

- 400g semolina flour
- 180g warm water

FOR THE SAUCE

- 200g cavolo nero
- 2 garlic cloves
- 25g flat-leaf parsley
- 60g parmesan
- 2 tbsp full-fat crème fraîche
- 1 lemon
- 4 tbsp Sourdough Crumbs (optional; page 74)
- extra virgin olive oil
- fine sea salt
- black pepper

1 To make the cavatelli dough, pop the semolina flour into a bowl and pour in the water. Use your hands to bring the two together into a shaggy dough. Once you've got a cohesive mass, tip the whole lot out onto a work surface and knead for 4–5 minutes into a smooth-ish ball. Now wrap with cling film to prevent the dough from drying out and rest for at least 5–10 minutes. This will give the semolina in the dough a little time to hydrate. Once the dough has had its first rest, knead again for 4–5 minutes until it's super smooth – you'll see the difference after just a few turns! Wrap and rest again, this time for at least 30 minutes.

2 Once rested, flatten the dough into a disc. Cut the disc into long strips and then, working in batches, roll them into ropes roughly 2cm in diameter. Use a bench scraper or knife to cut the ropes into equal-sized pieces, roughly 2–3cm chunks. Using the back of a fork, roll a little dough piece down the tines, creating a little dimple in the back of the pasta with your thumb. Repeat with the remaining dough. Dust the cavatelli with a little semolina and arrange them neatly on a tray. These will hold for a day in your fridge, but I like to use them straight away.

3 To make the sauce, bring a pot of water to a rolling boil and season generously with salt. Remove the stalks from the cavolo nero, roughly chop them and drop into the water for 3–4 minutes. You want them super soft – you can't really overcook them, so let 'em go. While they're bubbling away, roughly chop the cavolo leaves and peel the garlic. Drop the leaves, parsley (stalks and all) and peeled garlic cloves into the pot and cook for another 3–4 minutes.

4 Once everything is super soft, transfer to a blender or food processor using tongs or a spider, reserving the cooking water. (If you're using a Nutribullet or closed-top blender, let everything cool down a little before you blend!) Grate the parmesan and add it and the crème fraîche to the blender and blend until super smooth and bright green. You're looking for a thick, pourable consistency, so add a splash of the cooking water if you need to loosen things up a bit.

5 Cook the cavatelli in a pan of boiling salted water for 2–3 minutes. While they cook, pour the sauce into a pasta pan and gently warm it over a low heat. Spoon the cooked pasta straight into the warm sauce and toss to coat. If you need to add a little pasta water to loosen things up, go ahead. Have a taste and finish with salt, black pepper, lemon zest and a big squeeze of lemon juice. Divide among warm plates and top with extra parm, the sourdough crumbs and a drizzle of olive oil.

Homemade Gnocchi with Smashed Peas & Crème Fraîche

SERVES: 4
DIG IN
TOTAL: 1 HOUR 55 MINS, PLUS RESTING
PREP: 35 MINS, PLUS RESTING
COOK: 1 HOUR 20 MINS

This has to be one of my favourite ways to enjoy gnocchi. Light fluffy pillows, blanched then fried in brown butter until nutty, golden and crisp, paired with a bright, zippy, lemony crème fraîche sauce packed with sweet spring veggies and parmesan cheese.

FOR THE GNOCCHI

1kg Maris Piper potatoes (to yield roughly 500g mash)
110g '00' flour, plus extra for dusting
5g cornflour
2 egg yolks
fine sea salt

FOR THE SAUCE

160g frozen peas
180g asparagus
25g basil
15g unsalted butter
3 tbsp crème fraîche
80g parmesan
1 lemon
olive oil
fine sea salt
black pepper

1 Preheat the oven to 200°C fan/220°C/425°F/gas mark 7.

2 Stick the potatoes onto a baking tray, use a small knife to pierce a couple of holes in each and slide them into the oven for an hour or so, or until tender all the way through. You want to be completely confident they're cooked, so if in doubt, give them another 10 minutes. A knife should glide in one side and out the other with minimal effort.

3 While the potatoes are still hot, cut them in half. Scoop out the cooked potato onto a tray or into a bowl. If you've got a potato ricer, simply pass all that potato through so you have lots of fine strands of potato. If not, push the potato through a fine-mesh sieve, using a bench scraper or spatula. It's important to work with the potato while it's still warm – if you let the mash go cold before you start working with it, you'll end up with a gummy mess, so work as quickly as you can.

4 Sprinkle the flours and a generous couple of pinches of fine sea salt all over the little strands of mash. Start gently mixing them through the potato, being careful not to start kneading or working the dough – you're aiming to coat each little strand in flour, distributing everything evenly. Once you're happy everything is evenly distributed, drop the egg yolks on top. Using a bench scraper or knife, start chopping the yolks into the potato mixture. Once they've begun to blend into the mix, bring the dough together and start to gently knead it.

5 The gnocchi will need a bit of structure, and a gentle 1–2-minute knead will give the dough some strength. You want to keep working the dough until it is homogenous and there are no obvious streaks of yolk or flour. Once you're happy, cover it with a tea towel and leave to rest for 10 minutes. While it's resting, get your frozen peas out to thaw slightly.

6 Once rested, lightly flour your worktop and cut the dough ball into four pieces. We're going to roll these pieces into long sausage shapes, so I like to cut the dough ball lengthways. This way you're starting to roll a piece of dough that's already halfway to being a log. Roll each of the pieces into a sausage shape roughly 25–28cm long, and line them up on your chopping board. Try to make them as even as you can, but don't stress if they're not perfect,

Continued overleaf ⟶

PASTA & GRAINS

nothing is. Grab a long knife, ideally one that can cut all four logs at the same time, and cut them into little pillows. You can make them as big or small as you like here, it's up to you! Dust them with a little extra flour and set aside while you bring a pot of water to the boil and set up a large bowl of iced water. Season the water generously with salt, then drop the gnocchi in and cook for 1 minute, or until they start to float to the surface. I do this in batches – you want to give the gnocchi plenty of room to float about and cook evenly. Once the gnocchi are cooked, transfer to the ice bath. Once cool, remove from the bath and toss with a little olive oil. These are now ready to be crisped up in a pan, warmed through sauce, or popped into the fridge in an airtight container.

7 Add all but a handful of the peas to a blender or mortar and pulse/smash until pulpy. Trim the woody ends and slice the asparagus into 1cm pieces and roughly chop the basil. Bring the pot of water back to the boil and blanch the asparagus and that extra handful of peas for 1 minute, then drain and set aside.

8 Preheat a large frying pan over a high heat. Add a good glug of oil and let it get nice and hot. Add your blanched gnocchi and cook for 3–4 minutes until golden brown. Keep the gnocchi moving regularly. Add the butter and cook for 1–2 minutes a side, or until the gnocchi is glazed and nut brown. Add a splash of water, the smashed peas and the crème fraîche. Toss everything together to create a beautifully green, creamy sauce. Season with salt and pepper. Add the lemon zest, grated parmesan, blanched veggies and chopped basil. Keep tossing everything together and adding more water until glossy and the gnocchi is just coated with sauce. Adjust the seasoning if you need to and finish with lots of lemon juice.

9 Divide among warm plates, top with more grated parmesan, a few twists of black pepper and get stuck in.

SHOOT FROM THE HIP

If you fancy making this and asparagus is out of season, you can use other frozen spring veggies that are good to go all year round: broad beans are my go-to.

HOW TO SCALE

What happens if I end up with 523g of mash?! or 489g?! A surefire way to land the gnocchi plane is to work out the addition of flours and other 'stuff' by percentage. Grab your digital scale and weigh your mash. Now, work out the amount of flour you need based on that weight. The percentage weight of the mash you need for each flour is: flour – 20–22%, cornflour – 1%. So, if you have 1kg of mash, you'll need 220g (22% of 1000g) of flour and 10g (1% of 1000g) of cornflour. Add roughly 1 egg yolk for every 150g of mash, and you're laughing.

Pumpkin Ravioli with Taleggio Fonduta

SERVES: 4
DIG IN
TOTAL: 110 MINS
PREP: 50 MINS
COOK: 60 MINS

This is the pasta you roll out when you're looking to impress. There's plenty of technique on display here, and the payoff is absolutely delicious. Of all the filled pasta shapes, a classic ravioli is up there with the best. It's also a great place to start if this is your first pasta-making rodeo. It's as simple as folding up little parcels or filling and pressing them closed with your fingers – no fancy rolls, crimps or twists here. It's an intuitive process and a great way to get the hang of working with fresh dough, dialling in hydration and getting creative with different fillings. The sauce is all about the cheese. A sweet base of onions, tangy crème fraîche and nutty, buttery taleggio come together into a fondue of sorts, that clings to the pasta beautifully. A little thyme and balsamic add fragrance and some acidity. This is a proper plate of food!

FOR THE FILLABLE PASTA DOUGH

250g '00' flour

100g whole eggs (roughly 2)

50g egg yolks (roughly 2–3)

semolina, for dusting

1 You can make the pasta in a food processor or by hand. To make it in a food processor, tip the flour, whole eggs and yolks into the bowl. If your eggs don't quite weigh the right amount, use water to make up the difference. Whizz until you've got a rough, shaggy dough. Tip the whole lot out onto a clean work surface and knead for 4–5 minutes until smooth-ish, then wrap in cling film and rest for 30 minutes. To make it the old-fashioned way, tip the flour out onto a clean worktop and use a bowl large enough to hold the whole eggs and yolks to make a well in the centre. Tip the eggs and yolks into the well and use a fork to beat the eggs and yolks together. Gradually bring more and more flour into the egg mixture until it is very thick, then use your hands to bring everything together into a rough, shaggy dough. Knead for 8–9 minutes until you have a firm, smooth dough. Wrap and rest for 30 minutes.

2 Once the dough has had a rest, unwrap and knead again for 3–4 minutes. You'll see the dough transform on this second knead into a super smooth, supple ball. Wrap and rest again while you make the filling.

3 Preheat the oven to 170°C fan/190°C/375°F/gas mark 5. To make the filling, peel and scoop the seeds from the pumpkin. Cut into 4–5cm chunks and toss on a baking tray with a tiny lick of olive oil and a pinch of salt. Slide into the oven and roast for 35–40 minutes until completely tender all the way through, but not coloured. Turn off the oven. Allow to cool slightly before adding to a bowl with the grated nutmeg and parmesan. Add a little olive oil and use a fork to mash until homogenous. The sauce is super rich, so we're not going to add heaps of butter or cream here, just a clean, sweet, well-seasoned pumpkin mixture. Set aside to cool.

4 Unwrap your pasta dough and cut it in half. Open your pasta roller to the largest setting and use a rolling pin to roll one of the pieces of dough out until it's just about thin enough to pass through the machine. If you try and squash it through when it's too thick, you'll knacker your pasta machine. It's best to get your dough as close to the thickness of the setting you're starting on. Pass the pasta through the machine, working down the levels, getting thinner and thinner, until you can just about see your hand through the dough. Now fold the pasta in half, lengthways, and in half again into quarters. Return the pasta to the thickest setting, and repeat the process. This will continue to knead the pasta while also giving you a much more

Continued overleaf ⟶

PASTA & GRAINS

FOR THE FILLING

½ Delica pumpkin, crown prince squash or similar

¼ nutmeg

20g parmesan

olive oil

fine sea salt

FOR THE TALEGGIO FONDUTA

2 onions

10g thyme sprigs

100g full-fat crème fraîche

200g taleggio, rind removed

aged balsamic vinegar, for drizzling

olive oil

fine sea salt

black pepper

TEXTURES

The filling for stuffed pasta is all about getting your hydration right. Add too wet a filling to your dough and it'll break down your pasta and have a watery mouthfeel. Too dry, and the pasta will be claggy. Delica pumpkins have a very sweet, dense flesh, much drier than that of a butternut squash, which makes them perfect for stuffing into ravioli. After a long, slow bake in the oven, the flesh dries out even further, leaving behind a rich, creamy pumpkin that requires only a bit of nutmeg and parmesan to sing.

SHOOT FROM THE HIP

The typical sauce for a pumpkin-stuffed pasta is butter and sage, so if you want to sub in something more classic, that's the one for you. Gently melt 40g of unsalted butter in a pan and, when just warm and starting to sizzle, drop in sage leaves. Cook for 1–2 minutes, but don't let the butter brown. Add some pasta water, season to taste and get the pasta in there. Finish with a little lemon juice and grated parmesan, if you like.

---

uniform shape. Repeat this lamination process twice before rolling the pasta to the second-thinnest setting. Cut the pasta lengthways into three sections.

5 To shape the ravioli, add 6 little blobs of squash, equally spaced along one sheet. Using a very lightly damp brush or finger, moisten the pasta around the filling and fold the pasta up and over. Use two fingers to separate each of the little squash islands, pressing down firmly to seal in the filling. Now squeeze as much air out of the little parcel as you can before sealing the top. Run your fingers around each of the squash balls, pressing firmly to ensure the seal is super strong. Use a cutter or a sharp knife to cut out the pasta, leaving as much excess as you like. Repeat with the remaining pasta and filling. Lay onto trays lined with a little semolina.

6 Place a medium saucepan or pasta pan over a medium heat. Thinly slice the onions, add 1 tablespoon of olive oil to the pan and, once warm, add the onions. Season with salt and reduce the heat to medium-low. Cook, stirring regularly, for 30–35 minutes until caramelised and golden brown. Pick the thyme leaves from the stems and add half to the pan for the final 5 minutes of cooking. Once caramelised, add the crème fraîche to the pan and melt through the sauce. Bring to a bare simmer, reduce the heat to the lowest setting and tear in the taleggio in small chunks. Gently melt it through the sauce and remove from the heat.

7 Cook the ravioli in a pot of salted boiling water for 1–2 minutes, or until tender. Transfer to the sauce using a spider or slotted spoon and gently warm over a very low heat. Coat the pasta with the fonduta, adding a few splashes of water as needed to achieve a texture you're happy with. You want the sauce to be just a hair looser than you'd like as it hits the plate; it'll tighten up as it sits. Once the pasta is nicely coated and a little looser than you'd like, divide among warm plates and finish with a drizzle of balsamic vinegar, a few twists of pepper and a few extra thyme leaves.

CHEF'S TIP

While you're shaping your pasta, lay a damp cloth or sheet of cling film over the sheets while you work, this'll stop them from drying out – pasta that's too dry will crack when folded. Once you've made the ravioli, you can eat them all straight away or freeze them for another day. You can cook them straight from frozen, just drop them straight into boiling water and add 30 seconds or so to the cook time.

PASTA & GRAINS

FLOUR

BLT Bread 154

Stuffable Pitta Breads 156

Foolproof Focaccia 158

Semolina Flatbreads with Scapece 160

Garlicky Spinach & Cheese Pide 162

Sheet-tray Pizza alla Puttanesca 164

Bagels, Oniony Cream Cheese & Hot Honey 166

Olive Oil Buns, Grilled Mortadella & Taqueria Pickles 168

English Muffins 171

Chive Milk Bread 172

Baguettes & Homemade Salted Butter 174

& WATER

I've lost count of the number of times when I've asked someone about the best thing they ate at a restaurant, only for their eyes to widen as their brain zips back to the crusty, warm roll they were served with crunchy salty butter at the top of the meal. Sometimes, a good bake can eclipse everything else in the kitchen.

Bread is powerful, it's been around for a very long time, and it flicks a special switch in our brains.

In this chapter, we're walking into the wonderful world of breadmaking. Making bread is about as close to kitchen magic as you'll get. Learning the feel and texture of different doughs, playing with hydration levels and discovering the world of fermentation are the foundations of breadmaking. Baking bread is to create and manage a living thing. Yeasts and ferments breathe and eat, and you'll learn to control how much

and when they do their thing, ultimately dictating the texture, colour and flavour of your bread. All the recipes in this chapter are made with widely available flours and instant yeast. You can also make them all without a stand mixer or any fancy equipment. All you really need is flour and water, and you can start baking. So, let's get going.

GLUTEN

Starting with the right flour is key to success in the baking department. The main differences between flours lie in the texture and the flour's potential to create gluten. Texture refers to how finely the wheat has been milled, while gluten potential is dictated by how much protein is found in the wheat. The protein content of the flour denotes its classification – the higher the protein content, the more potential gluten. Flours with a higher protein content are known as 'hard' flours and those with lower, 'soft'. If you're making bagels, baguettes or pizza, reach for the hard stuff, as you'll want as much gluten development as possible. For cookies, cakes and pastry, go for 'soft' flour. Check the nutritional information on your bag of flour. You're looking for the percentage of protein here. A plain flour will usually have a protein content of 8–11%, a strong bread flour can sit anywhere between 12 and 15%.

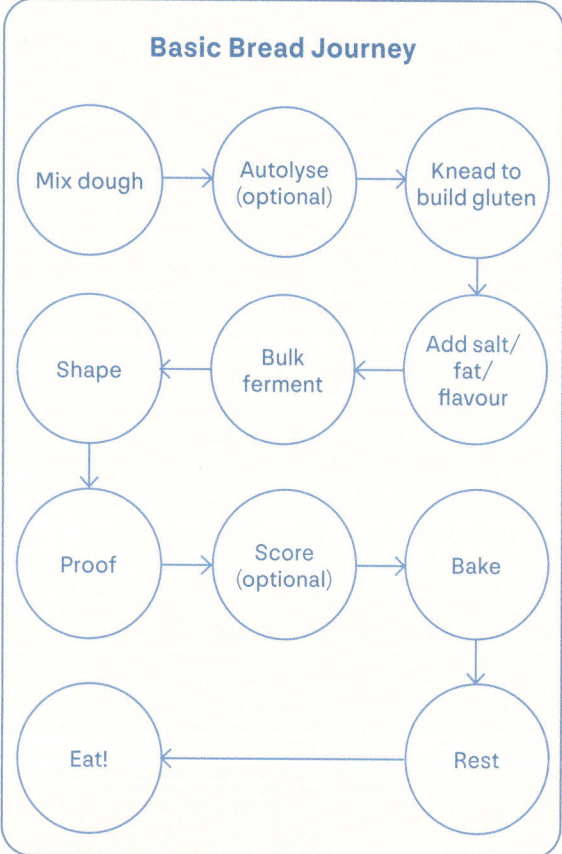

Basic Bread Journey

Mix dough → Autolyse (optional) → Knead to build gluten → Add salt/fat/flavour → Bulk ferment → Shape → Proof → Score (optional) → Bake → Rest → Eat!

Ballpark protein percentages in flour

Cake/pastry flour – 7–9%

Plain flour – 9–11%

'00' flour – 10–12%

Semolina – 12–13%

Strong bread flour – 12–15%

To transform potential gluten into actual gluten, you need to add water. When you add water to flour, two handy little proteins get to work. The glutenin and gliadin proteins are what give your dough stretch and strength. Once hydrated, they unravel and start to bond with one another, creating a network of strong, stretchy gluten. This is a natural process and gluten development doesn't need any more than a splash of water to occur (this is how no-knead breads work!),

FLOUR & WATER

but it does take a while. We can accelerate the process via kneading, squashing, stretching and agitating the dough, rubbing the proteins up against one another and forcing them to bond faster.

Gluten development isn't always desirable. Gluten adds chew and stretch to bakes so for something like a cookie or a shortbread, where you want the texture to be crumbly and melting, the aim is to create just enough gluten to hold everything together, but not so much as to make the bake chewy or tough. Using a 'soft' flour helps with this, but you'll also notice that when you incorporate the flour in these recipes, you're instructed to mix (or knead!) until everything is just combined and homogenous.

The aim of the game when making any bread is to strike a balance between how much fermentation you encourage (how much flavour and rise the yeast will give you) and gluten development, encouraging the dough to develop enough strength to actually hold on to all that air you've created with your fermentation.

Autolyse

(aw-toe-leez) What is it? It's an optional extra step in breadmaking when the flour is hydrated a day ahead of adding any other ingredients. Sometimes a little yeast is added too, but the main goal is to allow the flour and water to combine, and the flour to fully hydrate. This can take anywhere between 20 and 60 minutes. The autolyse process gives your dough improved strength and texture, and encourages a slower fermentation, improving flavour. It also drastically reduces the kneading time and makes any shaping much easier.

YEAST AND DOUGH FERMENTATION

Generally speaking, without yeast, breads lack rise and that funky, fermented flavour. You can make leavened bread without yeast, like soda bread, but we're sticking with yeast here. We'll also be using dried yeast rather than the fresh stuff favoured by commercial bakers. This is purely down to what is easily accessible – you can buy fresh baker's yeast, but it expires (dies) pretty quickly. Dried yeast comes in two forms: instant and active. I favour the instant stuff as it reduces faff in a recipe. You can add it directly to a dough mix and it'll spring into action. Active dried yeast requires activation before you mix it through a dough.

When you add instant yeast to a dough and hydrate it, it comes to life and starts looking for food (sugar/carbohydrates). The yeast eats the sugar and begins creating by-products that are essential to breadmaking – it chucks out CO_2 gas which, gives the dough lift and life. If allowed to proof long enough (a cold, overnight proof in the fridge) it'll run out of oxygen and begin to produce funky, fermented flavour compounds plus a bit of ethanol (alcohol). If you've ever left a dough in the fridge for a little too long, it might smell a little boozy and sour – well that's the ethanol! It's also what gives sourdough its signature sour flavour. As the yeast causes the dough to rise, we knead and deflate the dough as we work with it. Luckily for us, the yeast continues to work away, and you can deflate and proof dough a handful of times before the yeast is exhausted and can't carry on.

It's important to remember that the amount of yeast you're adding to your dough just dictates how long the cycle of proofing will take. The more yeast you add, the quicker the ferment. Even if you add just a tiny amount of yeast, the same fermentation process happens, it just takes much longer. Most standard bread recipes look for a bulk proof of about 1 hour and a secondary proof of 30–45 minutes. A standard measure to achieve this is 7g of instant yeast to 500g of flour (hence the existence of those little 7g sachets). The baker's percentage sits between 1 and 2% and this favours speed over flavour. BLT Bread (page 154) sits in this category and can be made in a handful of hours. The slower the fermentation (the proof) the better and more complex the flavour. For breads like baguettes we make a pre-ferment, a long overnight proof that builds that lactic, funky flavour we can then combine with a fresh dough to whip up the bread. Focaccia uses very little yeast but ferments for a long time and takes a day or two to make. The longer the ferment, the more time the yeast has to produce flavour compounds.

FLOUR & WATER

Always check the use-by date on your yeast. If you don't, you'll risk a few wasted hours waiting for a dough to rise that was never going to. It's almost as disappointing as making bread and forgetting to put the salt in, which happens more than you'd think in professional kitchens. If you're using one of the tins of yeast, write the date you opened it on the side. If it was over 6 months ago, it's time for a new tin.

> **Test your strength**
>
> When making bread, a great way to test the strength is to stretch the dough out super thin like a drum skin. If your dough is weak, it'll tear almost immediately. Knead it some more and it'll stretch a little but still tear when put it under a little pressure. Your dough has developed lots of gluten when you can stretch it and it creates a thin, almost transparent 'windowpane'.

HYDRATION AND BAKER'S PERCENTAGES

Managing hydration is critical when you're making bread. Hydration refers to exactly how much water or liquid you're adding to your flour and will ultimately dictate the texture of your dough. The more water you add, the slacker and looser the dough will be. For a classic white loaf, the hydration sits at about 60–65%, so for every 500g of flour used, you'd add about 300g of water. For a focaccia, the hydration is far higher, typically closer to 80–90%, whereas lower hydration doughs result in denser, chewier breads with a tighter crumb (smaller holes) like pretzels and bagels – picture a focaccia, a much wetter dough, with huge bubbles and an erratic, unpredictable crumb. If you want a super tender dough or batter, you can use alcohol to hydrate your flour. The Fritto Misto recipe on page 182 uses vodka and beer to inhibit gluten development to make a shatteringly crisp, tender batter – smart!

A handy way to look at breadmaking (and baking in general) is to break down recipes into percentages. This allows you to decode what's going on and understand how different ratios of ingredients affect the texture, flavour and colour of your final product. It also makes scaling recipes up or down really simple, and you can play with the percentages yourself. The percentages are always determined by their relative proportion to the total amount of flour. Flour is always 100%, then the other ingredients follow. I've popped a few of the recipes into the percentage table below to demonstrate how the different ingredients increase and decrease in percentage.

ADDING FAT AND ENRICHING DOUGHS

An enriched bread dough is one made with any combination of added fat, sugar and dairy. If you add extra sugar, butter, oil, eggs etc. to a dough, bang, it's officially enriched. In contrast to simpler, lean doughs, baking the enriched variety can be a little intimidating. Brioche can be a sticky customer, doughs can split (just like mayonnaise or chocolate), they can be a nightmare to shape and building a good gluten structure can be a devil. When you're making bread, goal number one is to develop a good, strong gluten structure. Enriched doughs require a very strong gluten network to accept and hold on to all of the extra fat and sugar. Adding fats and sugars will act as 'shorteners', i.e. they shorten the gluten chains within your dough, weakening the structure. A good example of where shortening is used to change texture is shortbread (the clue's in the name here, folks). Shortbread has a very high fat content (butter) and the dough is worked as little as possible in order to prevent lots of gluten development. This results in a delicate, crumbly, buttery, 'short' texture. The difference between shortbread and other enriched bakes (like brioche) is that shortbread isn't leavened (made with yeast or other significant raising agent) so doesn't require that strong network of gluten. Enriched

	FLOUR	WATER	YEAST	SALT	SUGAR	OIL
BLT Bread	100%	65%	1.2%	2.4%	1.2%	N/A
Foolproof Focaccia	100%	90%	0.8%	2%	N/A	3%
French Baguette	100%	69%	1.3%	2.25%	N/A	N/A

doughs need to have sufficient structural strength to hold on to all of the air bubbles the yeast will provide. Think of it as an inflating balloon: if the balloon is very weak, as more and more air is introduced, it'll just pop. Similarly, without enough structural strength, as the dough proofs and grows, it won't be able to support itself and will simply collapse. As soon as you start adding different bits and bobs to a complex, super strong, gluten-rich dough, it'll change straight away. When you make bread, the moment you add any sugar and butter to the dough, you slacken everything out, then have to briefly re-work the dough to bring it back.

BAKING AND STEAM

We've arrived at the best bit – baking. You want to bake hot, hotter than you think. Most of the bread recipes in this chapter call for temperatures north of 220°C fan/240°C/460°F/gas mark 9; this is to encourage the bread to puff and 'spring' as it hits the oven. You've created a big, puffy, fermented ball of dough and it still has heaps of potential to grow. As it meets the heat of the oven, the air trapped inside the bread will expand and 'spring', causing the bread to rapidly expand. The first 5–10 minutes of a bake are crucial to the end texture. If the bread springs and expands properly, the crumb and interior texture will be open and even. The role of steam in the bake is to prevent something called case hardening. Case hardening is when the outside of the dough sets too hard, too soon in the oven, before the interior can fully puff and aerate, inhibiting the rise of the dough. Adding moisture to the outside of your bake helps keep the elasticity in the dough for longer, allowing for more puff. You can chuck a cup of water into the oven, add a few ice cubes or even fill a spray bottle with water and then use it to spritz the dough as it bakes.

SHAPING AND SCORING

Baking in a tin is a lovely way to bake if you're relatively new to the bread game. The more you bake bread, the more you come to realise that more than half the battle is dough shaping. Even baking a simple loaf of bread in a tin requires a few precise movements, tactical turns and gluten manipulation. When you shape a loaf, you arrange the gluten network into a tense ball or log that will expand in a controlled, even way. The goal is to create surface tension. More on that in the recipes...

In a couple of the recipes, I ask you to score your bread. What does this mean, and why should you do it? When bread hits the oven, it expands. The gluten structure that is holding on to all that air will expand too, to such a degree that it'll need to break to allow the bread to rise in the oven properly. When you score the dough, you basically tell the bread where to break and control exactly how it expands. You also create what bakers call an 'ear' – a crispy edge where you slashed the dough. To score like a pro, pick up a baker's lame. They're dead cheap and are a superior scoring tool.

BONUS: ADDING FLAVOUR

If you want to add more flavour to your baking, beyond the funky fermented notes that yeast brings, you can take a few different routes. You can infuse your water with flavour, you can add mix-ins like herbs, spices or seeds through the dough, add them to the top like you would a bagel or sesame bun, or add a soak or a flavoured fat (oil/butter) after baking. If you're adding mix-ins, you need to let the dough relax before adding them. If you go in too soon while the dough is super tight and tense from kneading, the gluten network will resist the new ingredients, and you won't have a nice even mix. Give it a few minutes to slacken out, chuck the garnish in, and gently mix until it's incorporated. If properly mixed, you'll see that the seeds or chives just below the surface of the dough are shrouded with a super thin, almost transparent layer of dough. This is a great sign – it shows the dough has sufficient gluten development and your flavourful bits have been incorporated nicely.

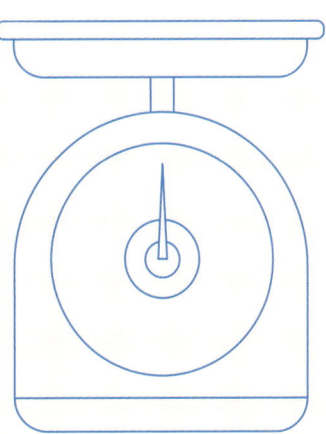

FLOUR & WATER

BLT Bread

- MAKES: 1 LOAF
- EYES CLOSED
- VE
- TOTAL: 1 HOUR, PLUS PROOFING
- PREP: 15 MINS, PLUS PROOFING
- COOK: 45 MINS

This is the only place to start when it comes to classic leavened loaves. Good ol' fashioned white bread. I like to call it BLT bread, because that's the best thing you can do with it. This recipe covers the basics of breadmaking and will deliver you a perfect, comforting loaf of bread to share with those you hold dearest.

500g strong white bread flour, plus a little extra for dusting
6g instant dried yeast
6g caster sugar
12g fine sea salt
350g room-temperature water
olive oil

> **CHEF'S TIP**
> Bake the crust dark! Colour = flavour and a pale loaf is a sad loaf. Be brave, bake until your loaf is a deep, mahogany brown.

> **SHOOT FROM THE HIP**
> You can bake this without a tin, if you like. Simply follow the shaping steps and transfer to an oval-shaped piece of parchment paper rather than the tin. Preheat a heavy baking tray upside down in the oven. Slide the loaf on the parchment onto the baking tray and follow the baking instructions.

1 Tip the flour, yeast, sugar and salt into a bowl and mix together. Add the water and use your hand to combine the ingredients, massaging the mix and making sure every bit of dried flour is incorporated into the dough. Once you've got a shaggy dough, tip it out onto a clean work surface and begin to knead. Knead for 5–6 minutes until you have a smooth-ish ball. Cover and rest for 5 minutes.

2 Once rested, knead again for another 5 minutes until you have a super smooth, supple dough. The dough will still be quite sticky, so lift it up and slap it down onto your surface then fold it over itself, repeating this action until you have smoother dough that's a little easier to handle. Shape the dough into a ball, lightly oil a clean bowl and drop the dough inside. Cover with cling film or a damp cloth and prove at room temperature until doubled in size. This will take between 50 and 75 minutes, so keep an eye on it.

3 To shape the dough, tip it out onto a lightly floured surface. Encourage the dough into a rough square shape, being careful not to fully deflate it but knocking it back a little. Grab the top two corners and fold them into the middle of the dough. Now grab the top of the dough and gently roll it down into the middle of the dough, forming a rough log shape. Be sure to create a little tension in the surface of the loaf as you go. Imagine you're rolling up a sleeping bag or carpet. Once it's a rough log shape, drop it into a 2lb/900g loaf tin. Cover with an oiled piece of cling film and proof at room temperature until doubled in size. This will take 45–60 minutes.

4 Preheat the oven to 235°C fan/255°C/480°F/gas mark 10. Slide a baking tray into the bottom of the oven to preheat.

5 Once fully proofed, remove the cling film, grab a sieve, add a few spoons of flour and dust a fine layer over the top of the loaf. Use a very sharp knife or a razor blade to cut a slash straight down the middle of the dough from top to bottom, roughly 1cm deep. Don't hesitate here or saw at the dough with your knife. Cut in one smooth, confident movement.

6 Place the loaf into the oven and chuck a couple of ice cubes onto the preheated tray. Bake for 14–15 minutes before reducing the oven temperature to 170°C fan/190°C/375°F/gas mark 5 for another 25–30 minutes until the crust is deep golden brown. Remove from the oven and allow to sit in the tin for 1 minute before tipping out and cooling on a wire rack. Cool for at least 45 minutes before slicing to allow the crumb to set. If you slice too soon, you'll squash your loaf!

Stuffable Pitta Breads

- 🍴 MAKES: 8 PITTA
- 👨‍🍳 EYES CLOSED
- ✅ VE
- ⏱ TOTAL: 35 MINS, PLUS PROOFING
- 🪵 PREP: 20 MINS, PLUS PROOFING
- 🍳 COOK: 15 MINS

There are some things in this world that are infinitely better when they're homemade. The pitta bread you buy in the shops is, for the most part, dry, crumbly rubbish. These are easily some of the easiest breads to make, and demonstrate a few foundational flatbread-style baking techniques. Once you've whipped up your dough, you can experiment with how thick or thin you make your pitta, how wide you roll them out and how you cook them. All of these little variations make a subtle difference to the end product and are a cheap, easy and tasty way to experiment. I love to stuff my pittas with Za'atar Chicken Livers (page 122), tahini sauce (page 72) and Chopped Salad (page 72).

500g strong white bread flour, plus extra for dusting
10g instant dried yeast
10g fine sea salt
20g caster sugar
300g room-temperature water

> **SHOOT FROM THE HIP**
> A nice way to add a nutty flavour to pitta bread is to use a percentage of wholemeal flour. You'll still want to have a portion of strong white bread flour in there so the bread has plenty of gluten, but a 60:40 (white:wholemeal) split is lovely.

1 Put the flour in a large bowl and mix through the yeast, salt and sugar. Tip in the water and use your hand (held in a claw shape) to incorporate the water into the dry ingredients. Mix until you have a rough, shaggy dough. Tip the dough out onto a clean work surface and knead for 8–10 minutes. The dough will be a little sticky to begin with, but don't be tempted to add any more flour as we've got our hydration dialled in. As you knead, the dough will become less and less sticky as it gains strength.

2 After 8–10 minutes of kneading, the dough should be smooth and supple. If you shape it into a rough ball and apply some tension to the top of the dough, it shouldn't tear, rather it should stretch and mould to your movement. If you see the dough tearing, knead it for another couple of minutes and then try again! Once you're happy with where you are, shape the dough into a ball, add to a lightly greased, clean bowl and cover. Proof at room temperature for 40–50 minutes until doubled in size.

3 Preheat the oven to the hottest setting (250–275°C fan/270–295°C/500+°F/gas mark 10+) and put a heavy baking tray upside down in the bottom of the oven to preheat.

4 Once doubled in size, pull the dough out of the bowl and use a bench scraper to divide it into 100–120g portions: you should have eight portions. Flatten each piece out into a disc then carefully fold the outside edge into the centre, working your way around the perimeter of the disc. Once you've brought the whole outside edge in, it should start to bunch into a ball. Flip it over so the seam is facing down, and use your hand in a claw to roll the dough in circles, using the friction of the dough against the work surface to tighten up the ball. Repeat with the remaining dough balls, cover them and leave to relax for 10–12 minutes.

5 After they've had time to relax, dust the balls with a little flour and use a rolling pin to roll the balls out into rough circles 16–18cm across and until they're roughly the thickness of a pound coin (2–3mm). I roll them from the middle out, turning the dough 90 degrees with every roll, until I have a shape I'm happy with! Don't worry, these don't need to be perfect.

6 Lift your pitta off the surface and carefully lay it onto the preheated tray in the oven. Close the door and cook for 1 minute before flipping over and cooking for another 30 seconds or so. Keep flipping until the pitta has puffed up like a balloon. Once it's puffed, it's cooked! Remove from the oven and wrap in a clean tea towel. Let the pitta steam in the towel for 2–3 minutes before tearing open and stuffing with whatever your heart desires.

Foolproof Focaccia

- MAKES: 1 LARGE FOCACCIA
- EYES CLOSED
- VE
- TOTAL: 50 MINS, PLUS PROOFING
- PREP: 25 MINS, PLUS PROOFING
- COOK: 25 MINS

This recipe is so easy and almost, just almost, impossible to mess up. I say that with confidence, as there's little to no kneading, no technical shaping or complex dough-making here. Whipping up this focaccia is as simple as mixing the ingredients, folding it over itself a handful of times and leaving it alone until it has that signature bubbly texture. This is free-form breadbaking at its gnarly, wild best!

450g water
4g instant dried yeast
500g '00' flour
15g olive oil, plus extra for drizzling
10g fine sea salt
3 rosemary sprigs
flaky sea salt

> **CHEF'S TIP**
> When handling and folding your dough, always oil or wet your hands to stop things getting too sticky. This is an example of a very high-hydration dough. It's become more and more trendy to work with doughs that have higher hydrations for a moist and irregular crumb. They can be a devil to work with, but thanks to this focaccia's rustic nature, you needn't worry about making anything uniform.

1 Add 420g of the water to a large bowl. Tip in the yeast and flour and bring together with your hands until there are no dry lumps of flour left in the bowl. Don't worry about kneading too much here, just make sure you've got all the flour hydrated.

2 Cover the bowl with cling film, or pop it inside something airtight, and leave for 1 hour at room temperature to autolyse. Once it's had an hour or so, mix the remaining water with the olive oil and fine sea salt. Tip the mixture over your dough and use your hands to squash it into the dough. It'll look a bit weird to begin with, but keep mixing until the dough comes back together.

3 Turn the dough out onto a clean work surface and give it a brief knead – it will be sticky but don't worry. Use a bench scraper to scoop the dough back up and into a clean bowl. Let it hang out for 30 minutes then give it a fold. Dunk your hands into cold water or rub with olive oil, reach under the top side of the dough, grab it and stretch it up and over the main body of the dough. Turn the dough 90 degrees and repeat the fold again. Complete four folds, one on each side. This counts as one turn. Leave the dough for another 30 minutes, then fold again. Let it rest for 30 minutes before completing another turn.

4 Cover and place the dough into the fridge overnight for a long, slow proof. If you want same-day bread, you can let the dough hang out at room temperature, and it will be ready to bake in roughly 2–3 hours.

5 When ready to bake, line a roughly 20 x 35cm baking tray with parchment paper and a glug of olive oil. Shape the dough into the lined tray and carefully encourage it to fill the tray. Try not to knock much air out of the dough. If it doesn't want to stretch and keeps shrinking back, cover and leave for 10 minutes, then try again. Cover and leave to proof at room temperature until the dough is super puffy again. If shaping straight after the folds, this will take 2 hours. If after time in the fridge, this will take roughly 20–30 minutes.

6 Preheat the oven to 230°C fan/250°C/480°F/gas mark 10.

7 Strip the rosemary leaves from the sprigs and sprinkle them all over the dough with a generous shower of flaky sea salt. Drizzle with olive oil and lightly wet your hands. Use your fingers to dimple the dough all over, being careful not to over-press the dough.

8 Slide into the oven for 20–25 minutes until golden brown and baked through. For an extra crispy crust, I remove it from the tin and slide it back into the oven directly onto the shelf for 7–10 minutes, until golden all over.

Semolina Flatbreads with Scapece

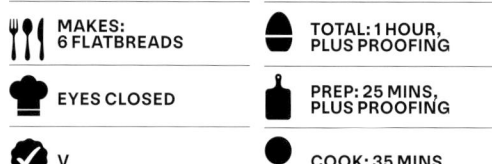

MAKES: 6 FLATBREADS

EYES CLOSED

V

TOTAL: 1 HOUR, PLUS PROOFING

PREP: 25 MINS, PLUS PROOFING

COOK: 35 MINS

It's good to have a flatbread recipe in the locker. These are similar in construction to the pitta breads on page 156, but have a slightly higher hydration and are gently fried in olive oil. The resulting bread is super soft, pillowy and has a lovely chewy, crunchy texture thanks to the semolina. It's a really versatile flatbread and can be topped or served with a whole host of different garnishes.

FOR THE SEMOLINA FLATBREADS

- 320g water
- 7g instant dried yeast
- 8g caster sugar
- 400g strong white bread flour
- 100g semolina, plus extra for dusting
- 10g fine sea salt
- olive oil

FOR THE SCAPECE

- 2–3 courgettes
- ½ garlic clove
- 15g mint
- 2 tbsp red wine vinegar
- 250g ricotta cheese
- extra virgin olive oil
- flaky sea salt
- black pepper

1 In a large mixing bowl, combine the water, yeast and sugar and stir to combine. Tip in the flour, semolina and salt and use your hand to mix the ingredients together, making sure all the flour is hydrated and there are no dry spots remaining. Once you've formed a shaggy dough, turn the dough out onto a clean surface and knead for 8–10 minutes. As you work the dough, notice the texture change from shaggy, to smooth but rocky, to smooth and springy. You can also achieve this in a stand mixer fitted with a dough hook attachment.

2 Rest the dough for 5 minutes then briefly knead it again for 2 minutes before shaping it into a ball and placing in a clean bowl. Cover and proof at room temperature until roughly doubled in size – this will take 45 minutes–1 hour, depending on the temperature of your room.

3 Once proofed, knock the air out of the dough and divide it into 6 equal pieces. Form the dough into little balls (page 170) and place onto a tray dusted with semolina. Cover loosely with an oiled piece of cling film, then chuck them in the fridge and forget about them for a day or two.

4 While the bread proofs, make the scapece. Use a sharp knife or mandoline to cut the courgettes into 5mm-thick coins. Preheat a large frying pan over a medium-high heat and add a generous layer of olive oil. Once hot, working in batches, drop a handful of sliced courgettes in and swirl them around in the hot oil. Cook for 3–4 minutes, or until they're tender, starting to brown and look a little shrivelled. Pull from the hot oil and drain on kitchen paper. Repeat with the remaining courgettes.

5 Finely grate the garlic clove, pick the mint leaves from the stems and finely chop. Add to a medium mixing bowl along with a splash of olive oil and the vinegar. Tip in the fried courgettes and toss with the marinade. Season generously with salt and plenty of black pepper. Set aside.

6 When you're ready for a flatbread, preheat a large frying pan over a medium heat. Add a glug of oil, pull out a dough ball and stretch it out in plenty more semolina. Once the oil is shimmering, drop the heat to medium-low and carefully lower in the bread, laying it away from you. It should sizzle as it hits the oil. Cook for 2 minutes, shaking the pan to move the bread around for even colouration, before flipping it and cooking for another 2 minutes. Remove and transfer to a rack to cool a little. Cook as many breads as you like.

7 Tip the ricotta out onto a plate and dress with the fried, marinated courgettes. Serve with the flatbreads.

SHOOT FROM THE HIP
These breads work well with so many different toppings, dips and sides. Try fresh burrata, torn black olives and basil, roasted peaches, sherry vinegar and pancetta, or use them to wrap up a few Pomegranate Lamb Ribs (page 242).

NOTES
You can leave the dough balls in the fridge for up to 3 days. They'll become funkier and more complex as they ferment, and even when a little over-proofed, they are still delicious when freshly cooked. Whip up a batch and make them through the week.

Garlicky Spinach & Cheese Pide

MAKES: 5 PIDE
EYES CLOSED
TOTAL: 45 MINS, PLUS RESTING
PREP: 25 MINS, PLUS RESTING
COOK: 20 MINS

I was in Istanbul when I tried 'Turkish pizza' for the first time. Ordered to go, when the doorbell rang, instead of a giant stack of square boxes, what entered were long thin ones, stuffed with delicious, dough-boats, cheese heavy and topped with sucuk (a Turkish sausage similar to chorizo), garlicky spinach, peppers or fresh cut tomatoes. They're dead easy to make at home, use a very low-effort dough and don't require a raging-hot pizza oven to bake to crispy, chewy perfection.

FOR THE DOUGH

375g strong white bread flour, plus extra for dusting

4g dried yeast

½ tsp fine sea salt

½ tsp caster sugar

220g warm water

2 tbsp olive oil

FOR THE SPINACH CHEESE FILLING

4 spring onions

200g feta

250g low-moisture mozzarella

25g parmesan

1 tbsp Aleppo pepper

1 garlic clove

200g baby spinach

1 lemon

olive oil

FOR THE GARLIC BUTTER

100g unsalted butter

1 garlic clove, crushed

1 rosemary sprig

1 To make the dough, mix the flour, yeast, salt and sugar in a bowl. Pour the warm water into the bowl along with the olive oil. Mix together into a shaggy dough then tip out onto a clean work surface and knead for 6–7 minutes until you have a smooth, springy dough. Divide into 115–120g pieces then shape into balls (see page 170), add to a lightly greased tray or airtight container, well spaced, cover and pop into the fridge overnight.

2 To make the filling, trim and thinly slice the spring onions and tip into a bowl. Crumble in the feta and coarsely grate in the mozzarella and parmesan. Add the Aleppo pepper and mix. Peel and thinly slice the garlic clove. Place a large sauté pan over a medium heat and add a generous glug of olive oil. Add the garlic and sizzle for a minute, then add the spinach leaves with a tiny splash of water. Toss and turn the leaves in the garlicky oil until fully wilted. Use the back of a spoon to squeeze out as much water as you can from the spinach before finishing with a little grated lemon zest and juice.

3 To make the garlic butter, drop the butter, garlic and rosemary into a small pan and place over a medium heat. Allow the butter to melt and start to sizzle before removing from the heat. Set aside for the garlic and rosemary to infuse for 5 minutes or so.

4 Preheat the oven to the hottest setting (250–275°C fan/270–295°C/500+°F/gas mark 10+) and pop a large baking tray upside down in the bottom of the oven. If you have a pizza oven, preheat it to about 350°C.

5 Dust a dough ball with a little flour and, using a rolling pin, roll it out into a long, thin oval shape. Grab a handful of the cheese mixture and run it down the centre of the oval, leaving a 2–3cm border. Top with a few pinches of the garlicky spinach. Fold the edges of the dough up and over the cheese mix, leaving just the centre exposed. At either end, pinch about 5cm of the dough together to form a seam on top of the bread. Now grab the ends of the pride and stretch it out, giving it a little lift as you do so, slapping it onto the work surface. Repeat with the remaining dough, spinach and cheese.

6 Use a thin baking tray or a baking peel to manoeuvre the pide. Working in batches, slide the pide into the oven onto the preheated tray and bake for 10–12 minutes. I can usually cook about three at a time. If using a pizza oven, it'll take about half the time. Whip out of the oven and brush the freshly baked dough with the garlic butter.

Sheet-tray Pizza alla Puttanesca

- SERVES: 4–6
- EYES CLOSED
- P
- TOTAL: 1 HOUR, PLUS PROOFING
- PREP: 35 MINS, PLUS PROOFING
- COOK: 25–30 MINS

A no-knead, do-it-with-your-eyes-closed kind of bake, a crispy, light dough topped with a no-cook sauce and a handful of delicious toppings, and a great way to approach pizza making with a home oven. The base dough recipe is very similar to the Foolproof Focaccia (page 158), just with a slightly lower hydration percentage and with an abbreviated process.

FOR THE DOUGH

390g room-temperature water
2g instant dried yeast
500g '00' flour
8g fine sea salt
10g olive oil, plus extra for drizzling
3 tbsp unsalted butter, softened

FOR THE TOPPING

1 garlic clove
1 tsp dried oregano
1 tsp dried chilli flakes
400g good-quality tinned chopped tomatoes
250g low-moisture mozzarella
½ red onion
25g nonpareille capers
40g good-quality black olives, pitted
12 tinned anchovies
12 boquerones-style pickled anchovies
pinch of fresh oregano leaves
extra virgin olive oil
fine sea salt
black pepper

1. Starting the evening before you want to bake your pizza, pour 360g of the water into a bowl, add the yeast and flour and use your hand to bring it together. Make sure all of the flour is hydrated and there are no dry spots of flour anywhere. Cover and set aside for 1 hour at room temperature to autolyse.

2. Mix the remaining water with the salt and olive oil. Once the dough has rested, tip the mixture over the top and use your hands to cut it into the dough. Cover again and let rest for 15 minutes. Dunk your hands into cold water or rub with olive oil, reach under the top side of the dough, grab it and stretch it up and over the main body of the dough. Turn the dough 90 degrees and repeat the fold again. Complete four folds and let the dough rest again for 15–20 minutes. Fold the dough again then turn it out onto the work surface. Shape into a ball, then transfer to a lightly oiled bowl. Cover and place in the fridge overnight.

3. Preheat the oven to 250°C fan/270°C/500°F/gas mark 10. Grab a rimmed baking tray that's roughly 40 x 30cm. Spread the softened butter across the tray then drizzle with a little olive oil. Remove the dough from the fridge and lift it out of the bowl. Transfer to the tray, drizzle generously with oil and use slightly oiled hands to press the dough evenly across the prepared tray. Cover loosely with cling film and let rest for 10–15 minutes.

4. While the dough rests, put the garlic clove, oregano and chilli flakes in a blender with 3 tablespoons of olive oil and blitz until the garlic is very finely chopped, then pour in the tomatoes. Season with salt and pulse the ingredients together to just mix them. Coarsely grate the mozzarella and finely dice the red onion.

5. Return to the dough and squash it right into the corners of the tray, making sure it's even all the way across. Pop any larger bubbles by tearing a little and press your fingers all over the dough to knock out as much as you can, leaving only a few tiny bubbles. Spoon a layer of the sauce over the pizza (you might not need it all) before topping with the cheese, diced onion, capers and olives.

6. Slide into the oven and bake for 20–25 minutes until golden and the cheese is melted and bubbling. Remove from the oven and add the anchovies, alternating between the two varieties. Transfer the pizza to a rack set over a tray and return to the oven for 3–5 minutes to crisp up the crust even more.

7. Let the pizza rest for 5 minutes before topping with the fresh oregano. Cut into squares with scissors and serve.

Bagels, Oniony Cream Cheese & Hot Honey

- MAKES: 9 BAGELS
- TOTAL: 75 MINS, PLUS PROOFING
- ROLL YOUR SLEEVES UP
- PREP: 50 MINS, PLUS PROOFING
- V
- COOK: 25 MINS

Most home cooks take one look at a bagel with its shiny crust, unique shape and signature chewy texture and think 'that must be hard to make'. Wrong! Bagels are easy to make, shape and bake and they're hard to beat fresh from the oven. As a Londoner who used to live in Brooklyn, I've eaten my fair share of bagels (or beigels). Whether it's a salt beef on Brick Lane or a BEC (bacon, egg and cheese) from the bodega, a good bagel never fails to deliver the pleasure only a baked good can.

FOR THE BAGELS

- 500g strong white bread flour
- 10g instant dried yeast
- 20g dark brown sugar
- 10g fine sea salt
- 290g warm water (about 30°C)
- 75–100g bagel seasoning (sesame seeds, poppy seeds, everything mix)
- light olive oil

FOR THE BOIL

- 2 litres water
- 100g black treacle
- 10g bicarbonate of soda

TO SERVE

- 6 spring onions
- 280g cream cheese
- hot honey
- flaky sea salt
- black pepper

1 Tip the flour and yeast into a bowl with the sugar and fine sea salt. Blend the dry ingredients together before pouring in the warm water. Use your hand to bring the ingredients together into a shaggy dough and keep mixing until there are no dry spots left. Tip the dough out onto your work surface and knead for 8–10 minutes until it is smooth, springy and has lots of strength. You can test this a few ways, but my go-to is the windowpane test (page 152).

2 Once you're happy with the gluten development, pop the dough into a bowl lightly greased with olive oil and cover. Allow to prove at room temperature for about 1 hour, or until doubled in size. Once proved, you either knock the dough back, reshape into a ball and slide into the fridge for 12–24 hours to cold ferment, or go ahead and shape.

3 Once ready to shape, tip the dough back out onto your worktop and divide into 90–100g pieces. Flatten each piece into a disc and form into a ball (page 170).

4 Line a couple of trays with little oiled squares of parchment paper and set the bagel balls out on them to double in size. Make sure you give them plenty of space to grow and cover them loosely with plastic wrap. They should take about an hour to get super puffy, but if you've gone for the cold ferment option, they might take closer to two to get there. When your bagels are just about proved, preheat the oven to 210°C fan/230°C/445°F/gas mark 8 and set up a tray lined with parchment.

5 Once proofed, gently scoop the balls up and use your thumb and forefinger to poke a hole through the centre, being careful not to de-gas the surrounding dough. You can then gently open up the bagel hole to your desired size with your fingers.

6 Add the water for the boil to a saucepan along with the treacle and bicarbonate of soda. Whisk to combine and place over a high heat. Bring to the boil then carefully lower in your proved bagels on the paper, peeling it off once they're floating. Cook for about 1 minute on each side before scooping them out with a slotted spoon or spider. Dab them dry and transfer to the lined baking tray.

7 Sprinkle with bagel seasoning at this point, while the bagels are still a little damp, so the seasonings adhere. Slide into the oven and bake for 15–17 minutes, until a deep golden brown. Whip them out and allow to cool on a rack for at least 15–20 minutes.

8 Thinly slice the spring onions and combine with the cream cheese in a bowl. Season with a little salt and lots of black pepper. Split the bagels in half and toast, if you like. Spread with cream cheese and top with hot honey.

Olive Oil Buns, Grilled Mortadella & Taqueria Pickles

MAKES: 8 BUNS

ROLL YOUR SLEEVES UP

TOTAL: 55 MINS, PLUS PROOFING

PREP: 40 MINS, PLUS PROOFING

COOK: 15 MINS

Having a good bun recipe up your sleeve is very handy, and this is my go-to. This recipe is adapted from a classic brioche dough. I love the flavour the olive oil brings, and the resulting bun is a little lighter than its buttery counterpart. There are a few techniques at play here, and they can be a little finicky, but once you've turned out your first batch of squishy, shiny, rich olive oil buns, you'll be rushing to make your next. You can stuff these with anything your heart desires, and they of course make amazing burger buns. Whip up a batch and use them for the cheeseburger recipe on page 196 or do as I do and fill them with potato chips, grilled mortadella, mustard and heaps of my favourite Taqueria-style pickles!

FOR THE OLIVE OIL BUNS

150g room-temperature water
110g whole milk, plus a splash extra
3 whole eggs
10g dried yeast
500g strong white bread flour, plus extra for dusting
15g fine sea salt
12g caster sugar
50g extra virgin olive oil

1 Tip the water, milk, 2 eggs and the yeast into a bowl and use a fork to beat everything together. Once mixed, add the flour, salt and sugar and use your hand to bring everything together into a shaggy dough in the bowl. You should have no dry lumps or bits of flour left in the bowl; keep working in the bowl until you get there. Once your dough has come together, tip it out onto a clean work surface and knead for 7–8 minutes, or until the dough begins to develop a smooth, tacky texture. It'll start out very sticky, but don't worry, the more you work it, the easier it is to handle.

2 Once kneaded, toss the dough back into the bowl and cover with a damp cloth or tea towel and leave the dough to rest for 15 minutes or so. The gluten will relax a little and allow you to incorporate the olive oil much easier. Add half of the olive oil to the bowl with the dough and start cutting it into the dough with your hands. It'll look pretty wild to begin with, but keep working the dough in the bowl and it'll eventually come together. Once the olive oil has been incorporated into the dough, add the other half and repeat. Knead for another 7–8 minutes until you have a super smooth, elastic dough. Form into a ball, pop into a clean bowl, cover and let proof at room temperature for 1–1½ hours until doubled in size.

3 While the dough proofs, make the pickles. Peel the carrot. Use a mandoline or sharp knife to cut the carrot and jalapeños into 1cm-thick slices. Peel and slice the onion and garlic, using a mandoline to cut the onion into very thin rounds and thinly slice the garlic. Preheat a medium frying pan over a medium heat. Add a shot of olive oil and, once hot, add the carrots and cook for 2–3 minutes until beginning to soften a little. Tip in the onion, garlic and jalapeños and toss together, cooking for 1–2 minutes until the onions are just starting to soften. Toss in the bay leaves (give them a scrunch beforehand), cumin seeds and oregano and cook for 1 minute, then add the vinegar, sugar, salt and 100ml of water. Bring to the boil, then reduce to a simmer and cook for 3–4 minutes before tipping into a container and allowing to cool. These will sit in your fridge happily for a week or so.

Continued overleaf →

NOTE
I discovered these addictive pickled carrots and jalapeños on the counter of a torta stand in Oaxaca. I'm yet to find a sandwich pickle I like better. Usually made with white vinegar and very little sugar, I like the extra funk that apple cider vinegar brings to the recipe and brown sugar rounds the whole lot out.

CHEF'S TIP
These buns freeze really well. Simply cool after baking, add to a sandwich bag and freeze. Defrost at room temperature then refresh in a warm oven.

FLOUR & WATER

FOR THE TAQUERIA PICKLES

1 carrot

5 fresh jalapeños

1 white onion

3 garlic cloves

2 bay leaves

1 tsp cumin seeds

1 tsp dried oregano

250ml apple cider vinegar

50g light brown sugar

1 tsp fine sea salt

extra virgin olive oil

TO SERVE

18 slices of mortadella

5–6 slices Swiss or provolone cheese

2 tbsp mayonnaise

2 tbsp Dijon mustard

100g salted Chipsticks

4 Once proofed, tip the dough out onto a lightly floured surface and knock the air out of it. Cut into eight 100–120g pieces then shape into balls. Flatten each piece out into a disc and carefully fold the outside edge into the centre, working your way around the perimeter of the disc. Once you've brought the whole outside edge in, it should start to bunch into a ball. Flip over so the seam is facing down and use your hand in a claw to roll the dough in circles, using the friction of the work surface to tighten up the ball.

5 Line a couple of baking trays with parchment paper and place the little dough balls on there with plenty of space between them. Cover loosely with cling film or a damp towel and proof at room temperature until doubled in size – this will be a bit quicker than the bulk proof, taking only 30–40 minutes.

6 Preheat the oven to 180°C fan/200°C/400°F/gas mark 6. Beat the remaining egg with a splash of milk and brush the buns generously. You can cover the buns with seeds or spices at this point, if you like. Bake the buns in the oven for 12–15 minutes, or until puffed, golden and cooked through. Once baked, whip the buns out of the oven and allow them to cool for at least 15–20 minutes.

7 Place a pan over a medium heat and lay in your slices of mortadella in a few little piles. Cook for 2–3 minutes until crispy before flipping and topping with slices of cheese. Add a splash of the pickle brine then cover the pan to steam and melt the cheese. Combine the mayo and Dijon mustard. Split the buns open and spread over the Dijonnaise. Top with grilled mortadella, a handful of pickles and a handful of Chipsticks. Add a lid and devour.

SHOOT FROM THE HIP
You can flavour these buns with seeds or spices before baking. Sesame is a classic, but why not try an everything bagel-style crust. Either sprinkle the seeds or seasoning directly onto the egg wash or carefully roll the buns in the topping. Be generous, some will fall off during the bake.

English Muffins

- MAKES: 10 MUFFINS
- ROLL YOUR SLEEVES UP
- V
- TOTAL: 65 MINS, PLUS PROOFING
- PREP: 40 MINS, PLUS PROOFING
- COOK: 25 MINS

Just like pitta, crumpets or a French baguette, English muffins are a bread that blow the shop-bought rubbish out of the water and are best enjoyed fresh from the griddle. A light, enriched dough is rolled in polenta for a crunchy exterior, punched out into muffins and gently toasted on either side in olive oil. This is a bread that kicks off the baking in a pan and is then finished in the oven, building a different style of crust and interior crumb. Once cooked, these are pretty perfect with just about anything stuffed inside.

350g whole milk
10g instant dried yeast
25g caster sugar
500g strong white bread flour
12g fine sea salt
70g unsalted butter, softened
200g polenta or coarse semolina
olive oil

CHEF'S TIP

It's sometimes hard to be sure exactly where your muffins are at on the way to being cooked. To be sure, you can use a thermometer. Insert the probe into the middle of a grilled muffin and see if it needs to hit the oven or not. If the middle is 90°C or hotter, it's good to go; anything lower than that and it'll need a flash in the oven. No thermometer? Stick 'em into the oven, just to be safe.

1 Pour the milk into a small saucepan and place over a low heat, gently warming it to just below blood temperature. A good way to test this is with your little finger. You want the milk to feel a neutral temperature – not warm but not cold. If you have a thermometer, you're going for about 35°C.

2 Once warm, pour into the bowl of a stand mixer or mixing bowl, tip in the yeast and sugar and whisk together. Add the flour and salt and use the dough hook or your hand to bring the ingredients together into a shaggy dough. If using a stand mixer, knead for 3–4 minutes on low speed before incorporating the butter, a little at a time, making sure the last addition has been accepted by the dough before adding the next. You can do this by hand, too, just keep kneading and adding the butter a little at a time. Once your dough is smooth, shiny and has plenty of strength, form it into a ball, transfer to a clean bowl, cover and allow to proof at room temperature for 1–2 hours, or until doubled in size.

3 Preheat the oven to 180°C fan/200°C/400°F/gas mark 6.

4 Dust your worktop generously with polenta and tip the proofed dough out onto it, trying not to de-gas or knock all of the air out. Dust the top of the dough generously with more polenta then use a rolling pin to gently roll the dough out to a disc about 2–3cm thick. Take a 9–10cm ring cutter, punch out 10 muffins and transfer them to a polenta-lined tray. If you don't have a ring cutter, you can use a can, a glass or anything else that does the job. These are a rustic bake so make them rustic! Any trimmings can be re-rolled and punched out. Simply ball back up, briefly knead and then rest for 5–10 minutes before rolling and cutting. Cover the muffins with oiled cling film or a damp cloth and leave to proof again at room temperature for 15–20 minutes.

5 Preheat a large frying pan over a medium-low heat for a good 5–6 minutes. Add a layer of olive oil and allow it to warm up. Working in batches, lay the muffins into the warm olive oil. You should see and hear a mild sizzle, but nothing too crazy. If there is no sizzling at all, the oil isn't quite hot enough. Cook gently for 3–4 minutes, or until a deep golden brown on one side and then flip over. Keep an eye on things – it's easy to lose track of how hot the oil is, and these can burn quickly!

6 Transfer the griddled muffins to a rack set over a baking tray to rest. If you need to, you can slide them into the oven for 5–7 minutes to finish cooking (see Chef's Tip).

7 Once cooked, let the muffins hang out for 5 minutes before tearing them open and serving.

Chive Milk Bread

- MAKES: 1 LARGE LOAF
- DIG IN
- V
- TOTAL: 70 MINS
- PREP: 30 MINS
- COOK: 40 MINS

A fond food memory is frantically eating a hot slice of toasted, squishy white bread, covered with Marmite at the kitchen table before running to catch the school bus. This almost daily occurrence demonstrates my prioritising of food over pretty much anything, especially punctuality. There's something about the way white bread toasts that is irresistible, a wafer-thin layer of crisp shrouding a fluffy, steamy interior. When saturated with butter and Marmite it is about as good a breakfast as I can think of. I wanted to create a turbo version of that white bread – super fluffy, super indulgent – and add an extra flavour to ramp up the savoury edge. So, here's chive milk bread.

FOR THE TANGZHONG

70g whole milk

35g strong white bread flour

FOR THE MAIN DOUGH

250g whole milk

5g instant dried yeast

400g strong white bread flour, plus extra for dusting

7g fine sea salt

35g caster sugar

50g unsalted butter, softened

20g chives, finely chopped

FOR THE EGG WASH

2 egg yolks

splash of whole milk

1 Start by making the tangzhong. Put the milk and flour into a small saucepan and place over a medium heat. Whisk together into a loose paste and cook, whisking constantly, for 2–3 minutes, or until the mixture thickens into a gluey paste. Switch your whisk for a spatula and clean the sides of the pan, making sure you've got all that milk and flour incorporated.

2 Pour the milk for the dough into the pan with the tangzhong. If your milk is icy cold from the fridge, this will help take the chill off it so the yeast doesn't take for ever to wake up. Mix the tangzhong loosely through the milk before tipping in the yeast.

3 Add the milk mixture to the bowl of a stand mixer fitted with the dough hook attachment. Add the flour, salt and sugar and drop in the butter. Set your mixer to medium speed and mix for 6–7 minutes, or until you have a loose, slightly rough but homogenous dough. It won't be fully smooth and elastic at this point, as the gluten still needs to develop a little further. Let the dough hang out for 5 minutes before turning the machine to high speed. Let the dough go for another 5–6 minutes until super smooth, shiny and elastic. To test if the dough is ready, complete a windowpane test. Stretch a small piece of dough out from the main mass, if you can see light passing through without the dough breaking, you're in business. If it tears easily, keep kneading!

4 Once you're happy with the dough, let it rest again for 5 minutes before adding the chopped chives. Mix into the dough on low speed until fully incorporated. Cover the bowl with a damp cloth or piece of cling film and let the dough bulk proof (proof as one big, uninterrupted mass) at room temperature for 1–2 hours, or until super puffy and at least doubled in size.

5 Once your dough has had its first proof, it's time to shape it! Tip the dough out onto a lightly floured surface and divide it into three roughly equal pieces. Use a digital scale to weigh each piece and adjust if you need to, cutting a tiny bit off the biggest piece and adding to the smallest.

6 Now take each piece of dough and roll it into a long rectangle roughly 15cm wide and 40–50cm long. Fold each long side into the middle then roll up the strip from the bottom into a tight little spiral. Repeat with the remaining dough pieces so you have three little spirals.

7 Once you've got your three spirals of dough, nestle them into a buttered and lined loaf tin (roughly 20 x 13 x 10cm, but don't panic if it's a regular 2lb/900g loaf tin). You want to line all the sides with parchment so getting the loaf out later is super easy. Cover the dough with a damp cloth or cling film and proof again at room temperature for 1–2 hours until very puffy – it should at least reach the top of the tin!

8 Preheat the oven to 180°C fan/200°C/400°F/gas mark 6.

9 Mix the egg yolks and milk together and generously glaze the top of the loaf. Slide into the oven and bake for 35–40 minutes until puffed, golden and fully cooked. To check the loaf is cooked, you can insert a probe thermometer into the centre. If it hits 95°C, you're golden. If the loaf is browning too fast during the bake, loosely cover it with foil.

10 Once baked, allow the bread to cool for 10 minutes before removing it from the tin, and letting it cool completely on a rack. If you slice it too early, the bread won't be set and you won't have that perfect cloud-like fluff you want. Once cool, slice into wedges, toast and devour.

> **CHEF'S TIP**
> Don't add your mix-ins too early! This recipe is perfumed with the gentle, oniony hum of chives. These are added once your dough has established itself as a strong, smooth, stretchy mass. If you add them before you've built that network of gluten, the bits get smashed to pieces and the chives will almost purée as they get mixed through the dough. We want a light fluffy crumb, holding on to those delicate chopped chives. You also need to let the dough relax for 5–6 minutes before adding any bits. For more tips, head to page 153.

Baguettes & Homemade Salted Butter

- MAKES: 4 MEDIUM BAGUETTES
- DIG IN
- V
- TOTAL: 1 HOUR, PLUS PROOFING AND RESTING
- PREP: 35 MINS, PLUS PROOFING AND RESTING
- COOK: 25 MINS

What sticks out as the best bread I've ever had was one enjoyed at Raymond Blanc's lovely Le Manoir aux Quat' Saisons. It's a very old-school spot, with silver service and a classic bread service, with waiters waltzing around the room carrying a great big basket overflowing with a whole host of different breads. You could pick between granary, semolina, soda bread or a little baguette. I went for the baguette with salted butter. Bread and butter is a spartan offering, so the two must be perfect and, bravo Raymond, they were. I ate about five over the course of lunch and I've been trying to recreate them ever since. Here's my version. It's a pretty hands-off recipe, but it does take a bit planning, preferments, plus a few confident shaping moves. It's still easier than making sourdough, I promise.

FOR THE POOLISH

150g strong white bread flour

150g room-temperature water

3g instant dried yeast

FOR THE DOUGH

220g room-temperature water

12g fine sea salt

4g instant dried yeast

385g strong white bread flour, plus extra for dusting

1 Begin by making the poolish. Add the ingredients to a bowl and use a spoon or spatula to mix until fully incorporated and there are no dry spots of flour left. Cover and pop in the fridge for 18–24 hours or leave at room temperature for 10–12 hours. The poolish will slowly rise, fall and then be covered with little holes where the bubbles have burst. It looks a little bit wrong and 'broken' but it's supposed to. Stick with me.

2 Add all of the ingredients for the dough to a bowl and tip in the poolish. Bring everything together to form a rough dough, using your hands to cut the poolish into the other ingredients. You can be quite rough with the dough at this point – the goal is to get everything well combined. Once everything has come together, tip out onto a clean work surface and knead for 4–5 minutes. You're not after a super smooth, strong, elastic dough at this stage, you're just starting the engines for the dough to develop its own gluten. Cover and pop into the fridge for 12–15 hours. It'll slowly ferment and build strength overnight.

3 Remove the dough from the fridge, tip it onto a lightly floured surface and cut into four roughly equal pieces. Shape each piece into a ball (page 170) and let rest for 5–10 minutes. One by one, gently pat the dough balls out until they're a rough square. You want to knock out any larger bubbles but try not to fully de-gas the dough. Grab the top of the square and slowly roll it back towards you into a little log, pushing down gently to seal along the seam and create some tension across the top of the dough.

4 Allow the logs to rest for 5 minutes. Dust the dough very lightly with flour and then, starting in the middle, gently roll the dough back and forth, drawing your hands outwards, to elongate the logs into longer, 40–45cm baguettes. Just be mindful of how big your baking surface is – if you roll them too long, they won't fit! When you get to the end, apply some more pressure and create pointy little tips. You want to be gentle but firm and confident when rolling these, and pop any large bubbles that you see sticking out.

Continued overleaf ⟶

A BAGUETTE TIMELINE
DAY ONE – 8pm, mix poolish (5 mins)
DAY TWO – 8pm, mix dough (25 mins)
DAY THREE – 8am, shape, proof and bake (2–3 hours)

FOR THE BUTTER

600ml good-quality double cream

8g flaky sea salt

> **CHEF'S TIP**
> Steam is so important in this bake. I fill an empty spray bottle with water so I can spritz the baguettes a few times while they bake. You can buy the bottle or simply upcycle an empty one. Just be sure to thoroughly clean it before use!

> **NO COUCHE**
> No dramas. Baguettes are typically proofed using a flax linen cloth known as a couche. It's essentially a stiff, robust piece of fabric that can be bunched up to support lots of delicate baguettes as they ferment. We're going to replicate the couche with standard tea towels and some parchment paper.

> **SHOOT FROM THE HIP**
> The baguette recipe is pretty down the line, it's hard to mix things up here. The butter, however, is more of a blank slate. You can use crème fraîche to make a funky, tangy butter or blend flavours through your butter. Confit garlic is lovely, citrus zest, Marmite, roasted chillies… the list really is endless.

5 Preheat the oven to 250°C fan/270°C/500°F/gas mark 10 and add a baking stone, steel, or upturned, heavy baking tray to the bottom of the oven.

6 Cut four lengths of parchment paper just long and wide enough to sit underneath the baguettes. Transfer each dough to a piece of parchment. Grab a large clean tea towel and sit the first baguette on top. Dust with flour and pull the tea towel up so it sits snug with the side of the baguette, repeat with the remaining breads, tucking the tea towel up and in between each dough. Cover and proof again for 45–50 minutes. You're looking for the dough to be light and puffy, but still have a little bounce when gently prodded. If the dough doesn't spring back, it may be over-proofing and you'll want to get it into the oven quickly.

7 Before baking, dust the baguettes with flour and use a sharp knife or razor to score the top. Holding your blade at an angle, slash 3–4 cuts along the baguette, each cut 10–12cm long. Don't be too precise here, you want to cut with one smooth, swift movement. Transfer the baguettes to the preheated oven and add some ice cubes or a good splash of water to the bottom of the oven. Spritz the baguettes with water and shut the door. Bake for 10 minutes before turning the temperature down to 225°C fan/245°C/460°F/gas mark 9 and baking for 22–25 minutes, or until a deep golden brown. Briefly open the door after 10–11 minutes to let any excess steam out before closing again. Once baked, remove from the oven and let them rest for at least 15 minutes before slicing.

8 To make the butter, tip the cream into the bowl of a stand mixer fitted with the whisk attachment or food processor. Whip on a high speed for 4–5 minutes until the cream passes through soft and stiff peaks and begins to curdle. It'll go from looking like terrible whipped cream to butter in the blink of an eye and can splash buttermilk all over the place, so once you're nearly at the splitting point, lower the speed of your mixer. You'll be left with about 280g of fresh butter and 320g of buttermilk. Set up a bowl of icy water and submerge the butter in it. Squash and massage the butter under the water to wash away any excess buttermilk then transfer to a board or bowl. Sprinkle with the salt and then fold it into the butter.

9 Serve the warm baguettes with the fresh salty butter.

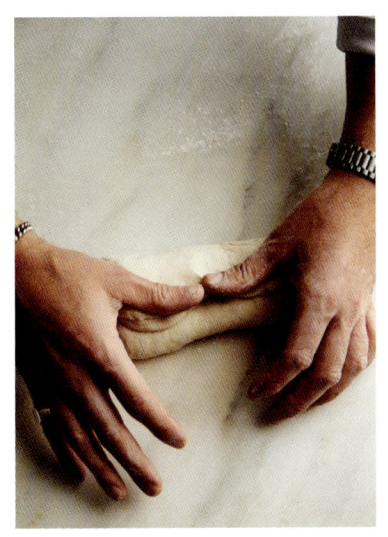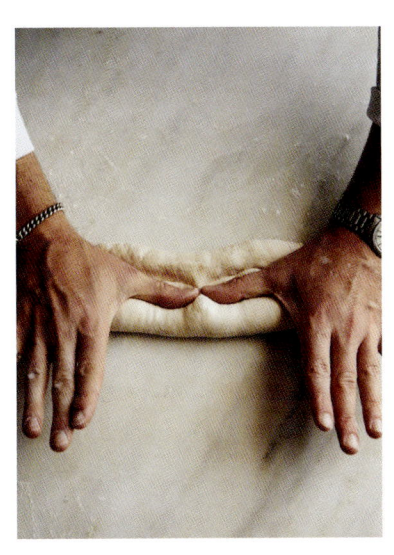

FLOUR & WATER

A FLASH

Beer Batter Fritto Misto & Lemon Mayonnaise 182

Sizzled Broccoli with
Blood Orange & Chilli Dressing 185

Pastrami-spiced Bavette with Charred Cabbage 186

Fried Skate Wing, Green Nam Jim
& Herb Salad 188

Crispy Sea Bass with Grated Tomatoes & Aioli 190

Peppered Clam Frites 191

Tuna Acqua Pazza 194

A Very Good Cheeseburger 196

Cod Schnitzel Holstein 198

Crispy Chicken Breast with Caper Pan Sauce
& Remoulade 200

IN THE PAN

For me, cooking with pans is up there with grilling over fire as the best way to cook. Perhaps years behind a restaurant stove with the things clasped in my hands fused us together. Who knows…? What I do know is that nothing delivers satisfaction quite like cooking something perfectly in a frying pan.

Pan cooking is immediate. You can see, touch, smell and hear your ingredients changing right in front of you. Cooking in pans is also more conducive to learning. Being able to see, smell, touch and hear what you're cooking lends far more teachable moments and means you can be much more precise in your decision making. It's remarkable how much meat, fish and vegetables benefit from being thoroughly coloured in a frying pan, cooked until just a few degrees under perfect, and then allowed to rest. This technique is something you are trained to do on any half-decent 'hot' or 'pans' section of a restaurant kitchen and, once you master it, it will serve you for years to come. Learning to cook with and understanding the potential of the humble frying pan unlocks a whole world of flavour. Before we start, head to page 34 to check out different pans and different materials.

CREATING CONTRAST

Searing, sautéing and pan roasting are all about creating contrast. The red-hot temperatures we'll be cooking at in this chapter will create crispy, caramelised, golden-brown crusts and deeply toasted exteriors. Good pan cookery is about treating the interior and exterior of a product separately. For example, when you order your steak medium-rare, you don't expect a limp, pale, pink piece of meat to arrive. If you were to cook the steak to medium-rare all over, that's what you'd get. When cooking a steak in a searing-hot pan, your goal is to create as much caramelised flavour on the exterior while slowly bringing the interior up to your desired doneness. It's this contrast that makes steak, crispy skinned fish, fried rice and crispy charred broccoli so endlessly delicious. The exterior is deep, rich, toasty, smoky and sometimes (intentionally) charred. There's a method to the madness and it's largely based on something called the Maillard reaction… Heard of it?

THE MAILLARD REACTION

Named after the bloke who discovered it – French scientist Louis Camille Maillard – the Maillard reaction is one of the key players when it comes to adding proper flavour to your food. Don't confuse the Maillard reaction with caramelisation (the cooking of sugars); it is the browning of both sugars AND proteins. Before it can brown, the surface of your ingredient needs to dry out and dehydrate. For a quicker sear and better colour, blot your ingredients dry with kitchen paper. The reaction can take place at a whole range of temperatures, it just depends on how long you've got and how much contrast you want to create. North of 125°C, the Maillard reaction really starts flying, with the proteins browning and caramelising pretty quickly. The reaction can still occur below this temperature, it just takes a good deal longer. In essence, the hotter the environment, the faster the reaction and the higher the contrast.

Conductive heat

Perhaps the quickest way to apply the Maillard reaction to any ingredient is to use conductive heat – the transfer of thermal energy between two or more things in direct contact. When you put your pan on the hob to heat up, that's conductive cooking. When you then add a steak to that hot pan, that's another layer of conductive cooking! The key is contact, and the tasty Maillard reaction can really get going when you press something cold into a very hot pan.

> ### What's fond?
>
> Just as the surface of your ingredient caramelises, any residue or liquid that comes off the ingredients can caramelise onto the bottom of your pan. This crispy, gnarly layer is known as 'fond', derived from the French word for foundation. Many sauces and braises start with this layer of flavour, built up through the caramelising of different proteins and vegetables – the dish then uses this foundation of flavour. The most classic example of how to transfer this sticky, caramelised goodness into a flavour bomb is by deglazing your pan and making a pan sauce.

> ### Help, it's sticking!
>
> The solution to ingredients that weld themselves to your pan is twofold: dry ingredients and sufficient heat. Make sure your fish or chicken skin is bone-dry before it hits the pan; if you're cooking something without skin (like an egg), your pan needs to be at the right heat. If you sprinkle a little water into the preheated pan, it should zip across the surface.

Things get exciting when you add fat to the equation. To sizzle and sear with purpose you need to introduce fat to the pan to facilitate super-efficient heat transfer. You don't always need metal to use conductive heat – deep-frying counts too. When you submerge an ingredient in hot oil, you expose every inch of its surface to direct contact with heat. It's a very effective way of browning and caramelising proteins.

Basting achieves the same effect. When you toss butter into a hot pan, allow it to melt and sizzle, and start spooning it over whatever you're cooking, you're enveloping the ingredient in hot fat. This increases the points of contact with heat and therefore caramelises it faster. Butter-basting a steak at the last minute is akin to deep-frying – it encourages a deep, rich golden-brown finish. Bear in mind that while deep-frying offers full-surface browning, it can't quite hit the same temperatures as the hot metal of a frying pan.

Choose the right fat

Now, people who say you can't sear and cook over a high heat with olive oil are losers. I use olive oil in most of my meat and fish cookery, and it does a bang-up job. It has a slightly lower smoke point than vegetable or sunflower oil, but it's the oil I want to eat 99% of the time so it's my fat of choice. I probably wouldn't use an expensive extra virgin olive oil – designed for finishing – to make fried rice or deep-fry fritto misto. It's a waste of money. I also consider how much of the oil will actually end up on my plate. If I'm searing chicken breasts and then making a pan sauce, I'll use butter or olive oil as they're more delicious than vegetable oil. Smoke points do matter to an extent, as they indicate at what point oils start to break down and eventually burn, but not as much as you think. Don't sear or deep-fry with butter or fancy olive oil and you'll be fine. As for smoke-free fats, they don't really exist. Cooking things in hot pans gets smoky, get used to it! If things are getting super smoky, remove from the heat and leave the oil to cool naturally. Do not add water.

Preheating

In almost all recipes that require a pan to brown something, I will ask you to preheat it. While you're prepping your ingredients (your mise en place), get your pans on the heat. This ensures when you come to add your fat and ultimately your ingredients, the pan is ready to rock. A preheated pan helps food caramelise, makes it more non-stick and allows you to cook quickly and efficiently. Adding an ingredient to a pan is like opening the oven door – the temperature drops.

Overcrowding

The enemy of the Maillard reaction is water. It gets in the way of crispy chicken skin, crackly fried rice and crisp fried seafood. A few times in this book, I'll ask you to work in batches. When you add a cold ingredient to a hot pan, there is an exchange of energy. The preheated pan is ready to transfer all that energy into the ingredient and kick-start the cooking. When searing, the goal is to balance the amount of heat energy your pan can offer with the amount of food you throw into it. You don't want to add small quantities of ingredients at a time – if you don't add enough, it'll burn. Conversely, if you cook four big steaks in a pan that can only offer the heat to sear two the temperature of the surface of the pan will drop and not be sufficient to sear.

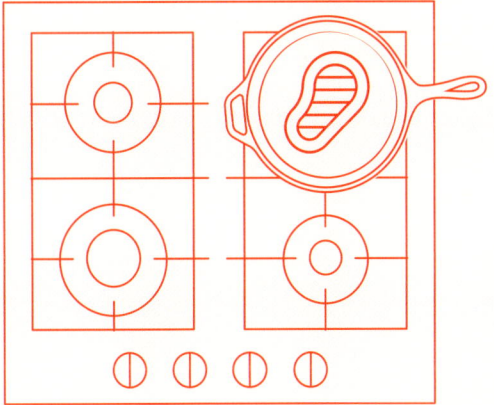

A FLASH IN THE PAN

Beer Batter Fritto Misto & Lemon Mayonnaise

SERVES: 4
EYES CLOSED
P / DF
TOTAL: 40 MINS
PREP: 30 MINS
COOK: 10 MINS

From pan to plate in a matter of seconds, *fritto misto di mare* is probably one of the best expressions of 'a flash in the pan'. This is one of the two recipes in this book that calls for a deep-frying set-up, and no, you don't need a plug-in deep fryer to make this plate of food. When cold, effervescent batter hits very hot oil, the moisture in the batter wants to evaporate very fast and you're left with a shatteringly crisp batter all around your seafood.

FOR THE FRITTO MISTO

12 medium raw shell-on prawns
3–4 small fillets of fish (lemon sole, red mullet or john dory would be delicious)
4–6 fresh sardines, cleaned and butterflied
3–4 whole squid or small cuttlefish
2 lemons
110g rice flour, plus a little extra
120g plain flour
1 tsp baking powder
1 tsp honey
200ml very cold sparkling water
150ml lager beer
50ml vodka
a few ice cubes
handful of fresh sage leaves
vegetable oil, for frying
fine sea salt

1 Start by preparing the seafood. You can ask your fishmonger to do most of the heavy lifting here, but you'll need to de-vein your prawns and portion up the fish and squid. Use a pair of kitchen scissors to snip the shells down the back of the prawn. Start between the shell where the tail and the head meet. Use a paring knife to make a cut down the back of the prawn between the snipped shell and lift out the vein. Repeat with the remaining prawns.

2 Cut the fish into bite-sized pieces, leaving the sardines whole if they're small enough, and score and portion your squid into similar sized chunks. If you've not scored squid before, the goal is to cut a shallow criss-cross into the flesh of the squid. If you're nervous about cutting all the way through the squid, you can use a table knife to get the hang of things before graduating to a chef's knife. Use a mandoline to slice one of the lemons very thinly. Cut the other into wedges.

3 Once your seafood has been prepped, pop it into the fridge while you make the batter and the mayonnaise. Put the rice flour and plain flour in a bowl with the baking powder and honey. Don't add the sparkling water, beer and vodka just yet, we want to mix it just before we go to fry.

4 To make the lemon mayonnaise, tip the yolks, mustard plus the grated zest and juice of both lemons into the bowl of a food processor. Add a good pinch of salt and whizz together. With the machine running, stream in the oils, one by one, until you have a thick, rich mayonnaise (if you need a few more tips on mayonnaise making, head to page 60), Season to taste with extra salt and lemon juice if you need to.

Continued overleaf ⟶

CHEF'S TIP

What should you do with all that oil? This is probably one of the questions I'm asked the most when I write a recipe that involves deep frying, and the answer is so simple. Don't throw away the bottle, wait for the oil to cool down, pass it through a fine sieve or a coffee filter to remove any solids left over from the cooking, then pop it back in the bottle. You can reuse this oil a few times before discarding.

FOR THE LEMON MAYONNAISE

2 egg yolks

2 tsp Dijon mustard

2 lemons

200ml extra virgin olive oil

200ml vegetable or sunflower oil

fine sea salt

5 Preheat a large saucepan filled halfway with vegetable oil to 180°C. Have a thermometer on hand to monitor the temperature as you go – the enemy of crispy fried seafood is oil that isn't quite hot enough. Add a few extra spoons of rice flour into a clean bowl. Whisk the sparkling water, beer and vodka into the batter dry ingredients and drop in a couple of ice cubes. The batter should have the texture of single cream and just hang on to your ingredients. It shouldn't be too thick.

6 Once your oil is up to temperature, drop the prawns into the bowl of rice flour and toss to coat. Dust off any excess then pass the prawns through the batter, allowing the excess to drip off, before carefully lowering them into the hot oil. Fry for 1 minute before whipping them out onto a rack set over a tray to drain. Season them straight away with fine sea salt.

7 Now run through the same process with the fish, sardines and squid, cooking each for just shy of a minute until they're just cooked, golden brown and crisp. The sliced lemons and sage leaves should get the same treatment right at the end. The whole process should take about 5–6 minutes tops.

8 Pile your crispy fried seafood onto a large serving platter. Add wedges of lemon and the fried lemon and sage leaves. Serve with a generous dollop of zippy lemon mayonnaise and something to sip on.

DEEP-FRYING TIPS

Never overfill your pot with oil! I only ever fill it to just over halfway up the sides of the pot. When you drop something into oil that has a high water content (pretty much any fresh raw ingredient), the water in the product will evaporate and cause the oil to bubble vigorously. If you add too much to your hot oil too quickly, or the oil is too close to the top of the pan, it can 'boil over' and flood your hob with hot oil. This can be dangerous but is super easy to swerve. I also like to have everything set up before I get to frying. A digital thermometer is a must, a slotted spoon or spider is good to have ready to go, as well as somewhere for your fried bits and bobs to land – a rack set over a tray or a tray lined with kitchen paper are perfect for this.

SHOOT FROM THE HIP

Any and all of the seafood is interchangeable. You don't need to include all of it, you could include scallops or langoustines if you're feeling boujie, or you could just fry prawns if you really like prawns! The main thing to focus on is choosing ingredients that can be cooked in a flash. A lovely vegetable fritto misto is also a delicious thing to eat – think thinly sliced squash or pumpkin, tenderstem broccoli, spring onions, leeks and mushrooms.

Sizzled Broccoli with Blood Orange & Chilli Dressing

- SERVES: 4 AS A SIDE
- EYES CLOSED
- VE / GF
- TOTAL: 30 MINS
- PREP: 10 MINS
- COOK: 20 MINS

If I had it my way, all broccoli would be cooked like this. I like to call it the sear and steam technique, and it works for so many different veggies. Cooking in pans is about transferring heat in one direction and we're going to take full advantage of that here, hard searing the broccoli until sizzled, caramelised and a little smoky before adding a shot of water to steam it through.

FOR THE DRESSING

- 2 shallots
- 2 garlic cloves
- ½ fennel bulb
- 3 red chillies
- 2 oranges or blood oranges
- 1 tsp fennel seeds
- 2 star anise
- 60ml white wine vinegar
- 60ml olive oil, plus extra for frying

FOR THE BROCCOLI

- 500g purple sprouting broccoli
- olive oil
- fine sea salt
- black pepper

1 To make the dressing, peel and finely dice the shallots and garlic, and finely dice the fennel and chillies, de-seeding the chillies if you want to. Grate the zest of the oranges then top and tail them. Cut away the rind and pith of the oranges and then, working over a bowl, cut out the segments. Allow the bowl to catch any juice and then give the leftover pulp a good squeeze to get everything out of it. Pop the segments into the bowl of juice and set aside.

2 Tip the fennel seeds and star anise into a small saucepan and place over a medium heat. Toast for 4–5 minutes, or until fragrant, then add the vinegar. Warm the vinegar with the spices and pour the whole lot into a bowl and allow to infuse for a few minutes. Tip the 60ml of olive oil into the saucepan and return to medium-low heat. Tip the orange juice and segments into the warm olive oil and cook for 3–4 minutes. The segments will begin to break down and release more juice into the olive oil, infusing it with flavour. Remove from the heat and allow to infuse.

3 Preheat a frying pan over a medium heat and add a good glug of olive oil. Once warm, add the diced shallots and fennel with a pinch of salt. Cook gently for 6–7 minutes until translucent. Add the chilli and garlic and cook for 1 minute. Turn off the heat and set a sieve over the pan. Pour in the infused vinegar, discarding the spices, then pour the olive oil and orange into the sieve. Use a spoon to work the infused oil and orange through the sieve, discarding the bitter pith. Whisk everything together and season to taste with salt and a little more vinegar if you need it. This dressing will keep in the fridge for a few days in a sealed container.

4 Now, to the broccoli. Sometimes purple sprouting can come in fat bunches with all the spears joined by one big trunk. If your broccoli is bunched up at all, break it down into individual spears.

5 Preheat a large frying pan over a high heat. Add plenty of olive oil and, once hot, drop the broccoli into the oil. Season generously with salt and pop another pan or a weight on top of the broccoli to weigh it down into the pan. Sear the broccoli for 2–3 minutes over a high heat until you can smell it caramelising and starting to char. At this point, drop the heat to low and add a splash of water to the pan. Pop a lid on and allow the water to steam the broccoli through for 1 minute. The underside of the broccoli will be well seared, caramelised and a little burnt, with the tops just steamed through, still retaining plenty of bite. Sear and steam – perfect!

6 Scoop the broccoli out and transfer to a serving plate. Dress generously with the spicy orange and chilli dressing and tuck in.

Pastrami-spiced Bavette with Charred Cabbage

- SERVES: 4
- EYES CLOSED
- GF
- TOTAL: 35 MINS
- PREP: 15 MINS
- COOK: 20 MINS

I love pastrami, but making it takes a seriously long time. You've got to brine a hulking great lump of beef for about a week, then poach it and then smoke it. You can achieve a very similar flavour profile following a few little tricks. Searing your steak in a smoking-hot pan will encourage a charred flavour that mimics the smoking process. The hot, fruity black pepper and coriander-heavy spice that forms that iconic jet-black bark is really special, but will burn in that pan if you apply it to the steak too soon. As the steak rests, we're going to brush it with mustard and then roll it in the heady mix for a solid little workaround. Serve with simple, vinegary charred cabbage and a dollop of mustard.

FOR THE PASTRAMI SPICE MIX

- 15g black peppercorns
- 10g coriander seeds
- 2 juniper berries
- 2g dried chilli flakes
- 2g garlic powder or granules
- 15g light brown sugar
- 15g fine sea salt

FOR THE BAVETTE & CABBAGE

- 2 hispi, pointed or sweetheart cabbages
- 50g unsalted butter
- 4 x 250g bavette steaks
- 4 tbsp Dijon mustard
- 1½ tbsp apple cider vinegar
- wholegrain mustard
- olive oil
- fine sea salt and flaky sea salt
- black pepper

1. To make the pastrami spice mix, place a small frying pan over a medium heat. Add the peppercorns, coriander seeds and juniper berries and toast for 1–2 minutes, or until super fragrant. Using a pestle and mortar or a spice grinder, grind to a coarse texture. I like to have texture through the spice mix, so it isn't all powdered – this way the pops of flavour are more intense. Add the chilli flakes, garlic powder, sugar and salt and mix.

2. Roughly chop the cabbages, discarding the woody stem, and cut the butter into cubes.

3. Place a heavy frying pan or cast-iron pan over a high heat. Thoroughly dry and lightly season the steaks with fine sea salt. Don't go mad at this point, there's a good amount of salt in our spice rub and we want to be liberal with that. Once smoking hot, add a shot of oil and lay in the steaks. Cook for 3–4 minutes total, rolling the steaks around in the pan to caramelise and char all sides. Bavette comes in lots of different shapes and sizes – some pieces are very thin, some are thick – so you'll need to use your gut. If you're using a digital thermometer, you're shooting for an internal temperature of 49°C when the steak leaves the pan. It'll rest up to a perfect medium.

4. Pull the steaks out of the pan and brush with the Dijon mustard. Season liberally with the pastrami spice mix, covering the whole steak. Set the spiced steaks onto a warm tray or plate to rest while you cook the cabbage.

5. Scatter the chopped cabbage into the hot pan and scatter the cubed butter over the top. Cook, undisturbed, for 4–5 minutes over a high heat. The underside will char and caramelise while the top begins to steam. For the last minute, pop a lid over the pan to build up some steam and cook the cabbage through. Season with flaky sea salt and move the cabbage around the pan. Finish with the cider vinegar and spoon onto warm plates.

6. Cut the rested steaks into thick slices and transfer to the plates, pouring over any resting juices. Finish with a dollop of wholegrain mustard and serve.

> **CHEF'S TIP**
> When you slice your bavette, make sure you slice it against or across the grain! You'll be able to identify which way the grain is set as it looks like little lines running down the steak. You want to carve across those lines for a tender, juicy steak.

Fried Skate Wing, Green Nam Jim & Herb Salad

🍴	SERVES: 2	⬬	TOTAL: 25 MINS
👨‍🍳	EYES CLOSED	🫗	PREP: 15 MINS
✅	P / DF	🍳	COOK: 10 MINS

Skate is a fantastic fish with a unique texture and flavour and really sings when cooked hot and fast in a pan. It's not dissimilar in flavour to white crab or the natural sweetness of a scallop, and has enough heft and body to stand up to the punchy nam jim. I like to serve this with little mounds of sticky rice to chew on in between bites. Dead moreish and perfect with a cold beer on a hot day.

FOR THE NAM JIM

2 green chillies

2 garlic cloves

25g coriander

1 tbsp fish sauce

2 tbsp light brown sugar

4 limes

FOR THE SKATE WING & SALAD

20g chives

15g mint

15g Thai basil

10g shiso/perilla leaves (if available)

¼ red onion

2 skate wings, trimmed (ask your fishmonger to help here)

vegetable oil

fine sea salt

sticky rice, to serve (optional)

1 First, prepare the nam jim. Remove the stems from the chillies and peel the garlic cloves. Roughly chop them both and add to a large mortar. Slice the stems from the coriander (saving the leaves) and roughly chop, then add to the mortar. Pound the ingredients into a thick, smooth, green paste. Add the fish sauce, brown sugar and the juice of 2 of the limes, mix thoroughly and have a taste. It should be well balanced between spicy, sour, sweet and savoury. You can adjust to your taste as you like with extra fish sauce, lime juice, chillies or sugar.

2 Prepare a bowl of iced water and lightly season it with salt. Cut the chives into 4–5cm lengths, pick the leaves from the mint and separate the basil and coriander leaves (from the nam jim) into bite-sized lengths. Tear the perilla into bite-sized pieces, if using. Thinly slice the red onion then add the whole lot to the bowl to crisp up. The water will take some of the raw funk and bite out of the red onion, so you can eat more of them!

3 Preheat a heavy frying pan or cast-iron pan over a high heat (you may need two or to work in batches). Thoroughly dry the skate wings and season with fine sea salt. Pick up the wing and take a look at either side of the bone – you'll notice that one side is a little thicker than the other. Add a good layer of vegetable oil to the hot pan and lay the skate in, thick side down. Cook for 4–5 minutes, undisturbed, until the surface is golden brown and crisp. Flip the fish and cook for 2–3 minutes on the underside. Once cooked, remove the skate from the pan and allow it to rest for 1–2 minutes.

4 Drain the herbs and onion and toss into a bowl. Season with salt and the juice of a lime and toss together into a punchy salad.

5 Serve the fish with a little of the nam jim spooned over top. Add a small pot of extra nam jim on the side, then slice the final lime into wedges and serve alongside the fish, with the nam jim pot and a generous handful of the dressed herb salad. Serve with sticky rice, if you like.

> **CHEF'S TIP**
> Cooking fish on the bone in a pan is not only for the chefs, it's also an easy win for home cooks. It's simultaneously fun to do, and it keeps the fish super juicy. A little metal skewer is all you need to monitor exactly how your fish is cooking: try to pass the skewer through the fish, if you meet any resistance, then you're going to want to keep cooking that thing. Does the skewer glide straight through? Bingo. It's cooked!

Crispy Sea Bass with Grated Tomatoes & Aioli

- SERVES: 4
- EYES CLOSED
- P / DF
- TOTAL: 30 MINS
- PREP: 10 MINS
- COOK: 20 MINS

Truly summery cooking often has a very short ingredient list, and this is no exception. Cooking a piece of fish in a hot pan is one of life's great joys and can deliver such incredible satisfaction to both the cook and whoever is lucky enough to eat it. I'm going to show you my favourite way to cook fish with just a little olive oil, salt and a hot pan. A raw grated dressing for caramelised veggies, roasted chicken or crispy fish is a great way to reinterpret the classic tomato sauce. It's full of life and acidity and really lifts the caramelised fish. Bread is a must and please trim your asparagus, don't snap it!

4 x 200g portions of sea bass, sea bream or trout
2 large ripe tomatoes
2 tsp sherry vinegar
12–14 asparagus spears
4 tbsp homemade Aioli (page 209)
25g basil
1 lemon
Focaccia (page 158), to serve
extra virgin olive oil
fine sea salt and flaky sea salt
black pepper

1. Season your fish liberally with fine sea salt and pop into the fridge for 20 minutes to dry cure. Remove from the fridge and rinse in iced water. Thoroughly dry the skin and flesh.

2. Slice the tomatoes in half and use the coarse side of a box grater to grate the flesh into a bowl. Hold the skin of the tomato with the flat of your hand and rub it against the teeth of the grater, the pulp will travel through leaving just the skin in your palm. Discard the skin and take a look at your tomato in the bowl. If it looks very watery, drain off some of the excess. Season generously with salt, the sherry vinegar and extra virgin olive oil. Mix and set aside.

3. Trim the woody ends from the asparagus and nip off any of the barbs that look tough or particularly thick. Bring a pan of water to the boil and season heavily with salt. Don't drop the asparagus in just yet, just have everything ready to go.

4. Preheat a large frying pan over a high heat. Be bold with the heat of your pan. It's very hard to burn the skin of a sea bass before it's cooked through, especially on a domestic hob, so give it hell. Add a generous amount of olive oil to the pan, allow it to heat up, begin to shimmer and lightly smoke. Make sure the skin is bone dry then very carefully add the sea bass portions to the pan, laying the fish away from you. Add a weight to the fish to ensure an even crisp and cook for 1–2 minutes, undisturbed. At this point, you can remove the weight as the fish will no longer try to flex or buckle.

5. Keep an eye on the fish as it cooks and notice the heat travel up through the skin and into the fillet. You can watch as the fish turns from a silvery translucent to grey to opaque white as it comes to temperature. We want to cook the fish 90% on the skin side before flipping. When the fish is just about to be flipped, drop the asparagus into the pan of water. Cook for 1 minute, then drain. Dress with salt, black pepper and olive oil.

6. Flip the fish and remove the pan from the heat. Allow the heat of the pan to just kiss the flesh side before removing from the pan and allowing to rest for 1 minute.

7. Add a dollop of aioli to the plate and then flood the rest with your grated tomato dressing. Pile on the asparagus, torn basil and crispy fish. Serve with a twist of black pepper, a sprinkle of flaky sea salt on the skin, a lemon wedge and some focaccia for mopping.

Peppered Clam Frites

- SERVES: 2
- ROLL YOUR SLEEVES UP
- P / GF
- TOTAL: 55 MINS
- PREP: 15 MINS
- COOK: 40 MINS

Mussels and chips, or moules frites as they're known on the continent, are a wonderful thing to eat, but I'm here pitching a new way with shellfish and potatoes. Enter, peppered clam frites. Peppercorn sauce is a hard-hitting classic and a sauce recipe that I think every home cook should have in their locker. Sure, it's right at home on a piece of seared sirloin or a filet mignon, but for me, it has plenty of applications away from the classic steakhouse serve.

FOR THE PEPPERCORN SAUCE

1 tbsp black peppercorns
4 shallots
1 garlic clove
25g thyme sprigs, tied into a bunch
4 tsp green peppercorns in brine
50ml bourbon whiskey or brandy
500ml good-quality fresh fish or chicken stock
250ml double cream
25g chives
15g tarragon
1 lemon
olive oil
fine sea salt

1 Start with the sauce. Tip the black peppercorns into a dry frying pan and toast over a medium heat for 4–5 minutes, or until they're fragrant and the pan is starting to smoke a little. Tip into a mortar or a spice grinder and crush very coarsely. I like to leave plenty of texture in the pepper here – you want to know it's there in a good peppercorn sauce.

2 Peel and finely dice the shallots and peel and finely grate the garlic clove. Place a large sauté pan over a medium-high heat and add a healthy dose of olive oil. Once hot, add the shallots and thyme with a pinch of salt and cook for 3–4 minutes until just translucent and the edges are starting to caramelise. Add the garlic and cook for just 1 minute before adding the black pepper and green peppercorns. Cook for another minute, to marry the spices with the shallots and garlic before adding the whiskey or brandy and reducing to a glaze. Be careful when you're adding the alcohol to a hot pan – if you're cooking over gas, it's likely that the alcohol will flare up and flambé. That's fine, and quite fun – just be prepared! Once the alcohol has almost entirely evaporated, add the stock, bring to the boil and reduce by two-thirds. You want things pretty rich here, so don't be shy. Finally, add the cream, bring back to the boil and reduce again. You're looking for a café au lait colour, nothing too dark, but a sauce with plenty of body. Have a taste: don't be tempted to fully season the sauce at this point, the clams are going to deliver some salinity to the dish, so hold off until they're in the mix. If you want to adjust the pepper, add some extra from your mill.

3 Give your clams a very good rinse under running cold water. Agitate them in a bowl under a running tap to wash away any excess grit or sand that might be trapped within the shells. Discard any clams that are open and won't close or have cracked shells. Cover again with cold water, add 1 tablespoon of fine sea salt and stir through the clams. Leave for 15 minutes. The salt will encourage the clams to open and release any last grit. Wash again, drain and set aside.

Continued overleaf →

A FLASH IN THE PAN

TO SERVE

1kg live clams, cleaned

fine sea salt

300g French fry-style oven chips

4 Prepare the chips according to the package instructions. I find an air fryer is an excellent cooking vehicle for oven chips, but a standard fan-assisted oven, set at around 220°C fan/240°C/460°F/gas mark 9, will do a fine job, too. Be sure to spread your chips out evenly across one or even two baking trays to ensure maximum crisp. We want them crunchy! Alternatively, you can fry them.

5 Once your chips are about 3 minutes from being perfect, bring your sauce back to the boil. Once very hot, tip in the clams and add a lid. Cook for 3–4 minutes, shaking the pan now and then, until all the clams have opened and are fully cooked. Finely chop the herbs and add them to the pan along with the grated zest and juice of the lemon. Have a taste and adjust the seasoning.

6 Fill large bowls with handfuls of chips and then spoon the saucy clams over the top, saturating the chips with the sauce. Serve with napkins and get stuck in.

SURF & TURF

It might seem a little strange using chicken stock to make this, but trust me, it really works. Chicken stock and seafood can work together extraordinarily well, the meaty base offering a great platform for the clam's natural sweetness. Peppercorns have an inherent fruity quality that is often overlooked, with home cooks focussing on the heat that the spice delivers. When toasted, the fruity qualities come to life and, after being liaised with meat stock, gives sauce au poivre a fragrance that lifts those sweet clams.

CHEF'S TIP

It's very important to check that the clams you're cooking are alive! If they're open when you buy them, give them a sharp tap on your work surface or any flat surface. If the clams are alive, the shell will gently close. If they're dead, they'll remain open. Similarly, any clams that do not open after the cooking process should also be discarded.

SHOOT FROM THE HIP

Mussels are a little cheaper than clams and will make a fine replacement if they're easier to get hold of. This might depend on the time of year as well as what your fishmonger has on the counter. Mussels are in season from September through to late April. Make sure you use fresh, live clams or mussels, not the precooked rubbish that comes in vacuum bags.

Tuna Acqua Pazza

- SERVES: 4
- TOTAL: 25 MINS
- ROLL YOUR SLEEVES UP
- PREP: 10 MINS
- P / DF
- COOK: 15 MINS

This is my take on acqua pazza, or fish poached in 'crazy water'. It qualifies as a 'take' as traditionally, fillets of white fish are gently poached in this punchy liquid, but I like to use the crazy water to dress a seared and sliced tuna steak. The acqua pazza is a heady mix of spicy, nearly raw garlic, red chillies, white wine, the juice from cooked clams, tomatoes, olive oil and herbs. The tuna gently poaches in the residual heat of the sauce, giving you an amazing contrast of raw, seared and just-cooked fish. It's a stunning plate of food and a really great way to experiment with different textures and seafood.

4 garlic cloves
2 red chillies
300g cherry tomatoes
1 fennel bulb
25g flat-leaf parsley
15g mint
4 fresh 2.5cm-thick tuna steaks
1 tsp fennel seeds
20–25 clams or mussels, cleaned
250ml dry white wine
handful of good-quality mixed olives
1 lemon
extra virgin olive oil
fine sea salt and flaky sea salt
black pepper
bread, to serve

1 Slice the garlic cloves as thinly as you can, think Goodfellas thin. Cut the chillies into thin slices, seeds and all. We want a bit of kick in our acqua pazza, but if you don't like it hot, you can remove them. Cut the tomatoes in half lengthways, and then into quarters. Cut the fennel into thin wedges. Finely chop the parsley leaves (a few stems in there is fine, too!) and tear the mint leaves into small pieces.

2 Preheat a frying pan over a high heat. Pat your tuna steaks dry and season them generously with salt. Add a good glug of olive oil to the pan and then, one by one, sear the tuna steaks on each side for a minute or so. You want to build a bit of colour on the bottom of the pan and get a good colour on the steaks, so go hard! Remove them from the pan and let them hang out while you whip up the sauce. Don't worry, the sauce takes about 10 minutes to make, they're not gonna go stone cold.

3 Sit the pan back over that high heat and make sure the pan is very hot, then add another generous glug of oil to the pan and drop in the fennel wedges. Cook for a few minutes until lightly coloured then add the garlic, chilli and fennel seeds. Cook for 1 minute then drop in the clams or mussels and tomatoes. Toss the clams in the spicy, garlicky oil then add the white wine and pop a lid on top. Cook for 2–3 minutes, or until the shells have opened and the clams are cooked through. Whip the lid off and add the herbs and olives. Mix them through the sauce and have a taste. Finish with a squeeze of lemon juice and adjust the seasoning.

4 Cut the tuna steaks into chunky slices and season with flaky sea salt, brushing them with a little olive oil. Transfer the sliced tuna steaks into warm bowls and spoon over plenty of the acqua pazza. Serve with good bread and a lick of extra virgin olive oil.

> **CHEF'S TIP**
> To get super clean slices on your tuna, use your sharpest, longest knife. Try to cut the fish in one clean movement, starting with the heel of your knife and pulling all the way back in one motion, gliding through the fish. If you saw away at the steak, it can tear and break, we want beautiful slices! If your knife isn't quite long enough, you can repeat the same smooth cut a few times.

A Very Good Cheeseburger

- SERVES: 4
- ROLL YOUR SLEEVES UP
- TOTAL: 40 MINS, PLUS RESTING
- PREP: 15 MINS
- COOK: 25 MINS, PLUS RESTING

The best cheeseburger is not a smash burger. It's served thick, cooked pink and topped with cheese, onions and big fat pickles. Find some really good beef, make a proper, 200g patty and then cook your burger like you would a steak. Nothing mixed in, no egg or breadcrumbs, just beef and salt. This, paired with a good sear and a long rest (yes, a rest!) will show you that quality beef, adorned with a few simple toppings, is the surefire path to a very good cheeseburger.

800g very good-quality aged beef mince, roughly 80:20 lean to fat ratio
1 white onion
4–6 chunky bread & butter pickles
8 slices of Red Leicester
4 sesame Olive Oil Buns (page 168) or store-bought sesame brioche buns
4 tbsp Dijon or yellow mustard
olive oil
fine sea salt
black pepper
ketchup, to serve
oven chips, to serve

1 Divide the beef mince into four equal, 200g portions. This is the same portion that most steakhouses use, it's generous and for good reason. A hefty patty will allow you to achieve some seriously good caramelisation on the outside, while being able to cook the burger to a perfect pink. Shape the mince into patties. They should be ever so slightly larger than your buns in diameter. They'll shrink a little as they cook. There's nothing worse than seeing a bun with a tiny little meatball inside and calling it a 'burger'. Don't be afraid to work the meat a little bit in order to get the shape you're after. Pop the patties onto a rack set over a tray and allow them to hang out for 20–30 minutes to dry out the exterior. You can pop them in the fridge overnight to properly dry out the surface, if you have time, just be sure to allow them to come to room temperature before cooking.

2 Before you start cooking, make sure everything is ready to rock. Once that burger hits the pan, the clock is ticking. Finely dice your onion and a couple of the pickles.

3 Season the burgers liberally with fine sea salt. Place a large, heavy frying pan over a medium-high heat. Make sure your pan is nice and hot before you lay in the patties. You should hear a good sizzle as they hit the pan. Now let them sear and cook on that first side for a good 3–4 minutes. You'll see the crust starting to form and the colour of the meat will start to change as the heat travels through the patty. Flip the burger and sear the other side. At this point, add 2 slices of cheese to your patties. Pop a lid or an upturned heatproof bowl over the pan to create a little steam and help to melt the cheese.

4 I like a medium cook on the burger – I want it to be nice and pink in the middle. To achieve this, you want to cook it about 3 minutes a side and then rest the burger for a good 5 minutes in the pan. The residual heat will finish the cooking.

5 Time to build. Warm the buns and slice in half. Add a healthy dollop of mustard to the bottom of each bun and top with the rested burgers. Add a little diced onion and pickle to the top of the burger and spread the top bun with ketchup and a little extra mustard. Top with the lid and transfer to plates. Add some extra pickles and a heaped side of oven chips and serve.

CHEF'S TIP

If you cook this burger like you cook a steak, you'll get it right every single time. This is a thick burger patty, and you can absolutely stick a digital thermometer into it to gauge how things are cooking in the middle. You also need to rest this guy. I like to leave it in the pan, allowing the residual heat to keep things nice and warm while the burger rests.

Cod Schnitzel Holstein

- SERVES: 4
- ROLL YOUR SLEEVES UP
- P
- TOTAL: 55 MINS
- PREP: 25 MINS
- COOK: 30–35 MINS

This is my take on an absolute classic, Schnitzel à la Holstein. Ordinarily, this is made with bashed-out veal cutlets, but as my partner is pescatarian I go for cod. I actually find it's much easier to cook breaded fish in this fashion than meat: there's no panicking about doneness; once it's browned, it's ready. The other flavours are like peas in a pod: brown butter, lemon, parsley, capers and anchovies come together to produce a stunningly simple but delicious dressing. A big fat pile of chips on the side wouldn't go amiss, either.

4 x 120g cod loin portions
150g plain flour
6 eggs
250g panko breadcrumbs
2 lemons
200g unsalted butter
4 tbsp capers
75g flat-leaf parsley
1 tin of good-quality tinned anchovy fillets
olive oil
fine sea salt and flaky sea salt
black pepper

> **SHOOT FROM THE HIP**
> You can add seeds or spices to the breadcrumb coating for an extra pop of flavour; some mixed sesame seeds, fennel or cumin seeds would be delicious.

1 Grab a large piece of parchment paper and fold it in half. One by one, pop the cod fillets between the two halves and use a rolling pin or frying pan to gently bash them out flat. Take your time and try to get them as thin as you can. You're shooting for thinner than a pound coin.

2 Set up your breading station: that's one bowl of flour, one with 2 beaten eggs and one of breadcrumbs. Season the breadcrumbs, flour and eggs well with salt and pepper. Season the cod fillets with salt and carefully pass them through the three bowls, dusting off the excess flour and allowing excess egg to drip away before thoroughly coating with the panko.

3 To segment the lemons, use the paring knife to remove the top and tail, before cutting away the peel and pith. Working over bowl to catch the juice, use your knife to carefully cut out each of the segments, cutting either side of the white pith that separates them. Work your way around the lemon methodically, until you have just the husk of the lemon left. Squeeze it over the segments and juice in the bowl and discard.

4 Preheat the oven to 120°C fan/140°C/275°F/gas mark 1.

5 Grab a large frying pan and cover the base with a generous layer of olive oil. Place over a medium heat; once the surface of the oil starts to shimmer (if you've a thermometer, aim for 180°C), carefully layer in the schnitzels, one or two at a time depending on the size of your pan. Fry for about 3 minutes on each side until golden brown and crispy (just be careful when flipping them as they are a little delicate) – they'll be fully cooked by the time they're looking delicious. Pop onto a rack set over a baking tray and slide into the oven to keep warm. Fry the remaining cod.

6 Tip the oil out into a heatproof bowl and set aside. Return the pan to the heat and add the butter. Melt the butter, allow it to foam and then caramelise in the hot pan. It'll turn nut brown and smell like toasted hazelnuts. Once your butter has reached this point, crack in the eggs, season with salt and pepper and fry to your liking. Once cooked, remove the eggs and throw the capers into the residual butter. Cook for 30 seconds before adding the lemon segments, lemon juice and parsley. Season and mix together.

7 Divide the crispy cod among warm plates and top each with a fried egg and some of the brown butter sauce. Finish with a couple of anchovies. Pour yourself a cold beer and get stuck in.

CHEF'S TIP
You can breadcrumb the fish in advance to save on some time before you hit the pans. To make sure the breadcrumbs don't go soggy, store the schnitzels buried in a little extra panko, above and below the fillets. You should have a little left once you've crumbed the fish!

NOTES
While cod is relatively sturdy when raw, you want to be a little careful when you're bashing it out from fillet to schnitzel. Go gentle or you'll break down the muscle fibres too much and the fish will be super delicate and hard to work with.

Crispy Chicken Breast with Caper Pan Sauce & Remoulade

SERVES: 2
ROLL YOUR SLEEVES UP
GF
TOTAL: 40 MINS
PREP: 15 MINS
COOK: 25 MINS

One of the most unjustly cooked things on earth is the chicken breast. They're about as lean as a piece of meat can get and the margin for error is therefore minimal. That being said, nailing a chicken breast is remarkably simple, as long as you follow a couple of very simple steps. You want to get as much colour onto the skin as possible. I treat a skin-on chicken breast like a piece of fish, cooking it most of the way through on the skin side, using the heat of the pan tactically, not exposing the delicate, lean breast meat to too much of its ferocity. Once you've got the colour, it's all about temperature. As soon as the middle of the breast hits 67–69°C, rest it. Once rested, douse it in delicious, simple pan sauce and get stuck in. Honestly, if you take anything from this book, I'd love for it to be how to cook a chicken breast really, really well in a pan. You've got this.

2 skin-on chicken breasts, ideally supremes	75ml white wine or 2 tbsp sherry vinegar
2 shallots	500ml good-quality chicken stock
½ small celeriac	½ lemon
1 tsp wholegrain mustard	20g soft herbs (dill, chives or tarragon)
2 tbsp thick Greek yoghurt	extra virgin olive oil
1 tbsp capers	fine sea salt
	black pepper

1 Lightly season the chicken breasts a good 20 minutes or so before you want to cook them and make sure they're at room temperature. Don't go mad, the caper sauce delivers a good thwack of salt.

2 Preheat the oven to 160°C fan/180°C/350°F/gas mark 4.

3 Once your chicken has had some time hanging out with the salt, pat it dry with kitchen paper or a clean towel. Preheat a heavy-based ovenproof frying pan over a medium-high heat. Once hot, add a generous glug of olive oil and lay the chicken breasts into the pan, skin side down. Drop the heat ever so slightly and add a weight on top to ensure an even, clean crisp across the whole surface of the chicken. Cook for 5 minutes.

4 Don't be afraid to check how the chicken is getting on now and then but give it a good 2 minutes before having a peek. You want the skin to achieve a deep golden-brown colour and become very crispy. Slide the pan into the oven for 5–6 minutes, or until the chicken hits an internal temperature of 68–69°C. Pull the pan out of the oven, flip the chicken over and cook for a minute before transferring to a plate to rest.

5 While the chicken is in the oven, prepare the remoulade. Peel the shallots and dice very finely. Peel and cut the celeriac into thin strips and then into a very fine matchsticks or julienne and add to a medium mixing bowl. Add the wholegrain mustard and yoghurt, mix together, then drop in the celeriac. Toss to coat and set aside.

6 Once your chicken is out of the pan and resting, return the pan to the medium-high heat, leaving behind all the chicken fat and olive oil. Add the diced shallots and cook with a tiny pinch of salt for 2–3 minutes, or until they turn translucent and start to crisp up. Add the capers and carefully deglaze the pan with the wine or sherry vinegar. Reduce by half then add the stock and crank the heat back up. Reduce by two-thirds or until thickened and rich with chickeny flavour. Taste as the stock reduces – it'll intensify in flavour and salinity as it cooks, so keep an eye on it. Finish with a squeeze of lemon juice.

7 Finely chop the fine herbs and add half each to the pan and remoulade. Toss through the sauce and remoulade. Cut the chicken into chunky slices and transfer to a warm plate. Cover generously with the pan sauce and add a healthy handful of remoulade to the plate.

PAN SAUCE
Pan sauce is about as simple a meat sauce as you can make. It's built in the pan you cook your steak, fish or chicken in and comes together while the meat rests. It requires a few key ingredients. Something acidic like wine or vinegar, something savoury like shallots, garlic or leeks and a good-quality stock are built up in the pan before being finished with herbs, cream, butter or olive oil. This is a very basic caper and shallot pan sauce that uses the chicken fat and olive oil in place of butter or cream to keep things nice and light.

CHEF'S TIP
Do not and I repeat, *do not*, cut open the chicken to check if it's cooked while it's cooking . . . I see so many people make this mistake and it's fatal for your chicken. Your thermometer is your best friend here, if you cut too early, your dreams of a juicy chicken breast will run out all over your chopping board. Use your thermometer or a metal skewer to test the internal temperature and only cut after resting.

A FLASH IN THE PAN

FROM

Baked Cod with Chorizo & Peas 206

Crispy Roast Potato & Artichoke Bravas 208

Smoked Aubergine & 'Nduja Lasagne 210

Dry-brined Chicken Legs with Sweet & Sour Peppers 212

Smoky Roasted Pumpkin & Fish Curry 214

Lamb Meatballs with Tomato, Yoghurt & Spiced Butter 216

Potatoes & Squash Baked in Cream 218

Crispy Pork Belly with Sesame Sauce 219

Baked Brill with Oven Chips & Warm Tartar Sauce 220

Roast Chicken with Schmaltzy Shallots & Mash 223

Garlic & Fennel Porchetta 226

THE OVEN

Whether you're planning on cooking a simple roast chicken, a piece of perfectly baked fish or a tarte tatin, the oven is an instrumental tool in producing some of the finest food, both sweet and savoury.

They also facilitate some of the best 'family meals'. With an oven, you can cook for one or two, but also have the capacity to turn out larger feasts, stunning centrepieces and showstopping bakes. There's a lot to learn about how your oven works and how best to use it to its full potential. Let's get into it.

HOW DOES YOUR OVEN WORK?

When we slide in a tray of spiced cod or artichokes and they come out crispy, what kitchen wizardry has taken place? Well, a combination of radiant and conductive heat, working in tandem with convection, cook your food from three different angles. Your oven is working overtime! But what do these three terms really mean? All of them use dry heat in different ways.

Every oven has at least one heating element. This is what chucks out heat into the oven (duh) and cooks things. As the element heats up, it emits rays of heat energy. Imagine standing next to a radiator or a roaring fire. You can feel the warmth coming off it, right? That's thermal radiation coming at you. The same thing happens in the oven with the heating elements. Whatever you're cooking in the oven sits on something hot, introducing a level of conductive heat (page 180) and then there's also convection to cover (more on that shortly). Following along? Good. Let's make it make sense in your home kitchen . . .

Decode your oven settings

Convection or 'fan-assisted' ovens are becoming commonplace these days. In fact, ovens that can do it all are now dominating home kitchens. How many times have you stood staring at the little control panels on your oven and thought 'what the hell am I looking at here?'. Well, let's break it down.

BOTTOM HEAT This is the baseline for an oven. A single heating element in the oven heats the space from the bottom up. It's your oven's gentlest mode.
Best for: long slow cooks, braises and ragùs.

TOP AND BOTTOM HEAT Introducing another source of heat increases the level of radiant heat and encourages a little more natural convection. I use this when baking as it allows bread and pastries to rise beautifully. If you're looking for something to set, like a custard tarts, this is the setting for you.
Best for: baking bread and delicate pastries, custard tarts, roasting delicate veggies.

FAN-ASSISTED/FORCED CONVECTION Turning on the fan in your oven significantly increases the amount of convection. As the hot air is whipped around the oven by the fan, it can cook and crisp foods much faster than regular, natural convection.
Best for: roasting chickens, crisping pork crackling, roasting chunky veggies.

FULL-SURFACE GRILL With no fan or bottom heat, the whole of the top heating element goes into overdrive, using 99% radiant heat to grill and roast your food from the top down. This is perfect for when you want to add colour and caramelisation to the surface of an ingredient.
Best for: grilled meats, finishing mac and cheese, cheese on toast, brûléeing sugar.

WARM A lot of ovens now have a warm setting that holds at a lower temperature and is useful either for extremely gentle cooking or to hot-hold cooked foods. That's a fancy term for 'keep them warm', but at a safe temperature.
Best for: warming plates, hot-holding roasts or sides, sterilising jars for preserves.

There are some fancier settings, too. You might be lucky enough to have an oven that has a proofing setting, can cook with steam and some can even clean themselves (boujie!). We're going to be focusing on just a couple of settings, but experiment and get to know your oven!

NATURAL VS FORCED CONVECTION (PLUS A NOTE ON AIR FRYERS)

A fan oven will heat up faster and cook more evenly, as air that's moving around rapidly transfers heat far better than air that is still. Used an air fryer? It's the perfect example. Despite their name, air fryers are not actually fryers, they're just really windy ovens, but they're closer to the cooking power of a fryer than a regular oven thanks to forced convection. Their compact size means they are more efficient at circulating air.

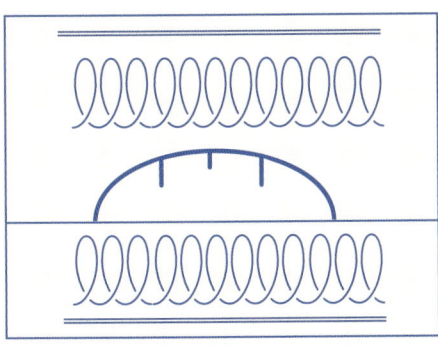

Thermal radiation directly heats the surface of the food

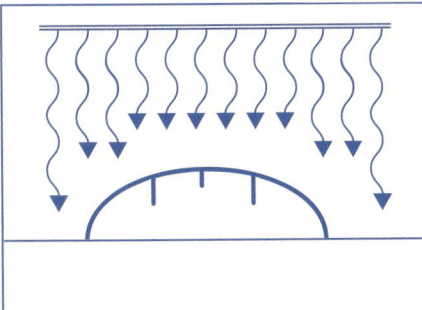

Convection – hot air next to the food heats its surface

WHEN TO USE YOUR FAN

Turn on the fan when you want your food to cook quickly and be exposed to as much heat as possible for the entire cooking time. Picture a roast chicken and you probably have a perfectly golden brown, crispy skinned bird in mind. When carved, there'll be tender, juicy, just-cooked breast and rich, tender dark meat. Dreamy. Fan-assisted cooking is perfect for these moments. When you're cooking something that demands a more homogenous texture – a braise or a gratin – it's best to avoid the fan. If your oven doesn't have fan assist, don't sweat it. Every oven recipe has the temperatures for different oven types and all will still work very well!

ROASTING VS BAKING

These terms are used interchangeably, but they are different. You can broadly categorise them by temperature, with baking usually happening at a slightly lower temperature than roasting. Annoyingly, this is not always the case, as a lot of bread-baking happens at very high temperatures and slow-roasting typically sits around the 150°C, which is pretty low... Don't get too hung up on terminology – focus more on what the ingredient or recipe requires from your oven in terms of time, temperature and setting.

TRAYS, TINS AND VESSELS

When shopping for baking trays, tins and roasting vessels, you want to buy cookware that is heavy and will conduct heat as efficiently as possible. I try to buy a good range of sizes, too. Some as wide as the shelves of the oven for making oven chips or cooking things that need lots of space, and some smaller ones for when I'm roasting a chicken crown. If you always use massive trays and tins, you'll limit the amount of airflow in your oven and the amount of flavour in your food. If you only have tiny trays, you won't be able to spread food out effectively, overcrowding and steaming where you want to caramelise.

HOT SPOTS

Every oven out there has hot spots. You'll notice them most when you're cooking a larger piece of meat, like a roast chicken or porchetta, especially if the oven is pretty full or there's a large piece of food or tray reducing the potential for convection. You'll be able to tell where the hot spots are by checking out what you're cooking: if one side or corner of your roast is browning a lot faster than the other areas. To combat this, place your food on the middle shelf and rotate the tray or dish as much as possible for even cooking. You can also crank up the fan setting and get the hot air really moving around the space, giving your food a better chance of avoiding hot spots and burnt bits.

KEEP THAT DOOR CLOSED

Consistent heat is key when using your oven. If your recipe calls for a temperature of 175°C, and you set your oven correctly, it'll race up to to 175°C, and then maintain it. As soon as you open the door, hot air rushes out and the temperature drops significantly. It takes the oven time to come back to 175°C and this then will affect the rate at which your ingredients cook. For consistent colour, texture and flavour, keep the door closed as much as possible!

FROM THE OVEN

Baked Cod with Chorizo & Peas

SERVES: 4
EYES CLOSED
GF
TOTAL: 50 MINS
PREP: 20 MINS
COOK: 30 MINS

This is one of those recipes where the whole is so much more than the sum of its parts. The chorizo and broad bean garnish is super versatile and can be spooned over so many different ingredients. Treat it like a warm dressing, and when you taste it, look for the same notes you're after in a vinaigrette or salad dressing. You want heat from the chorizo, sweetness from the peas and broad beans, richness from the pork fat and olive oil and a little hit of acidity from good sherry vinegar. Gently baking cod is one of the easiest ways to make the most of the fish and gives you plenty of space to nail the dressing.

4 x 120g cod loin fillets
2 tsp sweet smoked paprika
4 garlic cloves
150g frozen broad beans
100g frozen peas
2 shallots
125g spicy chorizo
280g long-grain rice such as basmati or jasmine
2 tbsp sherry vinegar
25g chives
6 tbsp thick Greek-style yoghurt
2 lemons
olive oil
fine sea salt

1 Preheat the oven to 200°C fan/220°C/425°F/gas mark 7.

2 Pat the cod fillets dry with kitchen paper and transfer to a parchment-lined baking sheet. Season generously with salt and dust with the smoked paprika. Grate 2 garlic cloves over the fish and drizzle with a generous dose of olive oil. Roll the fish around in the salt, paprika and garlic until thoroughly coated. Set aside.

3 Bring a medium saucepan of water to a rolling boil and season generously with salt. Set up a bowl of ice water and then drop the broad beans into the boiling water. Cook for 1 minute before fishing out and plunging into the ice water. Repeat with the peas. At this point, peel the little jackets off of the broad beans, if you like. Set aside.

4 Thinly slice the remaining garlic cloves, and peel and dice the shallots as finely as you can. Cut the chorizo into 1cm cubes.

5 Wash the rice thoroughly until the excess starch has been removed. Combine the rice with 340g of fresh water in a medium saucepan. Season with salt then place over a medium-high heat. Once boiling, cover with a lid and turn the heat right down. Cook for 8–10 minutes then remove from the heat and allow to rest for 10 minutes, with the lid on. Slide the cod into the oven and bake for 9–10 minutes.

6 While the rice is resting and the cod is cooking, make your dressing. Preheat a small frying pan over a medium heat. Tip in the chorizo and cook for 5–6 minutes until the fat has rendered and the chorizo is crispy. Add the diced shallots and half the garlic and cook for 2 minutes. Add the sherry vinegar, broad beans and peas. Finely snip the chives and add to the dressing.

7 Mix the yoghurt in a bowl with the grated zest from the lemons and some salt. Cut the lemons into wedges for later. Pull the cooked fish out of the oven. Spread the yoghurt over the base of some warm plates. Top with rice and a piece of baked cod and dress with lashings of the spicy chorizo and broad bean dressing. Finish with a lemon wedge.

Crispy Roast Potato & Artichoke Bravas

- SERVES: 4 AS A SIDE OR SNACK
- EYES CLOSED
- V / DF
- TOTAL: 85 MINS
- PREP: 20 MINS
- COOK: 65 MINS

A roasted Jerusalem artichoke is a pretty unique bite. They're sweet but also deeply savoury and when roasted with olive oil, they caramelise and take on an amazing chewy, crispy, unctuous texture. I think they work phenomenally well as part of the Madrid staple tapa, patatas bravas.

FOR THE POTATOES & ARTICHOKES

1kg small waxy potatoes (e.g. La Ratte, Charlotte or Jersey Royals)

800g Jerusalem artichokes

1 tbsp good-quality sherry vinegar

extra virgin olive oil

fine sea salt

FOR THE SALSA BRAVA

1 onion

2 garlic cloves

2 tbsp tomato purée

2–3 roasted piquillo peppers (optional)

1 tbsp sweet paprika

1 tbsp hot smoked paprika

20g plain flour

250ml vegetable or chicken stock, or water

2 tbsp good-quality sherry vinegar

2 tbsp vinegar-based hot sauce (I like Cholula)

olive oil

fine sea salt

1 Preheat the oven to 210°C fan/230°C/445°F/gas mark 8.

2 Scrub the potatoes and artichokes clean. Pop the potatoes in a saucepan and cover with cold water. Place over a medium heat, add a good pinch of salt and bring to a bare simmer. Cook for 10–12 minutes until just tender. Drain and allow to steam dry for 5 minutes. Use a heavy glass or mug to gently crush the potatoes one by one, just splitting the skins and exposing the interior.

3 Toss the artichokes and potatoes with plenty of olive oil and salt then tip onto a large baking tray lined with parchment paper. Make sure they're sitting in a single layer and are not overcrowding the tray, spreading them across two trays if necessary. Slide into the oven and roast for 55–60 minutes, tossing them every 10–15 minutes, until all the artichokes and potatoes have a tender interior and a golden crispy exterior.

4 While the veggies are roasting, make the salsa brava. Peel and finely chop the onion and garlic and place a saucepan over a medium heat. Add a shot of olive oil and, once warm, add the onion and garlic with a generous pinch of salt. Cook for 6–7 minutes until translucent, then add the tomato purée and roughly chop and add the peppers, if using. Crank up the heat to medium-high and toast the purée for 3–4 minutes before adding the paprikas and flour. Cook for another 2–3 minutes then add the stock or water, a little at a time, whisking in between additions. Once all the stock is in, tip the whole lot into a blender or use a stick blender to whizz until very smooth. Finish with the vinegar and hot sauce then season to taste. You're looking for a sauce the texture of thin double cream that is sharp, salty and spicy. If you need to let it down a little, add a splash more water or stock. To thicken, return to the heat and reduce. Pour through a sieve for an extra smooth finish and set aside.

> **NOTES**
> Salsa brava or 'brave sauce' is defined by a couple of key ingredients. You want to get your hands on a high-quality paprika for this and a very delicious sherry vinegar. The peppery heat of the paprika and sweet and sour notes from the sherry vinegar will give your sauce its signature, moreish twang.

FOR THE AIOLI

2 egg yolks

2 garlic cloves

1 tsp Dijon mustard

½ lemon

150ml neutral oil

100ml extra virgin olive oil

fine sea salt

5 To make the aioli, put the yolks, peeled garlic cloves, Dijon mustard and the juice of the half lemon in a blender with a pinch of salt. Add a splash of water and whizz until smooth. With the machine running, gently drizzle in the oils one by one until you have a thick, rich emulsion. Alternatively, you can make this with an immersion blender or in a pestle and mortar. For some more tips on emulsions, head to page 45.

6 Remove the potatoes and artichokes from the oven and drizzle with the sherry vinegar. Pile the crispy potatoes and artichokes onto a platter and drizzle generously with salsa brava. Add a heaping spoon of aioli to one side and serve.

SHOOT FROM THE HIP

If you're after a crispy, chip-like texture from your potatoes and artichokes, roast until tender and then allow to cool completely. You can then deep-fry them at 170°C for 5–6 minutes, or until golden brown and crunchy all over. While still warm, toss them with salt and vinegar for a more restauranty serve.

CHEF'S TIP

Jerusalem artichokes are full of natural sugars and, when you roast them, you'll notice a sticky, sugary caramel oozing onto your tray, similar to when you bake a sweet potato. This can be a nightmare to clean off the tray, so make sure it's lined with parchment paper!

FROM THE OVEN

Smoked Aubergine & 'Nduja Lasagne

- SERVES: 4–6
- EYES CLOSED
- TOTAL: 110 MINS
- PREP: 30 MINS
- COOK: 80 MINS

A good lasagne is all about the build. I want silky layer after silky layer: smoky aubergine ragù, a light, glossy béchamel, plenty of basil and stringy mozzarella. For a sauce that comes together in half an hour, this smoky ragù packs a heavyweight punch. The best thing you can do is make a big fat lasagne, eat half, then chill the leftovers. The next day, tip them out and cut into thick slices. You can then sear them in a non-stick pan until all of those layers are super crispy. Bliss.

4 aubergines
3 shallots
2 garlic cloves
1 tbsp fennel seeds
1 tsp dried oregano
100g 'nduja
800g good-quality tinned chopped tomatoes
50g unsalted butter
50g plain flour
750g whole milk
50g parmesan, plus extra to serve
300g fresh lasagne sheets or 325g dried lasagne sheets
250g grated low-moisture mozzarella
30g fresh basil leaves, plus a few extra to serve
extra virgin olive oil
fine sea salt
black pepper

1 Start by charring the aubergines. Place them directly over the flame of a gas hob for 10–12 minutes, have the stove set to max and use tongs to turn them now and then until the aubergines are soft, completely collapsing and the skin is charred and flaky. Remove from the heat and put in a bowl. Cover with a lid or plate and set aside for 5 minutes.

2 Peel and finely chop the shallots and preheat a saucepan over a medium heat. Add a generous layer of olive oil to the pan then add the shallots with a pinch of salt and cook or 5–6 minutes until translucent. The goal here is not to colour them too much. Peel and finely grate the garlic cloves and add to the pan with the fennel seeds, dried oregano and 'nduja. Stir through and cook for 2–3 minutes – the 'nduja will melt through the base and the raw edge will just cook off the garlic. Tip in the tomatoes, bring to a simmer and cook for 15–20 minutes.

3 Grab the burnt aubergines and use a small knife to remove and discard the stems and scrape away most of the burnt skin. Leave a small amount behind to add some extra smoke, but just a bit – too much can taste too bitter. Roughly chop the aubergine flesh and tip it into the tomato sauce. Season with salt and pepper and keep warm.

4 To make the béchamel, melt the butter in a medium saucepan over a medium heat. Once foaming, add the flour and whisk to a roux (the paste-like mix that is the base for thickening the sauce). Cook for 2 minutes or until the paste smells biscuity, then gradually pour in the milk in small increments, beating constantly to ensure that you have a smooth mixture before adding more milk. Once all the milk has been added, bring the mixture to the boil and allow it to thicken to the texture of thick double cream, stirring regularly. Once it's boiled, cook for a minute or so then remove from the heat, grate in roughly two-thirds of the parmesan, whisk through the sauce and season to taste with fine sea salt. Set aside.

5 Preheat the oven to 180°C fan/200°C/400°F/gas mark 6. Grab a dish (about 30 x 20cm) and start building your layers. Begin with a thin layer of smoky ragù sauce in the base of the dish, then a layer of pasta, a layer of béchamel topped with grated mozzarella, then pasta, then ragù, then torn basil leaves. Repeat until you've filled the dish. We want lots of thin layers here, so less is more with the fillings. Finish with a final layer of béchamel with dollops of the ragù on the top and sprinkle with parmesan.

6 Slide into the oven and bake for 30–35 minutes until bubbling and golden brown. Allow to cool for at least 20 minutes before topping with extra parm and basil leaves. Slice and serve.

Dry-brined Chicken Legs with Sweet & Sour Peppers

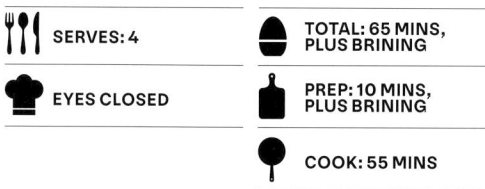

SERVES: 4
EYES CLOSED
TOTAL: 65 MINS, PLUS BRINING
PREP: 10 MINS, PLUS BRINING
COOK: 55 MINS

To dry-brine an ingredient is to coat it in salt at least a few hours ahead of cooking and allow the natural moisture within the ingredient to create a saline solution on the surface. That solution then works to penetrate the meat, seasoning it all the way through to the bone while the skin slowly dehydrates, ready to crisp and caramelise in the heat of the oven. Crank up the heat, get some good colour on the peppers, use fresh bay leaves (always!) and prepare to meet your new favourite midweek traybake.

1½ tbsp caster sugar
4 chicken legs
5 red peppers
3 white onions
3 garlic cloves
6–8 fresh bay leaves
3 tbsp red wine vinegar
300g fregola or giant couscous
5 tbsp tahini
5 tbsp thick Greek yoghurt
1 lemon
olive oil
fine sea salt
black pepper

1 Mix ½ tablespoon of the caster sugar with 1 tablespoon of fine sea salt and liberally season the chicken legs all over. If you've got time, you can leave these in the fridge overnight, or do this before you go to work, then whip them out when you get home. Don't have that kind of time? No bother, just salt them for at least 30 minutes. Don't forget to bring your chicken out to come to room temperature before cooking.

2 Preheat the oven to 250°C/270°C/500°F/gas mark 10.

3 Cut the peppers into chunky slices – I like to take the cheeks off the side of the peppers and leave them in large, organic shapes. Peel and halve the onions then cut them into 5mm-thick slivers and toss into a large roasting tin. Sit the peppers on top of the onions, skin side up. Drizzle the whole lot with lots of olive oil and sprinkle over a healthy pinch of salt, then slide into the oven and roast for 13–15 minutes, or until the peppers are starting to char and caramelise.

4 Thinly slice two of the garlic cloves and scrunch the bay leaves in your hands. Pull the tray out of the oven, stir the sliced garlic, bay leaves and remaining sugar through the peppers and onions, then top with the chicken legs. Slide back into the oven and reduce the heat to 190°C fan/210°C/410°F/gas mark 6. Cook for 40–45 minutes until the chicken legs are brown and the skin is crispy and caramelised. After 30 minutes, add the vinegar and stir through the veggies for the last 10 minutes and check in on the chicken legs. If they need a bit more colour towards the end, crank up the heat to 210°C fan/230°C/445°F/gas mark 8 for the last 5–10 minutes.

5 While the chicken cooks, cook the fregola in boiling salted water for 8–10 minutes until just tender. Drain and toss with a little olive oil to stop it clumping.

6 Mix the tahini and yoghurt in a bowl. Add the grated zest and juice of the lemon, a big pinch of salt and finely grate in the remaining garlic clove. Add a little ice-cold water to loosen the mix into a shiny, swoop-able texture.

7 Pull the chicken legs out of the oven and allow to rest for 5 minutes.

8 Spread some of the tahini across warm plates and top with fregola. Add a chicken leg to each and then cover with the jammy peppers, onions and bay leaves, will plenty of the roasting juices. Finish with a few twists of pepper and serve.

Smoky Roasted Pumpkin & Fish Curry

- SERVES: 4
- TOTAL: 50 MINS
- EYES CLOSED
- PREP: 10 MINS
- P / GF
- COOK: 40 MINS

I have fond memories of eating an extraordinarily spicy pumpkin and fish curry after one too many beers at a very good Thai restaurant in Melbourne. The pumpkin had been grilled, imbued with amazing smoke, the mackerel was smoked, the mussels were huge, plump monsters, steamed in the yellow curry sauce and just peeking from their shells. This is my at-home version. I've amended some of the ingredients to make it a little easier to pull off at home.

1kg delica or crown prince pumpkin (you can use squash, too!)
2 bird's eye chillies
1 white onion
3–5 tbsp good-quality Thai red curry paste
360g jasmine rice
200g smoked mackerel fillets
800ml coconut milk
1 tbsp palm or light brown sugar
4 tbsp fish sauce
4 limes
150g sugar snap peas or mange tout
5–6 makrut lime leaves
handful of Thai basil leaves (regular basil is tasty, too)
vegetable oil
fine sea salt

1 Preheat the oven to 220°C fan/240°C/460°F/gas mark 9.

2 Use a bread knife to cut your pumpkin in half then a spoon to scoop out the seeds. I like to leave the skin on my pumpkin for this, but if you want to whip it off, do so now. Cut the pumpkin into 2.5cm-thick moons, following the natural shape of the squash. Rub the squash with vegetable oil and salt and spread the pieces out on a roasting tray. Slide into the oven and roast for 35–40 minutes until tender, caramelised and starting to char.

3 Meanwhile, make the base for the curry. Halve one of the chillies lengthways. Peel the onion and use the coarse side of a box grater to grate the onion into a fine pulp. Preheat a large sauté pan over a medium heat and add a generous layer of vegetable oil. Add the halved chilli and grated onion and cook for 6–7 minutes until most of the moisture has cooked away and the onion starts to fry in the oil. Add the curry paste and cook for another 5–6 minutes and watch as the colour transforms from a light red into a deep, dark roasted maroon, staining the oil red as it goes.

4 Wash the rice 3–4 times in cool water to remove excess starch. Thoroughly drain then tip it into a medium saucepan and add 540g of fresh cold water. Add a tiny pinch of salt and place over a medium heat. Bring to the boil, pop a lid on then reduce to a simmer and cook for 8–9 minutes until the water has been fully absorbed and the rice is tender. Remove from the heat, lid still on, and leave to steam and rest for 10 minutes before fluffing with a fork.

5 Peel the skin from the mackerel fillets and flake into bite-sized pieces.

6 Once the oil has split from the curry-base mixture, tip in the coconut milk along with the mackerel skins and bring to a simmer. The skin will infuse the curry with smoky flavour. Cook for 10–12 minutes then add the sugar, fish sauce and juice of 2 limes. Cook for 1–2 minutes before having a taste. Adjust with more fish sauce, lime juice or chilli. Finish the curry with the flaked mackerel and peas right at the last moment. Remove the skin and discard.

7 Remove the lime leaves from the stalks, then stack them and cut into fine matchsticks. Pick the basil leaves from the stems and finely chop the chilli.

8 Divide the steamed rice among warm bowls. Remove the pumpkin from the oven and sit a couple of the roasted moons onto each bowl – don't worry if they break a little. Spoon over a generous helping of the curry then finish with lime leaves, chilli and basil. Serve with halved limes for squeezing.

SHOOT FROM THE HIP
You can make this vegetarian by omitting the mackerel and using a vegan fish sauce-style condiment. These are pretty readily available now but if you can't find one, a dash of soy sauce will add some of the salt and umami that the fish sauce delivers. You can use fresh seafood in this curry but for convenience, I like to use smoked mackerel.

Lamb Meatballs with Tomato, Yoghurt & Spiced Butter

- SERVES: 4
- EYES CLOSED
- TOTAL: 50 MINS
- PREP: 15 MINS
- COOK: 35 MINS

Growing up, there was a Turkish restaurant near us called Nemrut. I absolutely adored it and in tandem with my early exposure to Turkish pide in Istanbul (page 162), this restaurant cemented my love for Turkish cookery. This recipe is inspired by their *yogurtlu adana kebap*, a dish of spiced minced lamb over a bed of fresh bread, yoghurt and a lightly spiced tomato sauce and topped with hot spiced butter. This is a version that you can make at home without a huge charcoal grill; a midweek lamb dish that isn't traditional, by any stretch, but it's pretty delicious, if you ask me.

FOR THE LAMB MEATBALLS

1 tsp cumin seeds

1 tsp fennel seeds

1 tsp coriander seeds

1 tsp pul biber or Aleppo pepper

3 garlic cloves

1 jarred roasted pepper

50g flat-leaf parsley

500g lamb mince (20% fat)

1 tsp fish sauce

1 tbsp rose harissa

400g tinned chopped tomatoes

extra virgin olive oil

fine sea salt

1 Toast the seeds in a dry frying pan over a medium heat for 3–4 minutes until fragrant and beginning to smoke, then tip into a mortar and grind to a fine-ish powder. Drop in the pul biber and the peeled garlic cloves. Add a generous pinch of salt and smash the garlic cloves down and into a paste. Finely chop the pepper and add it to the mixture. Finely chop the stalks from the parsley and add to the mortar, too. Tip the lamb into a mixing bowl and add the pepper and parsley mixture, a good pinch of salt and the fish sauce. Use your hands to scrunch the paste through the meat and start to work the lamb in the bowl, almost as if you're working with a dough and trying to build gluten. You want to mix this until it starts to become a little sticky.

2 Preheat the grill to max and the oven to 220°C fan/240°C/460°F/gas mark 9.

3 Using slightly wet hands, form the lamb mixture into 12 little rugby ball-shaped meatballs. Lay them out on a roasting tray, toss with olive oil then slide under the grill for 4–5 minutes until one side is seared and slightly charred. Remove from the grill, and stir through the harissa, then slide the tray into the oven for 2–3 minutes before tipping in the tomatoes, seasoning with salt and returning to the oven for 9–10 minutes.

4 Meanwhile, peel the red onion whole and use a mandoline or sharp knife to slice it into very thin onion rings. Toss into a bowl, season with salt, add the juice of 1 lemon and the sumac, and use your fingertips to scrunch the seasoning into the onions. Set aside for 5–10 minutes. Roughly chop the parsley leaves (left over from making the meatballs) and toss through the mix.

> **NOTE**
> You can absolutely make this on the barbecue! If you fancy a smokier finish on the lamb, simply roll the meatballs over a very hot grill for 8–10 minutes until charred and smoky on the outside and just pink in the middle. Whip up the tomato sauce in a pan and you're good to go.

> **SHOOT FROM THE HIP**
> This would work well served family style, too! Make up a big platter as part of a wider spread. Serve with iced crudités and dips (page 80), Chopped Salad (page 72) and a couple of pide (page 162).

FOR THE SPICED BUTTER

50g salted butter

50g pine nuts

1 tbsp Aleppo pepper

TO SERVE

1 red onion

2 lemons

½ tbsp sumac

4 Turkish flatbreads or pitta bread (to make your own, see page 156)

150g thick Greek yoghurt

pickled green chillies

olive oil

flaky sea salt

5 To make the spiced butter, melt the butter in a small saucepan over a gentle heat. Tip in the pine nuts, crank up the heat a little, and toast the nuts in the hot butter until the butter has turned nut brown and the pine nuts are golden. Add the Aleppo pepper and remove from the heat.

6 Pop the flatbreads on top of the lamb and tomato sauce to warm and refresh for the last 4–5 minutes in the oven, before cutting into chunks. Lay a few chunks of bread across warm plates and top each with a few spoons of tomato sauce and 3 of the lamb meatballs. Top with more tomato sauce, a few spoons of yoghurt and a little of the spicy pine nut butter. Serve with the remaining lemon cut into wedges, a pinch of the onion salad and a pickled chilli.

FROM THE OVEN

Potatoes & Squash Baked in Cream

- SERVES: 4–6
- EYES CLOSED
- V
- TOTAL: 3 HOURS 10 MINS
- PREP: 30 MINS
- COOK: 2 HOURS 40 MINS

Now, most dauphinoise recipes will instruct you to layer up your veggies flat in the baking dish, buried in cream, but we're going to buck that trend here. Using a layer of jammy, caramelised onions as a foundation, you stick all of your sliced potatoes and squash, laced with black pepper and thyme, up on their sides. The resulting bake almost has a hasselback finish, with crispy layers, and a tender, garlicky centre. I like to eat this with pickled shallots and a vinegary green salad (page 70).

4 large white onions
25g thyme sprigs
50g unsalted butter
120ml dry white wine
400ml double cream
200ml whole milk
4 garlic cloves
¼ nutmeg
750g Charlotte, Desiree or similar waxy potatoes
500g butternut squash
25g sage
fine sea salt
black pepper
green salad (page 70), to serve
pickles, to serve

1 Peel the onions and use a mandoline or sharp knife to slice them to a thickness of 1–2mm. Split the thyme into two bunches and tie them separately.

2 Preheat a large saucepan over a medium heat and, once hot, toss in the butter. Allow the butter to melt, foam and start to sizzle then drop in the sliced onions, along with a healthy pinch of salt and one of the thyme bunches. Cook for 25–30 minutes over a medium-low heat until light golden, jammy and caramelised. Deglaze the pan with the white wine, scraping up any colour from the bottom of the pan.

3 While the onions cook, tip the cream and milk into a saucepan. Peel and thinly slice the garlic cloves and drop them into the pan along with the other bunch of thyme. Place over a medium heat and bring to a bare simmer. Drop the heat to the lowest setting and let the mixture tick over and infuse for 10–15 minutes. Pass through a sieve to remove the thyme and garlic, then return the infused mix to the pan and season to taste with salt and nutmeg.

4 Peel and thinly slice the potatoes. You can use a mandoline or sharp knife for this job. If using a knife, try to make sure the potatoes are all the same size. You're shooting for a thickness of 2–3mm. Once sliced, rinse the potatoes in cold water before thoroughly drying. Peel and remove the seeds from the butternut squash. Cut into slices a similar size to the potatoes. I like to cut the half squash down the middle lengthways and then cut across into smaller slices. Pick the sage leaves.

5 Preheat the oven to 165°C/185°C/350°F/gas mark 4.

6 Tip the caramelised onions into the bottom of a 30 x 20cm baking dish. Start stacking your slices of potato and squash together with the sage leaves. Every 10–12 slices, incorporate a slice of cheese. Use your judgement to distribute the herbs and cheese throughout the whole bake, saving a handful of cheese for the top. Lay the little stacks of veggies on their sides onto the bed of onions. Pour the hot, garlicky cream mixture over the top. Season the top of the bake with black pepper and dot with pieces of the remaining cheese. Cover with a sheet of parchment paper then wrap tightly with foil.

7 Slide into the oven and bake for 1½ hours, then remove the cover, crank the oven up to 190°C fan/210°C/410°F/gas mark 6 and return the bake to the oven for 30–35 minutes to colour. Remove from the oven and allow to rest for 5 minutes before serving with green salad and pickles.

Crispy Pork Belly with Sesame Sauce

- SERVES: 4
- ROLL YOUR SLEEVES UP
- DF
- TOTAL: 195 MINS, PLUS DRYING
- PREP: 15 MINS, PLUS DRYING
- COOK: 180 MINS

This is a bulletproof trick to nailing crispy, juicy pork belly every single time. All you need is some salt, a sheet of sturdy foil and a couple of hours. I serve this with a moreish sesame sauce, modelled on a Japanese-style roasted sesame dressing, steamed rice, some spicy chilli oil and a vinegary, salted cabbage salad.

FOR THE CRISPY PORK BELLY

1–1.2kg piece boneless pork belly

1 tsp ground white pepper

2 tsp toasted sesame oil

fine sea salt

coarse sea salt

FOR THE SESAME SAUCE

1 tbsp caster sugar

1 tbsp rice vinegar

90g tahini

1–2 tbsp light soy sauce

50g toasted sesame seeds

FOR THE SALTED CABBAGE

½ white cabbage

½ white onion

25g mint

2 tbsp rice vinegar

fine sea salt

TO SERVE

steamed rice

pickled ginger

crispy chilli oil (optional)

1. Preheat the oven to 150°C fan/170°C/325°F/gas mark 3.

2. Flip your pork belly so it's skin side down. Season the meat well with fine sea salt and rub with the white pepper and a little sesame oil. Lay out two sheets of foil and place the seasoned belly, skin side up, in the middle. Carefully fold the edge side of the foil in towards the pork, making sure they cover the sides and reach right up to the skin. You're aiming to make a foil tray, encasing the meat but leaving 100% of the skin exposed. Cover the skin with a handful of coarse sea salt. Pop the foil-wrapped belly onto a baking tray and slide into the oven to cook for 2–2½ hours. Check in on the pork after an hour or so. As the pork cooks, it'll naturally shrink, so you'll need to adjust your little foil boat accordingly. Scrunch the edges back towards the meat so they're snug, being careful not to spill any of the fat.

3. Once the pork has had 2–2½ hours at 150°C, whip it out and crank the oven up to 250°C fan/270°C/500°F/gas mark 10. Brush the coarse sea salt off the skin of the pork, then carefully remove it from the foil tray onto a roasting tray. Pour the pork fat from the foil tray into a bowl and reserve for another time (I like to add a few spoonfuls to the steamed rice). Slide the pork back into the oven for 25–30 minutes to puff the crackling and caramelise the exterior of the pork. Remove from the oven and rest for at least 30 minutes.

4. To make the sesame sauce, pop the sugar, vinegar, tahini and soy sauce into a blender or bowl and whizz or mix together until smooth. Add ice-cold water as needed, to loosen, until you have a creamy sauce. Finish with the sesame seeds and set aside.

5. To make the salted cabbage, use a mandoline or peeler to finely shave the cabbage and onion. Finely chop the mint leaves. Tip everything into a bowl, season with salt and set aside for 10 minutes. Dress with rice vinegar just before serving.

6. Use a serrated knife to carve the pork belly into slices and serve with warm rice, pickled ginger, the cabbage salad and a generous spoonful of the sesame sauce and, if using, chilli oil.

Baked Brill with Oven Chips & Warm Tartar Sauce

SERVES: 4–6
TOTAL: 95 MINS
DIG IN
PREP: 25 MINS
P
COOK: 70 MINS

This might be my death row meal. As somebody who grew up in the UK, it's sort of the law that we eat fish and chips, and this is my dream version. A brill is a brilliant fish to bake whole. It is super forgiving, cheaper than some of their other flatfish family and has a wonderful flavour. When cooked, it produces an amazing, gelatinous fish stock that blends with the olive oil and lemon as it bakes, creating its own sauce. It's so easy and feels incredibly cheffy. I *love* oven chips, and these are made in the same way you might make a roast potato – for me, it's the best way to do it. Whip up a tartar hollandaise and you're off to the races.

FOR THE OVEN CHIPS

- 2kg Maris Piper potatoes
- 3–4 rosemary sprigs
- vegetable oil
- sea salt and malt vinegar, to finish

FOR THE BAKED BRILL

- 1–1.5kg brill, whole, gutted and cleaned
- handful of mixed herbs (optional)
- 2–3 lemons
- olive oil
- fine sea salt

1 Start with the oven chips. Peel and cut the potatoes into chunky chips and tip into a large saucepan. Cover with cold water and season generously with salt. Place over a medium heat, bring to a bare simmer and cook for 7–8 minutes until just tender. Drain, spread out on a rack or tray and allow the chips to steam dry for at least 10 minutes. Preheat the oven to 220°C fan/240°C/460°F/gas mark 9. Fill a deep roasting tray with 1cm depth of vegetable oil and slide it into the oven. Once hot, whip it out and carefully lower in the chips one by one. Turn to coat them in the hot oil then return to the oven for 20 minutes, turning them regularly, until lightly golden. Drain the excess oil from the chips, turn the oven down to 200°C fan/220°C/425°F/gas mark 7 and return to the oven for 30–35 minutes to finish cooking.

2 Line a large baking tray with parchment paper and add a drizzle of olive oil. Use a pair of sturdy kitchen scissors to snip away the frilly, flexible skirt that runs up either side of the fish. I start at the tail end and cut up towards the head, pulling the skirt away from the main body of the fish as I go. Season generously with olive oil and salt, stuff the herbs, if using, into the cavity and thinly slice the lemons, shingling them over the top of the fish.

3 Slide the brill into the 200°C oven and bake for 25–30 minutes, checking as you go. Baking a flatfish on the bone like this can take a little time, and the best way to understand what's going on inside is to use a thermometer. You're shooting to take it out of the oven when the thickest part of the fillet next to the bone is somewhere between 60 and 64°C. With a good rest, this will give you pretty perfectly cooked flat fish. If you don't have a thermometer, you can use a cake tester or metal skewer to test the temperature. Simply insert it into the thickest part of the fish, leave it for a few seconds, then touch it to your lip. It wants to feel quite warm, but not hot. Once your brill is where you want it, whip it out of the oven and rest for 10–15 minutes – don't worry, it won't go cold!

4 While the brill and chips cook, make the tartar hollandaise. Peel and finely chop the shallot, finely chop the tarragon, chives, cornichons and capers, and set them all aside. Melt the butter in a small saucepan. Set up a small saucepan filled a third-full with water and set a heatproof mixing bowl over the top, ensuring the base

Continued overleaf →

FOR THE WARM TARTAR SAUCE

1 shallot
25g tarragon
25g chives
80g cornichons
40g capers
200g unsalted butter
3 egg yolks
1 lemon
1 tbsp Dijon mustard
a few dashes of Tabasco sauce
fine sea salt
black pepper

doesn't touch the water. Add the egg yolks to the bowl with the juice of the lemon. Place over a low heat and bring the water to a very gentle simmer, barely bubbling. Whisk together the egg yolks and lemon juice and cook, whisking all the time, for 5–6 minutes until the mixture has doubled in volume and has thickened significantly. Be careful not to overcook the eggs here: if you think things are getting too hot, whip the bowl off the pan and keep whisking. Once your egg yolks are thick and fluffy, turn the heat off underneath the pan.

5 Slowly pour in the melted butter, a little at a time, whisking the whole time, until fully incorporated. You will end up with a rich, thick emulsion. If things are getting too thick, add a little extra lemon juice or warm water. Add the remaining ingredients and beat them through the hollandaise. Season with salt and 15–20 twists of black pepper and keep warm over the pan of water, whisking now and then.

6 Scoop the chips out of the oven tray into a bowl and blot away any excess oil. Strip the rosemary leaves from the sprigs and finely chop, sprinkle them over the chips with salt and plenty of malt vinegar. To finish the fish, remove the lemons and place them to one side. Use a small knife to cut through the skin down the centre of the fish. Peel away the skin to reveal the flesh beneath. Drizzle with a little olive oil, season with salt and spoon over any juices from the tray. You can either serve the fish like this, or remove the fillets and serve them separately. I like serving the fish whole, with the chips, a bowl of warm tartar sauce, the roasted lemon slices and some fresh wedges.

SHOOT FROM THE HIP

You can substitute any flatfish in for brill, and use any size. Individual lemon or Dover soles are amazing, plaice is stunning and a big fat turbot is a real treat if you're feeling fancy or it's your birthday. Talk to your fishmonger and they'll recommend something delicious. Cooking times will vary, with smaller fish cooking in 12–15 minutes and much larger fish taking 45–50. Trust your gut and look out for those key temperatures. A large green salad (page 70) on the side of this will really set things off. You could even up the amount of herbs to bring the best out of the brill!

CHEF'S TIP

You might have some tips for making hollandaise with an immersion or stick blender, but making it this way yields a much nicer, fluffier texture. Make your sauce right at the last minute and keep warm over the pan of water so it doesn't split. If it does split, whisk in a few tablespoons of warm water from the pan!

NOTES

Hang on to the skirt from the brill and use the bones, head and any leftovers to make a very delicious fish stock. Simply add the fish pieces to a pan and cover with 50% white wine and 50% water, add a few aromatic veggies if you like, bring to a bare simmer and cook for an hour. Strain, reduce a little and you're done!

Roast Chicken with Schmaltzy Shallots & Mash

- SERVES: 4
- ROLL YOUR SLEEVES UP
- GF
- TOTAL: 120 MINS, PLUS RESTING
- PREP: 20 MINS, PLUS RESTING
- COOK: 100 MINS

Because of their dramatically different cooking times, the pro move when cooking chickens is to separate the breast and legs. We'll roast the crown in a hot oven until perfectly cooked; while it rests, the legs hang out in the oven and finish cooking. As the chicken roasts, it's going to render and yield a load of chicken fat to the bottom of the pan and we're going to have some shallots waiting to soak it all up. Seal the deal with garlic, red chillies and herbs, make a super quick gravy and serve it all with the buttery mash of your dreams.

FOR THE CHICKEN & SHALLOTS

1.8–2kg good-quality chicken
12 round shallots
1 garlic bulb
15g thyme sprigs
25g rosemary sprigs
2 red chillies
250ml white wine
750ml good-quality chicken stock
2 tsp cornflour (optional)
10g chives
2 tbsp sherry vinegar
olive oil
flaky sea salt
black pepper

1 OPTIONAL: Starting at least 3 hours but up to two days before you want to eat, season the chicken with roughly 10g of fine sea salt inside and out. Sit the chicken onto a rack set over a tray and slide into the fridge to air dry. The salt will draw moisture out of the skin, season the meat and improve the texture of your chicken. Pull the chicken back out of the fridge at least 1 hour before you want to roast it to allow it to come to room temperature. If you do this, skip the seasoning in the recipe!

2 Preheat the oven to 240°C fan/260°C/500°F/gas mark 10.

3 To prepare the chicken for roasting, first remove the wishbone. Pull any skin away from the front of the cavity where the neck meets the breasts and use a small, sharp knife to expose either side of the wishbone. Trace up the bone with the tip of your knife to the breastbone to expose both sides. Cut down and through the bottom of each side and then pull out the wishbone. Cut the skin where the legs meet the back of the breast then cut close to the leg, leaving as much skin on the crown as possible. Pop the legs out of the sockets and cut them away from the spine, being careful to keep your knife snug to the bone and to remove the oyster with the leg. Now, cut just below the ribcage towards the front of the breast down into the spine on either side of the crown. You can now push the crown forward and remove it from the spine.

4 To make the mash, prick the potatoes with a fork and put them on a baking tray. Slide into the oven for 60–70 minutes until they're completely tender. While still hot, cut in half and use a tea towel to hold the potatoes as you push them, cut side down, through a sieve into a large saucepan. The flesh will pass through the sieve and you'll be left with just the skin. Use a spatula or the back of a spoon to push any remaining potato through the sieve and into the pan. You can eat the skins, if you like, but we don't need them here! Place the pan over a medium heat and add the butter and milk, a little at a time, stirring until fully incorporated. Beat together until you have a rich, silky mash. Season with salt and keep warm.

Continued overleaf →

FROM THE OVEN

FOR THE MASH

1.5kg potatoes (Maris Piper, King Edward or similar)

150g unsalted butter

200ml whole milk

fine sea salt

SHOOT FROM THE HIP

I've kept it simple here, but a dollop of mascarpone and a spoonful of wholegrain mustard would be delicious in the mash. For more of a spring serve, wilt chopped gem lettuce and peas in the chicken stock as it reduces or try adding chopped figs and a splash of balsamic vinegar.

THE MAGIC NUMBER

The golden temperature for chicken breast is 72°C. Roast your breast on the crown until the thickest part hits 67°C, then whip it out of the oven and let it rest. Rest it for almost as long as you cook it, and allow the temperature to climb the last 5°C. The carry-over cooking time (the temperature of the breast will rise by 5–10°C during resting) is not to be overlooked and is the secret to the best roast chicken breast around.

CHEF'S TIP

You can make this start to finish in just shy of two hours, but if you've got time, season the chicken a few hours ahead and leave it in your fridge to air dry. You can do this up to two days ahead of roasting. Also, removing the wishbone from your chicken before roasting is not only a surefire way to make carving the bird as easy as possible but the yield on the breast will be much higher. Leftovers? Whip up the chicken pozole on page 104.

---

5 Preheat a large frying pan over a medium heat. Add a shot of olive oil, pat the chicken legs dry with kitchen paper inside and out and rub all over with olive oil. Season generously with flaky sea salt then lay into the pan, skin side down. Sear and crisp the skin for 5–6 minutes before removing and repeating with the crown. Try to get an even colour across the skin, but don't sweat too much if there are a few lighter patches.

6 Grab a large roasting tin or cast-iron pan and slide it into the oven to preheat. Top, tail and peel the shallots, leaving them whole. Cut the top off the garlic bulb, just enough to expose the top of the cloves, sit on a small sheet of foil, drizzle with oil, season with salt and wrap up tightly. Stuff the thyme and half of the rosemary inside the cavity of the crown. Remove the preheated tin or pan from the oven, add the shallots, the whole chillies, a good pinch of salt and a glug of olive oil. Toss to coat, drop in the parcel of garlic and sit the chicken crown and legs on top.

7 Slide the tin back into the oven and turn down the heat to 220°C fan/240°C/460°F/gas mark 9. Roast the chicken for 20–25 minutes until nice and brown then turn down to 200°C fan/220°C/425°F/gas mark 7 and roast for another 20 minutes, or until the thickest part of the breast has hit 68–69°C. Now whip the tin out of the oven, lift the crown out to rest on a tray, and slide the legs back in for another 25–30 minutes.

8 Remove the legs from the oven and lift out of the tin. To make the gravy, lift the garlic, chillies and herbs out of the tin and place it over a high heat on the hob. Add the white wine to deglaze the tin and scrape up the flavour. Bring to the boil and reduce until it's almost all gone, and the shallots are nice and shiny. Whip the shallots out of the tin and add the chicken stock. Reduce by two-thirds until rich and delicious. As soon as it's tasting perfect, lower the heat. At this point, if you want to thicken it, add the cornflour to a small bowl along with 3–4 teaspoons of the gravy. Stir the gravy into the cornflour to form a paste then whisk the paste through the rest of the gravy. Bring back to the boil and the sauce will thicken a little.

9 Squeeze the garlic out onto your chopping board and chop the remaining rosemary and roasted chillies into it. Add the mixture into the sauce and season to taste with salt and pepper. Put the shallots in a separate bowl, dress them with finely chopped chives and sherry vinegar and keep warm. Take your rested chicken crown and use a small, sharp knife to remove the breasts. Carve into thick slices and cut the legs into drum and thigh. Serve the roasted chicken with spoonfuls of buttery mash, the vinegary shallots and plenty of the rosemary and chilli gravy.

Garlic & Fennel Porchetta

- SERVES: 6–8
- DIG IN
- DF / GF
- TOTAL: 170 MINS, PLUS SALTING
- PREP: 40 MINS, PLUS SALTING
- COOK: 130 MINS

The classic Italian porchetta is made using a whole boneless middle of pork. That's the loin, the belly, and all the skin that surrounds them both. Not only is it very expensive and it probably won't fit in your oven, it's quite tricky to cook the belly and nail the cook on the loin. One Is packed with fat, the other is the leanest part of the pig! To solve this problem, make your porchetta with pork belly. They're so much easier to cook than the classic, are really easy to roll, offer that amazing spiral finish and are full of rich, porky flavour and still tick all of the textural boxes that the classic recipe does.

3.5–3.8kg boneless pork belly, skin scored
3 tbsp fennel seeds
1 tbsp black peppercorns
2 tbsp dried chilli flakes
15 garlic cloves
100g flat-leaf parsley, plus a little extra for the salad
25g rosemary sprigs
1 lemon
1 orange
2kg La Ratte, Jersey Royals or similar baby potatoes
1 litre good-quality chicken stock
500g kale
olive oil
fine sea salt

1 Start by butterflying and salting your pork belly. Before you get going, weigh the whole piece then measure out 2% of the total weight in fine sea salt. To butterfly the belly, lay the pork skin side down on the chopping board. Identify the thickest part of the belly and position that towards your dominant hand, or the hand you hold your knife in. Grab a long, sharp knife and make a cut along the middle of the belly halfway up from the chopping board. Imagine you're opening the belly up like a book, slicing through the middle of the belly, parallel to your chopping board in long strokes until you almost reach the end – don't cut all the way through! You can roll up the top half of the belly as it cuts away from the bottom half, this pressure helps the knife do its job and makes it easier to see what's going on. It doesn't have to be perfect, by any stretch, you're just opening up the pork belly to offer more surface area to soak up the porchetta flavours. Be sure to keep the half of the pork belly with the skin on completely intact.

2 Once butterflied, cover the belly, flesh and skin side with the measured salt, roll up into a loose log with the skin on the outside and pop onto a rack set over a tray. Set aside in the fridge for at least a couple of hours, and up to overnight.

3 Preheat the oven to 230°C fan/250°C/480°F/ gas mark 10.

4 To make the seasoning for the middle of the porchetta, start by toasting your spices. Put the fennel seeds and peppercorns in a dry frying pan over a medium heat and toast for 2–3 minutes until fragrant, then tip into a mortar or spice grinder and grind to a pretty fine powder. Mix the chilli flakes through. Lay out the salted pork belly, skin side down and open up the butterflied section. Season the inside of the belly liberally with the fennel, pepper and chilli mixture.

5 Peel and add 13 of the garlic cloves, together with the parsley (stalks and all) and rosemary leaves, to a small food processor or blender and blend to a paste, adding a little olive oil if you need to, to help get things moving. You want this pretty fine, so a processor or blender is handy, but you can hand-chop this if you want to. Use your hands to massage the herb mixture into the pork belly. Add the grated zest of the lemon and orange, then roll the pork belly up into a tight spiral, starting at the butterflied piece and rolling up towards the skin end.

Continued overleaf ⟶

228 FROM THE OVEN

> **CHEF'S TIP**
> For the ultimate, 360° crispy skin experience, ask your butcher to leave some extra skin attached to the belly where the pork loin has been removed, this way you can tie it all the way around the porchetta. Be sure to cook the porchetta on a rack set over a tray so every single side can get super crispy.

> **NOTES ON PORK BELLY**
> You're going to want to call your butcher for this recipe! Don't be afraid, pick up the phone and start chatting with them. Ask them for a boneless piece of pork belly from the thinner end (it's a little easier to roll). Be sure to do this a couple of days ahead so you've got time to air-dry your pig in the fridge for that perfect, crispy crackling.
> This recipe is super easy to scale up and down: you can either make the whole belly and cut it down into smaller joints (give 'em away to happy friends and family!) or just buy a smaller piece of belly. As the porchetta is one big log, the same size all the way down, the cooking time doesn't change all that much.

> **SHOOT FROM THE HIP**
> The holy trinity of garlic, fennel and chilli are going to be the main players in this recipe, but you can season your pig with whatever you like. Swap in for any spices and herbs that you're into. Calabrian chilli paste with chopped prunes and thyme is amazing; orange, Aleppo pepper and caramelised onions would be incredible. Your pig is your canvas, so get creative.

6 Cut 10–12 lengths of butcher's twine about 35–40cm long. Lay them out spaced apart by roughly 2–2.5cm then sit your porchetta on top, with the seam facing up. Starting in the middle, tie the porchetta tightly into the spiral shape. Pick up the two ends of each length of string and pass one under the other at least 3 times before pulling tight – this will ensure the strings won't slip as you go to tie each off for the second time. Tie all the strings off and trim any excess. Flip the porchetta over and rub away any excess moisture or herbs that might have made their way onto the skin (these will burn!), and make sure the skin is bone dry before rubbing the whole surface with a little olive oil. Add a good handful of salt and rub that into the skin, too. Tip the potatoes into a deep roasting tray and season with a little salt and olive oil. Set the porchetta on a rack over the top and then slide into the oven.

7 Roast at 230°C for 30–35 minutes then drop the oven temperature to 145°C fan/165°C/330°F/gas mark 3, pour the stock over the potatoes and cook for another 2–2½ hours until the centre of the porchetta hits 73–75°C. Top up the potatoes with a little water if you need to. The initial hot cooking stage will start to blister and crisp up the skin and then the long slow cook will render the fat and perfectly cook the pork belly, the potatoes gently poaching in the pork fat and stock underneath.

8 Whip the porchetta out and let it rest for at least 30–35 minutes. Segment the zested orange and lemon and tip into a bowl, squeezing the leftover bits over the top. Thinly slice the remaining garlic cloves. Preheat a large saucepan over a medium heat. Add a generous glug of olive oil and tip in the garlic. Infuse the oil with the garlic for 2 minutes then pile in as much of the kale as you can. Add a tiny splash of water, season with salt and pop a lid on. Wilt the kale in the garlicky oil, stirring every now and then and adding the rest of the kale as you go. Cook for 25 minutes, or until dark and very tender. Finish with the citrus segments and juice.

9 Carefully snip and remove the butcher's twine, then carve your porchetta into slices with a serrated knife. Warm a large platter in the oven before adding a bed of the braised kale. Top with slices of porchetta and serve with the potatoes.

BACK

Melted Courgettes & Mozzarella on Toast 234

Slow-roasted Tomatoes over Rice 236

Slow-cooked Squid with Black Olives 238

Braised Chicken 'Pizzaiola' 240

Tingly Pork Ragù with Noodles & Salted Cucumbers 241

Pomegranate Lamb Ribs & Parsley Salad 242

One-pot Mushroom Bourguignon 244

Spiced Short Ribs with Dates & Warm Hummus 245

Toulouse Sausage with Lentils & Horseradish Salsa Verde 248

Beef Cheek & Scotch Bonnet Pie 250

Lamb Shoulder with White Beans & Chard 252

BURNER

Slow cooking takes time, patience and planning, but the payoff is magical. It can transform tough cuts of meat into majestic, banquet-worthy plates, elevate and transform the textures of vegetables, as well as offer seafood a new dimension.

Set up your slow cook, stick it on the back burner or slide it into the oven, walk away and return to some serious flavour and mind-bending texture. With a bit of knowledge and experience, you and your slow cooking can really hit your stride. In colder months, make way for big bold pies, slow-roasted vegetables, rich braises, deep caramelised stews and, of course, ragù. That isn't to say summer is a no-go – slow-roasted tomatoes, squid stews and ox-tongue tacos are all hits in the warmer months.

WHAT IS SLOW COOKING?

Slow cooking is a catch-all term for any cooking method that aims to alter the texture of an ingredient through prolonged exposure to heat.

A good slow cook is all about layering flavour, and there are a few things to remember before you get started. The decisions you make now will affect the results and how your recipe will 'behave' down the line. Deciding how much you caramelise your meat, how finely you dice your vegetables, how much milk, stock or wine you add, whether you make a bouquet garni or use dried herbs will all have a knock-on effect at the end of the road. For example, if you're serving a ragù with pasta, think about how the sauce will interact with your chosen shape: do you want big chunks of shallot in there? Will they slide straight off a ribbon of pappardelle? Of course they will, so dice them finely. Do you want a richer sauce? Add more chicken stock and a little butter. Want depth of flavour? Use some good red wine. Every decision will be distilled into a beautiful sauce down the line, so take a moment and think it through.

BRAISING TOUGHER CUTS

Right, this is where tough cuts come into their own. All those golden bits of connective tissue and collagen are about to transform into sticky, unctuous gelatin and here's how. When collagen is heated in the presence of water it begins to convert into water-soluble gelatin, which melts into stocks and sauces, giving them body. This process begins as soon as collagen is heated above 50°C, and tops out at about 90°C. The hotter the braise within this range, the quicker the conversion. This is why braising liquid is so important – it maintains a temperature of 90–95°C and never allows the meat to get too hot, too quickly. As the meat comes up to temperature in the liquid, all that tough collagen just melts away, the meat becomes incredibly tender and the dish is transformed. Magic.

KEEP THINGS CHUNKY

With a long, slow cook, any vegetables that get lobbed into the braise are going to have to endure some seious cooking. I usually leave everything pretty chunky, so there's some texture at the end. For example, I halve chillies, leave shallots and garlic cloves whole and cut leeks into chunky rings. Trust me, if you start with super fine dice, a few hours later you'll have mush.

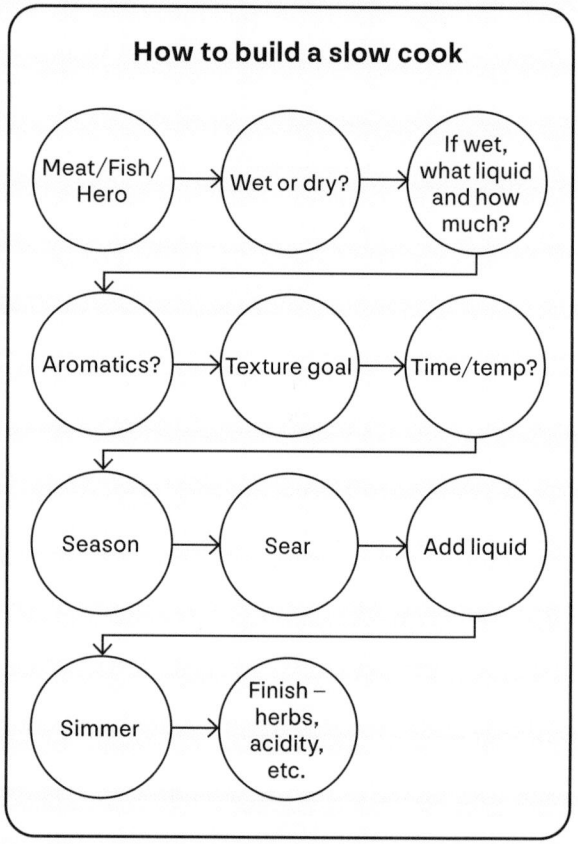

BOUQUET GARNI

My go-to in the winter months, a bouquet garni is essentially a little bundle of flavour you drop into a stew, braise, soup, ragù or stock at the start of cooking. It's usually composed of hardy, winter herbs like bay, thyme, rosemary, savory and sage, but can also feature parsley, leeks... the sky's the limit. The handy feature of a bouquet garni is that you can pluck it out at the end of the cook, while still feel the benefit of adding a sh*t-load of herbs to your pot. It's very annoying counting out the bay leaves and rosemary twigs you put in at the top of the recipe, so, buy some butcher's twine and use it to tie up your herbs.

HOB VS OVEN

Does it make more sense to slow cook on your hob or in the oven? For me, the oven is the best route. Not only is it easier to forget about (you can go about your day without standing over the hob stirring), but the technique makes much more sense. If you cook something on the hob, the heat comes from the bottom and you're relying on the heat to convect through the liquid and distribute evenly throughout the pot. If you're using a casserole dish or cast-iron dish, you'll have a better shot at this as their thick, heavy walls conduct and distribute heat very well (big-up, Le Creuset). If you're using a standard pot, as the liquid thickens throughout the cook, the heat distribution will get worse, and worse, until the flame of your hob is just hammering the bottom of the pot, your braise catches and your day is ruined. The oven, on the other hand, is the superior braising vehicle. The heat envelopes the whole cooking vessel, an even amount of heat is applied to the whole dish, and you get a nice even cook and beautiful results. On the whole, I like to cook my braises in the oven with a cartouche, which allows liquid to escape and evaporate while protecting the top of the dish from the direct heat of the oven. Pretty neat, right?

How to make a cartouche

If you're not familiar with it, here's the 101. A lid and a cartouche are very different things. A lid is designed to lock moisture in and protect a braise from reducing in the heat of the oven. A cartouche is there to allow a little evaporation/reduction, while protecting the top of the braise from burning.

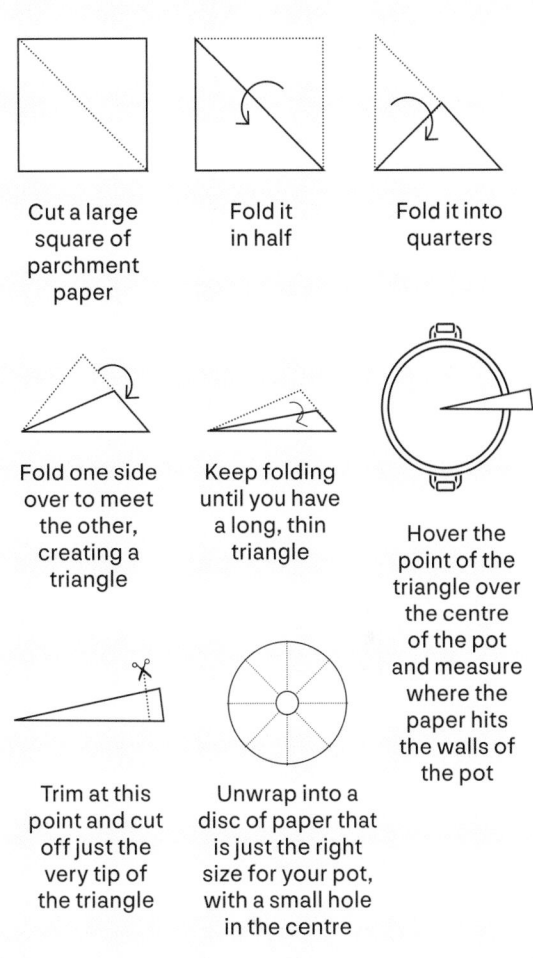

Cut a large square of parchment paper

Fold it in half

Fold it into quarters

Fold one side over to meet the other, creating a triangle

Keep folding until you have a long, thin triangle

Hover the point of the triangle over the centre of the pot and measure where the paper hits the walls of the pot

Trim at this point and cut off just the very tip of the triangle

Unwrap into a disc of paper that is just the right size for your pot, with a small hole in the centre

FINISHING MOVES

With any slow cook – be it stew, slow roast, ragù or braise – it's make or break at the last minute. You've spent hours cooking, the ragù is delicious, the meat has succumbed to the heat of the oven and now, for your final act, you're going to add a handful of choice ingredients to lift everything right at the last moment. Add butter or parmesan, a dash of lemon juice, chopped parsley or floral basil leaves... You've got heaps of options, so choose wisely. The goal with any last-minute additions is to bring new dimension to your braise while also highlighting the rich, slow-cooked depth of flavour. If everything tastes like it's been cooked for three hours, it can be a little flat. Sure, it'll still be very delicious, but it's these last few flourishes that take a braise from good to great.

BACK BURNER

Melted Courgettes & Mozzarella on Toast

- SERVES: 2
- EYES CLOSED
- P
- TOTAL: 40 MINS
- PREP: 10 MINS
- COOK: 30 MINS

Slow cooking in the summer months isn't something that is usually endorsed, but I love a comforting summer green veggie gently braised with olive oil and garlic. It offers a different way to enjoy summer produce and vegetables that are usually cooked quickly or served raw. Slow cooking encourages the vegetables to yield their crunch to the olive oil and garlic and be replaced by a more luxurious, soft, rich texture. It's unfamiliar and a lot of people would say it's 'overcooked' and they'd be, well, wrong. It's also the quickest slow-cook recipe you'll ever make. Lovely veg cookery. I eat mine outside in the sun with some fresh mozzarella, salted anchovies and grilled bread. Embrace the mush, slow-cook your courgettes.

- 4–5 courgettes
- 3 garlic cloves
- ½ tsp dried chilli flakes
- 25g basil
- 2 lemons
- 2 thick slices of sourdough
- 125g fresh mozzarella
- 4–6 salted anchovies
- extra virgin olive oil
- fine sea salt
- black pepper

1 Slice the courgettes into 1cm-thick coins. Try to keep them a consistent size so they cook evenly. Peel and thinly slice two of the garlic cloves.

2 Cover the base of a large saucepan with olive oil and place over a medium heat. When the olive oil is just warm, tip in the garlic and chilli flakes. Sizzle for 2–3 minutes until fragrant and the garlic has lost its raw hum then tip in all of the courgettes. Add half of the basil (whole, stalks and all, tied into a little bunch), plus a healthy pinch of salt. Stir the garlicky olive oil through all of the courgettes to thoroughly coat and lower the heat.

3 Cook, stirring occasionally, for 20–25 minutes until the courgettes have collapsed and have dulled in colour. Finish with plenty of black pepper, the remaining basil leaves and the grated zest and juice of 1 of the lemons.

4 Rub the sourdough with olive oil and toast in a griddle pan until crispy and lightly charred. Halve the remaining garlic clove and rub it over the grilled bread.

5 Divide the melted courgettes between warm plates and serve with the grilled bread, torn pieces of mozzarella, a few anchovies and lemon wedges.

CHEF'S TIP
For even cooking, cut your courgettes into equal-sized pieces and be sure to coat all the slices with a little of the oil and salt.

NOTES
You might think five courgettes for two people is a lot, but they shrink significantly as they braise. You've probably thought the same thing with a whopping great bag of spinach and then watched it shrink into insignificance. Both vegetables are made up of a lot of water and, as they cook, this vanishes and the mass decreases.

Slow-roasted Tomatoes over Rice

- SERVES: 4
- EYES CLOSED
- V / DF
- TOTAL: 2 HOURS 25 MINS
- PREP: 25 MINS
- COOK: 2 HOURS

Slow roasting a peak-season tomato delivers the most pure, intense expression of tomato flavour you can get. The technique can also elevate a slightly lacklustre, out of season fruit into something really special. If you've only got less than lovely tomatoes knocking about, this is a great cheat code to level up their flavour. You can play with the seasonings too – just salt and olive oil is a joy – but I've also enjoyed chopped rosemary, thinly sliced garlic and chilli flakes, gochujang, honey and grated ginger or dried mint, chopped black olives and diced red onions. Served over rice with a few simple garnishes it makes for a really comforting, clean plate of food.

1kg large ripe tomatoes
2 garlic cloves
25g thyme sprigs
150ml light soy sauce
30ml rice vinegar
4 eggs
300g sushi rice
100g frozen edamame beans or petits pois
1 bunch of spring onions
4 tbsp Japanese-style mayo (regular mayo will be delicious, also!)
1 tbsp toasted sesame seeds
1 tsp shichimi togarashi (optional)
sesame oil
fine sea salt
black pepper

1 Preheat the oven to 130°C fan/150°C/300°F/gas mark 2.

2 Halve the tomatoes lengthways, add to a bowl and drizzle with a good glug of sesame oil. Peel and thinly slice the garlic and toss into the bowl along with the thyme sprigs. Season well with 50ml of the soy sauce, 10ml of the rice vinegar and a little salt.

3 Tip the tomatoes onto a baking tray and arrange cut side up. Slide into the oven and bake for 1½–2 hours, or until very sticky, jammy and roasted. They will appear a little dry and dehydrated, but the interior will be super juicy and bursting with flavour.

4 While the tomatoes are slow roasting, it's time to work on the garnishes. Prepare the eggs for soft boiling according to the recipe on page 48. Plunge the eggs into boiling water for 6½ minutes, then transfer to a bowl of iced water. Peel the eggs then pop them in a bag with the remaining 100ml of soy sauce, 1 tablespoon of sesame oil and 20ml of rice vinegar. Leave in the fridge to marinate.

5 Wash the rice in cold running water to remove the excess starch. Drain and add to a lidded saucepan along with 375g of fresh, cold water. Add 1 teaspoon of salt and bring to the boil. Once boiling, reduce the heat to low and pop the lid on. Leave undisturbed for 10–12 minutes, then remove the lid and check if the rice is cooked. If the rice needs a little more time, add an extra splash of water and return it to heat for a couple more minutes, with the lid on. Once the grain is tender, allow to rest with a lid on for at least 10 minutes before fluffing with a fork.

6 When the tomatoes are ready, blanch the edamame or peas in a pan of boiling water for 1 minute and finely chop the trimmed spring onions. Divide the rice among warm bowls and top with a few roasted tomatoes. To each bowl, add a dollop of mayo, a pinch of sesame seeds, a halved soy-marinated egg, a little handful of spring onions, a pile of edamame beans or peas and a good dose of shichimi togarashi, if using.

> **SHOOT FROM THE HIP**
> A slow-roasted tomato makes a mean garnish for a big fat steak (page 270) or squashed between two slices of BLT Bread (page 154) with lashings of mayonnaise and togarashi.

Slow-cooked Squid with Black Olives

- SERVES: 4
- EYES CLOSED
- P / GF
- TOTAL: 70 MINS
- PREP: 15 MINS
- COOK: 55 MINS

Another relatively quick braise that transforms squid from raw, to firm to perfectly tender in just shy of an hour. As the squid slowly cooks, the flavour, along with the texture, also develops. Quick-cooked squid is sweet, saline and bouncy whereas slow-cooked squid develops an intense, savoury character that permeates whatever liquid it's being cooked in. The resulting braise is spectacular and anything cooked in the liquor will soak up that amazing seafood flavour.

700–800g fresh squid, bodies and tentacles, cleaned
3 shallots
½ fennel bulb
3 garlic cloves
1 long red chilli
1 tsp fennel seeds
1 tsp coriander seeds
25g thyme, tied into a bunch
250ml red wine
400g tin good-quality plum tomatoes
350g waxy potatoes
100g pitted taggiasche or kalamata olives
25g flat-leaf parsley
2 unwaxed lemons
extra virgin olive oil
fine sea salt
black pepper
Baguette (page 174), to serve (optional)
Aioli (page 209), to serve

1 To prep the squid, separate the tentacles from the bodies. If they're not too large, leave the tentacles whole, as they'll shrink a little bit when they cook. If you think they're too large, cut them in half. On one side of the squid bodies there is a natural seam that runs from the wide opening at the bottom to the top. Insert your knife into the bottom of the tube and cut along the seam, opening up the squid tube like a book. Use the back of your knife to scrape out any residue inside.

2 Lay the squid flat on your board and use a dining knife to gently score the inside in a cross-hatch pattern. Don't apply too much pressure, just use the natural weight of the knife to make shallow cuts along the squid. Repeat with the other squid bodies then use your sharp knife to cut it into bite-sized pieces.

3 Peel and finely dice the shallots, finely dice the fennel, peel and thinly slice the garlic and halve the chilli lengthways. Preheat a large pan or cast-iron pot over a medium-high heat and cover the base with olive oil. Season the squid with fine sea salt and briefly sear it in the hot pan, working in batches, until it's picked up just a little colour. Remove the squid from the pan, reduce the heat to medium and tip in the shallots, the fennel, plus the fennel and coriander seeds. Season with salt and cook for 5–6 minutes until translucent, then add the halved chilli and the garlic. Cook for 1–2 minutes then add the squid, thyme and wine.

4 Empty the tin of tomatoes into a bowl and use your hands to squash the tomatoes into bite-sized pieces. Tip them and their juice into the pan. Add 150ml of water to the tomato tin to rinse it out, adding it to the pan. Halve the potatoes and get those in, too. Make sure everything is submerged in liquid, season with salt and bring to a bare simmer. Reduce the heat to the lowest setting and let the braise tick over for 50–55 minutes until the squid is tender, the potatoes are cooked and the liquor has reduced and intensified. Add the olives for the last 5–10 minutes of cooking.

5 Fish out the bunch of thyme and finish the braise with finely chopped parsley and the zest and juice of a lemon. Serve with warm baguette, aioli and extra lemon wedges.

> **NOTES**
> Cuttlefish makes an amazing substitution for squid and is an affordable, delicious and readily available ingredient in the UK. They're larger and thicker than squid, so take a little more cooking, but they stand up to the braise really well. Pop into your local fishmonger and ask them about cuttlefish!

CHEF'S TIP
Scoring the squid before braising achieves two things: it tenderises the squid, speeding up that already speedy cook time, and it increases the surface area of the squid, creating hundreds of little crevices to hold on to the rich red wine and tomato sauce.

Braised Chicken 'Pizzaiola'

- SERVES: 4
- EYES CLOSED
- GF
- TOTAL: 1 HOUR 35 MINS
- PREP: 15 MINS
- COOK: 1 HOUR 20 MINS

To cook '*alla pizzaiola*' is to cook in the manner of a pizza maker and embrace a Neapolitan tradition of cooking cheaper cuts of meat gently in a tomato sauce. This is traditionally done with cheaper, tougher cuts of beef, but I love to swap in bone-in chicken thighs. This one is all about building flavour from the ground up. Served on a bed of polenta this makes a great midweek dinner or, simply with a piece of warm bread, a pretty perfect lunch.

8 bone-in chicken thighs
2 red onions
3 garlic cloves
1 long red chilli
1 tbsp fennel seeds
200ml white wine
800g tinned chopped tomatoes
25g fresh oregano, tied into a bunch
150g nocellara olives
125g fresh mozzarella or burrata
olive oil
fine sea salt
black pepper
polenta (page 120), to serve

1 Preheat the oven to 160°C fan/180°C/350°F/gas mark 4.

2 Season the chicken thighs with salt on all sides. Grab a large ovenproof frying pan, add a drizzle of olive oil and nestle the chicken, skin side down, inside. Place over a medium heat and bring the pan up to temperature, listening as the skin begins to sizzle. Cook for 7–8 minutes until the skin is brown and crisp. Once crispy, flip over and briefly sear the underside.

3 While the chicken is cooking, peel and finely dice the onions, peel and thinly slice the garlic cloves and thinly slice the chilli. Once all the chicken is browned, remove the thighs from the pan, leaving behind all that chicken fat and olive oil. Tip in the diced onions, season with a little salt and cook for 5–6 minutes until translucent, before adding the garlic, chilli and fennel seeds. Cook for 2–3 minutes then crank up the heat and dump in the white wine. Deglaze the pan with the white wine, scraping up any brown bits from the bottom before bringing to the boil and reducing the wine by half. Tip in the tomatoes and drop in the bunch of oregano. Stir and season with salt and pepper, bring back to the boil, reduce to a simmer and nestle in the chicken thighs. You want the chicken skin sticking out of the liquid, like alligators in a swamp. Scatter over the olives and then slide into the oven and cook, uncovered, for 1 hour.

4 Once the chicken has had an hour or so, crank up the heat to 200°C fan/220°C/425°F/gas mark 7 for the last few minutes to get some more colour on the skin. Allow to rest for 10 minutes before tearing over the cheese. Serve with warm polenta or fresh bread and olive oil.

> **BRAISING CUTS**
> Chicken thighs are the best cut of the bird for braising. They contain the hardest working muscles and benefit from low and slow cooking to break down tougher connective tissues and more robust dark meat. Braising on the bone boosts the chickeny flavour of your braise and keeps the meat super juicy.

> **CHEF'S TIP**
> I start my chicken thighs in a cold pan with a little olive oil, in a similar way you might cook duck. This way, you render as much fat as possible out of the skin and into the sauce for maximum roast chicken flavour.

Tingly Pork Ragù with Noodles & Salted Cucumbers

SERVES: 4
EYES CLOSED
DF
TOTAL: 90 MINS
PREP: 10 MINS
COOK: 80 MINS

You can have this really tasty, speedy ragù on the table in just an hour and a half. Sichuan peppercorns have a unique characteristic; they make your mouth tingly and numb. It's a moreish, different kind of spice than that of black peppercorns or even chillies. Paired with cooling cucumbers and chewy egg noodles, this ragù ticks all of the boxes.

1 cucumber
500g diced pork shoulder
2 pork sausages
2 white onions
15g ginger
5 garlic cloves
1 tsp Sichuan peppercorns
2 tbsp gochujang chilli paste
1 tbsp dark brown sugar
1 tbsp light soy sauce
2 tbsp sherry vinegar
390g dried egg or wheat noodles
4 spring onions
25g coriander
vegetable oil
fine sea salt

1 Start with the cucumber. Cut it into 1cm-thick rounds and stack the rounds into neat piles. Cut each pile into matchsticks. Put the cucumber matchsticks in a small bowl and season with 1 teaspoon of fine sea salt. Toss together and set aside.

2 Preheat a large cast-iron pan or saucepan over a medium-high heat. Add a thin coat of vegetable oil, lightly season the pork shoulder with salt and, working in batches, sear the meat, being careful not to overcrowd the pan as this will prevent the pork from caramelising. Take your time and build some good colour on the chunks of shoulder. Once browned, remove from the pan. Reduce the heat to medium, remove the casings from the sausages and add the sausages to the hot pan, using a wooden spoon to break the sausage down, rendering the fat from the sausages and browning the meat.

3 While the sausages brown, peel and finely chop the onions and finely grate the ginger and peeled garlic cloves into a paste. Add the onion to the pan with the sausages and cook for 3–4 minutes until translucent, then add the ginger and garlic paste. Coarsely crush the peppercorns using a pestle and mortar or spice grinder and add to the ragù. Mix through the onion and sausage, then cook for 2–3 minutes until super fragrant. Add the gochujang paste, sugar, soy sauce and about 500ml of water, bring to the boil then reduce to a bare simmer. Add the pork shoulder back to the pan and let the ragù tick over on a very low heat for 60–70 minutes, or until the pork shoulder is fork tender.

4 Once the ragù is cooked, use a couple of forks to shred the shoulder chunks and season with the sherry vinegar and add a little more soy if needed.

5 Cook the noodles according to the packet instructions. Once cooked, drain and briefly rinse under cold running water. Toss the noodles with a little of the sauce from the ragù and keep warm. Thinly slice the trimmed spring onions. Set up a bowl of iced water and use it to rinse the salt from the cucumbers. Cut the coriander into large stems and briefly refresh in the iced water. Divide the noodles among warm bowls, top with spoonfuls of the meaty ragù, a handful of the drained, salted cucumber, spring onions and some iced coriander.

BACK BURNER

Pomegranate Lamb Ribs & Parsley Salad

- **SERVES: 4**
- **EYES CLOSED**
- **TOTAL: 2 HOURS**
- **PREP: 15 MINS**
- **COOK: 1½–2 HOURS**

Pork might hold the limelight, but for my money, there isn't a rib out there offering better flavour and texture than lamb. They're hilariously easy to cook, and this recipe is, for the most part, pretty hands-off. Marinate them in something delicious and then bake, low and slow, on a rack in the oven. Finish with a handful of grassy parsley leaves, green chillies and plenty of lemon juice. You'll want to serve these with a cold beer and a fat stack of napkins.

FOR THE LAMB RIBS

22–24 lamb ribs	
1 tsp black peppercorns	
2 tsp cumin seeds	
1 tsp nigella seeds	
2 garlic cloves	
15g rosemary	
2 tbsp pomegranate molasses	
2 tbsp honey	
1 tbsp light soy sauce	
2 tbsp lemon juice	
fine sea salt	

FOR THE PARSLEY SALAD

- 100g flat-leaf parsley
- 2 green chillies
- 2 echalion shallots
- 1 lemon
- extra virgin olive oil
- flaky sea salt

TO SERVE

- 200g thick Greek yoghurt
- 50g honey

1 Put the lamb ribs in a bowl or a large plastic sandwich bag. Add the peppercorns, cumin seeds and nigella seeds to a small, dry frying pan, place over a medium heat and toast for 2–3 minutes until fragrant, before tipping into a mortar and coarsely crushing. Add the garlic cloves, peeled, plus a generous pinch of salt, then crush the cloves into the spices. Roughly chop the rosemary leaves and get them in there, too. Add the molasses, honey and soy sauce to the mortar and mix into a marinade. Tip over the lamb ribs and mix to coat. Marinate in the fridge for at least 30 minutes or up to 5 hours.

2 When ready to cook, preheat the oven to 140°C fan/160°C/325°F/gas mark 3. Line a baking tray with parchment paper and set a rack over the top. Lay the lamb ribs out on the rack leaving a little space between each rib. You might need to spread the ribs across a couple of trays, and that's fine!

3 Slide the tray of lamb ribs into the oven and cook, uncovered, for 1½–2 hours until the meat is super tender and the fat has rendered. Check on them after an hour and whip out any smaller ribs. As they're uncovered, the marinade will dehydrate, lacquering onto the meat as it cooks. You want to bake these pretty dark, so be brave: the soy and molasses might lead you to believe they're colouring too much, but have faith!

4 To make the parsley salad, first fill a bowl with iced water. Pick the leaves from the parsley and thinly slice the chillies. Peel and slice the shallots into thin rounds and separate into rings. Add the whole lot to the iced water for 10 minutes to crisp up and refresh.

5 Pull the ribs out of the oven – no need to rest these! Drain the shallots, chillies and herbs and dry in a salad spinner or on kitchen paper. Toss into a bowl and dress with olive oil, salt and lots of lemon juice. Serve a pile of the sticky lamb ribs with a dollop of yoghurt topped with honey and handfuls of the lemony parsley salad.

> **SHOOT FROM THE HIP**
> You can glaze these ribs with all sorts, just make sure there's a nice balance of sweetness, salinity and acidity. For a barbecue vibe, you could try smoked paprika, English mustard powder, maple syrup and apple cider vinegar.

One-pot Mushroom Bourguignon

- SERVES: 4
- TOTAL: 1 HOUR 50 MINS
- ROLL YOUR SLEEVES UP
- PREP: 20 MINS
- V
- COOK: 1 HOUR 30 MINS

This is a delicious braise that heroes mushrooms, but still has the heft and body of a classic beef bourguignon. It's far lighter, shines with rich red wine, sweet onions and heady thyme, and uses significantly less meat. Skip the meat and just use a good-quality beef stock to bring enough body and oomph to this recipe if you're that way inclined.

1kg mixed wild mushrooms (chanterelles, oyster mushrooms or similar)
350g small round shallots or pearl onions
200g Chantenay carrots
1 leek
2 garlic cloves
150g unsalted butter
50g plain flour
2 tbsp tomato purée
400ml full-bodied red wine
600ml mushroom or beef stock
1 tbsp dark soy sauce
25g thyme sprigs, tied into a bunch
3 fresh bay leaves
750g large Maris Piper potatoes
25g chives
olive oil
fine sea salt
black pepper
The Green Salad (page 70), to serve

1 Preheat the oven to 190°C fan/210°C/410°F/gas mark 6.

2 Make sure your mushrooms are free of grit or dirt. If the mushrooms are a little dirty, grab two bowls, filling the first with warm water from the tap and the second with cold water. Plunge the mushrooms into the first – the warm water will open up the pores of the mushrooms and rinse away any dirt – and swirl them around for 20 seconds max before transferring them to the cold water, repeating and then drying with a salad spinner or on clean towels. Once clean, tear the mushrooms into large pieces. Peel the pearl onions and Chantenay carrots, keeping them whole. Thinly slice the leek and peel and thinly slice the garlic cloves.

3 Preheat a large cast-iron pot or casserole dish over a high heat. Add a generous amount of olive oil and, once hot, tip in the mushrooms. Cook, undisturbed, for 2–3 minutes to get some real colour on the side touching the pan, then scoop out and set aside. Allow the pan to cool off a little before dropping in 75g of the butter. Once melted and beginning to foam, add the flour. Whisk together and cook over a medium-low heat for 10–12 minutes until very dark, whisking constantly. You're going for the colour of milk chocolate.

4 Add the tomato purée and whisk it into the hot roux. It'll sizzle and spit a little. Now add the leek with a pinch of salt and cook for 1–2 minutes before adding the garlic. Sweat for another 1 minute then tip in the onions, carrots, red wine, stock and soy sauce. Bring to the boil, stirring constantly, and watch as the roux thickens the braise. Once boiling, add the bunch of thyme (reserving a sprig or two) and the bay leaves, reduce to a simmer and add the mushrooms. Add 20 twists of black pepper and a touch of salt. Remove from the heat and set aside.

5 Peel the potatoes and use a sharp knife or mandoline to thinly slice them – you're aiming for a thickness of about 2–3mm. Stack the slices up into 8–10cm-high piles, then lay the stacks down on their sides around the perimeter of the pot, creating a halo effect. They should be half submerged in the braise and half exposed to the heat of the oven. Cut the remaining butter into small pieces and dot around the potatoes. Drizzle with a little olive oil, pick over the remaining thyme and season with salt.

6 Slide into the oven and bake for 50–60 minutes, until the braise has reduced and the potatoes are crispy on the top and tender underneath. Finish with finely chopped chives and serve with a vinegary green salad.

Spiced Short Ribs with Dates & Warm Hummus

- SERVES: 4–6
- ROLL YOUR SLEEVES UP
- DF
- TOTAL: 4 HOURS 30 MINS
- PREP: 30 MINS
- COOK: 4 HOURS

There's a restaurant I love on Shacklewell Lane in London called Oren. Oded and Lisa who run it are good friends and eating there never fails to put a smile on my face. Oded serves a meltingly soft beef cheek, glazed with beef sauce with hummus, and it's an absolute triumph. I've made this easy version for the home cook and have added a few little twists of my own.

FOR THE BRAISED SHORT RIBS

- 4–6 chunky bone-in short ribs
- 2 white onions
- 1 garlic bulb
- 1 red chilli
- 25g rosemary
- 4 star anise
- 2 cinnamon sticks
- 200ml red wine
- 1 litre good-quality beef stock
- 1 tbsp date molasses
- 2 tbsp red wine vinegar
- 5–6 medjool dates, pitted
- olive oil
- fine sea salt
- black pepper

1 Preheat the oven to 150°C fan/170°C/325°F/gas mark 3.

2 Season your short ribs generously with fine sea salt. Preheat a large casserole dish over a medium-high heat. Add a good glug of olive oil and work in batches to sear off the ribs. This is where the flavour begins, so make sure the ribs get good and brown. While the ribs sear, peel the onions and cut them into wedges, halve the garlic bulb and cut the chilli in half lengthways. I keep everything pretty chunky so it's easier to remove later on – if you dice too small it'll cook into oblivion, become one with the beef fat and stock and you won't get as shiny and sticky a glaze.

3 Once your beef ribs are seared, scoop them out of the pan, leaving behind all of the rendered beef fat and olive oil. Add the onions, garlic and chilli and brown them in the beef fat for 5–6 minutes until caramelised and dark. Drop in the rosemary and spices and tip in the red wine to deglaze your pan, then bring to the boil and reduce by half. Return the ribs to the pan and cover with the beef stock. Bring to a simmer, add a cartouche (page 233) and slide into the oven too cook for 3–3½ hours, checking now and then to monitor the liquid level – if it looks a little dry as it cooks, add a splash of water.

4 To make the pickled onion, peel and cut the onions into very thin rings using a mandoline or sharp knife. Split the chilli lengthways and add to a heatproof bowl with the onion rings and a pinch of salt. Add the sugar, vinegar and scrunched bay leaf to a saucepan and place over a medium heat. Bring to the boil then pour over the onions. Set aside to cool.

5 To make the hummus, tip the chickpeas plus the liquid from the jar into a saucepan. Place over a medium heat and bring to a bare simmer. Once warm, drain the chickpeas, saving the warm liquor, and add to a food processor or blender. Add the tahini, finely grate in the peeled garlic clove, and add the lemon juice and a healthy pinch of salt. Turn the machine on and drizzle in 50–60ml of olive oil. Add a little of the cooking water to loosen and adjust the texture to your liking. I blend my hummus for a good 8–10 minutes, seasoning to taste as I go and blending in a couple of ice cubes right at the end to add air.

Continued overleaf ⟶

FOR THE PICKLED RED ONION

2 red onions

1 long red chilli

40g light brown sugar

120g apple cider vinegar

1 fresh bay leaf

FOR THE HUMMUS

700g jar good-quality cooked chickpeas

70g tahini

1 garlic clove

1–2 lemons

olive oil

fine sea salt

FOR THE BULGUR SALAD

220g bulgur wheat

100g flat-leaf parsley

1 lemon

olive oil

fine sea salt

6 Now make the bulgur salad. Bring a pan of salted water to the boil. Rinse the bulgur wheat a few times with cold water, then drain and add to the boiling water. Cook for 10–12 minutes, or until just tender. Drain in a sieve and allow to steam for 6–7 minutes before adding to a bowl. Finely chop the parsley, stalks and all, and toss into the bowl with the bulgur, add the grated zest and juice of the lemon and a glug of olive oil. Toss together, taste and season with salt if needed.

7 Once the ribs are meltingly tender and the bones are easily removed, whip the dish out the oven. Allow the ribs to rest for 10–15 minutes before sliding the bones out and trimming away any sinew or unwanted bits. Set aside while you make the glaze. Set a sieve over a clean saucepan and pour in the cooking liquor and veggies. Gently press on the vegetables to get as much sauce as you can out of them. Skim a little of the fat from the cooking liquor, but not all of it – you want a good dose of beef fat in your glaze for a lip-smacking, shiny texture. Place the pan over a medium-high heat and bring the whole lot to a simmer. Add the date molasses and vinegar and reduce the liquor until you have a sticky glaze. Taste as you go, as the liquor will intensify while it reduces and become saltier. Once you're happy with the flavour, stop! Add your short ribs to the pan and spoon over the glaze. Swirl them about and get them good and coated. Drop in your dates and allow them to gently soak up some glaze and warm through.

8 Add a generous dollop of hummus to your warm plates. Divide the short ribs among the plates and sidle a few dates alongside. Spoon over the rich beef and date sauce, flooding the plate. Top the sticky, glazed short ribs with a pinch of pickled onions, finish with a drizzle of oil and serve with the bulgur salad on the side.

CHEF'S TIP

Getting the hummus texture just right is super important. We want it to be spoonable, luxurious and rich, but thick enough that it holds up when dropped onto the plate. Go steady with the water and finish with a few ice cubes to whip up the hummus for a silky-smooth finish.

NOTES ON SHORT RIBS

When buying short ribs, look for that intramuscular fat. You might have heard it referred to as 'marbling', a network of ivory-white fat running through the meat. This fat is essential if you want a juicy, tender rib. You also want a rib with a good meat-to-bone ratio. A big bone isn't everything and some folks say it adds bags of flavour to your glaze, and there's some truth to that, but we don't want to eat the bone, we're after what's attached to it – look for a decent bone, but even more meat. I debone my short ribs before serving, eschewing the theatre of the Fred Flinstone-esque style in favour of practicality.

Toulouse Sausage with Lentils & Horseradish Salsa Verde

- SERVES: 4
- ROLL YOUR SLEEVES UP
- GF
- TOTAL: 135 MINS
- PREP: 15 MINS
- COOK: 120 MINS

Cooking lentils in this style is a story of two halves. You first gently poach them and infuse them with earthy, vegetal notes; then, once they're almost cooked, they are finished with butter, lemon and a zippy horseradish salsa verde. I adore a Toulouse sausage – they have a distinct garlicky edge, but if you can't find them, just use whatever sausages you like. As the sausages cook, they render beautiful fats and juices into the lentils, giving them even more life and energy. It's proper old-school cooking at its best.

FOR THE LENTILS

- 200g dried puy lentils
- 2 onions
- 1 carrot
- 1 celery stick
- 1 leek
- 1 bouquet garni (bay, rosemary, thyme)
- 8 Toulouse-style sausages
- 150ml dry white wine
- 15g unsalted butter
- 1 lemon
- olive oil
- fine sea salt
- black pepper

FOR THE SALSA VERDE

- 200g spinach
- 25g flat-leaf parsley
- 10g tarragon
- 20g nonpareille capers
- 1 small garlic clove
- 2 tsp hot horseradish sauce
- extra virgin olive oil
- fine sea salt

1 Tip the lentils into a large saucepan. Chunk up one of the onions, the carrot, celery stick and the green half of the leek, saving the sweet white half for later. Add the bouquet garni, cover with cold water and season with salt. Bring to the boil, then reduce to the barest of simmers and cook for 20–25 minutes, or until you can squash a lentil between your thumb and forefinger, but they aren't completely tender. Once you're there, add a handful of ice cubes or a splash of cold water to slow down the cooking process. Allow the lentils to rest in the cooking liquor for 5–10 minutes before draining, reserving the cooking liquid and discarding the veggies and bouquet garni.

2 Preheat the oven to 180°C fan/200°C/400°F/gas mark 6 and finely chop the remaining leek and onion.

3 Place a large ovenproof sauté pan or cast-iron pot over a medium heat. Before it's hot, add a shot of olive oil and sit the sausages inside. Hear the sausages start to sizzle as the pan comes up to temperature and cook for 2–3 minutes on one side, then flip and repeat. Remove the sausages, add a little extra olive oil and toss in the onion and leek. Sweat with a pinch of salt for 3–4 minutes. Add the white wine and reduce until the pan is almost dry, then add the lentils and a few ladles of the cooking liquid – just enough to pool out of the lentils. Sit the sausages on top and slide into the oven for 10–12 minutes.

4 To make the salsa verde, bring a small pot of water to the boil. Add the spinach and parsley, stalks and all, and cook for 1 minute. Scoop out and refresh with cold water. Squeeze as much moisture as you can from the greens then add to a blender. Add the leaves from the tarragon, the capers, peeled garlic clove and horseradish sauce with a pinch of salt and a generous glug of olive oil and blend into a smooth, green salsa. Add a little cold water or extra oil if you need to get things moving. You want this to be thick, not too runny, so go easy.

5 Remove the lentils from the oven, whip the sausages off and add the salsa verde to the pan along with the butter. Swirl into the lentils until rich, bright green and emulsified. If you need to add a little more of the cooking liquor to loosen things up, go ahead, you want the lentils nice and saucy. Finish with the grated zest of the whole lemon and half the juice, adding more if you like. Spoon the lentils onto warm plates and top with the sausages.

Beef Cheek & Scotch Bonnet Pie

SERVES: 6–8

ROLL YOUR SLEEVES UP

TOTAL: 4 HOURS 30 MINS

PREP: 30 MINS

COOK: 4 HOURS

I started my London life in New Cross, surrounded by incredible Caribbean food. This one is inspired by that time. My mate and certified London pie king, Will Lewis (Willy's Pies) helped me out with this recipe. We've made a few pies together before and I knew he was the man to call for this one. Beef cheek is the perfect thing to stick in a pie. It's big, boisterous, and can stand up to a stout braise and the fruity, addictive heat of scotch bonnet.

FOR THE BRAISE

800g beef cheeks, shin or stewing steak

500g small round shallots

2 carrots

2 celery sticks

6 garlic cloves

1 tbsp tomato purée

25g thyme sprigs, tied into a bunch

1 tsp ground allspice

60g plain flour

440ml Guinness

500ml good-quality beef stock

2 tsp brown sugar

1–2 scotch bonnet chillies

olive oil

fine sea salt

black pepper

FOR THE PASTRY

400g self-raising flour, plus extra for dusting

200g beef suet

1 tbsp ground turmeric

2 tsp salt

280–300g whole milk, cold, plus a little extra for the egg wash

2 egg yolks

5g fresh thyme leaves

flaky sea salt

TO SERVE

300g frozen peas

chilli jam

1 Preheat the oven to 150°C fan/170°C/325°F/gas mark 3. Preheat a large saucepan or cast-iron pot over a high heat. Cut the beef cheeks in half and season generously with salt. Cover the base of the saucepan with a layer of olive oil and sear the cheeks on all sides. Peel the shallots and halve any larger ones so they're all roughly the same size. Peel and cut the carrots and celery into a 2cm dice. Peel the garlic cloves and roughly chop.

2 Remove the seared cheeks from the pan and set aside. Add the shallots, carrots and celery, reduce the heat to medium and cook for 10–12 minutes to pick up some good colour. Stir through the garlic and tomato purée and cook for 1–2 minutes, then add the thyme, allspice and flour. Cook for a good 3–4 minutes to cook out the flour, adding a little extra oil if the mix looks dry. Add the Guinness gradually, scraping the bottom of the pan to deglaze. Now add the beef stock, brown sugar and seared cheeks. Poke some holes in the scotch bonnets using a small knife and drop them into the braise (add both if you like it spicy). Bring to a bare simmer, cover with a cartouche (page 233) and slide into the oven to cook for 2½–3 hours, until the cheeks are soft but not completely falling apart. Once cooked, break the beef cheeks into bite-sized pieces, season to taste, then tip the mixture into a tray and allow to cool to room temperature.

3 To make the pastry, combine the flour, suet, turmeric and salt in a bowl. Add the cold milk gradually, using a fork to stir it through the dry ingredients, until you can form a shaggy dough. Use your hand to knead the dough in the ball until it's smooth and homogenous, then wrap it in cling film and rest for 5–10 minutes. Generously grease a 24–26cm oven dish or pie dish. Cut a third of the pastry away and set aside. On a floured surface, roll the large portion into a disc roughly 5mm thick and large enough to line your pie dish with plenty of overhang. Transfer to the prepared dish and encourage the pastry into the corners. Tip the cooled beef mixture into the dish. Dust the remaining pastry with flour and roll it out until it's large enough to cover the pie.

4 Beat the egg yolks with a splash of milk and a tiny pinch of salt and brush over the edge of the pie crust. Add the lid and use a fork to seal the edge. Trim the excess pastry and cut a vent in the middle of the pie. Chill in the fridge for 20–30 minutes.

5 Preheat the oven to 220°C fan/240°C/460°F/gas mark 9. Brush the top of the pie with egg wash and add some flaky salt and thyme leaves. Bake in the oven for 15 minutes, then turn the oven down to 180°C and bake for another 45 minutes. Allow to rest for 10–15 minutes before removing from the tin, slicing and serving with peas and chilli jam.

Lamb Shoulder with White Beans & Chard

SERVES: 6
ROLL YOUR SLEEVES UP
DF
TOTAL: 12 HOURS 30 MINS
PREP: 30 MINS
COOK: 10–12 HOURS

A lamb shoulder is a firm favourite and can be done literally hours before you eat it, ready to be liaised with something delicious (in this case, white beans) and plonked on the dinner table to be devoured. Now, you can cook a pretty good lamb shoulder in about 3 hours, but if you want ultra soft, super-luxe braised lamb, prep it the night before, set your oven to a balmy 100°C and leave the shoulder in there overnight. You'll wake up to a meltingly soft lamb, ready for a quick blast in a hot oven to crisp up. Serve with garlicky white beans, chard and a zippy romesco for a Sunday lunch.

FOR THE LAMB SHOULDER

- 2kg bone-in lamb shoulder
- 3 white onions
- 6 garlic cloves
- 2 red chillies
- 10 tinned anchovy fillets
- 25g rosemary sprigs
- 200ml white wine
- 500ml good-quality chicken stock
- 2 x 600g jars white beans
- 300g rainbow chard
- 1 tbsp sherry vinegar
- olive oil
- fine sea salt
- black pepper

FOR THE ROMESCO SAUCE

- 200g blanched almonds
- 1 tbsp sweet smoked paprika
- 350g jarred roasted peppers, drained
- 1 garlic clove
- 40ml sherry vinegar
- olive oil
- fine sea salt

1 Preheat the oven to 250°C fan/270°C/500°F/gas mark 10.

2 Rub the lamb with a little olive oil and season well with salt. Set a rack in a large roasting tin and sit the lamb on top. Slide into the oven and roast for 25 minutes until well coloured. Remove from the oven and set aside.

3 Peel the onions and cut into wedges, lightly crush half the garlic cloves and halve one of the chillies lengthways. Take a roasting tin large enough to sit your lamb in and place it over a high heat. Add 2 tablespoons of olive oil, add the onion, and sear for 4–5 minutes until browned on the cut sides. Drop in the crushed garlic, halved chilli, 5 of the anchovy fillets and half the rosemary. Cook for 1 minute, then add the white wine. Bring to the boil and reduce by half, then add the chicken stock and sit the seared lamb on top. Cover with a sheet of parchment paper then a sheet of foil and seal the foil tightly around the tin. Reduce the oven temperature to 100°C and slide the tin straight into the oven. Leave for 10–12 hours.

4 The next day, add the almonds to a small frying pan. Add 50ml of olive oil and place over a medium-low heat. Gently toast the almonds for 8–10 minutes until a rich golden brown, add the paprika and remove from the heat. Tip the drained peppers into a blender with the peeled garlic, toasted nuts and paprika oil. Add the vinegar and a pinch of salt then whizz into a smooth, thick romesco sauce. Add more oil to loosen and season to taste.

5 Pull the tin out of the oven and remove the foil and parchment. Carefully lift the braised lamb gently onto a roasting tin lined with parchment. Pour the liquid in the tin through a sieve and into a clean pan. Let it settle, then skim off as much of the fat as you can. Bring to a simmer and reduce until rich and delicious, tasting as you go.

6 Drain and rinse the beans. Peel and thinly slice the remaining garlic cloves and chilli and strip the rosemary leaves from the stems. Tear the leaves off the chard stems. Finely chop the stems and tear the leaves into large pieces. Preheat a large saucepan over a medium heat. Add a little of the lamb fat and drop in the garlic, chilli, chard stems, plus the remaining anchovy fillets and rosemary. Cook for 2–3 minutes until fragrant before adding the beans. Add the lamb sauce and warm through. Finish with the torn chard leaves, cook until wilted, then finish with the vinegar.

7 Crank the oven back up to 250°C. Slide the lamb back in and crisp it up in the oven for 5–6 minutes.

8 Serve the crispy lamb shoulder over the beans and chard with a bowl of the romesco sauce on the side.

TOASTING NUTS
If you're toasting nuts in a dry pan, you're only going to toast that little bit of the nut that is in contact with the pan. It's all too easy to burn them; for an even toast, you need to envelop the whole nut with heat. You can do this in an oven set at 150°C, or you can gently toast the nut in warm oil. Try out this technique when making the romesco!

OVER

Cipollata alla Siciliana 258

Burnt Leeks & Gribiche 260

Charred Lettuces & Bagna Cauda 262

Smoky Mussels with Rockefeller Butter 263

Barbecued Scallops with Chilli Butter & Raita 264

Cumin Lamb Skewers 266

Barbecue Whole Chicken with Hot Green Tahini 267

Grilled T-Bone, Embered Sweet Potatoes & Gorgonzola 270

Pork Chops with Peppers & Peaches 273

Stuffed Bass with Fregola, 'Nduja & Gordal Olives 276

FIRE

Cooking over fire is about as close to your ancestors as you'll get in the kitchen. It shouldn't be complex, but a whole host of products, gadgets and useless tech can cloud the way a little.

When it comes to kit, cooking and ingredients, less is always more on the barbecue. As well as keeping things very simple, always consider that your charcoal is one of your hero ingredients. The best barbecue recipes consist of a few ingredients, simply grilled and seasoned beautifully. Grilling is usually a social affair. You're rarely grilling for one (although I would highly encourage you to do so – be kind to yourself!) and I don't really go in for cooking a million individual sausages and burgers; it's too stressful and things are never ready at the same time. For me, the best way to approach grilling is to absolutely nail a couple of centrepieces. Not only are these more interesting (and impressive . . .) than a load of sausages, but they also make life much easier for you. Grab a big steak and a whole fish and feed a crowd without breaking a sweat. Keep it simple (stupid!), invest in a good grill and you'll never buy a disposable barbecue or a pack of pre-made burgers again.

GAS VS CHARCOAL

Gas barbecues are a bit naff. Sure, they're easy to use and clean – just turn them on and in about 15 minutes they're ready to rock – but you're missing out on some serious flavour. Charcoal is a bit more finicky to light, but don't be afraid of it, it's actually very easy, I'll show you how in a minute. As well as firing up quickly, gas barbecues can make temperature control very easy – with just the twist of a dial, you can drop or increase the heat in a flash, which is super handy and not as readily available to you on a charcoal grill. You can (and should) set up a charcoal grill with a hot zone and a cold zone. You do that by piling all your coals onto one side, creating a super-hot direct cooking zone for searing steaks, crispy fish skin and charring veggies. The other side of the grill is much cooler and used for indirect cooking, gradually bringing meat up to temperature or slowly softening aubergines. There are ways to control the heat on a charcoal barbecue that are far more fun and intuitive than turning a knob. I think the most important thing is that a gas barbecue doesn't offer real, heady, addictive smoky flavour . . .

The flavour that charcoal barbecues offer is just not achievable on a gas barbecue: hot fat dripping onto coals, flaring up and enveloping fish or meat with smoke is irreplaceable. It informs so much of what makes open-fire cooking and eating so enjoyable and I urge you to give it a go. If you're buying your first charcoal grill, go for a super simple piece of kit. A kettle or drum barbecue is a great place to start, and they can be picked up new or second-hand for a fraction of the price of a gas grill.

> ### Heat control
>
> As well as having cooking zones, and controlling air flow, don't be afraid to add more charcoal to control your heat. Folks often think they only have one shot at the barbecue title – one round of charcoal and that's that – but you can 'feed' your grill with more fuel as you go. Just make sure there's just enough heat left in the grill to light the charcoal that you're adding.

HOW TO LIGHT YOUR FUEL

What's the best way to light a charcoal barbecue? This seems to be the main speed bump on the road to barbecuing and it doesn't need to be. To light a barbecue, you will need three things:

- Charcoal
- A firelighter
- A box of matches

Believe it or not, you don't need a shedload of balled-up newspaper or a bottle of lighter fluid (that stuff is horrible, avoid at all costs). You can use a chimney starter, and I'd recommend investing in one if you plan to get into grilling. They're very cheap and make this job incredibly easy. Just pack them full to the brim with charcoal, light a firelighter on your grill and sit the chimney on top. In 20–30 minutes you'll have a basket of perfectly lit charcoal, ready to cook with. Tip it out into your barbecue and you're good to grill.

If you don't have a chimney starter, go down the volcano route. Pop your firelighter into the base of your barbecue and build a volcano of charcoal around it, leaving a few air gaps here and there (don't overthink it). If you're worried there's too much charcoal, drop another firelighter in there to be safe. Top off your cone-shaped pile with one final piece of charcoal and light the firelighters. Now don't touch it. Let it do its thing for 15–20 minutes before taking a look. I know it's tempting to poke and prod, but you'll probably knock it over and have to start again. If you're using a high-quality charcoal, this process is super quick, and you can start cooking a good bit before all the charcoal turns white. Hover your hand above the coals to gauge the heat. If it's hot and smells delicious, it's cooking time.

> **Flare-ups**
>
> Flare-ups occur when fat drips off a pork chop or steak, hits the hot charcoal and ignites. A little of this is actually good – it's how a whole heap of smoky flavour gets onto your food – but too much is not ideal as the food can get sooty, burnt and pick up ash from the grill. If you're cooking something super fatty and flare-ups are likely, have a little spray bottle of water, beer or a little diluted vinegar ready to spritz onto the fire to put it out.

GRILL ZONES AND AIR FLOW

Now you've got your barbecue locked in, your fuel sorted, and you know how to light it, it's time to set that thing up for success. You want to separate your grill into a hot zone and a cool zone. Naturally, the space in between the two will act as your medium zone (or purgatory, as I like to call it). Just pile your coals over to one side and have one side free of any heat. It's as simple as that. This gives you the ability to be agile with your ingredients – you can pull big steaks off to give them a break, rest burgers while you toast buns, and gently warm sauces and marinades away from the fierce direct heat.

RESTING RIG

As well as hot and cold zones on your grill, having a designated landing pad for cooked meats, fish and veggies is also super handy. I like to have a tray resting on one side of the grill full of something flavourful for ingredients to hang out in. Brown butter is perfect for this: just stick a pan onto the grill, add 100g of butter and cook until it's nut brown, then drop in smashed garlic cloves, aromatic spices and maybe some hard herbs like rosemary or thyme to add even more flavour. Pour this onto your tray and, once your steak or fish is cooked, transfer it to the flavour-bath of butter to rest.

> **How to make any grill non-stick!**
>
> Grills can get pretty gnarly over time, building up layers of sauce, grease and residue from the last thing you grilled. This crusty business is what makes your fish skin, burgers and pork chops stick to your grill. The best way to prepare your grill before cooking is to get it very hot, then brush it down with a wire brush or scourer to remove any chunks of debris, then rub it down with an oiled rag until the grates are black and shiny, allowing the charcoal to heat the oil in between each rub down. Repeat a few times and you'll have seasoned your grill just like a cast-iron or carbon-steel pan and it'll be pretty much non-stick!

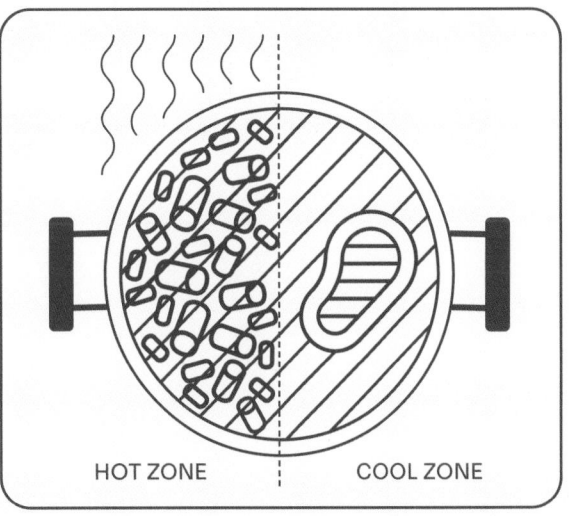

HOT ZONE | COOL ZONE

OVER FIRE

Cipollata alla Siciliana

- SERVES: 4
- EYES CLOSED
- DF / GF
- TOTAL: 35 MINS
- PREP: 15 MINS
- COOK: 20 MINS

This feels like a lovely place to start: a simple recipe that celebrates the humble onion, elevating it with just a very small list of ingredients and the magic of open-fire cookery. The smell of these little bundles gently grilling is to die for. Cipollata Siciliana literally means Sicilian onions – it's a classic street food from the Italian island that is utterly perfect on a hot day with a cold beer. They are a perfect little opener to an afternoon of grilling or the start of a larger feast.

500g piece of boneless pork belly, skin removed
16 chunky spring onions
4 garlic cloves
4 tbsp fish sauce
1 tbsp dried oregano
2 lemons
extra virgin olive oil
black pepper

1 Stick the pork belly into the freezer for 30 minutes or so before you want to slice it. Once cold, whip it out and flip it over so it's fat side down. Using your longest, sharpest knife, cut long, thin slices of pork belly, a similar thickness to bacon. Don't panic too much if they aren't wafer thin, just do your best. If your pork gets too warm and starts to soften up, stick it back in the freezer for 5–10 minutes. As the piece gets smaller, it will become trickier to cut thin slices. At this point, you can cut the pork into two pieces and cut slightly smaller slices from those (you can use toothpicks to secure them in place). Once sliced, set aside the pork.

2 Grade your spring onions according to size: you want to use your largest onion as your yard stick. I like to grill them in pairs or threes – it gives you more to wrap around than just a single onion. Bundle together the spring onions so each little pile is roughly the same size.

3 Wrap the little bundles of onions in strips of your pork belly, using toothpicks to secure the slices together and keep them from unravelling. As the pork cooks, it will contract around the onions but when raw they can be a bit flimsy. Wrap enough pork around the onions so that you have just the very green ends sticking out of the top of each little bundle.

4 To make the marinade, peel and finely grate the garlic cloves and add them to a small mixing bowl. Mix in the fish sauce, dried oregano and the juice of 1 of the lemons. Add a little olive oil and 20 twists of black pepper.

5 Light your barbecue, creating a hot zone and a cold zone. Allow the barbecue to pass through its hottest phase and start to cool. Once at a medium-high heat, pop the onions on the hot side of the grill. Cook for 5–6 minutes until the pork belly fat starts to render and spit a little. If things get a little hectic and flames start shooting up, you can move the onions to the cool zone and then back once the fire has settled. Roll the little bundles around, crisping up the pork belly and steaming the onions within. Once crispy and caramelised, start to brush them with the marinade and between each layer, grilling until it's lacquered on. Grill for 12–13 minutes until nicely glazed and completely cooked, then allow them to rest for a few minutes before cutting into bite-sized pieces. Drizzle with a little olive oil and serve with fresh lemon wedges.

Burnt Leeks & Gribiche

- SERVES: 4 AS A SIDE
- TOTAL: 35 MINS, PLUS COOLING
- ROLL YOUR SLEEVES UP
- PREP: 10 MINS, PLUS COOLING
- DF / GF
- COOK: 25 MINS

Cook the leeks in their skins, completely charring and burning the exterior before peeling back to reveal the lightly smoked, perfectly steamed sweet leeks inside. This is such a fantastic BBQ side, and would be stunning alongside a plate of grilled sardines or a couple of pork chops.

6 leeks
4 eggs, plus 2 egg yolks
2 tbsp Dijon mustard
2 lemons
150ml vegetable oil
2 shallots
60g dill pickles or cornichons
3 tbsp capers
20g dill
20g chives
10g tarragon
olive oil
fine sea salt
black pepper

1 Cut off the very tops of the leeks then pop the leeks into a bowl of water while you make the gribiche.

2 Bring a small pan of water to a rolling boil. Boil the four eggs for 8 minutes, then remove and plunge into iced water. Once cool enough to handle, gently crack the shells and return to the water for a minute or two. Peel the shells from the eggs, using the bowl of water to help wash away any shards of shell as you go. Set aside.

3 Add the yolks to a food processor along with the Dijon, the juice of 1 of the lemons and 2 tablespoons of water. Season with a good pinch of salt and turn on the processor. Slowly stream in the vegetable oil, creating an emulsion, then stream in roughly the same quantity of olive oil, stopping when you have super thick, almost jiggly mayonnaise.

4 Peel and finely dice the shallots and add to a small bowl with the juice of the remaining lemon. Set aside for 3–4 minutes. Finely chop the boiled eggs, pickles, capers, dill, chives and tarragon and add them to a mixing bowl. Drain the lemon juice from the shallots and tip them into the bowl, too. Add a couple of spoons of your mayonnaise and mix the sauce together. It should be chunky, with just enough mayonnaise to bind it together – don't go adding all the mayo at once, just bit by bit until you've got a texture you're into. If it's a little thick, you can add some lemon juice to loosen things up. Season with 35 twists of black pepper and a good pinch of salt.

5 Pull the leeks out of the bowl of water and shake off the excess water. Light your barbecue and when it hits peak heat, slap the leeks straight onto the hottest part of the grill. Roll them around, grilling all sides, until charred all over and collapsing. They'll look super burnt, but the interior will be gorgeous. This whole process will take about 10–15 minutes, depending on the ferocity of your barbecue.

6 Pull the leeks off the grill and let them steam for 5 minutes or so before cutting off the root then peeling back the first couple of layers of skin. The interior will be super soft and sweet. Transfer to a tray and dress with salt, pepper and a little olive oil before putting them on a warm plate and finishing with a generous dollop of gribiche.

CHEF'S TIP

We're back in the world of emulsions here. We want to make a super thick mayo to bind all the ingredients for the gribiche. For more of a deep-dive into how the magic of emulsification helps all this happen, how to nail basic emulsions and how to save a broken one, head to page 45.

Charred Lettuces & Bagna Cauda

- SERVES: 4
- EYES CLOSED
- P
- TOTAL: 35 MINS
- PREP: 10 MINS
- COOK: 25 MINS

This is sort of a hot, smoky version of a Caesar salad that involves burning lettuces and making a seriously punchy anchovy dressing. Burning brassicas is a tale as old as time, but one that we must keep telling, because it's utterly delicious, but burning lettuce is something that doesn't garner enough attention. This barbecued side couldn't be simpler: you blend together a bunch of ingredients into a dressing, grill a vegetable to smoky, tender perfection, then marry the two on a plate.

150g garlic cloves
15 tinned anchovy fillets, plus a few extra to serve
300ml whole milk
100ml water
1 lemon
6 baby gem lettuce
25g chives
25g parmesan
2 tbsp Sourdough Crumbs (page 74)
olive oil
fine sea salt
black pepper

1 Peel all the garlic cloves and add them, with the anchovy fillets, to a small saucepan. Pour over the milk and the water, place over a medium heat and, once it reaches a bare simmer, turn the heat down to low. Let the pan gently blip away for 15–20 minutes until the liquid has almost entirely reduced and the garlic and anchovies are soft and mellow.

2 Tip the whole lot into a blender or food processor and add the juice of the lemon and a touch of salt. Whizz into a smooth purée, then stream in 60–70ml of olive oil, or until you have a rich, thick dressing. Have a taste and add a little more lemon juice if you need to.

3 Halve the baby gems lengthways through the root. Season with salt and rub with plenty of olive oil. Light your barbecue and when it's just passed through its peak heat, get the lettuces onto the grill, cut side down. If you've got a pan weight (page 36) or something to weigh them down, get it on top now.

4 Cook the lettuces for 6–7 minutes on that cut side, until you see the green leaves on top starting to darken and change colour – this is the lettuce cooking from the bottom up. As soon as you see this change, give them another 30 seconds or so on the cut side, then flip. Grill for 30 seconds then pull them off to rest for a couple of minutes.

5 Toss the grilled lettuce into a bowl and add a few spoons of bagna cauda. Finely chop the chives and toss into the bowl. Grate in half of the parmesan, add 15–20 twists of black pepper and toss everything together. Tip out onto plates and top with coarsely ground black pepper, the remaining parmesan, a few extra anchovies and a few sourdough crumbs.

> **NOTES**
> What is bagna cauda? Well, it's different things to different folks, but in essence it's an anchovy and garlic sauce. Sometimes it's served hot, sometimes cold, sometimes made with milk, sometimes red wine. I like to make it into a room-temperature, salad dressing-style sauce, somewhere between a French anchoïade and a Caesar.

Smoky Mussels with Rockefeller Butter

SERVES: 4	TOTAL: 35 MINS
EYES CLOSED	PREP: 15 MINS
P	COOK: 20 MINS

This might be my favourite way to cook mussels: simply grilled over charcoal until they let you know they're cooked. With the classic moules frites preparation, you dress the mussels as they cook, whereas here, we're going to cook the mussels and dress them afterwards, which can help take some of the guesswork out of cooking them properly. Grilling mussels imbues them with the most amazing smoky flavour, a flavour that you rarely come across. Have your cold glass of wine and crusty bread at the ready . . .

80g English watercress
250g baby spinach
2 shallots
250g unsalted butter, softened
2 garlic cloves
20g tarragon
50g flat-leaf parsley
25g parmesan
1 tsp cayenne pepper
1 tbsp Worcestershire sauce
splash of Pernod or pastis (optional)
2 lemons
2kg live mussels, cleaned
flaky sea salt
black pepper
crusty bread, to serve

1 Bring a saucepan of salted water to the boil and set up a bowl with iced water. Plunge the watercress and spinach into the pan and cook for 1 minute, or until the pan comes back to the boil, then fish them out and plunge them into the iced water. Refresh, then squeeze as much moisture as you can from the blanched greens. Toss them into the bowl of a food processor.

2 Peel and finely dice the shallots. Preheat a small pan over your barbecue or a medium heat and toss in roughly 25g of the butter. Tip in the shallots with a pinch of salt and cook gently for 6–7 minutes, or until just softened. Empty the pan, butter and all, into the food processor.

3 Now, peel and grate in the garlic cloves, add the leaves of the tarragon and parsley, grate in the parmesan and add the cayenne, Worcestershire and, if using, the Pernod or pastis. Add the grated zest of both lemons and the remaining butter then whizz the whole lot into a smooth, green mix. Have a taste and season to taste with salt and pepper. I find it takes about 25 twists of pepper and a healthy pinch of salt. Scoop out into a bowl and set aside.

4 Tip the mussels into a large bowl or pan and rinse well under running water, shaking them to wash away any grit. To remove the beards (the little hairy rope that protrudes from the shell), grip it at the base and pull it down towards the hinge of the shell – it should come right out. If you need to, use a J-cloth or piece of kitchen paper to help you grip. Discard any mussels with cracked shells.

5 Make sure your barbecue is hovering between a medium and a high heat (too high and the mussel shells can crack and burn). Dry your mussels and add them to the grill, ensuring they aren't stacked up on one another and all are seeing a bit of heat from the charcoal. Add a lid or, if you don't have a lid, a sheet of foil over the top of the mussels to help cook them and trap in any smoke. Cook them for 3–4 minutes then lift the lid and have a peek.

6 Now, as soon as the mussel opens the flesh will be soft, tender and just cooked. If this is what you're after, whip them off, but you can keep cooking them if you want the meat to be a little firmer.

7 While the mussels cook, add the butter to a saucepan with a shot of water. Gently warm through, stirring the butter as it melts.

8 Once you're happy with the cooking, pull the mussels off the grill, discarding any that haven't opened, and spread them out onto a platter. Spoon over a generous amount of butter, being sure to get plenty into the shells and over the meat. Serve with cold wine and crusty bread.

Barbecued Scallops with Chilli Butter & Raita

- SERVES: 4 AS A STARTER
- EYES CLOSED
- P / GF
- TOTAL: 35 MINS, PLUS RESTING
- PREP: 15 MINS, PLUS RESTING
- COOK: 20 MINS

I'm not a huge raw scallop guy. For me, the best way to celebrate one of the jewels of the sea is to roast them hard on one side, rest them in butter and serve them with something super simple that'll elevate their natural sweetness. This is a lovely way to serve scallops, lightly spiced with a rich chilli butter and cooling mint yoghurt. I serve it as a small plate or a way to open up a larger barbecue feast.

300g full-fat Greek yoghurt
½ cucumber
15g mint
1 lemon
1 lime
1 tsp ground cumin
3 red chillies
1 garlic clove
15g rosemary sprigs
150g unsalted butter
14–16 large cleaned scallops
1 tsp medium curry powder
olive oil
fine sea salt

1 Before we get to grilling, let's make the raita. Set a sieve over a bowl and line with a J-cloth or a couple of pieces of sturdy kitchen paper. Tip the yoghurt into the sieve and pop into the fridge for at least an hour or so, and up to overnight, to thicken up. If at any point the yoghurt gets too thick, you can always let it back down with the whey collected in the bowl, or using lemon juice or olive oil.

2 While the yoghurt hangs out, coarsely grate the cucumber into a bowl. Season generously with salt and set aside for 10 minutes or so. Pick the mint leaves from the stems, then roll a little pile up into a cigar shape and thinly slice the leaves, repeating with the remaining mint. Squeeze as much moisture from the cucumber as you can then add to a bowl with the mint and hung yoghurt. Mix together and season with salt, grated lemon and lime zest and the ground cumin. I also add a shot of olive oil to boost the richness. Mix and set aside.

3 Light your barbecue and, once hot, toss the chillies with a little oil and salt. Grill the chillies until very charred on the outside, but not burnt to a crisp. Whip them off the grill and drop into a bowl. Cover and let the chillies steam for a minute or two before removing the skins and seeds. Chop the roasted chillies into a paste, peel and smash the garlic clove, remove the leaves from the rosemary sprigs and give them a rough chop. Add the lot to a small frying pan with the butter and set over the hot coals. Allow the butter to melt and the chillies, garlic and rosemary to infuse into the hot fat. Allow the butter to just start to brown before moving to the cooler side of the grill.

4 Once your barbecue is super hot, season the scallops with fine sea salt and the curry powder. Season from a decent height so you get an even spread of the curry powder. Rub with a little olive oil then place onto the grill, the larger flat side down. Cook for 2–3 minutes on that side (don't be tempted to turn them, just let them do their thing). We're shooting to cook the scallop 85% on this side, building a good crust and caramelisation before flipping. Once you've built up a good crust, give the scallops a prod. As they cook, they'll firm up, but before they become little golf balls the scallops will have a gentle bounce to them, with just a little give in the centre. Once you've landed here, give them a flip. Allow to cook for less than a minute before transferring to a tray. Spoon a little of the chilli butter over the scallops and allow them to rest for at least 2 minutes.

5 Swoosh the raita across a serving plate and dot the rested scallops over the top. Make sure the remaining butter is super hot before you pour it over the plate. Serve with a lemon and a lime cheek for squeezing.

CHEF'S TIP
Make sure those scallops are bone dry before they hit the grill! I love to cook scallops by touch. As with most proteins, their texture changes dramatically as they cook. With a big fat steak, it's actually very hard to tell what's going on inside purely by touch. The outside of the meat can feel super tough and you'll think the inside is well done when it's actually raw. Scallops have a very bad poker face, and when they've got a light bounce and have started to firm up, with just a little give in the middle, they're ready to rest.

Cumin Lamb Skewers

SERVES: 4
ROLL YOUR SLEEVES UP
DF / GF
TOTAL: 35 MINS, PLUS MARINATING
PREP: 15 MINS, PLUS MARINATING
COOK: 20 MINS

Spicy with chilli and Sichuan peppercorns and packed with cumin, these are stupidly easy to make and the thwack of flavour is out of this world. They're also dead fun to grill. As the fat renders it drips onto the coals and spits up plumes of lamb-scented smoke. I use a mixture of lamb shoulder interspersed with lamb rib meat. Both are rich in intramuscular fat and can take a really good grilling!

500g boneless lamb shoulder
6–8 lamb ribs
2 tbsp cumin seeds, toasted
1 tbsp hot chilli powder
1 tbsp ground cumin
½ tbsp Sichuan peppercorns, toasted and crushed
1 tsp cornflour
4 tbsp light soy sauce
2 tbsp olive oil
¼ white cabbage
2 tsp toasted sesame oil
1 tsp rice wine vinegar
fine sea salt
lime wedges, to serve

1 Grab your lamb shoulder and trim away any sinew from the meat. Be careful not to mistake fat for sinew: both are white, but sinew has a taut, silvery quality to it whereas the fat is chunkier and more malleable. Slide your knife under any sinew and cut it away, trying to leave as much meat behind as possible. Cut the meat away from the lamb rib bones: keeping your knife snug to the bone and angled slightly towards it, slide the blade along the bone, removing the meat cleanly. Cut the ribs and shoulder into even-sized pieces – I shoot for 2–3cm cubes/squares. You might not get everything exactly the same size, but if they're in the same ballpark, you'll be grand.

2 Mix the toasted cumin seeds, chilli powder, ground cumin, Sichuan peppercorns, cornflour, soy and olive oil in a small bowl in a bowl and tip in the lamb chunks. Mix thoroughly, coating every piece of lamb with a little marinade and a few peppercorns and cumin seeds. Cover and slide into the fridge overnight. If you can't afford overnight, let it hang out for at least 30–45 minutes.

3 Use a mandoline or a peeler to shred the cabbage into a bowl. Toss with a little salt, the sesame oil and rice wine vinegar. Set aside.

4 When you're ready to grill, thread the lamb onto skewers, one piece of shoulder, then a piece of rib, alternating as you go. Try to keep things as even as possible – IF you've cut the chunks more or less evenly, this should be super easy.

5 Light your barbecue and allow it to pass through peak heat and dip just below. It should still be hot, but not ripping hot. Grill the skewers for 8–9 minutes, turning them regularly, until charred and cooked through. Remove from the grill and allow to rest for a good 5–6 minutes before serving with your shredded cabbage salad and lime wedges for squeezing.

Barbecue Whole Chicken with Hot Green Tahini

It wouldn't be a barbecue without chicken. There are a million and one ways to grill a chicken, but this is my favourite, and you don't need to shove a can of beer anywhere. There are a few skills to take away from this recipe: deboning and brining a chicken, controlling the temperature of your grill, and learning how to properly rest and dress a piece of meat. Grilling a boneless chicken is a hell of a lot easier than bone-in and takes a lot of the guesswork out of making sure the chicken is cooked all the way through. You also can serve your guests crispy, juicy grilled chicken without them having to gnaw around any bones.

FOR THE BRINED CHICKEN

1 good-quality chicken
2 litres cold water
200g fine sea salt

FOR THE HOT GREEN TAHINI

100g tahini
1 garlic clove
25g dill
25g flat-leaf parsley
40g sliced pickled jalapeños
1 fresh jalapeño
1 lemon
olive oil
fine sea salt

1 First, debone the chicken. Remove the first two joints of the wing, the tip and the flat, leaving the drumette attached to the breast. Find the little ball of cartilage between the drumette and the flat and just slice through it. To remove the wishbone, lift the skin at the front of the chicken that covers the top of the breasts. Use your fingers to feel for a v-shaped bone that runs either side of the cavity, meeting at the top at the breastbone. Using the tip of your knife, slide along either side of the bone, revealing the entire v-shaped bone. Cut the cartilage that connects each side of the wishbone and then lift the bone up and out of the chicken, breaking it off at the breastbone.

2 Flip the chicken over and identify the backbone. Run your knife from the top to the bottom of the bone and begin to follow the carcass around, cutting away the meat, popping the leg joint out as you go, using the tip of your knife to follow the ribs and the central bones of the carcass all the way around. Once you've almost removed one of the breasts, be careful not to cut through the skin just above the breastbone and cut the base of the drumette away from the carcass. Repeat on the other side then lift out the central carcass, leaving the breasts, legs and drumettes all attached by one piece of skin.

3 To remove the leg bones, pop the chicken skin side down onto your chopping board and use your knife to trace along the thigh and drum bones, exposing them from beneath the skin. Slide your knife underneath and cut them away from the flesh. Repeat with the other half. You will now have a whole deboned chicken, with just the drumettes attached.

4 To make the brine, mix your cold water with fine sea salt in a clean container and stir until dissolved. Lower in the deboned chicken and pop into the fridge for 2 hours.

5 To make the green tahini, tip the tahini, peeled garlic clove, most of the dill and parsley, the pickled jalapeños and the fresh jalapeño into a blender. Add a splash of liquid from the pickled jalapeño jar and blend into a smooth, green sauce. Transfer to a bowl and season with salt and lemon juice.

6 Once brined, remove the chicken and discard the brine. Pat the chicken very dry with kitchen paper and rub it with just a little olive oil. Your chicken is ready for the grill!

Continued overleaf ⟶

TO SERVE

75g unsalted butter

2 garlic cloves

25g rosemary sprigs

8 spring onions

1 lemon

olive oil

flaky sea salt

black pepper

7 Light your barbecue and set up a hot zone and a cool zone. When the grill is at its hottest, pop a tray or frying pan over the heat and toss in the butter. Allow it to melt, foam and start to sizzle and brown before tossing in smashed garlic cloves and the rosemary. Season with a little salt and pepper and cook until fragrant and the butter has browned nicely. Remove from the heat.

8 Make sure your grill has passed through its peak heat stage and into a slightly more gentle, medium heat. Carefully lay the chicken, skin side down, onto the bars of the hot grill. You should hear a hiss as it hits the bars. Cook, undisturbed, for 8–9 minutes, checking the skin only after the chicken has had at least 5 minutes on the grill. Cook until the skin is super crispy and a little charred. Flip and finish the meat side for 4–5 minutes, or until fully cooked – if you've got a thermometer, you're looking for 68–69°C in the thickest part of the chicken. Once cooked, remove from the heat and let it rest on a tray, skin side up, sitting in the garlicky brown butter. Allow the chicken to rest in the tray on the cool side of the grill for 10 minutes, it'll finish cooking.

9 While the chicken rests in that garlicky butter, toss the spring onions with olive oil and grill for 2–3 minutes until blackened and wilted.

10 Spread the tahini over a serving platter, cut the chicken into portions and serve over the tahini. Spoon over some of the resting butter, dress with lemon juice, flaky sea salt and serve with the grilled onions.

SHOOT FROM THE HIP
You can replace the green tahini from this recipe with a whole host of sauces and condiments. Grilled chicken served with Chopped Salad (page 72) and Aioli (page 209) would be a beautiful summer dinner, or you could use nam jim (page 188).

CHEF'S TIP
I like to use a small, sharp knife when butchering chickens or other poultry. If you try to use a big, hefty chef's knife, it can be hard to manoeuvre and zip about the smaller bones. A smaller knife is nimble and agile, and can stay nice and snug to the bones, ensuring maximum yield and minimising waste

GRADIENT BRINING
The wet brine technique you've probably come across (and the one I recommend) is called gradient brining. This is where you dunk your chicken into a much saltier solution (somewhere between 10 and 20%) than the salt concentration you're after (1–2%) and then remove it when the desired salinity has been achieved. This can be a risky approach as if left in the solution too long, the bird becomes over-seasoned. However, with the right pointers, it's pretty easy to nail. I gradient-brine a lot of the chicken I cook as it's very consistent and always gives you a juicy, well-seasoned bird. I go for a 10% brine (100g salt dissolved in 1000g of water) for about 2–3 hours for a whole chicken.

Grilled T-Bone, Embered Sweet Potatoes & Gorgonzola

- SERVES: 4–6
- ROLL YOUR SLEEVES UP
- TOTAL: 70 MINS
- PREP: 10 MINS
- COOK: 60 MINS

Cooking a big fat steak to feed a crowd is the smartest thing you can do at a barbecue. I cook big steaks in quite a specific way, and while there are lots of different ways to reach the same goal, this is the one I like the best. What is the goal? A deep, dark, almost black caramelisation on the outside, with perfectly medium-rare, edge-to-edge pink meat inside (see Chef's Tip). I always serve steaks with garnishes that'll ramp up that beefy flavour. We're going to make a compound butter packed with big fat umami flavours to grill this steak with: anchovies, Worcestershire sauce and rosemary. Don't worry, the steak won't taste fishy, the anchovies are there just to level up that savoury kick.

1–1.5kg porterhouse or T-bone steak	25g thyme sprigs
4–6 sweet potatoes	200g gorgonzola dolce
500ml good-quality beef stock	1 lemon
250g unsalted butter, softened	25g chives
	olive oil
25g rosemary sprigs	fine sea salt
3 tbsp Worcestershire sauce	flaky sea salt
4 tinned anchovy fillets	black pepper

1 Before you do anything, pull the steak out of the fridge a few hours before you want to cook it. A big fat steak needs a really long time to temper and come up to room temperature so we can achieve that perfect, edge-to-edge pink. You can't expedite this process – it takes a long time and you can't rush it!

2 Preheat the oven to 180°C fan/200°C/400°F/gas mark 6. Rub the sweet potatoes with olive oil and salt and get them onto a baking tray. Slide into the oven and bake for 40–45 minutes until tender all the way through. Remove and allow to cool. While the potatoes are baking, pour the beef stock into a pan, bring to the boil and reduce by two-thirds until it's thickened a little.

3 Tip the butter into a food processor and whizz to soften it a little. Strip the leaves from the rosemary and finely chop. Add to the processor along with the Worcestershire sauce, anchovy fillets and the leaves from the thyme sprigs. Add 40 twists of black pepper and a good pinch of salt and whizz until everything is well combined. Tip into a bowl ready to brush onto your steak.

4 Light your barbecue and pile up the charcoal. Get your barbecue grate as close to the charcoal as possible – we're trying to maximise the amount of heat we can hit this steak with. Season your steak generously with flaky sea salt 15–20 minutes before you want to start grilling. I do it roughly at the same time I light the grill. This gives the salt ample time to penetrate the meat – it's a big fat steak and you want to give it a chance for the salt to do its job. If you don't have time to do this, season it with fine sea salt and slap it straight over the fire.

5 Get the steak on the grill over the direct heat and cook for a minute on each side. The grill will flare up and be super smoky, but don't worry, that's what we want! As soon as the steak has had a minute on each side move it over to the indirect side of the grill and rest for 3–4 minutes. While the steak rests, brush it generously with the butter. Repeat this process, hard-searing the steak with a rest in between until the thickest part of the steak is 47–48°C for medium-rare or 50–51°C for medium. The steak should be well blackened on the outside – to the untrained eye, it might look too dark, but don't worry, this is perfect. Once it hits the temperature you're looking for, pull it back onto the indirect side of the grill, brush with plenty more butter and

Continued overleaf ⟶

OVER FIRE

rest on a tray for a good 10–15 minutes. You can do this on the indirect side of your grill or somewhere warm.

6 While the steak rests, whip the rack off the grill and nestle the sweet potatoes in the embers. Turn the potatoes in the embers a few times, charring the skin and gently infusing the flesh below with smoke. Warm the reduced beef stock in the pan over the barbecue.

7 Carve the rested steak off the bone, and into slices. I keep the slices of fillet nice and chunky and the sirloin a little thinner. Brush any ash or embers off the potato skins and open them up, add a little of the steak butter and spoon in some gorgonzola and add some lemon zest. Finely chop the chives and add those to the potatoes too.

8 Pour any resting juices and melted butter from the tray into the beef stock. Spoon the warm beef sauce over the steak and finish with flaky sea salt. Serve.

NOTES

This recipe means a trip to your butchers and a digital thermometer, without a doubt! Not all butchers will carry steaks like this ready to go at the counter, so it might be worth giving them a call and ordering a T-bone or porterhouse a couple of days in advance, so you can be confident you can scoop up what you're looking for. You'll want a digital thermometer to be 100% confident your steak is where you want it – trust me, they're one of the best things you can buy for your kitchen.

CHEF'S TIP

To achieve perfect caramelisation on the outside and pink meat inside, get your barbecue incredibly hot and then hit the steak hard for a short amount of time before brushing with butter. Rest the steak and repeat the process, on, off, on, off, until the internal temperature is where you want it and the outside is super caramelised. You then rest the steak for a good amount of time in a warm place with lots of butter. Forget about bar marks. For me, they're all for vanity and do very little for flavour. You want to try and achieve a nice, even caramelisation all over the steak, not confine all of that flavour to a few criss-cross marks. Move the steak around the hottest part of your barbecue so that that every inch is hit by heat and then every inch will have plenty of flavour.

SHOOT FROM THE HIP

This is my favourite steak, but it might not be yours. They're also pretty massive, so if you're feeding just a couple of people or are just after something a little smaller, why not pick up a thick-cut ribeye or bone-in sirloin.

Pork Chops with Peppers & Peaches

- SERVES: 4
- TOTAL: 50 MINS
- ROLL YOUR SLEEVES UP
- PREP: 15 MINS
- GF
- COOK: 35 MINS

I've been making iterations of this recipe for years now, and this is undoubtedly my favourite version. Pork chops are a delightfully rich cut and, when grilled over charcoal with a little rosemary, are one of the most delicious things you can eat. They also love to be served alongside something sweet and spicy. Fruit is always my go-to choice here and using gorgeous summer peaches and scotch bonnets to make a dressing is really magic.

4 shallots
4 ripe yellow peaches
1 scotch bonnet chilli
3 tbsp sherry vinegar
4 thick-cut, bone-in pork chops, rind removed with plenty of fat left on
1 garlic clove
15g rosemary sprigs
700g jar good-quality cooked chickpeas
200g padron or baby peppers
2 courgettes
25g basil
olive oil
flaky sea salt
black pepper

1 Halve the shallots lengthways, leaving the skins on. Toss the halved shallots, 2 of the peaches and the chilli into a bowl. Add a shot of olive oil, a healthy pinch of flaky sea salt and toss everything to coat.

2 Light your barbecue, setting up a hot zone and a cold zone (page 256) and, once hitting its peak heat, tip the shallots, chilli and whole peaches onto the hot side of the grill. Cook the shallots for 4–5 minutes, cut side down, until very charred. Grill the chilli until soft, charred and tender, and the peaches until soft, caramelised and starting to collapse. Whip them all off the grill.

3 Peel the skin from the shallots and separate into petals – you'll see the charred surface give way to perfectly steamed, smoky shallot underneath! Chuck the roasted peaches into a bowl with the roasted scotch bonnet.

4 Scoop the pit out of the peaches and then, using a fork, mash the scotch bonnet and peach together with the sherry vinegar. Set aside.

5 Season the chops liberally with flaky sea salt. Go pretty hard – most of it is going to fall off into the barbecue, so don't be shy, pork can take lots of seasoning. Once the charcoal has cooled just a little, place a frying pan over the heat and sit the chops inside, fat side down. You can balance the chops against one another to help them sit up on the fat side as they render. The goal here is to melt and caramelise that thick fat cap on the top of the pork chop. This should take anywhere between 5–10 minutes, depending on the size of the fat cap and ferocity of your grill. Once 90% of the thick, opaque fat has turned translucent, you're good to go.

6 Remove the chops from the pan and lay them flat side down onto the grill. Grill on either side, flipping regularly, for 4–5 minutes or to medium doneness. If you've got a digital thermometer, you're shooting for an internal temperature of about 55°C before you pull them off the grill.

7 While your chops are grilling, smash the garlic clove and drop it into the pan of hot pork fat, pull it over to the cooler side of the grill and let it infuse. Finely chop the rosemary leaves and add that to the pork fat, too. You can brush this flavour-packed fat over the chops as they grill. Once your chops are where you want them, pull them off the grill and pour over a little of that pork fat. Rest them for at least 10–12 minutes.

Continued overleaf ⟶

8 Warm the chickpeas up a little over the grill; I like to do this in a saucepan with a little of their liquid. Add a few spoons of the remaining rendered, infused pork fat into the bowl with the spicy peach dressing. Season with salt and pepper and have a taste: it should be sweet, tart, fruity and spicy. Adjust as you like with vinegar, salt and pepper. Tip into a large mixing bowl with the warm, drained chickpeas. Add the roasted shallot petals and peppers, thinly slice the remaining peaches and the courgettes and add to the bowl along with the chickpeas. Tear in the basil and have a taste. Add a shot of olive oil and season if you need to.

9 You've got a couple of options now: you can serve the chops whole or carve the meat off the bone and into chunky slices. Serve the chops over the warm chickpea salad, pouring over any resting juice. Get stuck in.

> **CHEF'S TIP**
> Grilling pork can be a fiery business. Pork chops are packed with fat and can be a devil over live fire. A great way to swerve acrid, flame-licked pork chops is to start them off in a pan over your barbecue. This way, the majority of the fat is contained from the open flame or charcoal, resulting in fewer flare-ups. You'll also have a pan full of liquid gold in the form of rendered pork fat. You can infuse it with garlic and rosemary and brush it over your chops as they grill.

> **DRESSING TIPS**
> What we're essentially making with the scotch bonnet and peaches is a warm salad dressing. It's all about balance, check out page 16 for a bit of breakdown of how to make sure everything is working.

> **SHOOT FROM THE HIP**
> If you're cooking this recipe out of peak peach season, so many seasonal fruits will do a great job in the dressing. A plum version would be magical, as would cherries, apricots or early autumn figs.
> If you don't fancy chickpeas here, why not try these flavours in a sandwich? Whip up some Baguettes (page 174) or Olive Oil Buns (page 168) and serve the pork chops sandwiched inside, topped with that fiery peach dressing, fragrant basil and sweet roasted shallots. Stunning.

Stuffed Bass with Fregola, 'Nduja & Gordal Olives

- SERVES: 4
- DIG IN
- DF
- TOTAL: 90 MINS
- PREP: 30 MINS
- COOK: 60 MINS

This has to be one of my go-to recipes for when I've got mates coming over. It's light, delicious, challenging, and above all, fun to make! It's sort of the final boss of this book, as it requires a multitude of skills to pull off, but trust me, it's absolutely within your reach and you can (and will) nail this. The stuffing is packed with flavour: sweet shallots and fennel are spiked with garlic, spicy, meaty 'nduja, punchy gordal olives, lots of herbs and fregola. Some of summer's best flavours are stuffed inside this showstopper, so what are you waiting for? Get cracking.

1 large sea bass, gutted and scaled
1 tsp caster sugar
2 shallots
½ fennel bulb
1 jarred roasted pepper
2 garlic cloves
1 tsp fennel seeds
50g fregola or giant couscous
100ml dry white wine
150g 'nduja
150g gordal olives, plus a little brine
25g flat-leaf parsley
1 lemon
olive oil
fine sea salt and flaky sea salt
black pepper

1 Start by butterflying the fish. Roll the fish onto its spine and make a cut from the back of the belly cavity down towards the tail using your sharpest medium-sized knife or, if you have it, a fish filleting knife, keeping your blade snug to the spine. Use kitchen scissors to snip through the ribs that run up the belly and connect to the spine.

2 Now, starting at the top of the fish, draw your knife along the backbone towards the tail, freeing the first fillet from the bone. Be careful not to cut too far down and through the skin at the top – we want to keep that intact. Repeat on the other side, freeing up both fillets with just the spine in the middle. Use kitchen scissors to snip out the spine, leaving the tail attached. Use tweezers to remove the pin bones (optional) and cut away the rib bones from the belly. Mix the sugar with 2 teaspoons of salt and sprinkle the mix all over the fish, flesh and skin side. Pop into the fridge for 1 hour, then wipe away the brine and any moisture with kitchen paper. Return to the fridge while you make the stuffing.

3 Peel and finely chop the shallots and finely chop the fennel and roasted pepper. Peel and finely grate the garlic cloves. Preheat a frying pan over a medium heat and add a good glug of olive oil. Tip in the shallots and fennel with a pinch of salt and cook for 15–20 minutes until well caramelised and jammy.

4 Tip in the roasted pepper, garlic and fennel seeds and cook for a further 5–6 minutes then add the fregola. Crank up the heat, pour in the white wine and stir, deglazing the bottom of the pan. Now cook the fregola a little like a risotto, adding splashes of warm water as you go, but keeping the pan quite dry, until you have tender fregola and a rich, thick base for your stuffing. Remove from the heat and stir through the 'nduja. Roughly chop the olives and finely chop the parsley, folding them through the stuffing. Season with salt and pepper, a splash of olive brine and the grated zest of the lemon. Pop into the fridge to chill completely.

5 To stuff the fish, lay the fish skin side down on your chopping board. Lay the chilled stuffing up the centre of the fish in a line, being more generous the closer you get to the head, with just a little towards the tail. You probably won't need all the stuffing, but I'd rather you have a little too much than not enough! Fold one side of the fish over, enveloping the stuffing.

Continued overleaf ⟶

6 Cut 10 lengths of butcher's twine or string and space them evenly under the fish. Starting in the middle, tie off each of the pieces of twine, tight, but not super tight, sealing the stuffing inside the fish. Once the middle string has been tied, tie off the one closest to the head, and then the one closest to the tail, working inwards. Don't worry about any fancy knots, just tie them as best works for you. Some of your stuffing will fall out, and that's totally normal. Your fish is now stuffed and ready to cook.

7 Light the barbecue and allow it to pass through the peak of its heat and just start to ease off – you still want it to be nice and hot, so don't let it go too far. If you have one, lay an extra rack over the hottest part of the grill to preheat. Make sure the fish skin is very dry before brushing it generously with olive oil. Season all over with flaky sea salt then lay the fish on the rack. Cook for 4–5 minutes until that side is very crispy, then roll the fish onto the other side. Don't try and move the fish too early, or the skin might tear. Use a skewer to test how the fish is cooking. If it passes through the flesh with ease, it's ready.

8 Once the fish is cooked, remove it from the heat and, as always, let it rest for at least 5 minutes. Use scissors to snip away the strings then a sharp knife to cut the fish into chunky slices. If your fish isn't playing ball and won't slice cleanly, you can serve this with a fork and a spoon and simply break the fish into chunks! Serve the fish on a warm plate with lots of olive oil and lemon wedges.

> **CHEF'S TIP**
> Nailing any stuffing is all about texture. Lots of chefs use breadcrumbs to bind their stuffing together, but I find the result is quite stodgy. Grains are a fantastic way to give body to stuffings, and ever so slightly overcooking them is the secret. Not so far that they're mush, but just enough that they lend a sticky, tacky quality to the stuffing and help to give it some structure.

> **NOTE**
> We're going to butterfly the fish and remove the bones, so if you don't fancy doing that, ask your fishmonger to do it for you. I find it useful to take pictures of what I'm going for into the fishmonger with me, then chat through the recipe with them. They'll be able to recommend the best fish on the counter for the job and butterfly it for you.

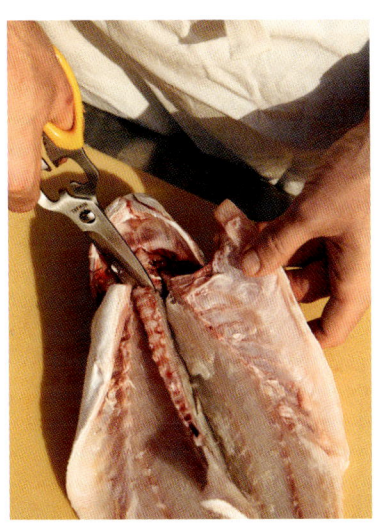

OVER FIRE

SWEET

Chocolate Mousse 286

Toasted Rice Panna Cotta with Plums & Olive Oil 288

Chewy Oatmeal Choc Chip Cookies 290

Sticky Date Puddings with Maple Toffee Sauce 292

Flourless Fondants 294

Rhubarb & Pistachio Choux Buns 295

Cheat's Apple Tarte Tartin 298

Brûléed Rice Pudding & Poached Cherries 300

Chocolate, Espresso & Marsala Baked Alaska 302

Doughnuts 'Myrtille' 305

Brown Sugar Tart 308

THINGS

'Room for dessert?' Yes. Always. My sweet tooth is long, and it continues to grow the older I get. I can rarely resist pudding and I don't usually try. Remember what I said about being a good eater? Well, the same applies to sweet things – that's your cue to never, ever skip dessert.

The pastry section is an interesting beast. It's the part of the kitchen that takes care of dessert, and often bread, too. This is, of course, a wider remit than the name suggests. The cooks working pastry will make mousses, tarts, custards, ice creams, temper chocolate, bake biscuits and brownies . . . if it's sweet, they're all over it. Strangely enough, while being home to some of the trickiest techniques in the kitchen and demanding a wealth of knowledge and experience, it's where some of the most inexperienced cooks are plonked on their first few weeks of being in a new kitchen. At my first serious cooking job, all the new chefs spent a month on the pastry section. Every morning, I faced the daunting task of making chocolate mousse and setting it into little dome-shaped moulds ready to freeze, pop out and cover with mirror glaze. As a cook with almost no experience this was tricky, but after I grasped the basics of whipping cream, making meringue and combining ingredients, I soon got the hang of it and pastry quickly became my favourite section.

The world of sweet things is all about precision, amazing food science, and bulletproof technique. In the savoury kitchen you can add a dash of this and a glug of that, chucking handfuls of salt here and there, but the pastry section doesn't offer you the same license. It's all about being precise and working with intent and, whether it's cream, eggs, sugar or chocolate, you need to really understand what's happening in the bowl in front of you. It's a different kind of cooking, and to become a well-rounded home cook, you need to know how to whip up a few classics. While I can't go into great depth on all things sugar, eggs, cream, chocolate and fruit (I've run out of pages!), I can give you a basic understanding of the mechanics of these ingredients, how they behave when they're hot and cold, whipped and infused, macerated and roasted.

THE CORE DESSERT TEAM

For me, good desserts revolve around a few core ingredients. Dairy, fruit and chocolate. There are plenty of tertiary ingredients that are drafted in to help elevate and enhance the flavours of these, but when I'm baking or making a dessert, my hero ingredients are usually sitting in one or more of these camps. I use sugar, caramels, salt and spices to platform and show off these main characters. Gentle spices and deep bittersweet caramels bring the best out of autumnal apples, vanilla infused into cream creates out-of-body good custards and blueberries boiled into jam are the star of a homemade doughnut.

SUGARS AND CARAMELS

Sweet things wouldn't be sweet without sugar. Sugar is at the heart of the sweet kitchen and a basic understanding of the different varieties and what they're best used for is super important.

CASTER SUGAR This hero of the sugar world is used across the board. It can be used to make syrup, caramel, and is a main character in the baking world. Its fine texture makes it perfect for dissolving into egg foams and sweetened whipped creams.

LIGHT BROWN SUGAR A soft sugar that has a caramel, molasses flavour. This adds more depth than caster.

DARK BROWN SUGAR Similar to the above, but a slightly more caramelised, bitter molasses flavour. Love a sticky toffee pudding? You like this sugar.

MUSCOVADO SUGAR A less refined brown sugar, with plenty of rich molasses flavour.

DEMERARA An unrefined, crunchy brown sugar that won't dissolve or melt when heated, great for topping apple pie or cookies with a crunchy layer of sweetness.

ICING SUGAR Super-fine milled sugar sometimes with added starches to inhibit clumping. Good for icing, pastry and dusting bakes.

HONEY, GOLDEN SYRUP AND MAPLE SYRUP These are examples of sweeteners that contain invert sugar. These sugars are more soluble, a little sweeter, and in some cases can extend shelf life.

That's a little run down of a few different types of sugar. Now it's time to use them, which usually means heating them up. Welcome to the world of syrups and caramel!

Syrups are a combination of sugar and water and can be made with any sugar. A 1:1 ratio of sugar to water will create what's known as a simple syrup. You can adjust the ratio depending on what you're planning to do with the syrup, and you can add heat to change the texture, too. If you heat syrup long enough and you take your syrup north of 160°C, you're in caramel country . . .

If you're making a direct caramel (just sugar, no water), simply tip your sugar into a dry pan and melt it. Don't overthink it, just melt it, shaking the pan now and then until everything is homogenous. A wet caramel, on the other hand, is a combination of sugar and water, brought to the boil and heated until the sugar begins to caramelise. Overall, you have more control of the colour and texture of your caramel using the wet method, however, wet caramels are when people run into issues with crystallisation. This is what happens when the sugar dissolved in water decides it would like to organise itself back into a solid state. As you boil a caramel and the water evaporates, there's less to get in the way of the sugar returning to its solid state. Adding a lid encourages any sugars that might be undissolved on the sides of the pan to hydrate and fall into the main body of syrup. You can use a damp pastry brush to sweep the crystals down into the caramel, but I use a lid for the first couple of minutes of making a wet caramel, and it never fails.

WHIPPING CREAM AND CUSTARD

A little cloud of whipped cream is the perfect crown to so many desserts, and here's a crash course. To be whipped, cream needs to have a fat content of at least 30%. Single cream can't be whipped – it doesn't have quite enough fat in it, sitting at 17–20%. Whipping cream has just enough fat (35–40%) to be whipped but still delivers a pretty light dessert, and then the big daddy, double cream, which weighs in at 40–50% fat, is practically begging to be whipped. When you agitate cream, you incorporate air. The fat in the cream holds on to the air, and the more air you whip, the thicker the cream becomes. Whip too much and you'll get butter. Not enough, and your cream will have no body.

When you whisk cream, always use a balloon whisk and a large mixing bowl to encourage as much air as possible. I rarely whip cream using electrical appliances like a stand mixer or an electric whisk to do this. The margin for error between great whipped cream and grainy, split whipped cream is pretty small and you have a much better feel and more control over the texture when using a hand whisk. If you do overwhip your cream and it looks grainy, or like it might be about to split, admit defeat and just keep whipping. You'll make butter! Never throw it away – you'll get a load of butter and buttermilk which are delicious.

Double cream is my go-to for most custards, mousses and whipped creams as it creates such a luxe texture and rich mouthfeel, but if you want to make light, airy pipeable, spreadable cream, you can add 15–20% whole milk to the weight of the cream. This reduces the overall fat content and will give you a whipped cream that has the texture of a light shaving foam.

EGG FOAMS

All the way back in Chapter One, we looked at the anatomy of an egg and how it can be whipped up into meringue and other light, airy foams. Calling whipped egg a 'foam' might sound a little cheffy, but it's super easy to make and this foam is behind some of your favourite desserts. There are heaps of egg foams out there, most being a combination of eggs and sugar or syrup. How you combine those two ingredients, and at what temperature, will determine the texture of your

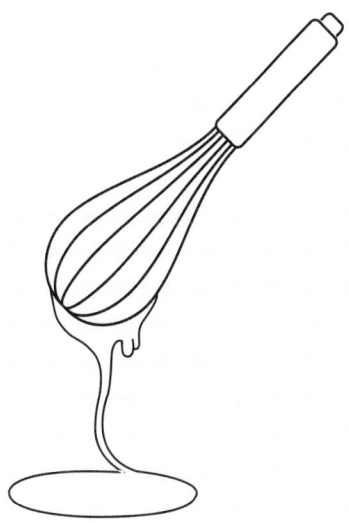

30% Sugar cane & vanilla bean

70% Cocoa liquor & cocoa butter

Dark: Look for 65–80%

55% Milk powder, cane sugar & vanilla bean

45% Cocoa liquor & cocoa butter

Milk: Anywhere between 45 and 65%

foam and what you can use it for. Whipping eggs to ribbon stage is probably the easiest of the foams, it involves whipping whole eggs with caster sugar until tripled in volume and super thick. The name describes a classic test for doneness where the mix is drizzled over itself and creates 'ribbons' of whipped egg that remain on the surface for a few seconds. We'll also make Italian meringue, which is a combination of egg whites and hot sugar syrup. The sugar syrup is poured into the whipped egg whites once it's hit a very precise temperature and the egg whites have a frothy, foamy texture. The hot syrup cooks the egg whites, stabilising the proteins. It's a shiny, fully cooked meringue and is ready to go straight after whipping.

CHOCOLATE

Chocolate is a magic ingredient that can deliver pleasure in the kitchen on a higher plane. The wonderful world of chocolate is deep and complex. Tempering, baking, caramelising and cooking chocolate can get super complicated, so we're just going to cover a few basics here. The main thing we're going to look for is the right chocolate with the right percentage. This refers to the percentage weight of the chocolate bar that is actually made with cocoa solids and cocoa butter, derivatives of the cocoa bean. There are other bits bobs in there too like sugar (we meet again!) and if you're using a milk chocolate there will be milk powder in there, too.

White chocolate is a bit different, as it doesn't contain any of the cocoa solids, it only contains the cocoa butter. This is what gives it the same mouthfeel and richness as other chocolate, and also what keeps it bright white and very sweet. The cocoa solids are what give dark chocolate its bitter character, and without any of these, white chocolate is dead sweet.

FRUIT

This is your opportunity to cook seasonally. Chocolate, dairy and eggs are always knocking about, but fruits come and go. You can incorporate fruit into your desserts raw or macerated, poached or roasted, but always use something that's at its best. Once you've picked your fruit, here's what you can do with it . . .

RAW Raw berries, stone fruits and citrus are all delicious. Be sure to peel any tougher skins and remove pips before serving. Taste the fruit and balance any tart, bitter flavours with increased sugar in the other components of the dessert.

MACERATED When you combine raw fruit and sugar, in the same way salt draws water out of ingredients, sugar does, too. The sugar and fruit juices combine to make a syrup and ever so slightly dehydrate the fruit, so the resulting flavour is a little more intense, and the fruit can take on a 'cooked' texture, while still retaining a fresh flavour.

POACHED Poaching fruit gently softens textures and flavours. Always use a flavour-packed liquid, whether it's wine, sugar syrup or fruit juice, and never let your liquid boil. Fruits are for the most part very delicate, so always remove whatever you're poaching from the heat a few minutes before it's done and let it cool down in the liquid. This ensures it doesn't overcook in the residual heat.

ROASTED You guessed it, this involves the oven! Toss your fruit with 10% of their weight in sugar and roast until just tender and a little behind the texture you're after – the residual heat will finish the cooking. For stone fruits you can turn the oven up quite hot; for softer fruits and berries, shoot for a lower temperature.

BALANCING SAVOURY AND SWEET

Throughout the recipes in this chapter, there are little splashes of savoury that help to balance out the sugar-forward recipes. In the tarte tatin recipe – essentially one massive caramel apple pie – savoury notes are really handy. Despite the presence of fruit, there's a shedload of butter and sugar in there and it needs to be brought out of the saccharine, sickly sweet zone back into the realm of balance. A generous pinch of salt levels out the caramel, a splash of vinegar helps to bring out the natural malic acidity of the apples and a few thyme leaves perfume the whole tart, boosting the autumnal vibes. A pinch of salt here, a blob of acidic crème fraîche there . . . all these little decisions help to give your desserts that edge above the rest.

A NOTE ON VANILLA

There's nothing quite like vanilla. For me, it's a hero ingredient, and a bowl of cool vanilla custard is a pretty great dessert in itself. Vanilla sparkles when given a creamy, neutral, rich, dairy stage on which to perform. A good amount of sugar and salt is also needed to bring out vanilla's perfume and brilliance. People don't often consider sugar as a seasoning, but it is. Infuse milk and cream with vanilla and taste it before and after you add sugar and then again with a pinch of salt. You'll notice the vanilla flavour explode off your spoon with the addition of each ingredient. It's a good food experiment and will demonstrate the power of seasoning. When buying vanilla, whole beans are best, but I know they're pretty expensive, and unless you're buying in bulk (which I'm pretty certain you're not), they can run to £3–4 each. If you don't want to use whole beans, buy a good quality vanilla paste. A teaspoon or so will deliver a similar level of heady fragrance to a fresh bean. Some people talk about terroir when it comes to vanilla – does it matter whether your vanilla is Tahitian or Madagascan? Sort of, but not really. These varieties will have subtle differences. Some are richer than others, some have an edge of liquorice or natural salinity. Unless you happen to be a bean sommelier, the likes of you and me and our panna cotta shouldn't worry too much.

> **Weigh everything in grams, please**
>
> Everything is measured in grams and it's my preference. It is a far more precise way to bake, and this game is all about precision. Not only is it the safest bet, it'll save you washing up that heap of cup measures and the annoying keyring full of tablespoons and half teaspoons taking up space in your kitchen cupboards. Just weigh everything straight into the mixing bowls or saucepans and you can be confident you got it right. Every. Damn. Time.

Chocolate Mousse

- SERVES: 4–6
- EYES CLOSED
- V / GF
- TOTAL: 40 MINS, PLUS SETTING
- PREP: 25 MINS, PLUS SETTING
- COOK: 15 MINS

This was the first dessert I learnt to make in a professional kitchen. It holds a special place in my heart, I have never grown tired of it, and it never fails to please those I feed it to. Chocolate mousse is all about deep, rich, dark chocolate and the perfect, light, fluffy texture. Don't skimp on the salt either. It's good all year round, but especially delicious in the height of summer with sweet poached cherries or crushed raspberries, or in winter with blood orange or poached rhubarb.

350g 70% dark chocolate
200g whole milk
70g caster sugar
120g egg yolks (about 6–7 yolks)
150g egg whites (about 5 whites)
180g double cream
200g full-fat crème fraîche
extra virgin olive oil, to serve
flaky sea salt

1 Cut your chocolate into very small pieces and put it in a medium heatproof bowl. Set a sieve over the top and set aside.

2 Pour the milk into a small saucepan and add 30g of the sugar. Place over a medium heat and bring to a bare simmer, being careful not to scorch the milk on the bottom of the pan. While the milk warms, add the yolks to a bowl and whisk in another 30g of sugar. Gradually pour the hot milk over the yolks and sugar while whisking continuously, to avoid any overcooking. Return the mixture to the pan and place over a medium-low heat.

3 Cook the milk and yolks, stirring constantly with a spatula, until the mixture reaches 79–80°C. Once you've hit that temperature, pour it straight through the sieve and over the bowl of chopped chocolate. Allow the chocolate to sit with the hot custard for 30 seconds before stirring together, the residual heat melting everything together. Set aside to cool a little, but not completely.

4 Tip the egg whites into a clean bowl and use an electric whisk to beat on medium speed to soft peaks. At this point, start sprinkling in the remaining 10g of sugar. Whisk until the egg whites have reached stiff peaks. Pour the double cream into a fresh mixing bowl and whisk to soft peaks. Be careful not to over-whip the cream here, so stop just before you think it's ready.

5 Add half of the whipped cream to the chocolate base and use a spatula to beat the two together until you have a smooth, slightly looser chocolate base. Add the remaining whipped cream and fold through a little more gently until the mix is homogenous again. Repeat the process with the whipped egg white. Take your time here making sure there are no streaks of egg white remaining in the mixture after each addition. Once all combined, season with flaky sea salt to taste. Pour the mousse into a 2-litre plastic container and pop a lid on top. Transfer to the fridge for at least 4–5 hours to fully set. You can make this mousse a day before you want to serve it.

6 Add the crème fraîche to a bowl and whisk gently to soft peaks – use a balloon whisk and do this by hand, you'll have much more control. Crème fraîche takes a little more whisking than double cream, it'll slacken out before it starts to thicken again, so stick with it. Use a large spoon to scoop portions of mousse into your serving bowls. Top with dollops of crème fraîche, flaky sea salt and a little olive oil.

> **CHEF'S TIP**
> A good mousse is all in bringing together the chocolate base, whipped cream and meringue. When you add the first quantity of cream, you can afford to be quite rough with the mousse. As the chocolate base takes on more of the cream and egg white, it becomes looser, lighter and more delicate. You want to be more and more mindful of your folding and how much air you're aiming to maintain in the mixture.

Toasted Rice Panna Cotta with Plums & Olive Oil

SERVES: 4–6
EYES CLOSED
V / GF
TOTAL: 80 MINS, PLUS SETTING
PREP: 35 MINS, PLUS SETTING
COOK: 45 MINS

Panna cotta is an achingly simple dessert that is all about texture. There are lots of different recipes out there for panna cotta, each delivering a different level of richness, a different level of wobble and varying infusions and flavours. Toasted rice makes for a spectacular flavour, with notes of earthy, roasted popcorn. Paired with a little vanilla it's very delicious. A panna cotta is a blank slate, why not try infusing the next one with cinnamon, bay leaf or warm toasted hazelnuts?

FOR THE PANNA COTTA

250g basmati rice

200g whole milk

600g double cream

1 vanilla pod

160g caster sugar

1 tsp fine sea salt

3 gelatine leaves (ideally platinum Dr. Oetker)

FOR THE POACHED PLUMS

4 plums

150g caster sugar

1 lemon

TO SERVE

extra virgin olive oil

1 Place a 25–30cm frying pan over a medium-low heat. Add the rice, shaking to spread it out across the pan, and cook for 10–15 minutes, shaking regularly, to toast evenly. After 8–10 minutes, the rice should have turned a light brown and should smell toasty. If patches are colouring too quickly, turn the heat down; you don't want to rush this. Keep cooking for another 5–6 minutes, or until the rice is a deep, nut brown and smells thoroughly toasted.

2 While the rice toasts, pour the milk and cream into a medium saucepan. Drag the back of a paring knife along the vanilla pod against a board to flatten it. Use the point of the knife to split it in half lengthways then use the back of the knife to scrape out the seeds. Add the seeds and the pod to the pan along with the sugar. Place the pan over a medium-low heat and very gently bring the cream and milk to just below a simmer. While the milk and cream are still hot, add the hot toasted rice to the pan and stir together. Remove from the heat and have a taste, add the salt, then taste again. Delicious. Cover and allow the milk and cream to infuse for at least 30 minutes.

3 Set up a big bowl of iced water, one large enough to house another bowl inside. Add the gelatine to the iced water and let it hydrate for 5 minutes until floppy. Place the saucepan back on the heat and gently reheat the infused milk and cream. Set a sieve over a fresh pan and pour the infused cream through, removing the rice and vanilla pod. Once hydrated, squeeze the excess moisture from the gelatine leaves and drop them into the milk and cream mixture. Whisk until the gelatine has fully dissolved before pouring into a bowl that fits into your ice bath.

4 Whisk the panna cotta mixture constantly as it cools, topping up the water with ice if you need to, until it heads below 10°C. If you don't have a thermometer, you're looking for the mixture to start to thicken and the vanilla seeds to stay at the surface. If left for 10 seconds and they sink to the bottom, keep whisking.

5 Once cool, pour your mixture into moulds, ramekins or espresso cups or into a larger container. Transfer to the fridge for at least 5–6 hours, ideally overnight.

6 Halve and de-stone the plums then cut each half into 4 slices. Add the sugar and 200ml water to a saucepan. Use a peeler to remove the lemon rind in strips and add to the pan along with the juice of half the lemon. Place over a medium heat and bring the syrup to a bare simmer.

7 Drop the plum slices in and cook for 5–6 minutes very gently, not letting the poaching liquor boil, until the plums are still a little firm but beginning to soften.

CHEF'S TIP
Cooling and 'churning' your panna cotta mixture over ice before pouring it into moulds helps the gelatine start to set – not only does this speed up the setting time, the little vanilla seeds are suspended throughout rather than all sinking to the bottom. This'll take 20–25 minutes, but is absolutely worth it.

Depending on the ripeness of your fruit, the time this will take will vary. Once tender, transfer to a bowl or container. Allow the poaching liquor to cool to room temperature before pouring it over the fruit. Ensure the fruit is fully submerged then transfer to the fridge to rest with the panna cotta. A minimum of 4–5 hours is lovely, overnight is better.

8 If set into individual moulds, briefly drip them into a bowl of warm water to loosen before tipping them out onto cool plates. If you set the mix as one, use a large spoon to take large scoops out and onto plates. Serve with the cool, syrupy plums and a drizzle of good quality, grassy olive oil.

SWEET THINGS

Chewy Oatmeal Choc Chip Cookies

- MAKES: 10 COOKIES
- EYES CLOSED
- V
- TOTAL: 30 MINS, PLUS RESTING
- PREP: 15 MINS, PLUS RESTING
- COOK: 15 MINS

There are a million recipes for chocolate chip cookies out there, and this one is mine. I think I probably went through 26 different formulas before I landed on this one. The amount of sugar, fat, egg and flour dramatically changes the texture and look of your cookie. On the road to amalgamating my two favourite cookies – the oatmeal raisin and the classic chocolate chip – I turned out super-thin, chewy cookies, big fat rocky cookies and almost everything in between. This is where I landed, a chewy, pretty classic-looking bake with crispy edges, a nice oaty flavour and just enough gooey chocolate right in the middle. A big shout out to my pal and all-round pastry genius Nicola Lamb who helped me develop this recipe, your wisdom knows no bounds!

110g unsalted butter, softened
100g light brown sugar
90g caster sugar
7g fine sea salt
8g vanilla extract
50g whole egg (roughly one!)
170g plain flour
1g baking powder
3g bicarbonate of soda
150g mixed chocolate (I like a 50:50 split of 70% dark and 60% milk)
50g oats

1 Add the butter, sugars and salt to a bowl or stand mixer fitted with the paddle attachment. Mix together until combined and homogenous but try not to incorporate heaps of air. Weigh the vanilla extract into a bowl and beat with the egg. Pour the egg and vanilla into the butter mixture and beat together until smooth, ensuring everything is evenly combined.

2 Sift the flour and raising agents together into the bowl and fold them through the mix. Roughly chop the chocolate and add to the bowl with the oats. Mix through the cookie dough until well distributed.

3 Use a spoon to scoop out 65–70g portions of dough and then roll into balls. Now you can choose whether to bake them straight away for a crunchier, thinner finish, rest in the fridge overnight for a chewy, thicker cookie or rest for just 1 hour for something in the middle. I like to freeze a couple for a later date. An emergency cookie from the freezer, served warm with ice cream, is a great card to play when you're craving something sweet at the drop of a hat.

4 When ready to bake your cookies, preheat the oven to 175°C fan/195°C/375°F/gas mark 5.

5 Line a baking tray with parchment paper or a silicone mat and add your cookie dough balls, well spaced apart. Slide into the oven for 12–14 minutes, or until the outside is nicely browned but the middle is a little paler. If baking from the freezer, add an extra minute to the baking time.

6 They'll puff in the centre a little, but will deflate and crack as they come out and cool. For a lovely dense, chewy cookie, use a glass or the back of a spoon to compress the cookie as soon as it comes out of the oven.

7 Rest for 5 minutes before transferring to a wire rack. Eat while still warm with ice cream, coffee or a glass of cold milk.

> **CHEF'S TIP**
> The amount of time you rest your cookie will change the way it behaves when baked. You can bake these cookies straight away, after 30 minutes in the fridge, or after an overnight rest, and they'll come out completely different! As the cookie rests, the butter firms up and the flour fully hydrates. This results in a slightly chunkier, chewy cookie. If you like your cookie to be a little thinner and more crunchy, bake them straight away!

Sticky Date Puddings with Maple Toffee Sauce

- SERVES: 8
- EYES CLOSED
- V
- TOTAL: 80 MINS
- PREP: 30 MINS
- COOK: 50 MINS

Sometimes, only a sticky toffee pudding will do. I didn't want to go too off-piste here: a few shots of strong coffee add a bitter back note to the sponge and the maple in the toffee lifts it out of the molasses rich depths of dark brown sugar and into somewhere a little more nuanced.

FOR THE DATE PUDDINGS

200g pitted medjool dates
300g water
1 tbsp molasses
2 tsp bicarbonate of soda
135g strong espresso/coffee
100g unsalted butter, softened, plus extra for greasing
290g soft dark brown sugar
150g eggs (about 3)
300g plain flour
4 tsp baking powder
½ tsp fine sea salt

FOR THE TOFFEE SAUCE

100g soft dark brown sugar
50g maple syrup
70g unsalted butter
240g double cream
flaky sea salt

TO SERVE

cold custard, ice cream or crème fraîche

1 Preheat the oven to 170°C fan/190°C/375°F/gas mark 5.

2 Tip the dates into a saucepan with the water, molasses and bicarbonate of soda. Place over a medium heat, bring to the boil, then cover with a lid and set aside for 15 minutes to soak. Tip in the espresso and use a stick blender to whizz the dates and liquid together into a chunky purée. Don't be too precious about it being super smooth.

3 Tip the butter into a large mixing bowl and add the sugar. Use a wooden spoon or spatula to beat them together until well combined. Incorporate the eggs, one at a time, until you have a smooth mixture. Sift over the flour, baking powder and salt and beat together until just combined. Pour in the date purée and fold through the mix.

4 Liberally grease 8 dariole moulds or large ramekins with butter. Divide the mixture among the moulds (the easiest way to do this is by transferring the mix to a jug and pouring it into the moulds), filling them three-quarters of the way up. Sit the moulds in a deep roasting tin or baking tray. Boil a kettle and pour the hot water into the tray until it comes just over halfway up the sides of the puddings. Carefully slide into the oven and bake for 25–30 minutes, or until a cake tester or skewer inserted into the puddings comes out clean.

5 While the puddings cook, make the toffee sauce. Put the sugar, maple syrup, butter and cream in a saucepan and bring to a rolling boil. Cook, whisking constantly, for 4–5 minutes then remove from the heat – it will darken to around the colour of milk chocolate. Season to taste with a little flaky sea salt.

6 Remove the puddings from the oven and allow to rest in the moulds for 5 minutes. Slide a round-ended knife or spatula around the edge of the puddings, snug to the mould, to loosen them, then turn them out into warm bowls. Top with a little of the maple toffee sauce, top with cool dairy of your choice, a little more sauce and a scrunch of flaky sea salt. Dig in.

> **NOTES**
> No dariole moulds or ramekins? Line a 900g loaf tin with parchment paper and tip the mixture straight in. Bake in the oven for 45–55 minutes, or until a cake tester inserted into the centre comes out clean. Allow to cool for 10 minutes before removing and slicing into thick slabs. Serve warm covered with the sauce.

Flourless Fondants

- SERVES: 4–6
- TOTAL: 25 MINS
- EYES CLOSED
- PREP: 15 MINS
- V / GF
- COOK: 10 MINS

A classic fondant recipe demands that you hit the cook time on the head, every single time, in order to turn out a little volcano of molten chocolate. Creating a mousse with eggs, butter and chocolate and gently baking is dead easy, but feels very cheffy. Finishing the mix with a hit of fresh citrus zest perfumes and lightens the whole dessert. Served with a scoop of vanilla or pistachio ice cream and a drizzle of olive oil, this dessert always delivers!

190g 70% dark chocolate, broken into small pieces

190g good-quality salted butter, cut into chunks

3 large eggs, plus 3 large egg yolks

90g caster sugar

8g mixed grated citrus zest (orange, lemon, lime)

TO SERVE

vanilla or pistachio gelato

olive oil

flaky sea salt

1 Preheat the oven to 180°C fan/200°C/400°F/gas mark 6.

2 Put the chocolate and butter in a heatproof bowl and set over a small saucepan filled with a little water, enough to come up about a quarter of the way up the sides of the pan, but not so much that the water touches the bottom of the bowl. Place the pan and bowl over a medium-low heat and bring the water to the boil. Once boiling, turn the heat right down to the lowest setting and allow the steam to gently warm the bowl, melting the butter and chocolate. Don't allow the pan to boil, if it does, remove from the heat completely. Just before everything has melted, whip the bowl off the pan and stir the butter and chocolate together – the residual heat will finish melting the remaining pieces. Once you've got a smooth, shiny, homogenous mixture, set aside to cool a little.

3 Add the whole eggs and egg yolks to the bowl of a stand mixer fitted with the whisk attachment, or a large mixing bowl. Use the mixer or an electric whisk to start beating the eggs together on medium-low speed and slowly add the sugar, one spoon at a time, shaking the grains into the eggs. Once all the sugar has been incorporated, increase the speed to medium and whip the eggs for 5–6 minutes until tripled in volume and thick. You should be able to pull the whisk up and out of the bowl and wave it across the top, the mixture creating a ribbon effect on the surface.

4 Season the chocolate mixture with a generous pinch of salt. Pour the whole lot into the bowl of whipped eggs and begin folding the two together. The chocolate will fall to the bottom of the bowl and the goal here is to marry the two components without knocking a load of air out of the eggs. Take a spatula and slide it to the bottom of the bowl before swooping around, up the side of the bowl and over the top. Repeat this movement, over and over, taking your time, and watch the egg mixture slowly deepen in colour as the two become more and more combined. Once completely homogenous, you're all done.

5 Arrange 4–6 small ovenproof bowls, mugs or ramekins on a tray and divide the chocolate mixture evenly among them. Slide into the oven and bake for 6–8 minutes, or until just warm in the middle. The top will have puffed up a little and set, but should still wobble a little when agitated. Remove from the oven and allow to rest for a minute or two.

6 Serve topped with a scoop of ice cream, a drizzle of olive oil and a pinch of flaky sea salt. Be careful, the bowls will be hot!

Rhubarb & Pistachio Choux Buns

- MAKES: 8–10 CHOUX BUNS
- ROLL YOUR SLEEVES UP
- V
- TOTAL: 85 MINS, PLUS COOLING
- PREP: 45 MINS, PLUS COOLING
- COOK: 40 MINS

When rhubarb is in season, chefs go absolutely bananas for it. Choux is a foundational pastry technique that should be in every cook's arsenal. Once you've mastered the choux bun, you can stuff it with whatever you like. With choux, it's all about texture: cooking out the paste and adding just the right amount of egg is crucial, so be sure to check out the Chef's Tip. I make the craquelin, rhubarb compote and pistachio cream in advance and have them waiting in the wings, then just bake the choux, assemble and serve.

FOR THE CRAQUELIN
50g unsalted butter, softened
50g light brown sugar
50g plain flour

FOR THE PISTACHIO CREAM
280g whole milk
1 vanilla pod
50g whole eggs
15g egg yolks
40g caster sugar
35g cornflour
40g crema di pistacchio
pinch of fine sea salt

1 To make the craquelin, tip the softened butter, brown sugar and flour into a bowl and use a spatula to combine the ingredients until you have a homogenous paste. It'll feel a little dry to begin with but keep going! Sandwich the mixture between two sheets of parchment paper and roll it out until it's roughly 3–5mm thick. You don't have to be mega precise here, just make sure the thickness of the craquelin is consistent, so it bakes evenly. Pop into the fridge or freezer to harden.

2 To make the pistachio cream, pour the milk into a small saucepan. Split the vanilla pod and scrape out the seeds, then add both the seeds and split pod to the pan. Place over a low heat and bring to a simmer, then remove from the heat and allow to infuse for 10–15 minutes. Meanwhile, put the whole eggs and yolks into a small mixing bowl and whisk in the sugar and cornflour. Bring the milk back to a simmer and, once hot, gradually whisk the milk into the egg mixture. Once fully combined, return to the pan and set back over a low heat. Cook, stirring constantly, for 5–6 minutes, or until the cornflour has thickened the mixture. Cook for roughly a minute longer, then pass through a sieve into a clean bowl. Beat the crema di pistacchio into the custard while it's warm and season with the pinch of salt.

3 To make the rhubarb compote, cut the rhubarb into even 1–2cm dice and tip two-thirds into a saucepan. Add the sugar, along with the finely grated zest and juice of the blood orange. Set aside to macerate for at least 30 minutes (up to overnight in the fridge). Once macerated, place over a low heat and bring to a bare simmer. Cook for 5–6 minutes, stirring now and then, until the rhubarb has broken down a little, with a few pieces still retaining their shape. Remove from the heat, stir through the remaining rhubarb and pour into a heatproof container. Cool completely before transferring to the fridge.

4 To make the choux, preheat the oven to 210°C fan/230°C/445°F/gas mark 8. Add the butter, water,

> **CREMA DI PISTACCHIO**
> I use pistachio cream for this recipe rather than a pure pistachio paste. It's far cheaper and more readily available. What's the difference? Paste is made using just pistachios, nothing else. Pistachio cream is made into a ready-to-use spread similar to a chocolate hazelnut spread and will have added stabilisers, fat and sugar. You can use pistachio paste in this recipe, but it's going to cost you!

Continued overleaf →

FOR THE RHUBARB COMPOTE

300g rhubarb

50g caster sugar

1 blood orange (or regular orange)

FOR THE CHOUX

60g unsalted butter

60g water

60g whole milk

½ tsp caster sugar

½ tsp fine sea salt

90g plain flour

120–130g whole eggs

TO SERVE

vanilla gelato

good-quality shelled pistachios

milk, sugar and salt to a medium saucepan. Place over a medium-low heat and bring to a simmer. Once the butter has completely melted, add the flour and use a spatula to quickly beat the mixture together into a rough dough. Lower the heat and keep working the dough in the pan, squashing and mixing it around the pan, for 4–5 minutes. The goal here is to dry out the paste a little. Keep working the paste and cooking it until there is a fine film around the walls of the pan, and the dough looks shiny. Tip into a clean mixing bowl and allow to cool for 6–7 minutes.

5 Beat the eggs in a bowl until homogeneous, then gradually beat them into the choux paste. Add them a little at a time, beating well between additions. It'll look broken and a little weird at first but keep going and it'll come together! Once you've incorporated 80 per cent of the beaten egg, test the consistency of your mix. It should just drop off a spatula, leaving a 'V' shape behind (see Chef's Tip). Incorporate the last 20 per cent of the egg mixture, bit by bit, if required. Transfer to a piping bag and set aside.

6 Line a large baking sheet with a silicone mat or parchment paper. Cut the piping bag and pipe the choux into evenly spaced mounds anywhere between 5–8cm wide and 3.5cm tall. This will create 8–10 large choux buns to stuff. Use a ring cutter to punch out discs of craquelin just large enough to cover the mounds. Gently press a disc on top of each mound. Slide into the oven and turn the heat down to 190°C fan/210°C/410°F/gas mark 6. Bake for 15 minutes, then briefly open the oven door to let any steam escape. Now lower the temperature to 160°C fan/180°C/350°F/gas mark 4 and bake for a further 15–20 minutes until golden brown. Remove from the oven and allow to cool on a wire rack.

7 Split each cooled choux bun in half across the equator. Briefly beat the pistachio cream to loosen it and then transfer to a piping bag. Open the choux bun, pipe on a layer of pistachio cream, a scoop of gelato and a big spoonful of rhubarb compote. Top with pistachios, another layer of pistachio cream, then the lid. Devour!

PIPING

Don't pull your hair out over super neat choux piping. Using a craquelin topper creates a crackled, sweet crust on top of the buns, hiding any piping sins and making even the dodgiest choux look amazing!

CHEF'S TIP

You want to add just enough egg to your choux paste so that it'll gently fall off a spatula, leaving behind a 'V' shape on the spoon. In France they call this 'le bec' or 'the beak', as it resembles a bird's beak. If your choux paste is too tight and not falling from the spatula, add a little more egg, but go steady.

Cheat's Apple Tarte Tatin

- **SERVES: 6–8**
- **ROLL YOUR SLEEVES UP**
- **V**
- **TOTAL: 115 MINS, PLUS COOLING**
- **PREP: 30 MINS, PLUS COOLING**
- **COOK: 85 MINS**

There are three main hurdles to jump when making a really good tarte tatin: simultaneously cooking the fruit perfectly, baking the pastry to golden puffed perfection, and making sure your caramel is just the right texture. Most recipes for tarte tatin demand you do all of these pretty much at the same time – making a caramel, sticking raw apples and pastry on top and sliding it into the oven, hoping it works out. We're going to cheat a little bit and treat the three elements separately. You can even bake this ahead of time and simply re-warm when ready to serve. I finish mine glazed with apple caramel and a big scoop of vanilla ice cream.

8 braeburn or cox apples
250g caster sugar
100g unsalted butter
2–3 thyme sprigs (optional)
1 tbsp vanilla paste
2 tsp good-quality apple cider vinegar
1 tsp flaky sea salt, plus a little extra
320g sheet all-butter puff pastry
500g cloudy apple juice
vanilla ice cream, to serve

1 Preheat the oven to 165°C fan/185°C/350°F/gas mark 4.

2 Peel and cut the apples into quarters and remove the cores. Try to keep them a consistent size and shape.

3 Put the caster sugar in a saucepan with 30g of water. Gently mix together to saturate all the sugar – it should look like wet sand – and make sure the sides of the pan are clean of water and sugar. Place over a medium heat and bring to a simmer, then cover with a lid and cook for 3–4 minutes before removing the lid and turning up the heat a little. Watch as the caramel changes to a deep golden amber colour. If you've got a thermometer, you're looking for 183–185°C. Remove from the heat and whisk in the butter, a little at a time. Be careful, as the caramel will boil and bubble up.

4 Strip the leaves from most of the thyme sprigs, if using, and add to the caramel with the vanilla paste, vinegar and salt. While still warm, pour into a 22–25cm tarte tatin dish or ovenproof frying pan and allow the caramel to cool.

5 Arrange the prepared apples on top, packing them tightly in a ring around the edge of the dish before filling in the gaps. Try not to trim or cut down the apples too much to plug the holes as, once they're cooked, we can squash the apples closer together. Place the frying pan over a medium heat and bring the caramel back up to temperature. Turn the heat down to medium-low and let the apples begin to soften and release some liquid. Cover loosely with a piece of scrunched-up and unfolded foil, slide the pan into the oven and bake for 10–15 minutes, or until the apples are just tender all the way through but not mushy. Allow the apples to cool to room temperature then pop in the fridge for 2 hours (or up to overnight). The longer you leave them, the softer the apples will get.

6 While the apples chill out, pour the apple juice into a medium saucepan and place over a medium heat. Bring to a simmer, then reduce the heat and let it tick over for 13–15 minutes, swirling the pan now and then, until it's reduced and becomes syrupy. You're looking for about 60–70g once reduced.

7 When ready to bake, preheat the oven to 180°C fan/200°C/400°F/gas mark 6.

8 Unfurl your pastry and, while still cold, cut it into a circle just larger than your apples. Lay it over the cooled apples and use a fork to prick lots of holes across the surface to allow steam to escape during baking. Use the back of the fork to tuck the sides of the pastry right the way up to the apples, nice and snug.

9 Transfer to the oven and bake for 40–45 minutes until the pastry is puffed, golden brown and crispy. Remove from the oven and let the tart rest for at least 25–30 minutes before turning it out. If it doesn't want to come out, rewarm it over a medium-low heat for 5 minutes. Serve warm with a dollop of ice cream, a few extra thyme leaves, if using, and a sprinkle of flaky sea salt.

SWEET THINGS

Brûléed Rice Pudding & Poached Cherries

- SERVES: 4–6
- ROLL YOUR SLEEVES UP
- V / GF
- TOTAL: 80 MINUTES, PLUS COOLING
- PREP: 20 MINUTES, PLUS COOLING
- COOK: 1 HOUR

This dessert delivers on every level. It's luxurious in a way that only cream-based desserts can be, it's rich and perfumed with vanilla, has the bitter crackle and crunch of burnt sugar and is crowned with glossy sweet and sour cherries. It's also hilariously easy to make restaurant-quality rice pudding at home, so forget Ambrosia. An utter delight to eat – the rice pudding pleasantly chilled, the layer below the burnished crust of burnt sugar gently warmed by the blowtorch. Cherries are one of the best fruits to offer a sweet and sour character to a dessert. This is a rich pudding and the lightly poached fruit, married with the tart molasses, is a gorgeous garnish.

FOR THE RICE PUDDING

2 tbsp unsalted butter

100g short-grain pudding rice

95g caster sugar, plus extra to brûlée

500g whole milk

500g double cream

1 vanilla pod or 1½ tsp vanilla paste

½ tsp fine sea salt

FOR THE SWEET AND SOUR CHERRIES

350g fresh ripe cherries

100g cherry molasses or pomegranate molasses

100g caster sugar

1 Preheat an ovenproof, lidded pan over a medium heat. Add the butter to the pan and let it melt, foam and start to sizzle. Once it's turned nut brown and smells like hazelnuts, tip in the rice. Stir to coat it with the hot butter and cook for 2–3 minutes to toast the rice ever so slightly. Now lower the heat and tip in the sugar, milk, 350g of the cream and the vanilla (if using the whole pod, split and scrape the seeds). Cook for 25–30 minutes, stirring regularly, until the mixture has thickened and the rice has started to soften.

2 While the rice is cooking, preheat the oven to 120°C fan/140°C/275°F/gas mark 1.

3 Pop a lid on the rice pudding and slide it into the oven to cook for 35–40 minutes, stirring a few times along the way. You'll notice it thicken as it cooks, the milk and dairy gently reducing.

4 Once the pudding has had about 40 minutes and the rice is tender, pull it out of the oven and stir through the remaining cream and the salt. You can serve it warm straight away or allow it to cool to room temperature before spooning it into dishes and refrigerating.

5 Halve the cherries and pry out the stones. Tip the halved cherries into a heatproof bowl. Put the molasses, sugar and 50ml of water in a pan and bring to the boil, stirring to dissolve the sugar, then pour the mixture over the cherries and stir to combine. Set aside to cool.

6 When ready to serve, dust the top of the rice pudding with a generous layer of sugar. Use a blowtorch or hot grill to caramelise and burn the sugar. Allow to set and become crunchy before topping with a few of the poached cherries and a little of the syrup.

Chocolate, Espresso & Marsala Baked Alaska

- SERVES: 6–8
- DIG IN
- V
- TOTAL: 80 MINS, PLUS FREEZING
- PREP: 40 MINS, PLUS FREEZING
- COOK: 40 MINS

A baked Alaska is a wonderfully retro dessert, and it shouldn't be lost to the past. The different textures and temperatures on the plate are a joy to eat. This combination of flavours is erring on the side of tiramisu: warm, torched coffee meringue envelops a bombe of sweet marsala and hazelnut parfait and rich chocolate espresso brownie. It's an amazing balance of sweet, bitter, salty and nutty. You can get ahead on every single element here: you can bake the brownie and parfait ahead and store them in the freezer, and you can even make the meringue mix in advance – just store it in an airtight container in the fridge and then re-whip before you pipe and toast.

FOR THE HAZELNUT MARSALA PARFAIT

60g egg yolks
140g caster sugar
60g water
100g mascarpone
240g double cream
50g egg whites
65g sweet marsala
70g toasted hazelnuts
tiny pinch of fine sea salt

1 To make the parfait, put the egg yolks in the bowl of a stand mixer fitted with the whisk attachment. Tip the sugar into a small saucepan and add the 60g of water. Shake the pan to dissolve the sugar, then set over a medium-low heat. Bring to a simmer and let it bubble away until it hits 120°C (use a digital thermometer to measure it). While the syrup comes up to temperature, whip the egg yolks at medium-high speed until light and fluffy. Once the syrup has reached 120°C, adjust the whisk to medium-low speed and slowly pour the hot syrup into the bowl. Once all the syrup is in, crank the speed up to high and whisk until the yolks are cooled to room temperature.

2 Put the mascarpone in a bowl and loosen it with a spatula. Fold the whipped egg yolks into the mascarpone a third at a time. In a separate bowl, whisk the cream to soft peaks. Fold the cream through the eggs and mascarpone in thirds. Whisk the egg whites to stiff peaks and then fold them through the mixture in thirds again. Pour the marsala into the mousse and stir through. Roughly chop the hazelnuts and fold through. Season with the tiny pinch of salt. Line a 15–18cm dinner bowl with a couple of layers of cling film with plenty of overhang. Pour the mousse inside, fold the cling film over the top and freeze for at least 4–5 hours, or until solid.

3 To make the brownie, preheat the oven to 160°C fan/180°C/350°F/gas mark 4. Line the base of a 20cm round springform cake tin with parchment and grease the sides with butter. Cut the butter into cubes, roughly chop the dark chocolate, and add both the butter and chocolate to a heatproof bowl. Set the bowl over a pan of simmering water and stir until melted, then remove from the heat and allow to cool a little.

4 Tip the eggs and sugar into a bowl and use an electric whisk (or stand mixer whisk) to whip until tripled in size. Pour the melted butter and chocolate mixture into the egg and sugar mixture and fold together. Sift the flour, espresso powder and pinch of salt over the mixture then fold in until incorporated. Add the espresso coffee and chopped milk chocolate and combine. Pour into the prepared tin and tap on the work surface a couple of times to create a flat, even layer. Bake in the oven for 20–25 minutes, or until a skewer inserted into the middle comes out just clean. Don't overbake these – it's okay if they are a little underdone, so lean towards keeping them nice and fudgy! Remove from the oven and allow to cool completely in the tin.

Continued overleaf ⟶

FOR THE ESPRESSO BROWNIE

150g unsalted butter, plus extra for greasing
150g dark chocolate
150g eggs
185g caster sugar
100g plain flour
20g espresso powder
pinch of fine sea salt
25g strong brewed espresso
100g milk chocolate, chopped

FOR THE COFFEE ITALIAN MERINGUE

120g egg whites
240g caster sugar
60g water
3–4g good-quality instant coffee powder

5 To make the meringue, tip the egg whites into the bowl of a stand mixer fitted with the whisk attachment. Add the sugar and 60g of water to a small saucepan and place over a medium heat. Bring to the boil and slowly bring up to 119°C. Once the syrup comes up to about 110°C, whip the whites on medium-high speed until they're just reaching soft peaks. Once the syrup has reached 119°C, adjust the whisk to medium-low speed and slowly pour the hot syrup into the bowl. Once all the syrup is in, crank the speed up to high and whisk until the whites are cooled to room temperature. After 3–4 minutes of whipping, add the coffee powder and whip it into the meringue. Continue mixing on high for 10–12 minutes until the bowl feels cool. If you want, you can add the meringue to a piping bag fitted with a star nozzle.

6 Remove the parfait from the freezer, pull it out of the bowl and unwrap. Use the rim of your bowl to create an indent on the top of your brownie. Trim around the line, then sit the parfait, flat side down, on top, creating a dome. Pop back into the freezer briefly to set.

7 Grab a serving plate and add a small blob of meringue to the base. Remove the Alaska from the freezer and stick it to the plate. Now, moving quickly, pipe or spread the remaining meringue onto the Alaska, covering it all the way down to the plate. Use a blowtorch to toast the meringue on the outside. I like to be quite generous with the torch and give the meringue a proper toasting, but you can go as charred as you like! Allow to sit and set for a minute or two, then slice and serve.

> **CHEF'S TIP**
> Making both pâte à bombe (imagine a meringue, but made with egg yolks) and Italian meringue is a simple but precise process. Make sure your thermometer probe isn't touching the bottom of your pot and is hovering in the syrup, or it'll trick you into thinking the syrup is ready. When you go to pour the syrup into your yolks or whites, make sure the whisk is on low speed, or you'll fling hot sugar all over your kitchen.

> **NOTE**
> This recipe makes a big brownie that'll then fit a parfait made in almost any dinner bowl. Eat the extras as snacks!

Doughnuts 'Myrtille'

MAKES: 12 DOUGHNUTS

DIG IN

V

TOTAL: 3 HOURS 30 MINS, PLUS PROVING AND COOLING

PREP: 1 HOUR, PLUS PROVING AND COOLING

COOK: 2 HOURS 30 MINS

If you head to the Savoie region of France, or anywhere in the Alps really, you'll find *tarte aux myrtilles,* a tart of almonds and wild blueberries. It's an absolute dream eaten with freshly whipped vanilla cream and a strong coffee. I've dragged this tart kicking and screaming back to London and combined it with a good old-fashioned British doughnut. This recipe is worth every step, and there are a few, so dig in – it's a great baking project that seriously pays off. There's a fair amount to do, so stagger everything and make the fillings before you get stuck into the doughnuts.

FOR THE BLUEBERRY JAM

600g blueberries

400g jam sugar

1 lemon

FOR THE ALMOND CUSTARD

140g blanched almonds

200g double cream

300g whole milk

130g caster sugar

40g cornflour

50g whole egg (about 1 egg)

60g egg yolks (about 3 yolks)

150g double cream

1 tsp almond extract

fine sea salt

1 To make the blueberry jam, put the blueberries, sugar and lemon juice in a large heavy-based saucepan and place over a medium heat. Crush the blueberries a little with a potato masher or fork. Bring to the boil, then reduce to a simmer and cook for 25–30 minutes. You're looking to hit a temperature of at least 104°C. As the jam cooks, you might notice a little bubbly scum forming on the top, just skim this off and ditch it. To check if the jam is ready, pop a plate into the freezer for 5 minutes. Whip it out, add a dollop of jam and return to the freezer for 5 minutes. Once cooled, run your finger through the jam; if it wrinkles up and has a little skin, then it's ready! If not, cook the jam a little longer. Pour into a shallow tray to cool completely before, transferring to a piping bag. Store in the fridge.

2 To make the custard, preheat the oven to 150°C fan/170°C/325°F/gas mark 3. Tip the almonds onto a baking tray, slide into the oven and roast for 10–12 minutes, or until a deep golden brown and toasted. While the nuts are roasting, pour the first quantity of cream and the milk into a pan, add half of the sugar, place over a medium heat and bring to a bare simmer. Tip the warm nuts into a food processor and blitz to a fine paste. Tip this paste into the warm milk and cream, whisk to combine, pop a lid on and let it hang out to infuse for at least 45 minutes.

3 Add the remaining sugar to a medium mixing bowl with the cornflour, whole egg and egg yolks. Whisk together until fully combined. Bring the milk mixture back to a bare simmer then gradually pour it into the egg mixture, whisking constantly. Return the mixture to the pan and place over a low heat. Cook, whisking thoroughly and constantly, until the cornflour is activated and thickens the custard. Once thickened, keep cooking for 1–2 minutes, or until the mixture starts to gently 'plop' and bubble. Pour the custard into a sieve set over a bowl and pass it through to remove any solids. Set aside to cool a little. Pour the second quantity of cream into a bowl with the almond extract and whisk to soft peaks. Try not to over-whip the cream here as you've still got to fold it through the custard, so stop a little before you think the cream is ready. Once at a luxurious soft peak stage, tip half into the custard and beat them together. Once combined, add the remaining cream and gently fold through the custard. Season with a touch of fine sea salt and transfer to a piping bag. Store in the fridge.

4 To make the doughnut dough, put the flour, sugar, yeast and salt in the bowl of a stand mixer. Mix to combine. Pour the milk into a small saucepan and heat until just warm to the touch, not hot. Whisk in the eggs and pour the liquid

Continued overleaf ⟶

FOR THE DOUGHNUTS

425g strong white flour, plus extra for dusting
40g caster sugar, plus extra for dusting
10g instant yeast
6g fine sea salt
225g whole milk
2 eggs
40g unsalted butter, softened
vegetable oil, for frying

> **NOTE**
> Once fried, the doughnuts will keep for a day or two in an airtight container. You can reheat them in a low oven then roll them in sugar ready to stuff. Once rolled in sugar, you'll want to serve them as soon as possible.

> **CHEF'S TIP**
> For the almond custard, it's important to combine the nuts and dairy while still warm, to extract the maximum amount of flavour. The infusion will not only be more intense, but it'll happen much quicker. The essential oils in the almonds are vibrant and brought to life by the heat of the oven and will transfer into the custard base while still warm.

> **SHOOT FROM THE HIP**
> If you can't be bothered to make jam, I understand – just buy yourself a good-quality jar. This recipe would work well with just about any jam I can think of. Rhubarb makes a very handsome swap.

into the dry mix. Add the dough attachment to the mixer and mix on low speed for 7–8 minutes. Once you've got a strong, springy dough, gradually add the softened butter, bit by bit, until fully incorporated. Mix for another 3–4 minutes on low speed.

5 Tip the dough out onto a lightly floured surface and briefly knead by picking it up and slapping it back down onto the work surface. The dough will be very sticky to begin with; persevere and it will become easier to work with – a bench scraper is handy here. Shape the dough into a rough ball and put it in a lightly floured bowl. Cover with a damp tea towel and leave to proof at room temperature for 60–70 minutes, or until at least doubled in size.

6 Cut twelve 7cm squares of parchment paper (if you're making small doughnuts, cut 20 squares) and grab a bench scraper or table knife. Set up a clean digital scale and dust it lightly with flour. Once your dough has proofed, punch the air out of it and turn out onto the work surface. Cut the dough into 60–65g portions for large doughnuts and 35–40g for smaller ones (use a digital scale to weigh your dough chunks). Shape each piece into a ball by flattening it out on the surface and tucking the corners in all the way around. Flip the dough over so the seam is flat against the work surface and, using the cup of your hand, roll the dough around to form a ball. The surface tension of the work surface and dough will form the doughnut into a smooth, uniform ball. Transfer the dough ball onto one of the parchment squares and slide under a damp tea towel. Repeat with the remaining dough. Leave to proof at room temperature for another 40 minutes or so, until at least doubled in size again. To set up the frying station you want a large pan, filled halfway with vegetable oil. Gradually bring this to 165°C, monitoring the temperature regularly. You'll also need a tray lined with kitchen paper to drain your cooked doughnuts on, plus a slotted spoon.

7 Fry your proofed doughnuts in batches. Carefully lower each doughnut into the oil, paper and all. If correctly proofed, they will float to the top straight away. Remove the paper and fry for 3 minutes until the underside is dark brown. Gently flip and cook for another 3 minutes until golden brown on both sides. You should have a lovely pale ring around the middle of the doughnut. Remove from the oil and drain on the lined tray. Repeat with the remaining doughnuts. Allow the doughnuts to cool before filling.

8 Roll the doughnuts in extra sugar and use a chopstick to create a little hole in the side around that blonde ring. Pipe in jam and then the custard on half of the doughnuts, and then the reverse on the other half. Serve straight away.

SWEET THINGS

Brown Sugar Tart

SERVES: 6–8
DIG IN
V

TOTAL: 2 HOURS 30 MINS, PLUS RESTING
PREP: 45 MINS, PLUS RESTING
COOK: 1 HOUR 45 MINS

My favourite dessert ever! A levelled-up custard tart. I love the classic, but swapping caster sugar for dark muscovado sugar transforms the custard from tasting predominantly of cream and nutmeg to having a complex, bittersweet flavour. I serve it with a blob of crème fraîche for some acidity. In its simplest form, making a custard tart is making pastry, rolling it out, blind-baking the case, then filling with custard and cooking until it's just set. Sounds simple, right? It can be a little daunting for first timers, but trust me, if you follow the steps and have a little patience, you'll be serving slices of custard tart to die for.

FOR THE PASTRY

235g plain flour

90g icing sugar, plus a little extra for dusting

40g ground almonds

2g fine sea salt

120g unsalted butter, very cold

50g whole egg (about 1 medium egg)

FOR THE CUSTARD

750g double cream

1 vanilla pod

200g egg yolks (about 10 yolks), plus 1 white

200g dark muscovado sugar

3g flaky sea salt

TO SERVE

good-quality crème fraîche

1 Start by making the pastry. Put the flour, sugar, almonds and salt in a bowl and mix to combine. Dice the cold butter and add it to the bowl. Using your fingertips, carefully rub the butter into the flour until it has a breadcrumb-like consistency. If you have a stand mixer, you can use the paddle attachment to complete this step. Once the mixture is fine and there are no visible chunks of butter left, beat the egg, add it to the bowl and bring everything together into a dough. Don't be afraid of giving it a brief knead – folks say you need to be super delicate with pastry, but at this stage the goal is homogeny. Make sure the pastry is a consistent texture throughout, it'll pay off later. Wrap and rest the pastry in the fridge for at least 30 minutes, up to overnight.

2 While the pastry rests, make the custard base. Pour the cream into a small saucepan and place over a very low heat. Split the vanilla pod lengthways and scrape out the seeds. Add the seeds and pod to the cream and stir them through. Bring the cream to just under a simmer, then remove from the heat and leave to steep for 30 minutes. Add the yolks (save the white for later), sugar and salt to a medium mixing bowl and vigorously whisk together. Muscovado sugar has a tendency to clump up, so give it hell (don't worry if there are some stubborn lumps, we'll sieve the base in a minute). Taste and adjust the salt as you like.

3 Once the cream has had time to steep, reheat it to just below a simmer. Slowly pour the hot cream over the eggs and sugar, whisking constantly, until fully combined. Allow to sit for 5–10 minutes, then pass through a sieve into a jug. Leave it to hang out for 10 minutes. You'll notice that the custard has a foamy layer on top – skim this off. If you want a perfectly clean, bubble-free tart, make the custard base the day before and rest it in the fridge overnight. If, like me, you don't mind a bubble or two, you can do all of this same-day.

Continued overleaf ⟶

NOTES ON SWEET PASTRY

I choose this pastry for almost every custard tart I make. It's an ironclad recipe and I'll use it for ever. Save yourself some time and double the recipe to make enough pastry for two tarts, then freeze half for a rainy day. When you're tucking the pastry into the case, use some of the trim to make a little bundle of dough and make a little tool that you can use to get the pastry right into the corners of the tart tin.

SWEET THINGS

4 Preheat the oven to 180°C fan/200°C/400°F/gas mark 6. Remove your pastry from the fridge and unwrap it. Dust your work surface with flour and begin rolling out the pastry. You want a rough circle big enough to line a 24–26cm tart tin and about the thickness of a pound coin (if you can't manage that thin, don't worry, anything south of 5mm is perfect). Pop your tart tin in the middle of the disc and make sure there's enough pastry around the edge for a good overhang.

5 You want to work quite quickly here: if your pastry warms up too much, it'll be hard to handle. If you think everything is getting a bit too warm, just pause and chill it for 10 minutes.

6 Roll the pastry around the rolling pin and carefully lay it into the tart tin, encouraging the pastry into the corners of the tin. Leave lots of overhang but keep everything snug to the tin. Scrunch up some baking paper and line the pastry. Tip in enough baking beans, dried beans or rice to weigh everything down then slide into the oven and bake for 20–25 minutes. Once the edges of the pastry are starting to take on colour and the kitchen smells like biscuits, whip the tart case out the oven. Remove the paper and baking beans, drop the temperature to 160°C fan/180°C/350°F/gas mark 4 and return to the oven for 10–15 minutes until the base of the tart is a dark nut brown. Remove from the oven and brush the interior of the tart with the egg white you saved: this is like a waterproof layer. If you've got any holes or cracks in your pastry at this point, use some excess pastry to plug it! Once your pastry is golden brown all over and egg-white waterproofed, use a serrated knife to trim away any excess pastry (some will have fallen away during the blind bake) and tidy up the edges.

7 Drop the oven temperature to 120°C fan/140°C/275°F/gas mark 1. Pop the tart in the oven and, with the oven door open, carefully pour the custard mix into the case. Fill to the very top and carefully slide it into the oven. If you have a blowtorch, briefly kiss the surface of the custard with the flame to remove any big bubbles. Bake for 45–50 minutes, or until the centre of the custard has the slightest wobble. Once you've hit this point, remove from the oven.

8 Allow the tart to cool to room temperature before removing it from the tart case and cutting it into slices. Serve with a dollop of good quality crème fraîche.

CHEF'S TIP

A chef once told me, 'you'd rather be looking at it, than looking for it'... I always make just a tiny bit more custard mix than I need. I know it would be smart, clever and sensible to make *just* the right amount of mix, but I always want to be sure I definitely have enough, so at the moment I pour the mix into the baked tart case I'm not left with a half-full tart and an empty jug. Tarts are a bit of work, and you don't need any added stress.
To get a clean slice, warm your knife with hot water or a blowtorch.

SHOOT FROM THE HIP

You can remove the nuts from the pastry recipe and replace them with 30g of extra flour. You can also infuse other spices into the cream with the vanilla, like cinnamon, tonka bean or bay leaves.

SWEET THINGS

CONVERSION CHARTS

DRY WEIGHTS

METRIC	IMPERIAL	METRIC	IMPERIAL	METRIC	IMPERIAL
5g	¼oz	225g	8oz	650g	1lb 7oz
8/10g	⅓oz	250g	9oz	675g	1½lb
15g	½oz	265g	9½oz	700g	1lb 9oz
20g	¾oz	275g	10oz	750g	1lb 10oz
25g	1oz	300g	11oz	800g	1¾lb
30/35g	1¼oz	325g	11½oz	850g	1lb 14oz
40g	1½oz	350g	12oz	900g	2lb
50g	2oz	375g	13oz	950g	2lb 2oz
60/70g	2½oz	400g	14oz	1kg	2lb 3oz
75/85/90g	3oz	425g	15oz	1.1kg	2lb 6oz
100g	3½oz	450g	1lb	1.25kg	2¾lb
110/120g	4oz	475g	1lb 1oz	1.3/1.4kg	3lb
125/130g	4½oz	500g	1lb 2oz	1.5kg	3lb 5oz
135/140/150g	5oz	550g	1lb 3oz	1.75/1.8kg	4lb
170/175g	6oz	600g	1lb 5oz	2kg	4lb 4oz
200g	7oz	625g	1lb 6oz		

LIQUID MEASURES

METRIC	IMPERIAL (US)	CUPS	METRIC	IMPERIAL (US)	CUPS
15ml	½fl oz	1 tbsp	180ml	6fl oz	¾ cup
20ml	¾fl oz		210ml	7fl oz	
30ml	1fl oz	⅛ cup	240ml	8fl oz	1 cup
60ml	2fl oz	¼ cup	265ml	9fl oz	
75ml	2½fl oz		300ml	10fl oz	1¼ cups
90ml	3fl oz	⅜ cup	350ml	12fl oz	1½ cups
100ml	3½fl oz		415ml	14fl oz	
120ml	4fl oz	½ cup	480ml	16fl oz/1 pint	2 cups
135ml	4½fl oz		530ml	18fl oz	2¼ cups
160ml	5fl oz	⅔ cup	1 litre	32fl oz	4 cups

OVEN TEMPERATURES

°C fan	°C	°F	GAS MARK	°C fan	°C	°F	GAS MARK
90°C fan	110°C	230°F	gas mark ½	170°C fan	190°C	375°F	gas mark 5
100°C fan	120C	250°F	gas mark ½	180°C fan	200°C	400°F	gas mark 6
110°C fan	130°C	250°F	gas mark ½	190°C fan	210°C	410°F	gas mark 6
120°C fan	140°C	275°F	gas mark 1	200°C fan	220°C	425°F	gas mark 7
130°C fan	150°C	300°F	gas mark 2	210°C fan	230°C	445°F	gas mark 8
140°C fan	160°C	325°F	gas mark 3	220°C fan	240°C	460°F	gas mark 9
145°C fan	165°C	330°F	gas mark 3	230°C fan	250°C	480°F	gas mark 10
150°C fan	170°C	325°F	gas mark 3	240°C fan	260°C	500°F	gas mark 10
160°C fan	180°C	350°F	gas mark 4				

INDEX

Page numbers in *italic* refer to illustrations

A

acidity 18, 30
Aioli 209, *209*
alcohol 31
almonds: Doughnuts 'Myrtille' 305–7, *306*
 Romesco Sauce 252, *253*
 Silky Almond Soup 96, *97*
anchovies: Bagna Cauda 262
 Cod Schnitzel Holstein 198–9, *199*
 Grilled T-bone 270–2, *271*
 Lamb Shoulder with White Beans 252, *253*
 Oeufs Mayonnaise 60, *61*
 Sheet-tray Pizza alla Puttanesca 164, *165*
 Tomato, Anchovy & Smashed Olive Salad 74, *75*
apples: Cheat's Apple Tarte Tatin 298–9, *299*
 Smoky Apple Vinaigrette 83
appliances 37
asparagus: Diner-style Stuffed Omelettes 52, *53*
aubergines: Smoked Aubergine & 'Nduja Lasagne 210, *211*
autolyse 151

B

Bagels, Oniony Cream Cheese & Honey 166, *167*
Bagna Cauda 262
Baguettes 174–6, *175*, *177*
Baked Alaska 302–4, *303*
baking 31, 205
balsamic vinegar: Jammy Balsamic Onion, Rosemary & Pecorino Topping 121
barbecues 38–9, 256–7

beef 24–6, *25*
 Beef Bone Broth & Tortellini 112–13, *113*
 Beef Cheek & Scotch Bonnet Pie 250, *251*
 Chopped Beef Tartare 84–5, *85*
 Grilled T-bone 270–2, *271*
 Pastrami-spiced Bavette 186, *187*
 Spiced Short Ribs 245–6, *247*
 A Very Good Cheeseburger 196, *197*
Beer Batter Fritto Misto 182–4, *183*
Bisque, Udon 110, *111*
black pepper 20
BLT Bread 154, *155*
blueberries: Doughnuts 'Myrtille' 305–7, *306*
bouquet garni 233
bread 150–3
 Baguettes 174–6, *175*, *177*
 BLT Bread 154, *155*
 Chive Milk Bread 172–3, *173*
 English Muffins 171
 Fennel Seed Soldiers 94, *95*
 Foolproof Focaccia 158, *159*
 Garlicky Spinach & Cheese Pide 162, *163*
 Olive Oil Buns 168–70, *169*
 Oniony Cream Cheese & Honey Bagels 166, *167*
 Pecorino Pain Perdu 62, *63*
 Semolina Flatbreads 160–1, *161*
 Sourdough Crumbs 74
 Stuffable Pitta Breads 156, *157*
 see also toast
Brill, Baked 220–2, *221*
brining 169
broad beans: Baked Cod with Chorizo & Peas 206, *207*
broccoli: Sizzled Broccoli with Blood Orange & Chilli Dressing 185
broths 93, 113
 Beef Bone Broth 112–13, *113*
 Brothy Chickpeas 98, *99*
 Chicken Wing Tea 108, *109*
Brown Butter, Orange & Almond Pilaf 126–8, *127*

Brown Sugar Tart 308–10, *309*, *311*
Brûléed Rice Pudding 300, *301*
Bulgur Salad 246, *247*
Buns, Olive Oil 168–70, *169*
burgers: A Very Good Cheeseburger 196, *197*
butter: Chilli Butter 264, *265*
 Garlic Butter 162
 Homemade Salted Butter 174–6, *175*
 Rockefeller Butter 263
 Spiced Butter 217
butter beans: Smoky Squash, Butter Bean & Citrus Soup 100, *101*

C

cabbage: Charred Cabbage 186, *187*
 Salted Cabbage 219
capers: Caper Pan Sauce 200–1, *201*
 Warm Tartar Sauce 220–2, *221*
caramel 21, 282, 283
 Brûléed Rice Pudding 300, *301*
 Cheat's Apple Tarte Tatin 298–9, *299*
 Maple Toffee Sauce 292, *293*
cartouches 233, *233*
cavolo nero: Creamed Cabbage Cavatelli 140
celeriac: Remoulade 200–1, *201*
chard, Lamb Shoulder with 252, *253*
cheese: Braised Chicken 'Pizzaiola' 240
 Cheesy Spelt 138–9, *139*
 Corn & Jalapeño Salad Topping 120
 Deep-dish Leek & Guanciale Quiche 64, *65*
 Fennel Seed Soldiers 94–5, *95*
 Fudgy Boiled Eggs & Comté 48, *49*
 Garlicky Spinach & Cheese Pide 162, *163*

Melted Courgettes & Mozzarella on Toast 234, *235*
Pecorino Pain Perdu 62, *63*
Pumpkin Ravioli with Taleggio Fonduta 144–6, *145*, *147*
Ricotta Dumplings with Cheese & Tomato Broth 136–7, *137*
Scapece 160, *161*
Sheet-tray Pizza alla Puttanesca 164, *165*
Smoked Aubergine & 'Nduja Lasagne 210, *211*
A Very Good Cheeseburger 196, *197*
cherries: Cucumber, Cherry & Almond Crunch Salad 78, *79*
Poached Cherries 300, *301*
chicken 26
　Barbecue Whole Chicken 267–9, *268*
　Braised Chicken 'Pizzaiola' 240
　Chicken Soup with Crispy Skin 102–3, *103*
　Chicken Wing Tea 108, 1*09*
　Crispy Chicken Breast with Caper Pan Sauce 200–1, *201*
　Crispy Rice with Za'atar Chicken Livers 122, *123*
　Dry-brined Chicken Legs 212, *213*
　Roast Chicken Pozole Rojo 104
　Roast Chicken with Schmaltzy Shallots 223–5, *224*
　stock 92, 108
chickpeas: Brothy Chickpeas 98, *99*
　Crispy Chickpeas 72, *73*
　Hummus 245–6, *247*
　Pork Chops with Peppers & Peaches 273–5, *274*
　Turmeric Coconut Curry 'Baked' Eggs 54, *55*
chillies 31
　Beef Cheek & Scotch Bonnet Pie 250, *251*
　Blood Orange & Chilli Dressing 185
　Chilli Butter 264–5, *265*
　Corn & Jalapeño Salad Topping 120
　Fish Crudo with Jalapeño & Apple 86, *87*
　Nam Jim 188, *189*
　Taqueria Pickles 170
chips: Oven Chips 220–2, *221*

Peppered Clam Frites 191–2, *193*
chives: Chive Milk Bread 172–3, *173*
　Chive Soft Scramble 46, *47*
chocolate 284, *284*
　Chewy Oatmeal Choc Chip Cookies 290, *291*
　Chocolate, Espresso & Marsala Baked Alaska 302–4, *303*
　Chocolate Mousse 286, *287*
　Flourless Fondants 294
Chopped Salad 72, *73*
chorizo: Baked Cod with Chorizo & Peas 206, *207*
Choux Buns, Rhubarb & Pistachio 295–7, *296*
Chowder, Fennel 'Nduja & Mussel 106, *107*
Cipollata alla Siciliana 258, *259*
clams: Peppered Clam Frites 191–2, *193*
　Tuna Acqua Pazza 194, *195*
coconut milk: Turmeric Coconut Curry 'Baked' Eggs 54, *55*
cod: Baked Cod with Chorizo & Peas 206, *207*
　Cod Schnitzel Holstein 198–9, *199*
coffee: Chocolate, Espresso & Marsala Baked Alaska 302–4, *303*
　Sticky Date Puddings 292, *293*
condiments 31
Cookies, Chewy Oatmeal Choc Chip 290, *291*
cookware 34
Corn & Jalapeño Salad Topping 120
cornichons: Warm Tartar Sauce 220–2, *221*
courgettes: Melted Courgettes & Mozzarella on Toast 234, *235*
　Scapece 160, *161*
couscous: Stuffed Bass with Fregola 276–8, *277*, *279*
Crab with Fresh Tagliolini 129–31, *130*
Craquelin 295–7, *296*
cream: Chocolate Mousse 286, *287*
　Hazelnut Marsala Parfait 302–4, *303*
　Homemade Salted Butter 174–6, *175*

Potatoes & Squash Baked in Cream 218
Toasted Rice Panna Cotta 288–9, *289*
whisking 283
cream cheese: Oniony Cream Cheese & Honey Bagels 166, *167*
Smoky Trout Rillette 81
Crème Fraîche Ranch Dip 80
crisps: Rosemary Crisps 84, *85*
Sweet Onion Tortilla 57
cucumber: Cucumber, Cherry & Almond Crunch Salad 78, *79*
Raita 264, *265*
Silky Almond Soup with Melon & Cucumbers 96, *97*
Tingly Pork Ragù with Salted Cucumbers 241
Cumin Lamb Skewers 266
curry: Smoky Roasted Pumpkin & Fish Curry 214–15, *215*
Turmeric Coconut Curry 'Baked' Eggs 54, *55*
custard 283
　Almond Custard 305–7, *306*
　Brown Sugar Tart 308–10, *309*, *311*

#

dates: Spiced Short Ribs with Dates 245–6, *247*
Sticky Date Puddings 292, *293*
deep-frying 184
desserts 282–4
Diner-style Stuffed Omelettes 52, *53*
dips: Crème Fraîche Ranch Dip 80
Smoky Trout Rillette 81
Spicy Peanut Hummus 81
Doughnuts, 'Myrtille' 305–7, *306*
dressings 68–9
　Blood Orange & Chilli Dressing 185
　Mustardy Beans & Hazelnuts 76, *77*
　Smoky Apple Vinaigrette 83
　Soy Vinaigrette 88
Dumplings, Ricotta 136–7, *137*

E

eggs 44, *44*
  boiling 48
  Chive Soft Scramble 46, *47*
  Chocolate Mousse 286, *287*
  Chopped Beef Tartare 84–5, *85*
  Deep-dish Leek & Guanciale Quiche 64, *65*
  Diner-style Stuffed Omelettes 52, *53*
  egg foams 283–4
  Egg Wash 172–3
  French Omelette 50, *51*
  Fudgy Boiled Eggs & Comté on Rye 48, *49*
  Merguez Ragù and Pickled Peppers 'Baked' Eggs 54, *55*
  Oeufs Mayonnaise 60, *61*
  Pecorino Pain Perdu 62, *63*
  Poached Eggs with Garlicky Greens 56
  Pommes Rösti with Crispy Sage Fried Eggs 58, *59*
  Slow-roasted Tomatoes over Rice 236, *237*
  Sweet Onion Tortilla 57
  Turmeric Coconut Curry 'Baked' Eggs 54, *55*
  whisking 45
emulsions 45
English Muffins 171
enriched doughs 152–3
equipment 32–9

F

fat 20–1, 24, 30
  breadmaking 152
  pan cooking 181
fennel: Fennel & Bitter Leaf Slaw 83
  Fennel 'Nduja & Mussel Chowder 106, *107*
Fennel Seed Soldiers 94, *95*
fish 27–9, *28*, 69
  Beer Batter Fritto Misto 182–4, *183*
  Fish Crudo with Jalapeño & Apple 86, *87*
  see also cod, mackerel *etc*
Flatbreads, Semolina 160–1, *161*
flavours 16–18, 41, 285
flour 150, 152
foams, egg 283–4
Focaccia, Foolproof 158, *159*
Fondants, Flourless 294
Fregola, Stuffed Bass with 276–8, *277*, *279*
French Omelette 50, *51*
Fritto Misto 182–4, *183*
fruit 15, 22–3, 284–5
  see also apples, cherries *etc*
Fudgy Boiled Eggs & Comté on Rye 48, *49*

G

garlic: Aioli 209, *209*
  Bagna Cauda 262
  Garlic & Fennel Porchetta 226–9, *227–8*
  Garlic Butter 162
  Garlicky Spinach & Cheese Pide 162, *163*
  Poached Eggs with Garlicky Greens 56
gluten 150–1, 152
Gnocchi with Smashed Peas 141–2, *143*
grains 116–17
Green Salad 70, *71*
green vegetables: Poached Eggs with Garlicky Greens 56
Gribiche 260, *261*
guanciale: Deep-dish Leek & Guanciale Quiche 64, *65*

H

ham: Pecorino Pain Perdu 62, *63*
hazelnuts: Hazelnut Marsala Parfait 302–4, *303*
  Mustardy Beans & Hazelnuts 76, *77*
herbs 15, 21, 22, 30, 233
hominy: Roast Chicken Pozole Rojo 104
Horseradish Salsa Verde 248, *249*
Hummus 245–6, *247*
  Spicy Peanut Hummus 81

I

ice cream: Chocolate, Espresso & Marsala Baked Alaska 302–4, *303*
ingredients 22–31
Italian meringue *303*, 304

J

jalapeño peppers: Corn & Jalapeño Salad Topping 120
  Diner-style Stuffed Omelettes 52, *53*
  Fish Crudo with Jalapeño & Apple 86, *87*
  Hot Green Tahini 267–9, *268*
  Taqueria Pickles 170
Jerusalem artichokes: Crispy Roast Potato & Artichoke Bravas 208, *209*

K

kale: Garlic & Fennel Porchetta 226–9, *227–8*
Kimchi Butter Fried Rice 124, *125*
knives 32, *33*

L

lamb 26
  Cumin Lamb Skewers 266
  Lamb Meatballs 216–17, *217*
  Lamb Shoulder with White Beans 252, *253*
  Pomegranate Lamb Ribs 242, *243*
Lasagne, Smoked Aubergine & 'Nduja 210, *211*
leeks: Brothy Chickpeas with Pancetta & Leeks 98, *99*
  Burnt Leeks & Gribiche 260, *261*
  Deep-dish Leek & Guanciale Quiche 64, *65*
lemon: Fish Crudo 86, *87*
  Lemon Mayonnaise 182–4, *183*
lentils: Toulouse Sausage with Lentils 248, *249*
lettuce: Charred Lettuces & Bagna Cauda 262

limes: Fish Crudo 86, *87*
liver: Liver Toast 108, *109*
  Za'atar Chicken Livers 122, *123*
long beans: Mustardy Beans & Hazelnuts 76, *77*

M

mackerel: Cured Mackerel with Soy Vinaigrette 88, *89*
  see also smoked mackerel
Maillard reaction 180–1
Maple Toffee Sauce 292, *293*
mayonnaise: Aioli 209, *209*
  Burnt Leeks & Gribiche 260, *261*
  Lemon Mayonnaise 182–4, *183*
  Oeufs Mayonnaise 60, *61*
meat 24–6
  braising 232
  cutting raw meat 69
  pan cooking 180–1
  salads 69
  stock 93
  see also beef, pork *etc*
meatballs: Fragrant Pork Meatball Noodle Soup 105
  Lamb Meatballs 216–17, *217*
melon: Silky Almond Soup with Melon 96, *97*
Merguez Ragù and Pickled Peppers 'Baked' Eggs 54, *55*
meringue 45
  Coffee Italian Meringue 303, 304
milk: Brûléed Rice Pudding 300, *301*
  Chive Milk Bread 172–3, *173*
  Pecorino Pain Perdu 62, *63*
mint 16
Mousse, Chocolate 286, *287*
Muffins, English 171
mushrooms: Cheesy Spelt with Pancetta, Mushrooms & Yolk 138–9, *139*
  One-pot Mushroom Bourguignon 244
mussels: Fennel 'Nduja & Mussel Chowder 106, *107*
  Smoky Mussels with Rockefeller Butter 263
  Stovetop Seafood Rice 132, *133*
Mustardy Beans & Hazelnuts 76, *77*

N

Nam Jim 188, *189*
'nduja: Fennel 'Nduja & Mussel Chowder 106, *107*
  Smoked Aubergine & 'Nduja Lasagne 210, *211*
  Stuffed Bass with Fregola & 'Nduja 276–8, *277, 279*
noodles: Fragrant Pork Meatball Noodle Soup 105
  Tingly Pork Ragù with Noodles 241
  Udon with Ginger Prawn Bisque 110, *111*
nuts, toasting 253

O

oatmeal: Chewy Oatmeal Choc Chip Cookies 290, *291*
Oeufs Mayonnaise 60, *61*
oils 30
Olive Oil Buns 168–70, *169*
olives: Braised Chicken 'Pizzaiola' 240
  Slow-cooked Squid with Black Olives 238–9, *239*
  Stuffed Bass with Fregola, 'Nduja & Gordal Olives 276–8, *277, 279*
  Tomato, Anchovy & Smashed Olive Salad 74, *75*
omelettes: Diner-style Stuffed Omelettes 52, *53*
  French Omelette 50, *51*
onions: Jammy Balsamic Onion, Rosemary & Pecorino Topping 121
  Pickled Red Onion 245–6, *247*
  Potatoes & Squash Baked in Cream 218
  Sweet Onion Tortilla 57
  see also shallots; spring onions
oranges: Blood Orange & Chilli Dressing 185
Oven Chips 220–2, *221*
ovens 204–5, *205*, 233, 312

P

Pain Perdu, Pecorino 62, *63*
pan cooking 180–1
pancetta: Brothy Chickpeas with Pancetta & Leeks 98, *99*
  Cheesy Spelt with Pancetta, Mushrooms & Yolk 138–9, *139*
  Diner-style Stuffed Omelettes 52, *53*
  Fennel & Bitter Leaf Slaw 83
  Pancetta, Sage & Nutmeg Topping 121
Panna Cotta, Toasted Rice 288–9, *289*
pans 34
Parsley Salad 242, *243*
pasta 116–17
  Crab with Fresh Tagliolini 129–31, *130*
  Creamed Cabbage Cavatelli 140
  Pumpkin Ravioli with Taleggio Fonduta 144–6, *145, 147*
  Rigatoni & Sunday Sauce 118, *119*
  Smoked Aubergine & 'Nduja Lasagne 210, *211*
  Tortellini 112, *113*
  White Sausage & Sage Pappadelle 134, *135*
Pastrami-spiced Bavette 186, *187*
pastry 64, 250, 308–10, *311*
peaches: Pork Chops with Peppers & Peaches 273–5, *274*
peanuts: Spicy Peanut Hummus 81
peas: Baked Cod with Chorizo & Peas 206, *207*
  Homemade Gnocchi with Smashed Peas 141–2, *143*
Pecorino Pain Perdu 62, *63*
Peppercorn Sauce 191–2, *193*
peppers: Merguez Ragù and Pickled Peppers 'Baked' Eggs 54, *55*
  Sweet & Sour Peppers 212, *213*
  Pork Chops with Peppers & Peaches 273–5, *274*
  Roasted Peppers, White Beans & Tuna 82
  Romesco Sauce 252, *253*
pickles 31
  Pickled Red Onion 245–6, *247*
  Pickled Shallots 70
  Taqueria Pickles 170

Pie, Beef Cheek & Scotch Bonnet 250, *251*
pilaf: Brown Butter, Orange & Almond Pilaf 126–8, *127*
pine nuts: Spiced Butter 217
pistachio paste: Rhubarb & Pistachio Choux Buns 295–7, *296*
Pitta Breads, Stuffable 156, *157*
Pizza alla Puttanesca 164, *165*
Plums, Toasted Rice Panna Cotta with 288–9, *289*
polenta: English Muffins 171
  Perfect Polenta 120–1
Pomegranate Lamb Ribs 242, *243*
Pommes Rösti 58, *59*
pork 26
  Cipollata alla Siciliana 258, *259*
  Crispy Pork Belly with Sesame Sauce 219
  Garlic & Fennel Porchetta 226–9, *227–8*
  Pork Chops with Peppers & Peaches 273–5, *274*
  Tingly Pork Ragù 241
  see also sausages
potatoes: Crispy Roast Potato & Artichoke Bravas 208, *209*
  Fennel 'Nduja & Mussel Chowder 106, *107*
  Garlic & Fennel Porchetta 226–9, *227–8*
  Homemade Gnocchi 141–2, *143*
  Mash 223–5, *224*
  One-pot Mushroom Bourguignon 244
  Oven Chips 220–2, *221*
  Pommes Rösti 58, *59*
  Potatoes & Squash Baked in Cream 218
  Slow-cooked Squid 238–9, *239*
prawns: Beer Batter Fritto Misto 182–4, *183*
  Stovetop Seafood Rice 132, *133*
  Udon with Ginger Prawn Bisque 110, *111*
preparation 40–1
preserves 31
pumpkin: Pumpkin Ravioli 144–6, *145, 147*
  Smoky Roasted Pumpkin & Fish Curry 214–15, *215*

Quiche, Deep-dish Leek & Guanciale 64, *65*

radicchio: Fennel & Bitter Leaf Slaw 83
Raita 264, *265*
Ranch Dip 80
Ravioli, Pumpkin 144–6, *145, 147*
Remoulade 200–1, *201*
Rhubarb & Pistachio Choux Buns 295–7, *296*
rice 116–17, 128
  Baked Cod with Chorizo & Peas 206, *207*
  Brown Butter, Orange & Almond Pilaf 126–8, *127*
  Brûléed Rice Pudding 300, *301*
  Chicken Soup 102–3, *103*
  Crispy Rice with Za'atar Chicken Livers 122, *123*
  Kimchi Butter Fried Rice 124, *125*
  Slow-roasted Tomatoes over Rice 236, *237*
  Smoky Roasted Pumpkin & Fish Curry 214–15, *215*
  Stovetop Seafood Rice 132, *133*
  Toasted Rice Panna Cotta 288–9, *289*
Ricotta Dumplings 136–7, *137*
Rigatoni & Sunday Sauce 118, *119*
risotto: Cheesy Spelt 138–9, *139*
roasting 205
Rockefeller Butter 263
Romesco Sauce 252, *253*
Rosemary Crisps 84, *85*

salads 68
  Bulgur Salad 246, *247*
  Charred Lettuces & Bagna Cauda 262
  Chopped Salad 72, *73*
  Cucumber, Cherry & Almond Crunch Salad 78, *79*
  Fennel & Bitter Leaf Slaw 83
  Fish Crudo with Jalapeño & Apple 86, *87*
  Green Salad 70, *71*
  Herb Salad 188, *189*
  Mustardy Beans & Hazelnuts 76, *77*
  Parsley Salad 242, *243*
  Roasted Peppers, White Beans & Tuna 82
  Tomato, Anchovy & Smashed Olive Salad 74, *75*
salsas: Horseradish Salsa Verde 248, *249*
  Salsa Brava 208–9, *209*
salt 16, 17, 18–20, 30
  cooking pasta and rice 117
  Dry-brined Chicken Legs 212, *213*
  gradient brining 169
sardines: Beer Batter Fritto Misto 182–4, *183*
sauces: Bagna Cauda 262
  Caper Pan Sauce 200–1, *201*
  Custard 283
  Maple Toffee Sauce 292, *293*
  Peppercorn Sauce 191–2, *193*
  Romesco Sauce 252, *253*
  Salsa Brava 208–9, *209*
  Sesame Sauce 219
  Sunday Sauce 118, *119*
  Tahini Sauce 72
  Warm Tartar Sauce 220–2, *221*
sausages and sausagemeat:
  Fragrant Pork Meatball Noodle Soup 105
  Merguez Ragù and Pickled Peppers 'Baked' Eggs 54, *55*
  Tortellini 112, *113*
  Toulouse Sausage with Lentils 248, *249*
  White Sausage & Sage Pappardelle 134, *135*
scallops: Barbecued Scallops 264–5, *265*
Scapece 160, *161*
sea bass: Crispy Sea Bass 190
  Stuffed Bass with Fregola 276–8, *277, 279*
sea bream: Fish Crudo 86, *87*
seafood 27–9
seasonal food 14, 23, 29
seasoning 16, 18–21
Semolina Flatbreads 160–1, *161*
Sesame Sauce 219
shallots: Pickled Shallots 70
  Schmaltzy Shallots 223–5, *224*

INDEX

shellfish 27–8
sherry vinegar: Cured Mackerel 88, 89
skate: Grilled Skate Wing & Green Nam Jim 188, 189
slow cooking 232–3
smell, sense of 17
smoked fish 27
smoked mackerel: Smoky Roasted Pumpkin & Fish Curry 214–15, 215
Smoky Trout Rillette 81
soups 93
   Beef Bone Broth 112–13, 113
   Brothy Chickpeas 98, 99
   Chicken Soup 102–3, 103
   Chicken Wing Tea 108, 109
   Fennel 'Nduja & Mussel Chowder 106, 107
   Fragrant Pork Meatball Noodle Soup 105
   Roast Chicken Pozole Rojo 104
   Silky Almond Soup 96, 97
   Smoky Squash, Butter Bean & Citrus Soup 100, 101
   Tomato Soup 94, 95
Sourdough Crumbs 74
Soy Vinaigrette 88
spelt: Cheesy Spelt 138–9, 139
spices 20, 30
spinach: Garlicky Spinach & Cheese Pide 162, 163
   Horseradish Salsa Verde 248, 249
   Rockefeller Butter 263
spring onions: Cipollata alla Siciliana 258, 259
   Oniony Cream Cheese & Honey Bagels 166, 167
squash: Potatoes & Squash Baked in Cream 218
   Smoky Squash, Butter Bean & Citrus Soup 100, 101
squid: Beer Batter Fritto Misto 182–4, 183
   Slow-cooked Squid 238–9, 239
   Stovetop Seafood Rice 132, 133
steak 19, 24
   Grilled T-bone 270–2, 271
Sticky Date Puddings 292, 293
stock 92–3, 108
Stovetop Seafood Rice 132, 133
sugar 17, 21, 31, 282–3
Sunday Sauce 118, 119
Sweet Onion Tortilla 57
Sweet Potatoes, Embered 270–2, 271
syrups 283

Tagliolini, Crab with Fresh 129–31, 130
tahini: Hot Green Tahini 267–9, 268
   Hummus 245–6, 247
   Tahini Sauce 72
Taqueria Pickles 170
Tartar Sauce 220–2, 221
tarts: Brown Sugar Tart 308–10, 309, 311
   Cheat's Apple Tarte Tatin 298–9, 299
tasting food 14, 16–18
tinned foods 27, 31
toast: Chive Soft Scramble 46, 47
   Liver Toast 108, 109
   Melted Courgettes & Mozzarella on Toast 234, 235
tomatoes: Braised Chicken 'Pizzaiola' 240
   Cheese & Tomato Broth 136–7, 137
   Crab with Fresh Tagliolini 129–31, 130
   Crispy Sea Bass with Grated Tomatoes 190
   Lamb Meatballs with Tomato 216–17, 217
   Merguez Ragù and Pickled Peppers 'Baked' Eggs 54, 55
   Rigatoni & Sunday Sauce 118, 119
   Sheet-tray Pizza alla Puttanesca 164, 165
   Slow-cooked Squid with Black Olives 238–9, 239
   Slow-roasted Tomatoes over Rice 236, 237
   Smoked Aubergine & 'Nduja Lasagne 210, 211
   Tomato, Anchovy & Smashed Olive Salad 74, 75
   Tomato Soup 94, 95
   Tuna Acqua Pazza 194, 195
tools 14–15, 32–7, 39
Tortellini 112, 113
Tortilla, Sweet Onion 57
Toulouse Sausage with Lentils 248, 249
trout: Smoky Trout Rillette 81
tuna: Roasted Peppers, White Beans & Tuna 82
   Tuna Acqua Pazza 194, 195
Turmeric Coconut Curry 'Baked' Eggs 54, 55

Udon with Ginger Prawn Bisque 110, 111

vanilla 285
   Toasted Rice Panna Cotta 288–9, 289
vegetables 22–3, 232
   Iced Veggies & Three Easy Dips 80–1
   see also peppers, tomatoes etc
vinaigrette 83, 88
vinegar 21, 30

watercress: Rockefeller Butter 263
white beans: Lamb Shoulder with White Beans 252, 253
   Roasted Peppers, White Beans & Tuna 82
White Sausage & Sage Pappardelle 134, 135
wine: One-pot Mushroom Bourguignon 244

Y

yeast 151–2
yoghurt: Raita 264, 265

ACKNOWLEDGEMENTS

First and foremost, I want to thank the many, many brilliant cooks I've worked with or for over the years. Thanks for giving me a job and inspiring me to be inquisitive, hungry and driven. So much of what is in this book I learnt from you all. A special thanks to Michael and Gareth, the two head chefs that changed how I cook for ever and became my good friends. To Conor, Donal, Lisa, Jackson, Arvin, Rob, Keoghan, Noah and Ben. Work never felt like work with you lot around.

Making a book is hard! From the tiny germ of an idea to being scooped up off the shelf, it takes a village, and oh boy did I find a good one. Thank you to my agent Emily Sweet for being a brilliant guiding voice from our very first chat over a beer; without you this book wouldn't be what it is today. Thank you to Will McSweeney for being the finest manager on the planet, who's better than you? To the wonderful Julia Pollacco, Sarah Hammond, Sim Greenaway and the whole crew over at HarperCollins for making this such a joyful process. Thanks also to copy-editor Laura Nickoll. The cover of my dreams was designed by the fantastic Luke Bird.

The photographs in this book surpass anything I could have ever dreamed of. To have four of the most talented people bringing these recipes to life was an utter privilege. Rosie Mackean, you're a star. Food styling is so much more than putting food on a plate. It's making people feel at ease, building trust, understanding the person behind the food and creating work that is so much more the sum of its parts. I'm lucky to have been able to work with you on this. To Emma Cantlay, thank you for bringing the best energy to set and for making a completely perfect tarte tatin. Thank you to Sam A. Harris and Evie Milsom for capturing it so beautifully, and to Rachel Vere for digging out some of the best props I've ever seen. It was an honour to watch you all in action. Thank you to Will Lewis for his pie wisdom, Nicola Lamb for being an endless fountain of pastry knowledge and to anyone else who lent an ear during the recipe development process. Recipes only work if they're well tested, and without a good crew of cooks around me, I could never have got through it all. Thanks to the amazing Caitlin Macdonald, Ben Benton, Chloe René, Nell Gordon-Hall and Anna Lawson.

To my parents, for being fiercely supportive and full of love. Special mention here goes to Mum for putting utterly delicious food on the table every day. Where would I be without 'too late to shop rice'? Dad, for always believing in me and being in my corner. You recognised my passion early, taking me to dinner and watching my eyes widen as I discovered the world of restaurants. To my beautiful sisters, Beccy and Mollie, you're my two biggest cheerleaders and you've inspired me since day one. Thank you to Frank the dog, for sitting with me for hours and hours on end as I wrote and rewrote, drafted and redrafted, punched the air one minute and sat in despair the next. You spent most of it asleep, but it meant a lot to me. Of course, to Nanny. You brought a love for food into my life like nobody else, eating tea with you and Grandpa was the best day of the week.

To my friends, you know who you are, thanks for putting up with all this cooking nonsense. I love you all! A special mention to my chief proofreader and the bloke who gave me my first proper writing gig, Lucas.

Finally, to Lou. I do it all for you. Thank you for allowing me the space to run off and play with food, knives and fire in sweaty kitchens for so many years and for waiting for me to come home from work in the middle of the night, smelling like fish and oil. I'll make you Sunday sauce for ever.

If anyone reading this is hungry for a career in food or food writing and is after some advice on getting started, please drop me a line. I'm always up for a chat.

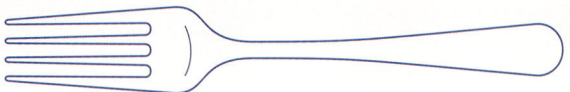

HarperCollins*Publishers*
1 London Bridge Street
London SE1 9GF

www.harpercollins.co.uk

HarperCollins*Publishers*
Macken House, 39/40 Mayor Street Upper
Dublin 1, D01 C9W8, Ireland

First published by HarperCollins*Publishers* 2025

10 9 8 7 6 5 4

Text © Ben Lippett 2025
Photography © Sam A Harris 2025

Ben Lippett asserts the moral right to be identified as the author of this work

A catalogue record of this book is available from the British Library

ISBN 978-0-00-871599-1

Food Stylist: Rosie Mackean
Prop Stylist: Rachel Vere
Illustrations: Shutterstock.com

Printed and bound by GPS Group in Bosnia and Herzegovina

All rights reserved. No part of this publication may be reproduced, stored in a retrieval system, or transmitted, in any form or by any means, electronic, mechanical, photocopying, recording or otherwise, without the prior written permission of the publishers.

Without limiting the author's and publisher's exclusive rights, any unauthorised use of this publication to train generative artificial intelligence (AI) technologies is expressly prohibited. HarperCollins also exercise their rights under Article 4(3) of the Digital Single Market Directive 2019/790 and expressly reserve this publication from the text and data mining exception.

WHEN USING KITCHEN APPLIANCES PLEASE ALWAYS FOLLOW THE MANUFACTURER'S INSTRUCTIONS